The U.S. Brewing Industry

D1413274

The U.S. Brewing Industry

Data and Economic Analysis

Victor J. Tremblay
Carol Horton Tremblay

The MIT Press
Cambridge, Massachusetts
London, England

TRINGALI

First MIT Press paperback edition, 2009
© 2005 Massachusetts Institute of Technology

Set in Palatino on 3B2 by Asco Typesetters, Hong Kong. Printed and bound in the United
States of America.

Library of Congress Cataloging-in-Publication Data

Tremblay, Victor J.
The U.S. brewing industry : data and economic analysis / Victor J. Tremblay, Carol
Horton Tremblay.
    p.   cm.
Includes bibliographical references and index.
ISBN 978-0-262-20151-3 (hc. : alk. paper)—978-0-262-51263-3 (pb. : alk. paper)
1. Brewing industry—United States—History—20th century. I. Title: US brewing
industry. II. Tremblay, Carol Horton. III. Title.
HD9397.U52T73   2005
338.4′766342′097309045—dc22   2004049939

10 9 8 7 6 5 4 3

for Jason, Mark, and Jeff

Contents

Foreword

Robert S. Weinberg

In the fall of 1940, about a month before my thirteenth birthday, I attended my first political debate. My grandfather had two tickets to a debate between Wendell Willkie (the Republican candidate for president) and Robert Jackson (an Assistant Attorney General who acted as a stand-in for an ailing President Roosevelt). This experience had a great impact on my future intellectual life.

Willkie was a successful but relatively unknown attorney/businessman who, as chairman of the Commonwealth and Southern Company (C&S), a large utility, had challenged the Tennessee Valley Authority's expansion into territories served by C&S's operating subsidiaries. After extensive litigation and negotiation, C&S sold the Tennessee Electric Power Company to the TVA, and Willkie emerged as a national figure. He was an executive who had stood up to the New Deal juggernaut. He may not have won, but he had not lost.

In the course of the debate, Willkie was extremely critical of massive government bureaucracy. Jackson argued that solving large and complicated problems required large bureaucracies. Then, to everyone's surprise, he admitted that big bureaucracies could and did make big mistakes.

Jackson then said something that hit me right between the eyes. I wrote this remark verbatim on my program, because I wanted to remember it: "In fact, I don't know which brand of wisdom I distrust the most. That of the theorists who have studied a business but never run one, or that of the executives who have run a business but have never studied it." I had often listened to my father and his friends argue about various business successes and failures, and I had not understood the basis of their disagreement. With two simple sentences Mr. Jackson had made me realize that, in the real world, there is both a theoretical view and a pragmatic (practitioner's) view of any business or organizational problem. This planted the seed that ten years later convinced me to leave physics for economics.

Finally, in 1966, after two and a half years as an Air Force Officer, two years on the staff at MIT, and ten years at IBM, I joined Anheuser-Busch as a Corporate Vice President (Corporate Planning) and a member of the Corporate Management, Marketing, and Technical Committees. Thus began my 36-year association with the brewing industry.

In 1971 I established R. S. Weinberg & Associates (RSWA). Since then I have worked with all but one of the major brewers in the United States. In 1979 RSWA launched *Brewing Industry Research Program*, a continuing study of the brewing industry in the United States. Each year we produce thousands of charts and tables analyzing all aspects of the brewing industry. These studies allow us to advise brewers about the existence and growth of new opportunities, investment bankers and law firms about the brewing industry, and government agencies about the impact of government policies on the brewing industry (with particular emphasis on avoiding unintended consequences). In 1997, RSWA became The Office of R. S. Weinberg.

The brewing industry is a fun industry to study. The relationships among the major players (i.e., the ultimate consumers; the brewers and their suppliers; the suppliers' suppliers; the wholesalers and the retailers; federal, state, and local government regulators; various environmental and community activists) are clear and well defined. Until recently it was a comparatively easy industry to study. It is not complicated. Since it is highly regulated, a hard-working and patient analyst can track down 85–95 percent of the data necessary to model it from various published government, industry, and trade sources.

The remaining 5–15 percent is another story. We have spent 30 years and more money than we can think about trying to build a true (complete) general-equilibrium model of the brewing industry (BIGEM). To date we have not been successful. When we started on this quest, in 1972, our "von Neumann factor" was about three years. That is, we believed our model would be completed by the end of 1975 or the middle of 1976 at the latest. We now have file cabinets full of interesting and useful partial-equilibrium models (PEMs). I believe we are close to finally developing BIGEM but we have not caught the "gold ring"; however, close counts only in horseshoes. As a practical matter, we regularly combine strings of our PEMs to form a valuable ersatz

BIGEM which may be used in the same manner that we would use a true BIGEM.

When Vic Tremblay first contacted me I was impressed with the ambitious project he and Carol had undertaken. My first reaction was that it was about time that some serious industrial organization scholars wrote a definitive study of the evolution of the brewing industry in the United States. For this reason I was pleased to make parts of our data base available to the Tremblays for this project. A review of the book's bibliography clearly shows that, although industrial organization economists have drawn many specific examples from the operations of the brewing industry, none have devoted a full book to the subject. The most comprehensive analyses published to date are chapters, generally 25–40 pages in length, in standard industry survey textbooks. (For examples, see Elzinga 2001 and Greer 2002.) The present volume is indeed a first. In fact it is the kind of book that I always wanted to write.

The U.S. Brewing Industry offers something to a wide range of readers, from brewery executives seeking to expand their qualitative and quantitative perspectives of the brewing industry (in response to Mr. Jackson's second criticism, to run a business but to never study it) to academics who desire an insight into the real world forces that actually shaped the brewing industry over time in order to develop a "feel" for the actual problems and uncertainties brewing executives face and of the major balls they have to juggle (in response to Mr. Jackson's first criticism, to study a business but never actually run one). The Tremblays have the "time and space" to show the reader how all of the pieces actually fit together. This is a particularly important point.

The ten chapters are presented in an order that focuses attention on how the interconnections between the various pieces affect the final outcome. After a brief introduction and summary, Tremblay and Tremblay discuss basic demand and cost conditions and industry concentration. This is followed by a discussion of how the major brewers have evolved and a discussion of the development of the import and domestic specialty market. The next two chapters discuss price and non-price behavior, including brand proliferation, trigger, and advertising strategies. The final chapters cover the measurement of the industry's economic performance and public policy issues.

The Professors Tremblay have hit a home run. In a single volume they provide the theorist with more than adequate basic knowledge of the fundamental operating dynamics of the brewing industry. At the same time, they provide brewing industry executives with an excellent demonstration of how the tools of economic analysis can improve even the most pragmatic managers' understanding of the environment in which they operate.

This is a book that I will recommend to all of my brewer clients and to all others who ask me for a starting point from which they can begin to develop an understanding of the economics of the brewing industry.

Preface

Our initial interest in the U.S. brewing industry derived from a growing dissatisfaction with the empirical inter-industry studies found in the field of industrial organization. As this line of research came under criticism during the 1970s, empirical research shifted to the study of a single industry. Industry studies flourished in the 1980s with Appelbaum's (1979, 1982) "new empirical industrial organization" technique, which used firm-level data to measure the degree of market power in an industry. The novelty of Appelbaum's work, the availability of firm-level data, and the dynamic nature of brewing motivated Victor to apply this technique in his 1983 dissertation of the U.S. brewing industry.

The economic issues at play in the brewing industry drew Carol's interest as well, and a collaboration began with our 1988 study of mergers. We have studied the U.S. brewing industry ever since. A veritable market laboratory, the brewing industry provides dramatic examples of many of the important topics in industrial organization, economic policy, and business strategy. Increasing industry concentration, the microbrewery renaissance, and scale-increasing technological change represent some examples. Brewers have also engaged in fierce advertising rivalries, brand proliferation, and mixed-pricing strategies, actions that have been shaped by the unique personalities of the beer barons as well as by economic considerations. The causes and consequences of rising concentration, the social costs of alcohol consumption and abuse, and the merits of higher excise taxes and more restrictive advertising laws in brewing are subjects of continued policy debate.

Over time, contributions from game theory and management strategy influenced our research on brewing. Explicit game-theoretic models of oligopoly explain how history and the idiosyncrasies of firms and industries affect rational firm behavior in imperfectly competitive markets. The implications of game theory are difficult to test, however, since many of the relevant idiosyncratic variables are unobservable. We attempt to overcome this weakness by studying the environment and the actions of individual firms, an approach found in the field of strategic management. Like Ghemawat (1997) and McAfee (2002), we have come to believe that a case study of an individual industry and its leading firms is the best way to understand and evaluate firm strategy, economic performance, and policy issues relevant to the industry.

We blend several approaches to analyze the economics of the U.S. brewing industry and to test prominent theories. First, we attempt to provide a detailed description of the industry and review relevant theoretical and applied literature. Whenever possible, we use regression analysis and hypothesis testing. In other cases, we use raw data to document various features of the industry. Finally, we provide historical examples of firm actions and outcomes, with an interest in understanding the strategies used by successful and failing brewers. We hope that those interested in the brewing industry and in the fields of industrial organization, applied game theory, and management strategy will find this blend of theory, history, and data analysis of merit.

We have given high priority to constructing a rich and extensive data set on the U.S. brewing industry. We believe that this is the most comprehensive data set of economic variables available for an oligopolistic industry. We wish to thank the individuals and institutions listed in appendix A for permitting distribution of the data.

This book represents the culmination of almost 25 years of research, and we owe a great deal of thanks to many colleagues and friends who have helped us along the way. First, we would like to thank our former professors at Washington State University and at the University of Wisconsin at Madison for enhancing our research skills in the fields of industrial organization, game theory, and econometrics: Yeon-Koo Che, Ray Deneckere, Greg Duncan, Bill Hallagan, Fred Inaba, Lane Rawlins, Larry Samuelson, and Stan Smith. We owe special thanks to Kenneth Elzinga and Douglas Greer for their valuable comments and suggestions over the years and for their work on brewing which has inspired much of our research. We would also like to thank our co-authors, colleagues, editors, and friends for providing many useful comments and facts: Steve Buccola, Doug Denney, Eric Dickey, Ulrich Doraszelski, Kellie Essary, Rolf Färe, John Gabriel, Alix Gitelman, Avi Goldfarb, Shawna Grosskopf, Natsuko Iwasaki, Joe

Kerkvliet, Yasushi Kudo, Byung Lak Lee, Stephen Martin, Jason Mann, Carlos Martins-Filho, William Nebesky, Jon Nelson, Dong Wong Noh, Kumiko Okuyama, Steve Polasky, Jim Ragan, Danny Sam, Tim Sass, Barry Seldon, William Shepherd, Michael Vardanyan, and Andreas Waldkirch. We apologize to those who have been inadvertently omitted. We are also grateful to the librarians at the Anheuser-Busch Corporate Library in St. Louis, Mary Lynn Butler and Ann Lauenstein, for answering our questions about brewing and providing access to the Library. We owe special thanks to our sponsoring editor John S. Covell for his faith and guidance, to H. Yan Ho for her reliable and able editorial assistance, and to Paul Bethge for his careful and skillful editing.

We cannot thank Bob Weinberg enough for his help and encouragement with this book. Bob, a scholar of management strategy and the leading expert on the economics of the brewing industry, has provided numerous insights that have enlightened our thinking about brewing and business strategy.

Last, but not least, we would like to thank our family and friends for their support and sage advice. These include Bud Horton, Pat Horton, Muriel Horton, the King family, George Stephenson, Louise Stephenson, Judy Thornley, Ed Thornley, Vince Tremblay, Jeri Tremblay, Jason Mann, and Mark Tremblay.

The U.S. Brewing Industry

1   Introduction

It is not from the benevolence of the butcher, the brewer, or the baker that we expect our dinner, but from their regard to their self interest.

—Adam Smith, *The Wealth of Nations* (1776)

The first recorded brewery in the American colonies was built in New Amsterdam in 1612. Brewing as we know it in the United States today emerged in the middle of the nineteenth century when a few German immigrants began making German-style lager beer instead of English-style ales, porters, and stouts. American consumers took to the lighter lagers such as those brewed by Anheuser-Busch, Coors, Miller, Pabst, and Schlitz, and by the late 1800s these firms had gained a competitive advantage.[1]

In the period 1880–1919, however, some states and some counties passed laws prohibiting the sale of alcoholic beverages. In 1914, Congress passed the Webb-Kenyon Act, which made it illegal to mail or ship alcoholic beverages into any state that banned alcohol consumption. The Eighteenth Amendment to the Constitution, effective in 1920, outlawed production, transportation, and sale of alcoholic beverages in the United States. The amendment put 1,568 firms out of the beer-making business.

Some brewers stayed in business by making soft drinks, malt syrup, and dairy products, but those that closed their doors for good suffered a dramatic loss in wealth. For example, the William J. Lemp Brewing Company of St. Louis, valued at $7 million before Prohibition, was sold to a shoe company for less than 10 percent of its former value. The Harvard Brewery of Lowell, Massachusetts, once valued at $4 million, was sold for only $275,000 (*Modern Brewery Age*, September–October 1983).

Alcohol consumption did not cease. Many people violated the law by making beer, wine, and distilled spirits at home or by visiting illegal bars called "speakeasies." According to Glover (2001: 22), New York had about 15,000 bars before Prohibition and an estimated 32,000 speakeasies during Prohibition. In the Chicago area, where an estimated 30 illegal breweries were in operation, Prohibition pushed the price of a 31-gallon barrel of beer from $10 to $55–$60 (*Chicago Tribune Magazine*, April 24, 1977). One study found that gross profits soared by more than 1,000 percent, but much of the illegal gain was spent on bribes to ensure that government officials ignored the illegal activities (Ronnenberg 1998). According to Miron and Zwiebel (1991), Prohibition caused the consumption of alcoholic beverages to decline by only 30–50 percent in the later years of the law, a decline that resulted more from higher prices than from Prohibition itself.

After concerns arose that Prohibition was ineffective, encouraged crime, and led to a general disregard for the law, it was ended in 1933 with the ratification of the Twenty-First Amendment. Breweries that had survived by pursuing other business activities quickly returned to brewing. The number of brewers of lager grew to about 700 by 1938. It has declined dramatically since then. From 1947 to 2001, for example, the number of traditional brewers of lager fell from 421 to 24 and the market share of the four largest brewers of domestically produced beer rose from 17 to 94 percent.

Some brewers that had been among the mightiest exited the industry. Of the top ten brewers in 1947, only two survive today: Anheuser-Busch and Pabst. Although Pabst is currently the fourth-largest firm, it is no longer a true brewer; all its beer is produced under contract by Miller. These post-Prohibition brewers specialize in large-scale production of lager beer, such as Budweiser, Miller Genuine Draft, and Coors Light. To distinguish them from import and smaller domestic micro-brewers, they are now called "traditional," "macro," or "mass-producing" brewers of "regular domestic beer."

While the mass producers were exiting the industry in droves in the second half of the twentieth century, several entrepreneurs began "crafting" beer on a small scale. Because of their size, the new enterprises were called "boutique" or "micro" breweries. In contrast to the traditional brewers, the microbreweries returned to the brewing practices of the past by making ales, porters, stouts, and darker lagers. The success of the smaller brewers has been as dramatic as the decline of the larger ones. From 1979 to 2001, the new market segment grew from two firms to more than 1,400.

The lone constant in the post-World War II brewing industry has been the continued success of Anheuser-Busch. From 1950 to 1956, Anheuser-Busch traded the top position back and forth with Schlitz. Since then, Anheuser-Busch has been the largest U.S. brewing company. Between 1950 and 2001, its share of domestic production rose from 5.83 percent to nearly 55 percent. Today Anheuser-Busch is the largest brewer in the world, and its Budweiser brand name is as synonymous with beer as Coke is with cola.

An important goal of this book is to document the changes that have occurred in the U.S. brewing industry, primarily during the period 1950–2000, and to explain why these changes have occurred. Previous studies are summarized, historical and current events are described, and both firm data and industry data are used to analyze how outside forces and the behavior of firms have affected the industry.

The approach of studying a single industry and its individual firms borrows from three traditions. The first involves a case study of the structure, conduct, and performance of a single oligopolistic industry (Scherer 1970). This descriptive approach focuses on the industry as a whole, and generally ignores the behavior of individual firms. The second is the new industrial organization approach, which uses game theory to predict the behavior of rational firms and their impact on competition and social welfare in imperfectly competitive markets. The third approach involves a descriptive and empirical analysis of the behavior and performance of the important firms within an industry. According to Scherer (1980: 291) and Spulber (as quoted in Ghemawat 1997: x), a study of individual firms can guide economic theory, provide insights into firms strategies, and make it possible to prescribe optimal management strategies that fit specific market settings.

In the end, all three traditions rely on the study of a single industry, and insights from each approach appear throughout the book. This blend of approaches should lead to a better understanding of the industry and the behavior of individual firms.

1.1   The Art of Brewing and the Different Styles of Beer

Archeological evidence indicates that beer is as old as civilization and may predate the invention of bread.[2] Scholars have traced the origins of brewing back more than 6,000 years and have established that ancient Assyrians, Babylonians, Chinese, Egyptians, Greeks, Romans, and Teutons all made beer. Evidence of the oldest brewery was recently discovered in the ruins of a 5,500-year-old Syrian city (*Modern Brewery Age*, March 26, 2001: 12). The building housed a bakery and a brewery with ovens for charring grain and large vats for fermenting. Several examples of ancient beer recipes indicate that these brews tasted quite different from the beer of today. For example, according to an article published in the *Cambridge Architectural Journal* (Samuel 1996), ancient Egyptians used emmer (a type of wheat) and malted barley to produce a fruity, sweet brew.

Today beer is made from four main ingredients: water, hops, yeast, and cereal grains. Malted barley, corn, rice, and wheat are commonly used grains, and fruits, herbs, and other spices are sometimes added as flavor enhancers. Beer is brewed by heating a mixture of grains and water to convert the starches in the grains to sugars and carbohydrates. The grains are then removed, and the remaining mixture, called wort, is boiled with hops and other flavorings. The wort is cooled, and yeast is added to start fermentation, a process that changes sugar into alcohol and carbon dioxide. Beer is then aged and filtered before being pasteurized (or micro-filtered) and packaged for consumption.

Beer has been packaged in many different vessels. Early containers included clay pots and blackjacks (leather bags coated on the inside with black tar to preserve freshness). In modern times, the standard measure of volume in the U.S. brewing industry is an American barrel, which contains 31 U.S. gallons (117.34 liters). Before Prohibition, beer was shipped to taverns in wooden barrels that were coated with tar to prevent contact with wood and the absorption of a woody flavor. Since Prohibition, the largest containers are the half-barrel (15.5 gallons) and the keg (usually 8 gallons or less). Still the industry continues to record sales in terms of 31-gallon barrels, a practice that is followed throughout this book. Since the 1950s, half-barrels and kegs have been made from stainless steel or aluminum. In 2000, 51 percent of the beer consumed in the United States was packaged in cans, 40 percent in bottles, and 9 percent in half-barrels or kegs (*Brewers Almanac* 2001).[3]

Brewers can alter a beer's flavor and other characteristics in a number of ways. Alcohol content can be increased by lengthening the fermentation time and by adding sugar. Fermentation at the bottom of the vessel produces a milder taste and less alcohol than fermentation at the top. Much of beer's flavor derives from malt (dried barley roasted in a kiln). As with coffee, roasting at a higher temperature produces malt that is darker and has a richer flavor. At one pole of the malt spectrum is "pale malt," which is used in lighter lagers. At the other is "black malt," which is roasted just short of burning. Substituting corn or rice for some of the malt produces a very dry and light-colored beer. Hops help preserve freshness and add bitterness to counter the sweetness produced by the grains. Water quality and mineral content are important to producing good beer, and some brewers advertise that they use water from "pure" or "crystal-clear" springs.[4]

Today, beer styles range from pale and watery to dark and hearty (table 1.1).[5] There are three general styles of beer: ale, bottom-fermented beer, and other styles. Ales are beers produced with top-fermenting yeast. Fermentation takes place at relatively high temperatures (about 55–70° Fahrenheit) and takes about 5–7 days, yielding a beer with a higher alcohol content than a lager. Ales tend to be dark and taste fruity and sweet. Bottom-fermented beer originated in Germany in 1836 and was first produced in the United States by John Wagner of Philadelphia in 1840. Bottom fermentation occurs at low temperatures (33–60°F) and requires 6–10 days. Because the process of making this style of beer involved longer storage time, it came to be called "lager," which means "storehouse" in German. Lager beer is noted for its mild flavor and light color.

While today's domestic microbreweries and import suppliers produce a variety of all-malt lagers, ales, porters, and stouts, the traditional mass-producing brewers focus on the production of a light lager style beer, called "regular domestic beer" or "lager." This encompasses traditional or regular lager, light beer, low-alcohol beer, malt liquor, dry beer, and ice beer (table 1.2). Regular lager is marketed at three price points: "popular-priced," "premium," and "super-premium." Malt liquor, dry beer, and ice beer are similar to regular lager but have a higher alcohol content. Light beer is lower in calories. Low-alcohol beer contains half the alcohol of regular beer.[6]

A number of factors contribute to the production and distribution of quality beer. Quality at the production stage requires superior ingredients, sterile brewing conditions, adequate aging, and consistent brewing practices. Inadequate aging, for example, produces "green" or immature beer that has an unpleasant flavor and aroma (Rhodes 1995; Goldammer 1999). Beer's quality is also affected by handling and

Table 1.1
The major beer styles.

Top-Fermented

Ales come in many styles. Classic examples include pale ale, which is amber in color and may be mild to quite bitter; brown ale, which is lightly hopped, sweet, and full-bodied; Scottish ale, which is dark in color and has a sweet, malty flavor; and bitter ale, which is highly hopped and has a very bitter taste. Alcohol content[a] varies by brand but normally ranges from 3.1% to 7.5%.

Barley wine is a full-bodied ale that requires a long aging period and has a very high alcohol content (7–15%)

Porters are dark brown, full-bodied, lightly hopped ales. The dark color results from a larger proportion of black malt. (Alcohol content: 4.3–6.3%.)

Stout is a stronger and more bitter porter brewed with more hops and black malt. (Alcohol content: 4–10%.)

Bottom-Fermented

A *bock* is traditionally a strong, dark, sweet, full-bodied beer. (Alcohol content: 5.9–13%.)

Lagers come in many styles. The term refers to any bottom-fermented light amber beer. Brands made with 100% malt have a golden color. Corn or rice adjuncts are added to produce most of the pale and light lagers found in the U.S. today. (Alcohol content: 3.9–5.4%.)

A *pilsner* (or *pilsener*) is a pale lager beer with a dry, crisp, highly hopped flavor. The style originated in the Czech town of Pilsen. The terms *lager* and *pilsner* are used interchangeably in most of the world today.

Others

Cream ale (a style developed in the U.S.) is light in color, highly carbonated, and often made by blending ale with lager. (Alcohol content: 4.8–5.5%.)

Steam beer is made with bottom-fermenting yeast (like a lager) but at higher temperatures (like an ale). This style originated in California in the Gold Rush days, when ice was very expensive. The name is now a registered trademark of the Anchor Steam Brewing Company of San Francisco. Anchor Steam is an all-malt beer with a creamy and mild hop flavor. (Alcohol content: 5.7%.)

Wheat beers are made with malted wheat as well as other grains. Two German styles, *Berliner Weisse* and *Weizenbier*, are top-fermented and have a hoppy and malty taste. *Hefeweizen* is a bottom-fermented wheat beer. (Alcohol content: 4.5–5.6%.)

---

a. Because alcohol content varies by brand, a range of values is provided for each style. The numbers in parentheses indicate the alcohol content by volume for various brands within each type. Alcohol content can be measured by weight or volume. Alcohol content of 5% by volume is equivalent to 3.98% alcohol by weight. Throughout this book, alcohol content is expressed by volume. See appendix C for further details.

Table 1.2
Major styles made by mass-producing brewers, listed in order of introduction into U.S. market. Numbers in parentheses: alcohol content by volume, calories per 12-ounce container.

Popular-priced lager A mild and pale lager that is usually lightly hopped and highly carbonated. Adjuncts can account for up to 65% of all grains. Examples: Busch (4.72% alcohol, 153 calories), Keystone (4.74%, 121), Milwaukee's Best (4.34%, 133), Old Milwaukee (4.53%, 145).

Premium lager A premium-priced, mild, pale lager. Colors range from very pale to gold. A premium lager has a slight malt flavor and is low in bitterness. These beers are brewed with 25–30% adjuncts. More rice than corn adjuncts are used to produce a "crisp" taste. Examples: Budweiser (4.65%, 142), Coors (4.55%, 137), Miller Genuine Draft (4.67%, 147).

Super-premium lager A mild golden-colored beer, normally with a higher hop and malt content than premium beer. Examples: Michelob (4.80%, 152), Killian's Red (5.00%, 161), Rolling Rock (4.64%, 142).

Malt liquor This style has "no legal or accepted definition" (Robertson 1984, 35; Apps 1992, 55). Its distinguishing feature is that it normally has about 20% more alcohol than premium lager. Because malt beverages with an alcohol content in excess of 5% cannot be called beer in some states, they are termed malt liquor. Examples: King Cobra (5.90%, 180), Magnum (5.92%, 160), Olde English 800 (5.96%, 167).

Light beer An extremely pale lager with fewer calories, a milder flavor, and a more watery body than premium lager. The usual adjunct is corn (50–65% of total grain). Examples: Bud Light (4.16%, 114), Coors Light (4.36%, 107), Miller Lite (4.18%, 96).

Low-alcohol beer A beer with half the alcohol of premium lager. Introduced in the mid 1980s, it is no longer produced by the major U.S. brewers.

Dry beer A highly carbonated malt beverage in which more of the sugars are fermented into alcohol, leaving little taste. Dry beer has about 10% more alcohol than premium lager. After initial success in the early 1990s, little dry beer is produced today.

Ice beer A beer made by freezing lager and then removing the ice crystals to produce a beer that is more concentrated and has about 10–20% more alcohol than premium lager. Examples: Bud Ice (5.5%, 148), Icehouse (5.5%, 149), Milwaukee's Best Ice (5.5%, 132).

distribution. Unlike wine, beer is a perishable product that begins to deteriorate once it is packaged. Shelf life is longer for beer that is refrigerated, pasteurized, and rich in hops, malt, and alcohol. Beer experts recommend that unpasteurized beer in kegs be consumed within 6 weeks. When pasteurized in cans or bottles, regular domestic beer should be consumed within 3 months, all-malt lager within 4 months, ale within 6 months, and double bock within 8 months. Very heavy barley wine can be stored for several years without spoiling. According to Elizabeth Alt, director of the U.S. Brewing Academy, regular lager can deteriorate significantly in a month if exposed to sunlight or temperature variation (*New York Times*, May 12, 1982). As

packaged beer becomes stale, it takes on a cardboard-like flavor. Expo-
sure to sunlight can cause beer to have a skunk-like odor. Brewing
errors can also cause beer to have a medicinal or metallic flavor (Klein
1995: 31–32).[7]

Domestic brewers normally produce quality beer that reaches consumers while fresh. Although individual consumers have strong opin-
ions about which brands are best, it is difficult to identify real quality
differences among different brands of the mass-producing brewers.
The palates of most consumers are not sufficiently sharp to distinguish
subtle differences between brands within a style. Another problem is
that most differences are horizontal rather than vertical (Tirole 1988). A
product characteristic is vertical when all consumers agree on its ranking. A good example is freshness, since all consumers prefer beer that
is fresh, *ceteris paribus* (all other things being equal). A characteristic is
horizontal if the optimal choice depends on the individual consumer.
For example, those who prefer a robust flavor will like a porter or a
stout, while those who prefer something milder will choose a lighter
beer.[8] Although beer rankings abound, they generally are influenced
by the reviewers' preferences for horizontal characteristics, as there is
little consistency among rankings.[9]

1.2 U.S. Beer Production and Consumption

With the exception of the Prohibition era, total U.S. beer consumption
grew between 1863 and 2000.[10] Figure 1.1 reveals that beer production
and consumption rose steadily from 1863 until the prohibition movement and then again from 1960 to 1980. The numbers are undoubtedly
biased downward in the nineteenth century, however, as home brewing was more common at that time. Production figures for the Prohibition period reflect the production of near or non-alcoholic beer (i.e.,
beer with less 0.5 percent alcohol by volume), a close substitute for
beer when spiked with absolute alcohol (ethanol). The growing difference between consumption and production after World War II reflects
growth in exports. In 2002, Americans consumed about 180 million
barrels of domestic beer and about 23 million barrels of imported beer.

Per-capita consumption exhibits a similar but more variable pattern.
Figure 1.2 plots domestic beer per-capita consumption from 1863
through 2000 and shows that consumption rose steeply before reaching a pre-Prohibition peak in 1914 at 21 gallons per capita. The data
also reveal the effectiveness of the prohibition movement after 1914,

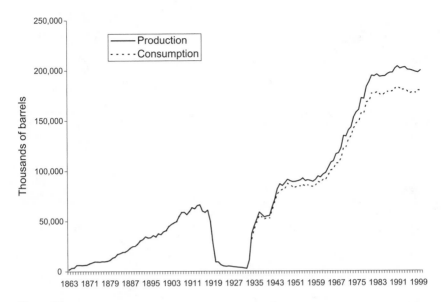

Figure 1.1
Total U.S. beer production and consumption, 1863–2000. Sources: U.S. Treasury Department, Bureau of Alcohol, Tobacco, and Firearms, as reported in *Brewers Almanac* (various issues).

the year that the Webb-Kenyon Act went into effect. After Prohibition was lifted, per-capita consumption increased rapidly from 1934 through 1936. This may have resulted from habit and the addictive nature of alcohol. The level of addiction would be relatively low immediately after Prohibition but would rise as more and more consumers developed a taste for beer and built up a tolerance for alcohol. Per-capita consumption rose rapidly again during World War II, declined during the 1950s and the early 1960s, increased before peaking in the early 1980s, and generally trended downward thereafter.

By world standards, the United States is a major beer-drinking nation (table 1.3). In 2001, U.S. per-capita beer consumption was about 22.0 gallons. The United States ranks 11th among developed countries in beer consumption, 34th in wine consumption, and 20th in spirits consumption. Most of the major beer-drinking nations are in Northern and Eastern Europe. The average consumer in the Czech Republic or in Ireland drinks almost twice as much beer as the average U.S. consumer. Per-capita beer consumption in France and Italy is less than half what it is in the United States.

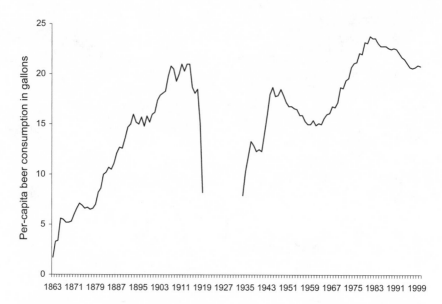

Figure 1.2
U.S. per-capita beer consumption, 1863–2000. Sources: U.S. Treasury Department, Bureau of Alcohol, Tobacco, and Firearms; U.S. Bureau of the Census as reported in *Brewers Almanac* (various issues).

1.3   A Profile of the Industry

The U.S. brewing industry is an important part of the national economy. Beer is one of the commodities used by the U.S. government to calculate the consumer price index (CPI). Beer accounts for about 58 percent of alcohol consumption in the United States (*Modern Brewery Age*, March 23, 1998; *Beer Industry Update: A Review of Recent Developments* 2002). In 2002, the industry accounted for more than $64 billion in sales, employed more than 850,000 U.S. workers, and paid $8.7 billion in federal and state excise and sales taxes. Today there are more than 2,200 beer wholesalers and more than 1,800 brewers and beer importers in the United States (Beer Institute 2002–2003).

It is common to divide U.S. brewers into three segments (sometimes called "strategic groups"). The first segment includes the traditional brewers that entered the market immediately after Prohibition and produce predominately domestic-style lager. Because of their early entry, their large size, and their style of brewing, they are called "traditional," "macro," or "mass-producing" brewers. Firms within this segment are sometimes distinguished by their geographic scope of

Table 1.3
Per-capita consumption (gallons) of beer, wine, and spirits for the leading 40 beer-drinking countries, 2001. Source: *World Drink Trends 2003*.

Beer rank		Beer	Wine	Spirits
1	Czech Republic	41.8	4.4	1.0
2	Republic of Ireland	39.8	3.1	0.6
3	Germany	32.5	6.3	0.5
4	Austria	28.2	8.2	0.4
5	Luxembourg	26.7	17.0	0.4
6	Denmark	26.1	8.2	0.3
7	Belgium	25.9	4.9	0.3
8	United Kingdom	25.7	4.6	0.4
9	Australia	24.6	5.3	0.3
10	Slovak Republic	22.8	2.9	1.2
11	*United States*	*22.0*	*2.0*	*0.5*
12	Netherlands	21.3	5.0	0.4
13	Finland	21.2	5.3	0.6
14	New Zealand	21.1	4.4	0.4
15	Venezuela	21.1	—	0.3
16	Spain	19.8	9.6	0.6
17	Canada	18.2	2.7	0.5
18	Hungary	16.9	8.2	0.8
19	Portugal	16.2	13.2	0.4
20	Poland	16.0	1.6	0.9
21	Cyprus	15.9	4.4	0.8
22	Switzerland	15.1	11.4	0.4
23	South Africa	14.7	2.4	0.2
24	Sweden	14.6	4.1	0.3
25	Norway	13.4	2.9	0.2
26	Romania	13.3	7.9	1.2
27	Iceland	12.9	2.1	0.3
28	Mexico	12.8	0.1	0.2
29	Brazil	12.3	0.5	0.4
30	Colombia	11.9	0.1	0.4
31	Malta	11.0	5.1	0.3
32	Japan	10.6	0.7	0.8
33	Paraguay	10.6	0.4	—
34	Greece	10.3	9.0	0.5
35	Argentina	9.8	9.0	0.1
36	France	9.5	15.0	0.6
37	Latvia	9.2	1.1	1.5
38	Russia	7.9	2.0	1.7
39	Italy	7.6	13.2	0.1
40	Chile	7.1	4.2	0.4

operation, as local, regional, or national producers. This distinction was especially important from the 1950s through the 1980s, as the large national firms gained share from the local and regional brewers. Among the regional producers still in existence are the Pittsburgh Brewing Company, the Latrobe Brewing Company, and the High Falls Brewing Company. Only three macrobrewers produce and market beer nationally today: Anheuser-Busch, Coors, and Miller.

The second segment consists of more recent entrants that started out with very small brewing facilities. Firms in this segment include brew pubs, restaurant-breweries that sell most of their beer on site, and microbreweries (small breweries that sell most of their beer off site). Firms in this segment generally brew European-style beer, which is called "domestic specialty" or "craft" beer to distinguish it from imported beer of the same style. Because several microbreweries are no longer micro in size, the larger microbreweries are called "regional specialty brewers." This general class, which includes brew pubs, microbreweries, and regional specialty breweries, is called the domestic specialty or craft brewers. Among the well-known domestic specialty brewers are the Anchor Brewing Company, the Boston Beer Company, the Sierra Nevada Brewing Company, and the New Belgium Brewing Company.

The third segment includes international producers who sell beer in the United States. Imported brands are far from homogeneous, however. For example, many of the brands from Canada and Mexico are similar to regular domestic beer, while most brands from England and Ireland are more like domestic specialty beer. The unifying feature of this group is that the imported brands sell for a substantial price premium, owing in part to the high cost of shipping beer to the U.S. market. Among the most popular imported brands are Corona (from Mexico), Heineken (from the Netherlands), and Labatt Blue (from Canada).

Figure 1.3 illustrates the relative popularity of the main styles of beer sold in the United States in 2001. Imported beer commands a market share of more than 10 percent. In spite of rapid growth and notoriety, domestic specialty beer has a market share of only about 3 percent, comparable to that of ice beer or malt liquor. The remaining styles of beer are brewed by the mass producers and have a sizable share of the market. What one might consider traditional American beer (i.e., domestic super-premium, premium, popular, and light beer) accounts for about 75 percent of all beer sales in the United States. Light beer is

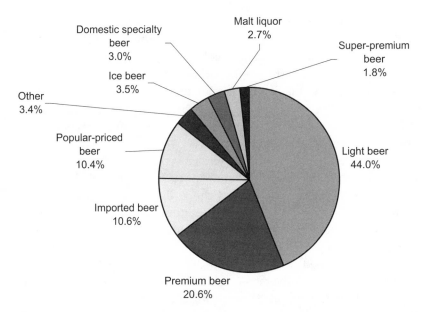

Figure 1.3
Market shares of leading beer categories in the United States in 2001. Source: See appendix A.

the most popular category, with a 44 percent market share. Of the five leading brands sold in the United States in 2001, all are American-style lagers: Bud Light (with a market share of total U.S. production at 18.7 percent), Budweiser (18.2 percent), Miller Lite (8.8 percent), Coors Light (8.6 percent), and Natural Light (4.5 percent).

1.4   Fundamental Questions and Overview

Because of their production dominance, considerable discussion is devoted to the mass producers and their core products. After all, Anheuser-Busch and Miller spill more beer than the specialty brewers produce.[11] The mass-producing sector is of particular interest because mass producers have continued to exit the industry and the reasons for this trend are not fully understood. One hypothesis is that technological change has made large-scale production more efficient. Another suggests that greater advertising competition has forced many local and regional brewers out of business. Chapter 2 sets the stage for this debate by showing how demand and cost conditions in the brewing industry have changed since World War II. Chapter 3 documents the increasing concentration among the mass producers, surveys previous studies, and provides evidence that scale economies and advertising competition have contributed to a high level of concentration.

Anheuser-Busch is currently the largest and most successful brewer in the world. The industry price leader and one of the most profitable brewers in the United States, Anheuser-Busch maintains a clear competitive advantage over other U.S. brewers. The sources of its success will be discussed in chapters to come.

On its rise to the top, Anheuser-Busch faced a number of challengers. In the late 1940s and the early 1950s, Anheuser-Busch traded the number 1 spot with Pabst and Schlitz. Schlitz, the last competitor to hold the top spot in brewing (in 1956), continued to challenge Anheuser-Busch through the mid 1970s. But Anheuser-Busch faced its stiffest competition from Miller. Philip Morris Inc., a successful cigarette producer, purchased Miller in 1969–1970 and vowed to capture the number 1 spot from Anheuser-Busch. The fierce battle that ensued led to brand proliferation and to escalating advertising spending among the leading brewers. At the local level, Anheuser-Busch also faced stiff competition from several strong regional brewers. For example, Coors operated regionally in the 1970s and was the leading brewer in Oklahoma in 1977, with a 59.6 share of the state's beer sales (*Beer Industry Update: A Review of Recent Developments*, 1982). Chapter 4 provides a brief history of the 13 most influential brewers and describes the strategies contributing to their successes and failures.

The emergence of microbreweries is of interest for two reasons. First, the sheer number of entrepreneurs who started brew pubs or microbreweries and their phenomenal success into the mid 1990s merits attention. Second, these small brewers have returned to the brewing practices of Europe, a strategy that has proven successful and changed the behavior of many mass producers. Today, most domestic mass producers offer European-style beers along with their flagship brands. Chapter 5 describes the microbrewery movement and the behavior of the leading domestic specialty brewers. Imports and their importance to the domestic market are also discussed in that chapter.

Another goal of the book is to evaluate the extent to which the behavior of brewers is consistent with game theory. The approach taken here borrows from the new industrial organization by focusing on game-theoretic analysis of optimal firm actions and from strategic management by investigating the strategic histories of firms (Ghemawat 1997; McAfee 2002). The best way to conduct such research is with a case study of an oligopolistic industry. Chapters 3, 6, and 7 examine the important strategies used in brewing and how they have influenced the evolution of the industry. The evidence suggests that game theory explains the behavior of brewing firms. Brewers used various pricing, advertising, brand-proliferation, merger, and "Hail Mary" strategies to compete in a "preemption race" in advertising and in a "war of attrition" that was thrust upon them by external forces.

Ongoing concentration and the dominance of Anheuser-Busch evoke concern about the industry's performance. Chapter 8 investigates the industry's efficiency, equity, and technological progress. In view of Anheuser-Busch's prominence, the market power exerted by that firm is estimated for several time regimes.

Chapter 9 provides a policy assessment of the industry. As many mass-producing brewers exited the industry by merging with other brewers, the U.S. Department of Justice established several important anti-merger precedents by successfully challenging mergers in brewing. These cases are reviewed, and policies needed to ensure an adequate degree of competition in brewing are discussed. Estimates of the external costs associated with drunk driving and alcohol abuse are summarized, and proposals by public health officials to mitigate the external costs of alcohol consumption and abuse, such as higher excise taxes and tighter advertising restrictions, are surveyed and assessed.

The final chapter provides predictions concerning the future of the brewing industry and offers suggestions for future research.

2   Basic Demand and Cost Conditions

We might as reasonably dispute whether it is the upper or the under blade of a pair of scissors that cuts a piece of paper, as whether value is governed by utility or cost of production.

—Alfred Marshall, *Principles of Economics* (1890)

Demand, cost, and regulatory conditions shape an industry and affect the behavior and the performance of individual firms. On the demand side of the market, producers who are unwilling or unable to meet the needs of consumers will fail. For example, if consumers' preferences vary geographically because of differences in customs, norms, or traditions, then national producers will benefit from offering products that cater to regional differences. On the supply side, the state of technology has an important influence on production, as new technologies enable firms to produce the same quantity of output at lower cost. Legal constraints may have a direct effect on demand and cost conditions as well as on the industry's structure. For example, the federal government could impose taxes that would increase costs, could ban advertising in an effort to curb consumer demand, or could prohibit large corporations from expanding further.

Several factors drive market demand and firm cost conditions in the U.S. brewing industry. Important demand factors include the price of beer, the price of substitutes (other alcoholic and non-alcoholic beverages), consumers' income, demographics, and the level of consumer addiction. On the supply side, the most important factor has been technological change.

Understanding the basic economic conditions of a market is important for at least two reasons. First, it allows one to assess the productive efficiency of an industry.[1] Second, effective policy recommendations require a thorough understanding of the industry. For example, a sales tax policy that is designed to reduce the consumption of a particular commodity will be less effective in markets with relatively inelastic market demand functions. This chapter discusses the basic economic conditions of the U.S. brewing industry, information that will be useful in later chapters.

2.1 The Demand for Beer

Economic theory predicts that an individual consumer's demand for beer is a function of the price of beer, the prices of substitutes and complements, the consumer's income, the product's characteristics, and the consumer's level of consumption capital. Important substitutes for beer include other alcoholic beverages, such as wine and distilled spirits, and soft drinks. Regarding product characteristics, there is little real difference among the brands marketed by the mass-producing beer companies. Nevertheless, beer producers may appeal to consumers from different socioeconomic classes—for example, by targeting heavily advertised name-brand products to the wealthy and generic or unadvertised brands to those with lower incomes. Thus, advertising may play an important role in promoting name brands and influencing demand.

The fact that alcoholic beverages are potentially addictive affects the demand for beer in a number of ways. First, price and income may have little effect on demand. Second, addiction will influence demand directly and will vary with an individual's consumption capital (Stigler and Becker 1977). For an addictive commodity, current consumption may be higher when past and expected future consumption are higher (Becker and Murphy 1988; Akerlof 1991). Third, peer pressure and advertising that promotes an image that drinking alcohol is the social norm may encourage alcohol consumption (Akerlof and Kranton 2000).[2]

At the market level, demographic factors also affect the demand for beer. Table 2.1 identifies the percent of the population that drinks beer by gender, age, race, household income, and region of the country for various years from 1980 through 2001. The figures indicate that men are more likely to drink beer than women and that beer is more popular for consumers aged 18–44 than for those 45 and over.[3] Racial differences exist and vary over time. Across all years, beer demand rises with household income. Residents of the Northeast and the West are

Table 2.1
Percent of population that drinks beer, by demographic category and year. Source: Simmons Market Research Bureau, as reported in *Beer Industry Update: A Review of Recent Developments* (various issues).

	1980	1985	1990	1995	2001
Adults	48.8	48.4	43.0	46.6	42.8
Males	62.0	59.9	54.8	57.5	—
Females	36.0	38.2	32.2	36.5	—
18–24	57.7	56.7	47.0	49.9	50.5
25–34	58.6	56.9	51.2	59.3	51.6
35–44	53.2	51.4	47.0	50.6	49.6
45–54	47.2	47.3	43.1	43.6	44.2
55–64	40.5	40.7	37.6	35.1	35.0
65+	27.5	30.6	26.2	31.7	26.0
Race					
White	48.9	48.4	43.2	47.3	—
African-American	47.3	49.0	41.1	42.1	—
Other	51.6	49.0	45.1	43.8	—
Household Income (×$1,000)					
60+	—	—	49.3	53.9	49.5
40–60	56.7	54.6	48.1	52.3	44.6
30–40	54.1	53.3	45.6	45.7	41.4
20–30	—	—	43.2	45.0	39.3
10–20	50.4	45.0	39.5	38.2	29.6
0–10	36.6	40.0	28.4	36.2	28.9
Region					
Northeast	50.4	52.1	45.4	49.3	—
East Central	47.9	46.3	—	—	—
West Central	54.2	50.9	—	—	—
South	40.5	43.8	38.1	43.1	—
Pacific	55.5	50.9	—	—	—
Midwest	—	—	46.7	46.5	—
West	—	—	44.5	50.0	—

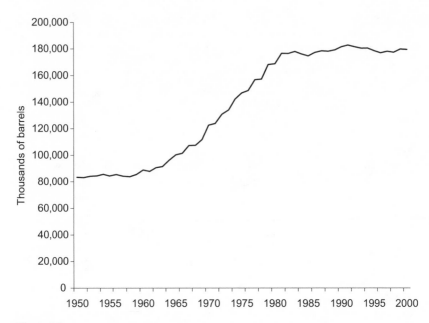

Figure 2.1
Total U.S. consumption of domestic beer, 1950–2000. Source: See appendix A.

more likely to be beer drinkers than residents of other regions. Per-capita beer consumption varies considerably across states. While annual per-capita beer consumption in the United States was 22 gallons in 2000, Utah had the lowest consumption rate at 12.9 gallons and Nevada had the highest at 32.1 gallons (*Beer Industry Update: A Review of the Evidence* 2001).[4]

Figures 2.1 and 2.2 show how beer consumption has changed from 1950 through 2000. Figure 2.1 details the impressive growth in total consumption from the early 1960s to 1980. Figure 2.2 reveals a similar pattern for per-capita consumption (i.e., consumption per person aged 18 years and older), but the trend declines after 1980. The coming of age of the baby-boom generation during the mid 1960s provides a partial explanation for these trends. Figure 2.3 tracks the trend in the primary beer-drinking population, those aged 18–44, revealing a pattern that mimics that of per-capita consumption.

The trends of other important demand determinants are depicted in figures 2.4 and 2.5. According to figure 2.4, the price of beer rose relative to the price of spirits and fell relative to the price of soft drinks from 1964 to 2000. The relative price changes for alcoholic beverages

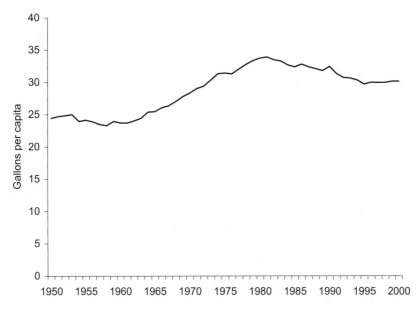

Figure 2.2
U.S. per-capita beer consumption, 1950–2000. Sources: See appendix A.

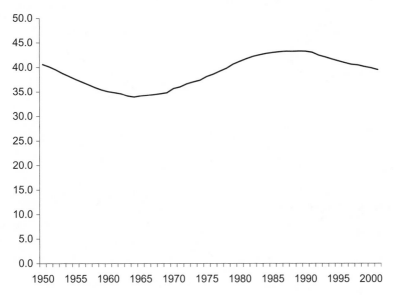

Figure 2.3
Percent of U.S. population 18–44 years old, 1950–2001. Source: See appendix A.

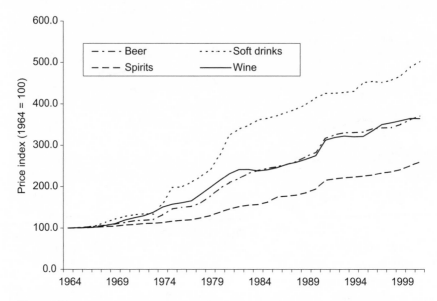

Figure 2.4
Price indices for beer, soft drinks, spirits, and wine, 1964–2001. Source: See appendix A.

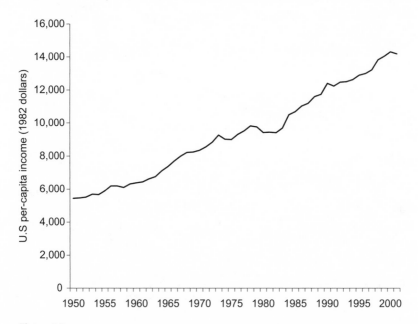

Figure 2.5
U.S. real disposable income per capita, 1950–2001. Source: See appendix A.

may be driven by a shift in demand away from spirits in favor of beer and wine. This is consistent with the trend in the percent of ethanol (or absolute alcohol) consumed in the form of spirits, which declined from 41.5 percent to 29.0 percent from 1960 to 2001; during this period, beer's share rose from 47.9 percent to 58.1 percent and wine's share rose from 10.6 percent to 12.9 percent (*Beer Industry Update: A Review of Recent Developments* 2002: 274). Figure 2.5 shows that real per-capita income more that doubled from 1950 to 2000. Since beer is a normal good, income growth may have been an important stimulant of demand, especially for premium and super-premium brands.

Considerable effort has been devoted to estimating the market demand for beer. Table 2.2 summarizes the main findings of seven recent studies. Although there is variability in the estimates, they all indicate that the demand for beer is inelastic, with a mean estimate of the price elasticity of demand of about −0.498. That is, a 10 percent increase in the price reduces the quantity demanded by about 5 percent. The majority of studies conclude that beer is a normal good but that income has a relatively small effect on demand. Regarding cross-price effects, most studies show that wine, spirits, and soft drinks are imperfect substitutes for beer, as the cross-price elasticity estimates are close to zero.[5] Studies that control for demographics find that demand rises with growth in the young adult population (Ornstein and Hanssens 1985; Lee and Tremblay 1992; Lariviere et al. 2000; Nelson 2003).

Table 2.2
Estimates of the price, income, and cross-price elasticities of the U.S. demand for beer. In studies with more than one elasticity estimate, mean values are reported. n.a.: not available.

Source	Price	Income	Cross-price Wine	Spirits	Soft drinks
Hogarty and Elzinga 1972	−0.889	0.430	n.a.	n.a.	n.a.
Ornstein and Hanssens 1985	−0.142	0.011	n.a.	n.a.	n.a.
Tegene 1990	−0.768	0.731	0.202	0.106	n.a.
Lee and Tremblay 1992	−0.583	0.135	n.a.	0.267	0.305
Gallet and List 1998	−0.730	−0.545	0.285	n.a.	n.a.
Nelson 1999	−0.200	0.760	0.140	0.062	n.a.
Nelson 2003	−0.174	−0.032	n.a.	n.a.	n.a.
Mean value	−0.498	0.213	0.209	0.145	0.305
Standard error	0.318	0.465	0.073	0.108	—

McGahan (1995) estimates U.S. beer demand for the period 1935–1939 and finds similar results to those of table 2.2. Her estimate of the income elasticity of demand is 0.40, and although she finds that soda, spirits, and wine are mild substitutes for beer, only the price of soda is significant. The one result that conflicts with table 2.2 is her price elasticity estimate of −10.30. According to McGahan, consumers had greater access to home-brewed beer after Prohibition, which made the demand for beer more elastic during the 1930s.

Debate continues over the effect of advertising on the demand for beer. Whether advertising provides consumers with useful information about product characteristics, signals product quality, or attempts to persuade consumers of the merits of one brand over another, a firm will advertise only if it leads to a sufficient increase in its demand. Advertising that attracts new customers or causes existing customers to buy more will increase market demand. If, however, advertising only induces current customers to switch brands, then it will have no effect on market demand. Grabowski (1977–78), Kelton and Kelton (1982), and Tremblay (1985b) find that a firm's advertising increases the demand for its products.[6] Demand estimates for the industry leader, Anheuser-Busch, will be discussed later in the chapter. For the market as a whole, most of the empirical evidence indicates that advertising has little or no effect on beer demand (Lee and Tremblay 1992; Gisser 1999; Nelson 1999; Coulson et al. 2001).[7] This is not surprising; advertising is unlikely to attract many new customers to an established market with well-known brands such as mass-produced beer. Nonetheless, the issue remains controversial among social scientists and public health officials.

The demand for beer has varied with time. First, beer consumption is seasonal, peaking in the warm summer months (*Brewers Almanac* 1998: 18). Second, the evidence indicates that the demand for milder foods and beverages began to increase in the 1950s.[8] In response, the major brewers started brewing lighter and lighter beer. In the early 1960s, the rule of thumb in brewing was "a bushel of malt to a barrel of beer" (*Printers' Ink*, January 19, 1962: 28), but this changed as the leading brewers started using fewer grains and hops to make beer. From 1950 to 2000, for example, the amount of malt used to brew a barrel of beer in the United States declined by more than 21 percent, and the quantity of hops declined by more than 62 percent. Figures 2.6 and 2.7 show how the amounts of grain, malt, and hops used to make a barrel

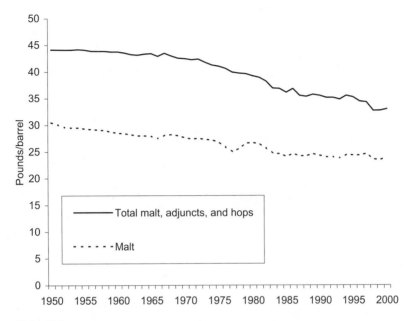

Figure 2.6
Total ingredients and total malt used to make beer in the United States. Source: U.S. Treasury Department, Bureau of Alcohol, Tobacco, and Firearms as reported in *Brewers Almanac* (various issues).

of beer have declined, indicating that the average domestic beer has become considerably lighter and milder since the 1950s. This shift in demand toward lighter products proved to be an important influence on firm success.

Consumers have also shown an increasing preference for premium over popular-priced beer. The popular-priced category commanded a market share of about 80 percent in 1950 (*Beverage World*, December 1991: 21), about 75 percent in 1960 (Greer 2002: 37), but only 10.4 percent by 2001. Rising income partially explains this change, as premium beer is likely to be more income-elastic than popular-priced beer. The main problem with this argument is that premium and popular-priced brands have very similar characteristics, which raises the question why so many consumers prefer the higher-priced premium brands. One likely explanation is advertising. Premium brands are heavily advertised, which enhances image and boosts demand. When a brand is high priced and has an image of high quality, then Veblen effects strengthen the persuasive power of advertising.[9] That is, consumers

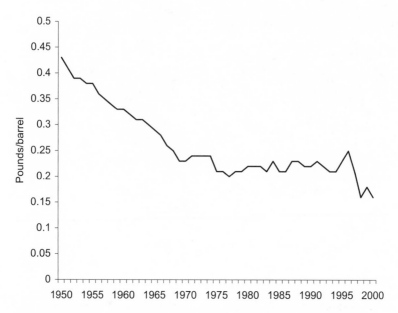

Figure 2.7
Total hops used to produce beer in the United States, 1950–2000. Source: U.S. Treasury
Department, Bureau of Alcohol, Tobacco, and Firearms as reported in *Brewers Almanac*
(various issues).

who want to impress their neighbors will prefer more expensive
brands that use advertising to reinforce a premium or super-premium
image. The trend toward consumption of beer in bottles and cans facil-
itates these image effects,[10] as it is easier to display consumption of
a super-premium brand when the name is in plain sight. The shift
toward brands with a premium image encouraged aggressive advertising of the premium brands by the national brewers. Advertising and
a growing demand for premium beer have important implications for
firm success and industry structure.

The demand for beer has also been estimated for several foreign
countries. The best studies include Clements and Johnson 1983
(Australia), Selvanathan 1995 (the United Kingdom), and Lariviere
2000 (Canada). In spite of cultural differences among countries, the
empirical results are surprisingly close to those of the United States.
Demand is inelastic; the effects of wine, spirits, and income are small;
and advertising generally has a positive but insignificant effect on
market demand.

2.2   Technology and the Cost of Producing Beer

From duality theory, all of the economically relevant aspects of a technology can be summarized in a cost function or a production function
(Varian 1992). A production function describes the maximum quantity
of outputs that can be produced in a particular period from a specified
set of inputs and state of technology. A cost function describes the
minimum cost of producing outputs in a particular period, given input
prices and technology. In most empirical representations of brewing
technology, output is measured in 31-gallon barrels, and inputs are
divided into three categories: labor, capital, and materials.

Understanding the nature of technology is important for several reasons. First, it provides information about the extent of economies of
scale and scope. Second, it allows one to assess the efficiency of firm
production. Inefficiency can result, for example, if production takes
place at the wrong scale, if firms waste inputs, or if firms use inputs in
the wrong proportions. Figure 2.8 depicts a variable-returns-to-scale
production function, $f(x)$, with a single input (x) and a single output
(q), and illustrates three types of inefficiency. If the firm employs x_1,
then pure technical efficiency is achieved if production equals q_1^{PTE}.
Scale and technical efficiency are reached when production takes place
on the constant-returns-to-scale frontier at point q_1^{OTE}. If the firm actually produces q_1, pure technical inefficiency exists and equals $q_1^{PTE} - q_1$
or segment AB. Scale inefficiency also exists and equals $q_1^{OTE} - q_1^{PTE}$
or segment BC. Following Färe et al. (1985), pure technical efficiency
(PTE), scale efficiency (SE), and overall technical efficiency (OTE) are
defined as follows:

$$PTE \equiv q/q^{PTE},$$

$$SE \equiv q^{PTE}/q^{OTE},$$

$$OTE \equiv q/q^{OTE}.$$

Overall efficiency is reached when the firm uses x^* to produce q^*,
which implies that $PTE = SE = OTE = 1$.

Understanding basic economic conditions allows one to evaluate the
productive efficiency of an industry. With estimates of market demand
and minimum efficient scale, defined as the minimum output needed
to reach scale efficiency, one can determine the industry structure that
will minimize the total industry cost of producing the socially optimal

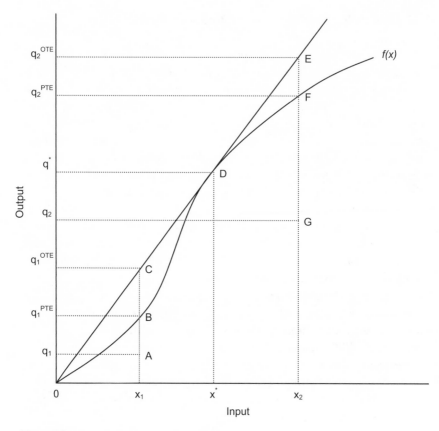

Figure 2.8
The production function and efficiency measures.

level of production (i.e., productive efficiency). This allows one to compare the actual with the cost-minimizing industry structure (Baumol,
Panzar, and Willig 1982).

Figure 2.9 shows how total, labor, and material costs of production
per barrel changed from 1950 to 1997. The real cost of brewing beer (in
1982 dollars) has typically ranged from $50 to $75 per barrel. Because
the quantities of materials per barrel were relatively stable over time,
much of the fluctuation in material costs resulted from changes in the
price of materials. Shrinking employment caused a slight decline in the
total cost of labor in spite of rising real wage rates. From 1950 to 1998,
for example, average annual real wages in brewing rose by about 88
percent, motivating firms to substitute capital for labor.[11]

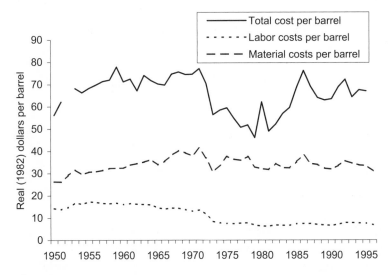

Figure 2.9
Input costs per barrel, 1950–1996. Source: See appendix A.

Labor strikes and consumer boycotts disrupt production and raise short-run unit costs (since some inputs are fixed). The most dramatic examples involve Anheuser-Busch and Coors in the 1970s. A 1976 strike by Anheuser-Busch workers lasted 95 days (*Wall Street Journal*, June 7, 1976; *Business Week*, April 21, 1980). A comparison of the company's cost per barrel in 1976 with the average cost per barrel in adjacent years reveals that the strike increased Anheuser-Busch's unit cost by about 8.4 percent. At Coors, management was accused of unfair labor practices, which led to a short strike and a boycott of Coors beer from 1977 through 1978 (*Business Week*, May 8, 1978 and September 29, 1980; Burgess 1993; Baum 2001). Coors's unit costs during the period exceeded the average for adjacent years by about 2.3 percent.

Advertising costs are important in many consumer-goods industries. In brewing, advertising accounted for more than 7 percent of the total or full cost in brewing from 1950 to 1996. If marketing and production are separable operations, one can define the full cost function as the production cost function plus the marketing cost function. On the production side, the goal of the firm is to invest in inputs in order to minimize the cost of producing the profit-maximizing level of output. On the marketing side, the goal is to invest in advertising and other

Table 2.3
Estimates of minimum efficient scale (MES), measured in millions of barrels.

	MES	Source
1935	0.1	McGahan 1991
1957	0.1	*Business Week*, March 9, 1957
1963	1.0	*Business Week*, April 13, 1968
1967	1.0	*Forbes*, November 1, 1967
1968	1.0	*Financial World*, February 28, 1968
1973	4.5	Scherer 1973
1982	4.5	*Business Week*, July 12, 1982
1990	>4.5	Elzinga 1990

promotional activities in order to minimize the cost of selling that output in the market (Färe et al. 2004; Vardanyan and Tremblay 2004).

Three studies provide empirical analyses of production technology in the U.S. brewing industry. Tremblay (1987) uses firm-level data to estimate a translog specification of a cost function. Kerkvliet et al. (1998) employ industry data to estimate a ray-homothetic specification of a production function (Färe 1975). Xia and Buccola (2003) estimate a generalized Leontief specification of a cost function using industry data. All three studies find statistical support for the hypothesis that the U.S. brewing industry experienced considerable technological change and productivity growth in the second half of the twentieth century.[12]

Evidence from several sources indicates that changes in technology caused scale economies to increase in brewing.[13] Table 2.3 summarizes estimates of the minimum level of output needed to reach scale efficiency, minimum efficient scale (MES), from trade sources and early economic studies. Estimates of MES went up, especially in the late 1960s and the early 1970s.[14] MES was estimated at about 100,000 barrels in the late 1950s and more than 4 million barrels by the mid 1970s.

An early technique designed to identify an industry's efficient scale of operation is the survivor test, an approach that assumes that the largest share of industry output will be produced by firms that operate at the most efficient size.[15] Although it captures more than just scale effects, the survivor test does identify the most successful size classes of firms over time. Table 2.4 provides survivor estimates for the U.S. brewing industry for five-year intervals from 1950 to 2000. The dominant size class was less than 1 million barrels through 1960 but rose

Table 2.4
Percent of production by size class for selected years. Size-class values are measured in millions of barrels. Production data are for all domestic specialty and mass-producing brewers. Sources: Tremblay 1987 for 1950–1983; Office of R. S. Weinberg for 1985–2000.

Size class	1950	1955	1960	1965	1970	1975	1980	1985	1990	1995	2000
0–<1	56.7	37.4	28.1	12.5	3.9	8.5	5.7	3.1	1.8	2.8	3.3
1–<2	10.2	17.5	15.9	8.6	7.7	1.6	0	1.0	0	1.6	1.9
2–<4	15.8	31.7	18.9	18.0	22.9	3.7	6.1	1.6	1.2	0	0
4–<6	17.3	13.4	27.5	26.3	20.6	20.4	0	0	0	0	0
6–<10	0	0	9.6	22.9	5.9	0	6.9	5.0	3.6	7.7	0
10–<18	0	0	0	11.7	20.9	26.9	32.1	17.3	14.4	5.9	5.9
>18	0	0	0	0	18.1	38.9	49.2	72.0	79.0	82.0	88.9

sharply to more than 18 million barrels by 1975. These results are consistent with table 2.3 for the 1950s but suggest that MES was much larger than industry experts realized thereafter.

Scholars have proposed three hypotheses to explain these survivor results. Keithahn (1978), Ornstein (1981), and Lynk (1984) argue that advances in technology increased the efficient scale of operation in brewing. Greer (1971, 1981) and Mueller (1978) claim that the growth in share of the largest size class follows from an advertising advantage enjoyed by large brewers. Sutton (1991) develops a model to show how both effects interact to boost sunk costs and the privately efficient scale of operation.

Kerkvliet et al. (1998) investigate how technical change affects the efficient scale of operation in brewing. They use industry data to estimate a production function and find that technological change substantially increased MES from 1960 to 1990. A scale-efficient firm had to produce about 600,000 barrels of beer (requiring a market share of 0.7 percent) in 1960 and more than 5.5 million barrels (requiring a share of about 2.9 percent) in 1990.

After assessing the evidence, Keithahn (1978) and Greer (2002) provide MES estimates more in line with the survivor test. Their work suggests that conservative estimates of MES were about 8 million barrels in 1970, at least 16 million barrels from 1980 to 1990, and 18 million barrels in 2000. The data that are available suggest that MES may have been even higher than 18 million barrels by the late 1990s.[16] Figure 2.10 plots the average cost (in 2000 dollars) against output levels for several firms of different sizes from 1993 to 2000. Average cost declines dra-

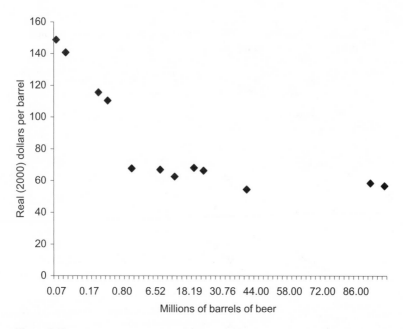

Figure 2.10
The average cost of production for various brewers. Source: *Beer Industry Update: A Review of Recent Developments* (various issues).

matically to about 1.2 million barrels and continues to decline to a lesser extent up to about 39 million barrels of production.[17] Although these numbers are only suggestive, as the data ignore potentially important firm effects, they imply that the degree of scale economies is substantially higher today than in the 1950s and the 1960s.

There are several reasons for the increase in MES in brewing. First, faster packaging equipment made large-scale production more efficient. Table 2.5 shows that the speed of canning lines has increased more than sixfold since the early 1950s. To operate a single canning line at an efficient rate, a firm had to produce only 330,000 barrels of beer in 1952 but more than 2 million barrels by 1987. Second, new technologies made it possible to automate many of the functions of modern breweries during the 1960s and the 1970s. Keithahn (1978) demonstrates that these innovations led to considerable reductions in labor costs. In 1973, for example, he found that the modern Schlitz plant in Memphis (built in 1970) had 45 percent lower labor costs and 4 percent lower overall costs per unit than its older Los Angeles plant (built in 1954). At the industry level, greater automation decreased the

Table 2.5
Maximum speed of a canning line and scale of operation needed to make efficient use of a single canning line. Efficient scale of operation measures annual production (million barrels) needed to operate one canning line efficiently, based on normal operating rates for U.S. breweries of a 250-day, three-shift operation (Keithahn 1978: 34–35). According to *Business Week* (September 13, 1969: 138), canning lines in the early 1950s operated at 300 cans per minute and cost $26,000; in 1969, canning lines operated at 1,200 cans per minute and cost about $90,000. In real terms, this amounted to $99,200 in the early 1950s and $265,500 in 1969. Estimates of number of 12-ounce cans that can be filled per minute are from the following sources: *Business Week*, September 13, 1969; Keithahn 1978; Tremblay 1987; Scherer 1996; Anheuser-Busch Customer Service Center (January 6, 2003).

	Maximum speed (12-oz. cans/minute)	Efficient scale of operation (millions of barrels)
1952	300	0.330
1966	750	0.820
1969	1,200	1.310
1978	1,500	1.630
1987	2,000	2.180
2003	2,000	2.180

amount of labor needed to produce an average barrel of beer by about 84 percent from 1950 to 1997. Third, cost savings associated with multi-plant operation have further increased the efficient scale of the firm. In the late 1940s and the early 1950s, innovations in water treatment allowed brewers to use water of consistent quality in all parts of the country.[18] Firms could then decentralize production, cut transportation costs, and expand their geographic markets. Falstaff and Pabst were the only multi-plant producers in 1948, but most of the major brewers operated more than one plant by 1956.[19] Scherer et al. (1975) find that national producers with three or four plants gained moderate cost advantages over single-plant producers because of efficiencies in marketing, investment flexibility, and risk management. More recently, industry analysts have estimated that efficient production requires five or six plants (*Modern Brewery Age*, March 16, 1992). By 2003, only the industry leaders, Anheuser-Busch and Miller, had five or more plants.

A superior marketing position, as is enjoyed by a large firm, also appears to be important. According to Porter (1976), television gave a marketing advantage to large national producers over smaller local and regional producers after World War II. If television is more effective than other media for advertising beer, then the relative cost of advertising to reach a certain number of potential consumers would

fall for national producers.[20] Hilke and Nelson (1984) find that unit
advertising costs are generally lower for national than for regional
advertising campaigns, and Tremblay (1985b) finds that the marginal
benefit of advertising is greater for national than for regional brewers.
Seldon et al. (2000) provide the most reliable estimates of brewers'
advertising costs by estimating a cost function for advertising with
quarterly data (1983–1993) from six major beer producers (Anheuser-
Busch, Coors, Genesee, Heileman, Pabst, and Stroh). Their results indicate that television, radio, and print advertising are substitutes but not
perfect substitutes in promoting sales. Using the same data set, Färe
et al. (2004) find that beer advertising exhibits mild economies of scale,
with minimum efficient scale ranging from 2.5 million to 3.5 million
barrels of production per year from 1983 to 1993.

The last issue of interest regarding brewing technology involves the
extent to which beer producers minimize production and marketing
costs. Kerkvliet et al. (1998) estimate a stochastic frontier production
function, assuming an exponential and a truncated normal error structure, and find a high level of efficiency on the production side of brewing. Their mean estimate of technical efficiency is 0.96, their scale
efficiency is 0.98, and their overall technical efficiency is 0.94.[21] On the
marketing side, Kelton and Kelton (1982) find that Miller was the most
efficient advertiser in brewing from 1951 to 1977. Much of Miller's
superior marketing efficiency is attributable to the success of Miller
Lite's advertising theme in the 1970s. In a study of the advertising productivity of Anheuser-Busch, Coors, Genesee, Heileman, Pabst, and
Stroh from 1983 to 1993, Färe et al. (2004) conclude that all but one firm
over-invested in television advertising. The one exception is Anheuser-
Busch, which was the most efficient advertiser of the group. Färe et al.
and Vardanyan and Tremblay also find that overall marketing efficiency and firm success are closely linked for these large brewers. Industry experts often claim that marketing efficiency is more important
than production efficiency for success in brewing (Scherer et al. 1975:
258), a viewpoint that is consistent with academic research and with
the relative success of Miller and Anheuser-Busch.

2.3   Estimation of Production and Demand

This section provides new estimates of an industry production function and a market demand function. We also estimate a firm demand
function for the industry leader, Anheuser-Busch. The specification of

the market demand function for beer follows from the discussion above and from Denney et al. 2002.[22] The empirical model is

$$Q_t = \alpha_0 + \alpha_1 P_t + \alpha_2 P_t^{\text{Cola}} + \alpha_3 P_t^{\text{Spirits}} + \alpha_4 \text{Inc}_t + \alpha_5 \text{Dem}_t$$

$$+ \alpha_6 Q_{t-1} + e_{t,D}, \tag{2.1}$$

where Q_t is total beer consumption in period t, P is the price of beer, P^{Cola} is the price of cola, P^{Spirits} is the price of spirits, Inc is disposable income, Dem is a demographic variable, and e_D is an additive error term. Dem is the proportion of the adult population (age 18 and over) in the age group 18–44. Marketing studies and table 2.1 show that people in this age group are more likely to drink beer than those over 44. Lagged consumption (Q_{t-1}) controls for habit or addiction, assuming a partial adjustment or myopic model of addiction.[23] Because the price and output of beer are determined simultaneously, equation 2.1 is estimated jointly with the supply relation described in chapter 8 using two-stage least squares.[24]

Table 2.6 reports the empirical results for the market demand function. All parameter estimates have expected signs, and most differ significantly from zero at traditional levels of significance. Consistent with previous studies, the results show that cola and spirits are substitutes for beer and that the demand for beer slopes downward. Income growth stimulates beer demand, indicating that beer is a normal good. Demand increases with the fraction of the population aged 18–44, and the significant coefficient on the lagged value of consumption

Table 2.6
Parameter estimates of the market demand for beer in the U.S., 1953–1995. Adjusted $R^2 = 0.998$; $F = 3223.9$.[a] Source: Denney et al. 2002.

Variable	Parameter estimate	$|t\text{-statistic}|$
Intercept ($\times 10^{-3}$)	8.529	0.218
P ($\times 10^{-2}$)	-3.871^{b}	2.680
P^{Cola} ($\times 10^{-2}$)	2.955^{a}	3.791
P^{Spirits} ($\times 10^{-2}$)	0.141	0.129
Inc	6.058^{b}	2.226
Dem ($\times 10^{-4}$)	11.597^{c}	1.988
Q_{t-1}	0.638^{a}	5.309

a. Significant at 0.01 level (two-tailed test).
b. Significant at 0.05 level (two-tailed test).
c. Significant at 0.10 level (two-tailed test).

Table 2.7
Own-price, cross-price, and income elasticity estimates of demand.

	Short run	Long run
Own price	−0.298	−0.745
Cross-price, beer-cola	0.191	0.478
Cross-price, beer-spirits	0.015	0.038
Income	0.085	0.213

is consistent with addictive behavior. Table 2.7 reports the resulting short-run and long-run elasticity estimates taking into account the habit-forming nature of beer consumption. In general, these elasticity estimates are in keeping with those of the previous studies reported in table 2.2. Consistent with economic theory, the estimates indicate that demand is more elastic in the long run than the short run.

Anheuser-Busch's inverse demand depends on its own output and advertising, its rivals' output and advertising, and the income and demographic variables described above.[25] For example, even though advertising has no effect on market demand, Miller ads may cause consumers to buy more Miller beer and less beer from Anheuser-Busch. The empirical model of Anheuser-Busch's inverse demand function is

$$P_{t,\text{A-B}} = \beta_0 + \beta_1 q_{t,\text{A-B}} + \beta_2 q_{t,\text{Other}} + \beta_3 A_{t,\text{A-B}} + \beta_4 A_{t,\text{Other}}$$

$$+ \beta_5 \text{Inc}_t + \beta_6 \text{Dem}_t + e_{t,\text{A-B}}, \tag{2.2}$$

where $P_{t,\text{A-B}}$ is the average price of Anheuser-Busch's beer in period t, $q_{\text{A-B}}$ is Anheuser-Busch's output, q_{Other} is the combined output of all other brewers (i.e., rivals' output), $A_{\text{A-B}}$ is the company's advertising expenditures, A_{Other} is the combined advertising of all other firms in brewing, and $e_{\text{A-B}}$ is an error term. The sample includes 52 annual observations from 1950 to 2001. Like the market demand model, the firm's price and output are endogenous variables, so the firm's inverse demand function and supply relation (discussed in chapter 8) are estimated jointly using two-stage least squares.[26]

Table 2.8 presents the empirical results. The estimated demand function for Anheuser-Busch beer shows that price is negatively and significantly affected by the firm's own output and the output of rivals. The other parameter estimates are small and insignificant. The values of the advertising parameters are of interest, however, as their signs

Table 2.8
Parameter estimates of demand for Anheuser-Busch (A-B) beer, 1950–2001. Adjusted $R^2 = 0.969; F = 257.72$.[a]

	Parameter estimate	$|t\text{-statistic}|$
Intercept	0.275	0.38
$q_{\text{A-B}}$ ($\times 10^4$)	-0.222[b]	1.72
q_{Other} ($\times 10^4$)	-0.105[a]	2.98
$A_{\text{A-B}}$ ($\times 10^4$)	0.017	0.07
A_{Other} ($\times 10^4$)	-0.013	0.17
Inc	-0.003	1.15
Dem	0.032	1.57

a. Significant at 0.01 level (two-tailed test).
b. Significant at 0.10 level (two-tailed test).

suggest that firms use advertising to compete for market share and that advertising is a strategic substitute (Bulow et al. 1985). That is, the firm's own advertising increases demand, and its rivals' advertising reduces the demand for Anheuser-Busch beer. This is consistent with market studies that show that advertising has little or no effect on market demand. Low levels of significance and a high R^2 are a concern and suggest that there may not be enough variation in the data to obtain reliable parameter estimates. Multi-collinearity plagues the data, with most pairwise correlations between variables exceeding 0.90. Still, omitting any of these variables might bias the results.[27]

The last function to be estimated is the industry production function. The new estimates below update the work of Kerkvliet et al. (1998) by expanding the sample from 1950–1992 to 1950–1995. The model specifies labor (L), materials (M), and capital (K) as inputs[28] and a ray-homothetic functional form (Färe 1975):

$$q = \ln \Theta_1 + \ln \Theta_2 D_{50}$$

$$+ D_{50}\left(\phi_1 \frac{L}{L+M+K}\ln L + \phi_2 \frac{M}{L+M+K}\ln M + \phi_3 \frac{K}{L+M+K}\ln K \right)$$

$$+ D_{72}\left(\phi_4 \frac{L}{L+M+K}\ln L + \phi_5 \frac{M}{L+M+K}\ln M + \phi_6 \frac{K}{L+M+K}\ln K \right)$$

$$+ e_{pf}, \tag{2.3}$$

where the Greek letters are parameters of the model and e_{pf} is an error term. The variable D_{50} equals 1 for the years 1950–1971 and 0

Table 2.9
Parameter estimates of production function, 1953–1995. Adjusted $R^2 = 0.989$; $F = 543.71$.[a]

Variable	Parameter estimate	$|t\text{-statistic}|$
Intercept	-0.721[a]	4.095
D_{50}	0.223	0.932
$x_L D_{50}$	0.123[b]	1.754
$x_L D_{72}$	0.251[a]	2.933
$x_M D_{50}$	0.094[a]	4.064
$x_M D_{72}$	0.151[a]	5.917
$x_K D_{50}$	0.104[a]	4.348
$x_K D_{72}$	0.126[a]	5.163

a. Significant at 0.01 level (two-tailed test).
b. Significant at 0.10 level (two-tailed test).

otherwise, and D_{72} equals 1 for the years 1972–1995 and 0 otherwise. These dummy variables control for a shift in the technology of beer production in 1972 (Kerkvliet et al. 1998), and this specification allows the intercept and slope parameters of the model to vary by technological regime.[29]

The production function is estimated by ordinary least squares.[30] The results are reported in table 2.9, where

$x_L \equiv (L \cdot \ln L)/x,$

$x_M \equiv (M \cdot \ln M)/x,$

$x_K \equiv (K \cdot \ln K)/x,$

and

$x \equiv (L + M + K).$

The parameter estimates are similar to those of Kerkvliet et al. (1998), and all input parameters are positive and significant. The results also confirm that the effect of each input on output is greater in the later regime. For example, the parameter value on the labor term x_L in the latter period ($\phi_4 = 0.251$) is more than twice that of the parameter value on x_L in the earlier period ($\phi_1 = 0.123$). The marginal product of each input is greater in the later period, a result that is consistent with the presence of technological change in brewing.

2.4 Conclusion

This chapter analyzes the basic demand and cost conditions of the U.S. brewing industry. Previous studies indicate that beer demand is price-inelastic and habit and demographic factors are important determinants of demand. Market demand is more responsive to price in the long run than in the short run, and consumers' income and the price of substitutes have small effects on the demand for beer. There is little evidence that advertising has a significant effect on the market demand for beer. Similar conclusions can be drawn from the beer demand studies of several foreign countries.

On the production side of the market, all the evidence indicates that there was considerable technological change in brewing between 1950 and 2000. The real cost of production declined and the efficient scale of operation increased. Once a firm has reached MES, the evidence also suggests that marketing efficiency is vital to firm success in brewing.

In view of problems with multi-collinearity with the Anheuser-Busch data, further research is needed to better understand the nature of beer demand at the firm level. The market demand and production function results are consistent with previous work.

Industry Concentration

... in many and perhaps most American industries high concentration is not a technological, marketing, or financial imperative.

—F. M. Scherer, *Industrial Market Structure and Economic Performance* (1970: 103)

Industry concentration is a fundamental aspect of market structure. A change in concentration can have a profound effect on the behavior of firms and the economic performance of the market. For example, static Cournot and Bertrand models of oligopoly with product differentiation predict that pricing will become more competitive as the number of rivals increases. Therefore, understanding the causes and consequences of industry concentration is crucial to assessing the role of government in the industry. One way to shed light on these issues is to study the history of concentration in a particular industry.

The U.S. brewing industry provides an excellent case study. Between 1947 and 2000, as figure 3.1 shows, the number of independent mass-producing beer companies decreased from 421 to only 24.

Early on, industry experts did not anticipate the extent to which concentration would increase. For example, Horowitz and Horowitz (1965: 152) conclude that "it appears unlikely that concentration in the brewing industry, at least with regard to the leading five firms, will increase to any great extent in the near future...." By the 1970s, however, forecasts became remarkably accurate. Elzinga (1973: 113–114) predicted that the "shakeout in the industry has not ended" and that the "industry could support at least thirty efficient and independent firms." Keithahn (1978: 128) expected firms to continue to exit the industry until there were approximately 20–25 independent brewers, and Mueller (1978) argued that concentration would continue to rise

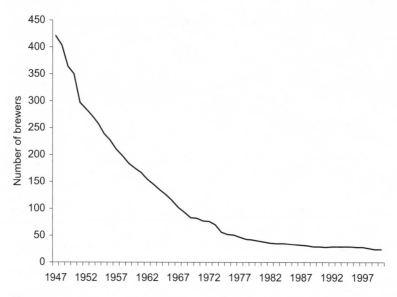

Figure 3.1
Number of independent mass-producing brewing companies, 1947–2000. Source: See appendix A.

and that Anheuser-Busch and Miller would come to dominate the brewing industry. Although the microbrewery revolution was unanticipated, these later forecasts are remarkably accurate for the mass-producing sector of the industry; there are currently 24 independent mass-producing beer companies, and the industry is dominated by the three national brewers: Anheuser-Busch, Miller and Coors.

The magnitude and duration of the transformation in the structure of the industry sparked speculation about its causes and economic consequences. At issue is the degree to which changes in technology and the marketing practices of leading brewers fueled increasing concentration. This chapter discusses the change in concentration and reasons for this change in the U.S. brewing industry. The economic consequences of increasing concentration in brewing will be discussed in chapters 6–8.

3.1   The Measurement and the Extent of Industry Concentration

An appropriate measure or index of concentration would account for both the number and the size distribution of firms within an industry. Consider, for example, two different industries, each with 100 firms.

The first might be classified as reasonably competitive if products are homogeneous and all firms are equal in size, while the second might be classified as imperfectly competitive if it is dominated by a few very large firms that produce differentiated products. To account for these differences, an index of concentration would assign greater weight to the size of the largest firms in the industry.

The two most commonly used indexes of industry concentration are the four-firm concentration ratio (CR_4) and the Herfindahl-Hirschman index (HHI).[1] For an industry with n firms that are ordered from largest (firm 1) to smallest (firm n), these indexes are defined as follows:

$$CR_4 \equiv \sum_{i=1}^{4} ms_i,$$

$$HHI \equiv \sum_{i=1}^{n} ms_i^2,$$

(3.1)

where ms_i is the market share of firm i. The concentration ratio measures the market share of the four largest firms in the industry, giving equal weight to the share of each of the four largest firms and no weight to the shares of other firms. The Herfindahl-Hirschman index measures the sum of squares of the market shares of all firms in the industry. Each firm's share receives weight, but greater weight is given to the shares of larger firms. Both CR_4 and HHI can range from 0 to 1, with a higher value indicating greater industry concentration. One can show that $HHI = \sum x_i^2 + 1/n$, where x_i is the deviation of the ith firm's market share from the industry mean market share (Scherer and Ross 1990: 73). This decomposition reveals that HHI rises with a decrease in the number of competitors and with an increase in the variance of market shares among competitors. When firms are of equal size, $\sum x_i^2 = 0$ and $HHI = 1/n$.[2] Because HHI accounts for the mean and variance of the size of firms in industry, HHI is generally preferred to other measures of concentration.[3]

Figure 3.2 depicts the trends in CR_4 and HHI (measured as an index ranging from 0 to 100) in brewing from 1947 to 2000 and reveals a consistent pattern of increasing concentration.[4] Even though firm size varies across brewers, the correlation coefficient between CR_4 and HHI is high at 0.95, a result that holds for many industries. In a sample of 91 U.S. industries, for example, Scherer (1980) finds that the average correlation between CR_4 and HHI is 0.94.

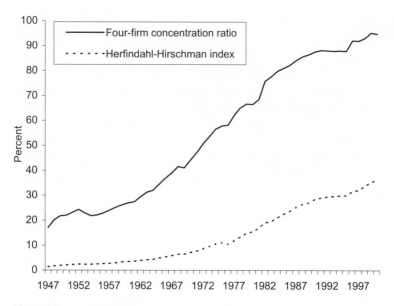

Figure 3.2
Concentration in the U.S. brewing industry, 1947–2000. Source: See appendix A.

One must be cautious when interpreting the national measures of concentration in brewing, however, since they are only accurate when the geographic market is national in scope. In several anti-trust cases from the 1950s and the early 1960s, the market for beer was defined as regional rather than national. The courts ruled that the market was a single state in the 1958 anti-merger case between the Pabst and Blatz brewing companies, but economic experts have shown that the market was substantially larger than one state (Elzinga 1986). In the Schlitz-Burgermeister case of 1961, the court identified the relevant geographic market as the western region of the country, which included the states of Arizona, California, Idaho, Montana, Nevada, Oregon, Utah, and Washington. This indicates that the national measures of CR$_4$ and HHI may understate the relevant regional level of concentration during this period.

The market became more national in scope by the mid 1960s. At that time, national brewers (Anheuser-Busch, Miller, Pabst, and Schlitz) came to dominate the industry, and most of the surviving brewers operated multiple plants in different regions of the country. To illustrate, the ten largest brewers operated 48 plants and had a combined market share of more than 66 percent in 1968. In addition, the stronger regional brewers were potential competitors in every region of the country by the late 1960s (Horowitz and Horowitz 1969). Greer (1981) defines the beer market as national by the 1970s.

Although such delineations may vary by industry, Scherer and Ross (1990: 82) and Shepherd (1997: 16) contend that once CR_4 exceeds 40 percent, the level of effective competition diminishes and an industry can be classified as an oligopoly. If one accepts this cutoff and the national market designation by the mid 1960s, then the brewing industry has been oligopolistic since 1968. This is consistent with Elzinga's (1971) characterization of the market as "concentrated" by the early 1970s. According to the standards established in the Merger Guidelines by the Department of Justice, brewing would be classified as "moderately concentrated" beginning in 1972 and "highly concentrated" beginning in 1982.[5] By the late 1990s, Greer (1998: 32) characterized the U.S. brewing industry as a "tightly-knit oligopoly."

3.2   The Causes of Increasing Concentration

Several factors influence industry concentration.[6] When the minimum efficient scale (MES) is large relative to the size of the market, productive efficiency requires just a few rivals and a natural oligopoly exists. Technological change that causes MES to rise will reduce the number of firms that can survive in the industry and drive up concentration. Individual firm effects may also be a factor. For example, an unusually lucky or successful firm will grow rapidly at the expense of its competitors and thereby increase concentration. In addition, a dominant firm may merge with rivals or pursue strategies that eliminate competitors. Government actions may affect entry or exit costs and the behavior of firms in ways that change industry concentration.

With more than 600 horizontal mergers and acquisitions of facilities and/or brands in the U.S. brewing industry since 1950 (Greer 2002: 32), one might think that merger activity has been an important cause of high concentration in brewing. As a hypothetical example, if the two largest firms (Anheuser-Busch and Miller) had merged in 2000, the market share of the leading firm would have increased from 53.61 to 75.67 percent and HHI would have jumped from 36.12 to 59.77. In spite of all the merger activity in brewing, effective enforcement of the anti-trust laws constrained the major brewers from expanding by merger. Weiss (1966), Elzinga (1973), and Tremblay and Tremblay (1988) find that most of the largest brewers gained little of their size through mergers from 1947 through 1983. Evidence on merger activity during the years 1984–2001, provided in chapter 7, supports this conclusion. Thus, the extensive merger activity in brewing involved primarily small or failing firms and had little effect on CR_4 and HHI.

Scholars disagree about the extent to which scale economies explain concentration in the brewing industry. Early studies by Elzinga (1973), Keithahn (1978), Ornstein (1981), and Lynk (1984) suggest that the dramatic increase in concentration resulted from new technologies that increased MES relative to the size of the market. The most reliable evidence from chapter 2 indicates that MES rose substantially for the mass producers in the post-World War II era. The implications of that research are summarized in table 3.1, which reports estimates of minimum efficient scale (MES*), scale efficiency (SE*), defined as the market share needed to reach MES*, the production of the average firm in the industry (Actual Average Scale), the number of firms needed to reach MES* (n*), and the actual number of mass-producing beer companies in the market (n). The estimates indicate that a brewer would need an annual level of production of about 0.1 million barrels in 1950 but 18.0 million barrels in 2000 to reach MES. This corresponds to a market share of 0.1 percent in 1950 and a market share of 9.9 percent in 2000. Scale efficiency did not appear to be a concern for brewers in 1950, as there were 350 firms in an industry that could efficiently sup-

Table 3.1
Estimates of MES, market share needed to reach MES, average actual scale, cost-minimizing number of firms, and actual number of firms. MES* is an estimate of minimum efficient scale (millions of barrels). SE* is an estimate of scale efficiency, measured as MES* divided by total beer production (percent). Actual average scale equals total beer production divided by the number of mass-producing beer companies (millions of barrels). n* is an estimate of the cost-minimizing number of firms, measured as total beer production divided by MES*, and n is the actual number of independent mass-producing beer companies.

	MES*	SE*	Actual average scale	n*	n
1950	0.1	0.1%	0.24	829	350
1960	1.0	1.1%	0.52	88	175
1970	8.0	6.4%	1.59	15	82
1980	16.0	9.1%	5.11	11	42
1990	16.0	8.5%	6.59	12	29
2000	18.0	9.9%	8.23	11	24

port 829 firms. The average firm was too small to reach MES by 1960, however, with 175 brewers forced to compete in a market that could efficiently support only 88 firms. Disequilibrium continued through 2000, as there were 24 brewers in an industry that could support only 11. This, at least partially, explains the impressive trend in concentration in brewing.

This evidence indicates that beer companies were forced to play a "war of attrition" game by 1960.[7] That is, changes in technology caused MES to increase and forced n firms to compete in a market that could profitably support only n^* firms, where $n > n^* > 0$. In this setting, existing brewers faced four strategic options: expand internally, merge with a competitor, find a profitable market niche, or exit the industry. Before exiting the industry, some brewers chose a "harvest" or "devolution" strategy which only delayed the company's demise. This strategy entails drastic cuts in advertising, physical maintenance, and other overhead costs, enabling the firm to profitably survive until its physical capital and product goodwill sufficiently depreciate. In this war of attrition, the mass exit of firms, called an "industry shakeout," would be the direct consequence of the increase in MES relative to the size of the market.

Gisser (1999) performs a formal test and finds support for the hypothesis that technological change drove concentration. One concern with Gisser's study is that it uses the change in the percent of beer sold in cans and bottles to measure the extent of technological innovation, a measure that rises steadily (e.g., the Pearson correlation coefficient between the index and a simple time trend from 1950 and 1997 is 0.92). Thus, his test may capture the effect of other relevant demand and cost variables that also vary with time.

Increasing scale economies brought about by technological change cannot fully explain concentration, however, as the leading brewers are much larger than required for scale efficiency. For example, in 2000 the scale of operation of Anheuser-Busch was more than 5 times MES and the scale of Miller was more than twice MES. This evidence supports Keithahn's (1978) position that the structural change in brewing is not a purely technological phenomenon.

Greer (1971, 1981) and Mueller (1978) agree, arguing that the growth of the largest brewers also comes from successful marketing campaigns. The advent of television in the late 1940s raised the marginal benefit of advertising for firms who were able to market and advertise nationally.[8] In the words of Mueller (1978: 98), "in an advertising war, all the advantages go to the national brewers." Along these lines, William Coors, retired president of Coors, laments that the "angel of death" of the small regional brewer was the "television tube" (*Modern Brewery Age*, September 13, 1999: 14). Likewise, an Anheuser-Busch executive stated that the company's use of television advertising in the 1960s put them "far ahead of the rest of the industry" (*Fortune*, November 1972: 60).[9] In 1952, the four national brewers (Anheuser-Busch, Miller, Pabst, and Schlitz) accounted for 84 percent of network television advertising but only 23 percent of sales (*Modern Brewery Age*, July 1953). In addition, a 1954 survey indicated that brewers felt that television advertising was the most effective medium for marketing beer (*Modern Brewery Age*, April 1954). The empirical work of Peles (1971a), Ackoff and Emshoff (1975a), and Tremblay (1985b, 1993) shows that advertising expenditures per barrel and the marginal benefits of advertising are greater for national than for regional producers. Thus, there is strong evidence to suggest that the advent of television advertising induced national brewers to increase their advertising efforts which in turn generated growth relative to the regional and local brewers.

These arguments are synthesized in the dynamic models of Sutton (1991) and Doraszelski and Markovich (2003). In the Doraszelski and Markovich framework, two firms play a preemption game in advertising. Once one firm gains a size or a strategic advantage from a string of lucky or successful advertising campaigns, the other firm scales back its advertising spending and industry concentration rises. This is consistent with the advertising advantage enjoyed by the national brewers and with the ensuing marketing battles that led to eventual dominance by Anheuser-Busch, Miller, and Coors.[10] In the Sutton framework, advertising raises sunk costs and ultimately industry concentration. The implication of these models is that industry concentration and the degree of firm asymmetries will depend on the size of the market, MES, advertising, and the degree of price competition.

To understand the important implications of this body of work, consider the simple case where an industry consists of n symmetric firms that produce homogeneous goods. Total revenue or sales at the market level (S) equals $n \cdot s$, where s is the equilibrium level of total revenue for the firm. Entry occurs until firm profits equal setup costs (F), which are assumed to be sunk. That is, $F = q(P - AC)$ in equilibrium, where q is firm output, P is the market price, and AC is average variable cost.

Using this condition and the definition of the price-cost margin ($PCM \equiv (P - AC)/P$), we can derive

$$S = \frac{nF}{PCM}. \tag{3.2}$$

Solving for $1/n$ yields

$$\frac{1}{n} = \frac{F}{PCM \cdot S}. \tag{3.3}$$

This suggests that tougher price competition (i.e., Bertrand instead of Cournot competition) will cause PCM and therefore the equilibrium number of firms (n) to fall, *ceteris paribus*. In the most basic framework, where the degree of price competition is constant, products are homogeneous, and sunk costs are exogenous, industry concentration (i.e., $1/n = $ HHI) falls as the size of the market increases relative to sunk costs. This simple relationship breaks down in the case of brewing, however, since products are differentiated and advertising expenditures may be endogenous.

Sutton extends the basic model to allow endogenous advertising spending to raise sunk costs. In this case, an increase in the size of the market has both direct and indirect effects. Like the basic model, an increase in S directly lowers concentration, *ceteris paribus*. Indirectly, a larger market induces greater advertising outlays, which increases sunk costs and industry concentration. In this case, a larger market need not support more firms since sunk costs rise with the size of the market.

As we discussed in chapter 2, technological change increased MES in brewing and the invention of television created new marketing opportunities for large advertisers. As MES rose relative to the size of the market, brewers found themselves competing in a war of attrition. Television advertising also set off a preemption game or race in advertising, a race that was won by the national brewers who could make effective use of this new advertising medium. Advertising attracted more consumers, and the national brewers built new and more efficient plants, in part because strict enforcement of the anti-trust laws prevented them from growing by merger. (See chapter 7 below; see also Keithahn 1978: 51–59, 122–128.) Although a few smaller brewers survived by serving niche markets, it appears that most lost market share and responded by cutting price in an effort to avoid excess capacity. Tough price competition deterred entry and few small firms

Table 3.2
Estimated value of a barrel of new and used plant capacity. The firm listed first in right-most column is the buyer.

	New	Used	Source and acquisition information[a]
1948	—	$15.00	*Newsweek*, November 30, 1953; Pabst-LA acquisition
1951	$25.00	$10.00	*Forbes*, March 1, 1968
1959	$30.00	$10.00	*Forbes*, April 15, 1959; Falstaff acquisitions
1964	$28.60	—	*Business Week*, March 14, 1964
1965	—	$12.67	www.americanbreweriana.org; Falstaff-Narragansett acquisition
1965	—	$16.76	*Fortune*, November 1972; Hamm-Heublein acquisition
1966	$30.00	$15.00	*Business Week*, July 30, 1966; Falstaff acquisitions
1969	$40.00	—	*Business Week*, September 13, 1969
1969	—	$37.10	*Fortune*, November 1972; Miller–Philip Morris acquisition
1975	$40.00	$20.00	*Fortune*, November 1975
1976	$40.00	$4.25	*Forbes*, October 1, 1977; Heileman acquisitions
1979	—	$8.68	*Forbes*, June 8, 1981; Heileman-Carling acquisition
1979	—	$22.73	Elzinga 1982; Anheuser-Busch–Schlitz acquisition
1980	—	$3.18	*WSJ*,[b] May 14, 1981; Stroh-Schaefer acquisition
1982	$59.59	$19.30	*Fortune*, May 31, 1982, *New York Times*, August 27, 1983; Stroh-Schlitz acquisition
1983	$50.00	$17.50	*WSJ*, February 3, 1983; Heileman acquisitions
1985	$62.50	—	Elzinga 1986: 217
1985	$60.00	$4.44	*MBA*,[c] March 17, 1986; S&P-Pabst acquisition
1986	—	$21.60	*MBA*, March 16, 1987; Bond-Pittsburgh acquisition
1987	—	$46.15[d]	*MBA*, March 26, 2001; Bond-Heileman acquisition
1989	—	$17.93	*MBA*, March 12, 1990; proposed Coors-Stroh merger
1993	—	$23.26	Weinberg, *MBA*, March 26, 2001; Hicks, Muse, and Co.–Heileman acquisition
1995	$51.00	—	*Forbes*, July 31, 1995; new Anheuser-Busch Brewery in Georgia
1996	—	$29.00	*WSJ*, July 2, 1996; Stroh-Heileman acquisition
2001	$66.67	$16.67	Interview with Danny Sam of Kona Brewing Co., July 1, 2002; Kona's purchase of equipment from several Hawaiian microbreweries
2002	—	$94.92[e]	*MBA Weekly News Edition*, June 10, 2002; South African Breweries–Miller

a. First firm listed is buyer.
b. *Wall Street Journal*.
c. *Modern Brewery Age*.
d. Although Alan Bond paid $1.2 billion for Heileman in 1987, Robert Weinberg estimates that Heileman was overvalued at $400 million [*Modern Brewery Age* (March 26, 2001)]. The rapid demise of Heileman supports his estimate. If valued at $400 million, Heileman would have cost $15.38 per barrel, a value more in line with other estimates during the 1980s.
e. This relatively high market value undoubtedly reflects product goodwill and the expected value of future market power as well as the value of the firm's assets.

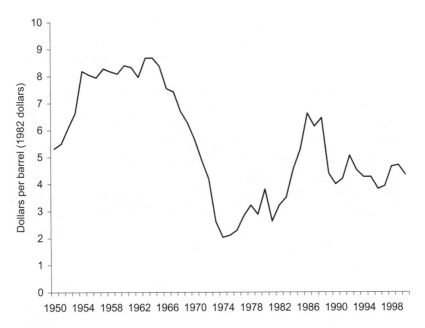

Figure 3.3
Real advertising expenditures per barrel for the U.S. brewing industry, 1950–2000.
Source: See appendix A.

survived. Thus, it appears that rising MES, higher sunk costs due to advertising, and tough price competition all contributed to high concentration in the brewing industry.

Available data indicate that sunk costs are indeed high in brewing. Table 3.2 provides data on the cost per barrel of new plant and equipment versus used plant and equipment for various years between 1948 and 2002. The data reveal that the price of a new brewery with 18 million barrels of capacity would have cost more than $1.2 billion in 2001. The data also indicate that a used plant is generally valued at about 50 percent of a new plant. Along with the fact that brewing equipment depreciates slowly,[11] these figures imply that both fixed and sunk costs are high in brewing. The deterrent effect of these costs on entry is borne out by the complete absence of entry into the mass-producing sector of the brewing industry since the late 1930s.

Although Sutton does not provide a formal test, he claims that one can observe the effect of advertising on concentration by investigating the behavior of the leading brewers during several distinct periods in brewing history. Sutton delineates three periods between 1953 and 1985, an analysis that is extended here.[12] Figure 3.3 plots real advertising expenditures per barrel at the industry level. Five advertising regimes can be identified between 1950 and 2000. The first regime or period, 1950–1964, represents a time when television advertising became important and advertising spending rose and remained well above the industry average of $5.56 per barrel. In the second period, 1965–1974, advertising intensity plunged, but 1974–1986 was an era of renewed advertising competition. Advertising spending declined again in the fifth period, 1987–1995, and stabilized when four companies came to dominate the industry in 1996. The advertising behavior of the leading brewers may differ, however, from the overall advertising trends of the industry. To track the potential differences in advertising strategies within the industry, brewers are segmented into three groups or tiers on the basis of their influence on the industry. The first tier consists of the leading national brewers. The second tier includes

Table 3.3
Classification of major brewers during five advertising regimes.

	Tier	
	First	Second
1950–1964	Anheuser-Busch	Ballantine
	Pabst	Carling
	Schlitz	Falstaff
		Hamm
		Miller
1965–1974	Anheuser-Busch	Falstaff
	Miller	Heileman
	Pabst	Schaefer
	Schlitz	Stroh
1975–1986	Anheuser-Busch	Pabst
	Miller	Coors
	Schlitz-Stroh[a]	Genesee
		Heileman
1987–1995	Anheuser-Busch	Heileman[a]
	Coors	Pabst
	Miller	Stroh
1996–2000	Anheuser-Busch	Pabst
	Coors	Stroh[a]
	Miller	

a. Stroh purchased Schlitz in 1982 and Heileman in 1996. In 1999, Miller, Pabst, and Yuengling purchased Stroh.

other large regional brewers that played a prominent role in the development of the industry. The third tier contains all other small regional and local brewers. This taxonomy of firms for each period is summarized in table 3.3.

The first period, 1950–1964, identifies a time of intense advertising competition. Anheuser-Busch, Pabst, and Schlitz marketed beer nationally and led the industry in sales for most of the period, placing them in the first tier. Also influential were the members of the second tier: Ballantine, Carling, Falstaff, Hamm, and Miller.[13] Figure 3.4 shows that the advertising intensities of the top two tiers tracked the upward trend of the industry and that firms in the first tier generally advertised more intensively than firms in the second tier.[14] This is consistent with the work of Tremblay (1985b and 1993) and with the hypothesis that large national producers were better able to exploit television advertising than regional or local firms. With a marketing advantage, first-tier and second-tier firms gained market share at the expense of smaller regional and local competitors. (See figure 3.5.) The sheer decline in industry profitability during the period, described in figure 3.6, reflects

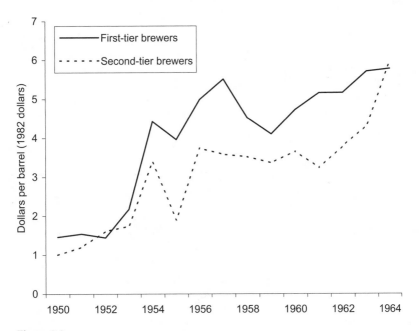

Figure 3.4
Real advertising expenditures per barrel for first-tier and second-tier brewers, 1950–1964.
Sources: See appendix A.

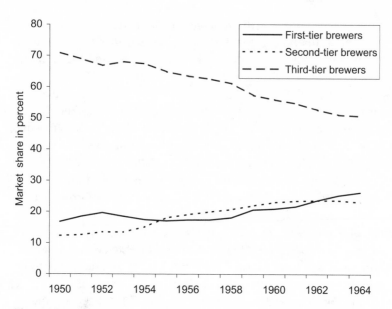

Figure 3.5
Market shares of first-tier, second-tier, and third-tier brewers, 1950–1964. Source: See appendix A.

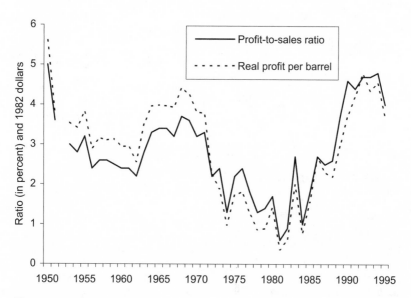

Figure 3.6
Profit-to-sales ratio and profit per barrel in the U.S. brewing industry, 1950–1995. Source: See appendix A.

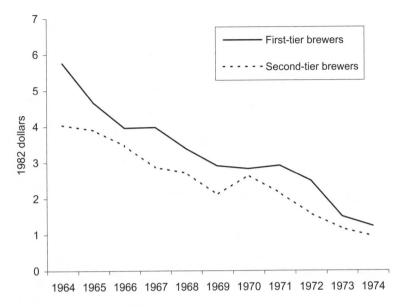

Figure 3.7
Real advertising expenditures per barrel for first-tier and second-tier brewers, 1964–1974.
Sources: See appendix A.

fierce price and advertising competition that forced many third-tier brewers out of business.

In the second period, 1965–1974, industry advertising intensity fell dramatically while industry profit rates became more stable through 1972. During this period, Miller joined Anheuser-Busch, Pabst, and Schlitz among the first-tier brewers. Ballantine, Carling, and Hamm faltered and fell from the second tier to the third. Ultimately, Ballantine was purchased by Falstaff in 1972. Carling sold one plant to Miller and another plant to National in 1966 and was purchased by Heileman in 1979. Hamm was sold to Heublein in 1965 and then to Olympia in 1975. During this era, the second tier included Falstaff, Heileman, Schaefer, and Stroh. Consistent with the overall industry data, figure 3.7 shows that advertising intensities of the first and second tiers steadily declined during this period.[15] In spite of an increase in industry profit rates between 1965 and 1969 (figure 3.6), figure 3.8 indicates that third-tier firms continued to lose market share to the industry leaders. Sutton argues that the growth and the greater advertising intensity of the national brewers implies that they continued to have a superior marketing position.[16] The period ended with a dramatic drop

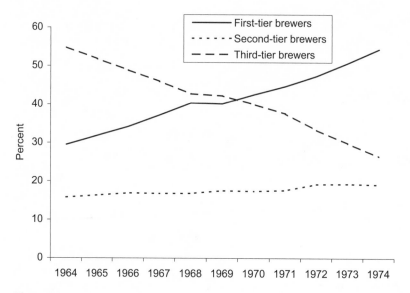

Figure 3.8
Market shares of first-tier, second-tier, and third-tier brewers, 1964–1974. Source: See appendix A.

in industry profits, in part because of rising costs and a recession in the early 1970s.

From 1975 to 1986, the major brewers fought for market share by stepping up their marketing efforts. A typical description of this "beer war" appeared in the September 4, 1978 issue of *Newsweek*[17]: "After generations of stuffy, family-dominated management, when brewers competed against each other with camaraderie and forbearance, they are now frankly at war. Marketing and advertising, not the art of brewing, are the weapons. Brewers both large and small are racing to locate new consumers and invent new products to suit their taste. Two giants of the industry, Anheuser-Busch of St. Louis and Miller Brewing Company of Milwaukee, are the main contenders." Fueling the battle was the purchase of Miller by Philip Morris in 1969–70. According to Mueller (1978: 99) and Weinberg (*Beverage World*, December 1991), Philip Morris subsidized Miller's operations during the mid 1970s in an effort to expand Miller's market share and make it the world's largest brewer. Indeed, Miller increased its brewing capacity from 9.0 million to 28.0 million barrels from 1975 to 1978, more than doubled its real advertising spending from 1974 to 1976, and introduced five new

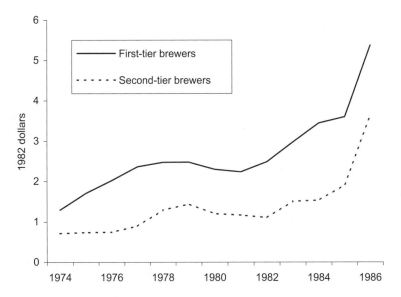

Figure 3.9
Real advertising expenditures per barrel for first-tier and second-tier brewers, 1974–1986.
Sources: See appendix A.

brands of beer in the mid 1970s. Of the new brands, Miller Lite was a big success. Growing demand for Lite and an expanded advertising budget caused Miller's market share to climb from fifth in 1974 to second by 1977. The rapid growth of Miller did not go unnoticed by the industry leader, Anheuser-Busch. A-B's president, August Busch III, challenged Miller to "bring lots of money" if it intended to contest A-B's number 1 position (*Business Week*, November 8, 1976: 58).

During this period, Anheuser-Busch, Miller, and Schlitz-Stroh were in the first tier.[18] Anheuser-Busch and Schlitz responded to Miller's challenge, but Pabst was unable to keep pace with the industry leaders and narrowed its geographic scope from national to regional in the early 1980s.[19] Thus, Pabst became a second-tier producer, along with three other strong regional producers: Coors, Genesee, and Heileman.[20] Figure 3.9 demonstrates that the advertising of first-tier firms intensified during the years 1975–1986 and was considerably higher than that of second-tier firms.[21] Beer profits increased from 1975 to 1977 (figure 3.6), and first-tier firms gained substantial share from third-tier brewers. (See figure 3.10.) The facts are consistent with Sutton's proposition that the advertising advantage of the leading firms put continued

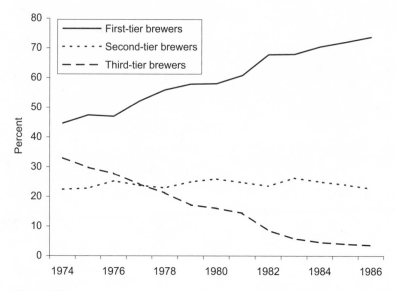

Figure 3.10
Market shares of first-tier, second-tier, and third-tier brewers, 1974–1986. Source: See appendix A.

financial pressure on smaller regional brewers, causing the weakest ones to exit the market and increasing concentration in the industry.

The period 1987–1995 is characterized by the expansion of a few large brewers. Coors moved into the first tier by becoming a national brewer and the third-largest brewer in the United States. In spite of Stroh's acquisition of Heileman in 1996, Stroh fell out of the first tier as its financial position deteriorated during the 1990s. Likewise, Genesee moved from the second tier to the third as its market share declined. Thus, Anheuser-Busch, Miller, and Coors are classified as members of the first tier and Heileman, Pabst, and Stroh as members of the second tier.[22] First-tier firms continued to invest heavily in advertising during this period, while advertising from the second tier began to dry up. (See figure 3.11.) As figure 3.12 shows, this was the first period in which first-tier brewers gained market share from second-tier firms. One explanation for enhanced profits is that more and more beer was being produced by firms with the newest and most efficient plants: Anheuser-Busch, Miller, and Coors. The market share of the three industry leaders rose from 64 percent to 81 percent from 1984 to 1990. Another potential cause, of course, is dampened competition, an issue that will be explored further in chapters 7 and 8.

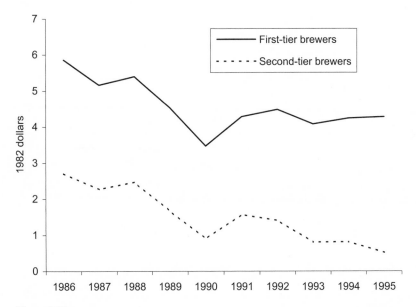

Figure 3.11
Real advertising expenditures per barrel for first-tier and second-tier brewers, 1986–1995.
Sources: See appendix A.

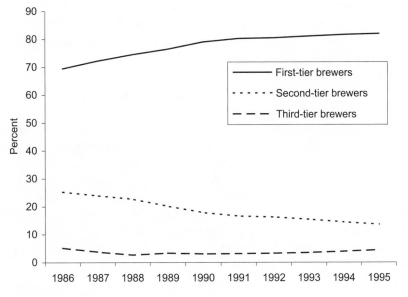

Figure 3.12
Market shares of first-tier, second-tier, and third-tier brewers, 1986–1995. Source: See
appendix A.

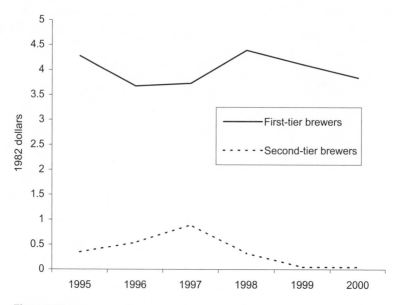

Figure 3.13
Real advertising expenditures per barrel for first-tier and second-tier brewers, 1995–2000.
Sources: See appendix A.

The present structure of the U.S. brewing industry was unfolding in the final period, 1995–2000. Three national producers dominate the industry: Anheuser-Busch, Miller, and Coors. Pabst and Stroh are the only other brewers of sufficient size to merit second-tier status, yet they have continued to decline. In 1999, Stroh went out of business, selling its brands and facilities to Miller, Pabst, and Yuengling, and all Pabst beer is now brewed by Miller. The three industry leaders continue to invest in advertising and gain market share, while firms in the second tier lose share and have almost given up on advertising (figures 3.13 and 3.14). By 2000, the top three brewers accounted for almost 89 percent of domestic beer production. Assuming no unforeseen circumstances, the mass-producing sector of the industry will soon consist of three national producers and a handful of regional niche brewers.

Although the evidence is consistent with Sutton's explanation for increasing concentration in brewing, another explanation is also consistent with the evidence. As discussed in chapter 2, consumers have shown an increasing preference for the premium brands of the national brewers at the expense of the popular-priced brands produced primarily by the local and regional brewers. The main weakness with this

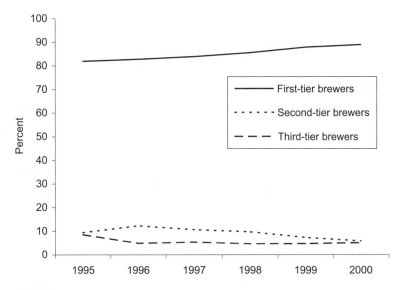

Figure 3.14
Market shares of first-tier, second-tier, and third-tier brewers, 1995–2000. Source: See appendix A.

demand-side argument, however, is that there is very little difference between premium and popular-priced beer. Since the major domestic brands became lighter in the 1950s and the 1960s, few consumers can distinguish one brand of domestic beer from another. In fact, some consumers dub the leading domestic brands "millcoorweiser" (*Consumer Reports* 2001). In view of their sameness, Greer (2002) argues that a premium image has more to do with advertising than with real product quality, an issue that will be discussed further in chapters 6 and 7. On the other hand, some consumers may prefer to pay a premium price for an advertised brand to impress their neighbors (i.e., Veblen effects) or to reinforce personal identity (Akerlof and Kranton 2000).

The national brewers have also pressured the regional brewers in other ways. First, they introduced their own popular-priced brands in the late 1950s and the 1960s to compete directly with the regional brands. Then in the 1970s, the major national brewers launched massive capacity-expansion programs. For example, Anheuser-Busch increased its capacity by almost 100 percent, Miller by almost 500 percent, and Schlitz by more than 80 percent from 1970 to 1979. To make use of the expanded capacity, the majors began to target their marketing efforts at particular regions of the country as well as the nation as a whole. In the state of Oklahoma, where Coors was the leading brand in the 1970s, Anheuser-Busch's market share increased from 12.6 percent in 1977 to 47.2 percent by 1985. At the same time, Coors's share of the Oklahoma market declined from 59.6 percent to 26.3 percent.[23] In the Northwest, stiff competition from the major brewers squeezed three formerly dominant regional brewers out of business: Rainier in 1977, Blitz-Weinhard in 1979, and Olympia in 1982.

Lieberman (1990) shows that large firms are more likely to survive an industry shakeout if they are more efficient than small rivals and are less likely to survive when equally efficient. Industry experts claim that Anheuser-Busch has established and cultivated a competitive advantage since the 1950s. On the demand side, Anheuser-Busch sells some of the most popular brands in the market. On the supply side, it owns the most efficient and strategically located plants. In contrast, several smaller brewers were inferior or unlucky, since they were located in regions of the country with stagnant demand and were unable to build state-of-the-art production facilities (Elzinga 1973;

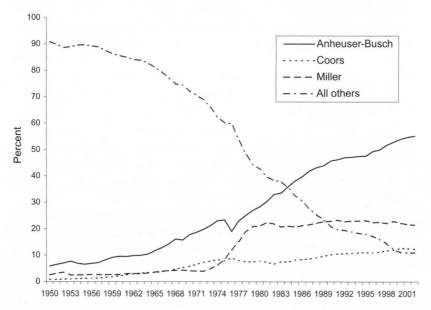

Figure 3.15
Market shares of leading brewers, 1950–2002. Source: See appendix A.

Tremblay and Tremblay 1988). Thus, concentration is due in part to the relative luck or success of the largest brewers. This is consistent with the trends illustrated in figure 3.15, which shows that the Coors, Miller, and especially Anheuser-Busch not only survived but gained market share through most of the period 1950–2002.

This discussion suggests that there is no simple explanation for the extent of concentration in the beer industry today. Several theories are consistent with the data. The evidence is clear that MES has risen relative to the size of the market and that consumers have switched from popular-priced brands to premium brands. It is also true that sunk costs are high and that they may have been increased by advertising and other marketing efforts of the major brewers. Further research is needed to unravel the relative importance of these factors.

3.3   Empirical Analysis of Concentration

To better understand the market forces that shape industry concentration, a linear regression model is estimated. Following Sutton, concentration will depend on MES relative to the size of the market. In addition, current as well as past advertising expenditures may affect sunk costs and, therefore, industry concentration.[24] Assuming that the influence of advertising on concentration over time follows a geometric lag, a Koyck transformation generates a tractable model (Hill et al. 2001). Specifically, concentration in period t depends on advertising in period t and on concentration in period $t - 1$. The regression model takes the form

$$CR_t = \alpha_0 + \alpha_1 Adv_t + \alpha_2 CR_{t-1} + \alpha_3 SE_t + e_t, \qquad (3.4)$$

where CR_t is industry concentration in period t, measured as HHI or CR_4, and Adv is industry advertising expenditures (in 1982 dollars). SE is MES divided by industry production, which is the market share needed to reach MES.[25] The parameter α_2 measures the rate at which the marginal effect of advertising depreciates; α_2 is expected to be positive but less than 1.[26] It can be shown that the Koyck transformation induces correlation between lagged concentration and the error term. The model is estimated using instrumental variables with lagged values of SE and Adv used as instruments.

The regression results from four alternative specifications of equation 3.4 are reported in table 3.4. The results from model 3.1, which

Table 3.4
Regression estimates of industry concentration. HHI is the dependent variable in models 3.1 and 3.2, and CR_4 is the dependent variable in models 3.3 and 3.4. Adv and SE are measured in period t. Absolute values of t-statistics are in parentheses. No autocorrelation is detected in any of the models.

Variable	Regression model			
	3.1	3.2	3.3	3.4
Intercept	−2.4114	−5.1154[a]	10.564	−2.1652
	(0.980)	(2.964)	(0.931)	(1.996)
Adv	0.01278[c]	0.0072[a]	0.0241	0.0070[a]
	(1.956)	(3.337)	(1.450)	(2.828)
HHI_{t-1}	0.56775[b]	0.7524[a]	—	—
	(2.147)	(6.473)		
CR_{4t-1}	—	—	0.5323	0.9035[a]
			(1.515)	(11.35)
SE	—	0.6435[a]	—	0.6388
		(2.231)		(1.198)
F	31.508[a]	680.507[a]	16.456[a]	3010.13[a]

a. Significant at 0.01 level (two-tail test).
b. Significant at 0.05 level (two-tail test).
c. Significant at 0.10 level (two-tail test).

measures concentration as HHI, imply that advertising significantly increases concentration at the 10 percent level. The effect of lagged concentration is also positive and significant, indicating that past advertising may have a positive effect on industry concentration through the link between past advertising and past concentration. The short-run multiplier or effect of advertising on concentration, α_1, is 0.0128 and the long-run multiplier, defined as $\alpha_1/(1 - \alpha_2)$ in the Koyck model, is 0.0296. Thus, only about 43 percent of the total, long-run effect of advertising is realized in the current period. Although none of the coefficients are significant in model 3.3 when concentration is measured as CR_4, a less preferred measure of concentration, the slope parameter estimates from models 3.1 and 3.3 are similar.

Models 3.2 and 3.4 include SE and show that scale economies relate positively to concentration in brewing, significantly so when concentration is measured by HHI. The inclusion of SE in the model improves the significance levels of all parameter estimates. In the CR_4 model, the advertising and lagged concentration parameters, insignificant without SE in the model, became significant at 1 percent. The insignificant coefficient estimate on SE in model 3.4 may result from multi-collinearity. The Pearson correlation coefficient for CR_{4t-1}, and SE is 0.897; the correlation coefficient for HHI and SE is 0.786 and appears to be less problematic. All in all, the parameter estimates are stable and the results support the hypothesis that both advertising and scale economies are important determinants of concentration in the brewing industry.

3.4 Conclusion

This chapter documents the departure of more than 300 independent mass-producing beer companies, and the corresponding trend in industry concentration, from 1950 to 2000. Initially, scholars debated whether concentration was powered by technological change or by the advertising advantage of the national brewers arising from the invention of television. Sutton (1991) and Doraszelski and Markovich (2003) provide formal dynamic models to show how advertising, MES, and price competition can affect industry concentration.

The evidence suggests that the high level of concentration in the industry stems from multiple causes. Both advertising and scale economies appear to be important determinants. All of the evidence indicates that MES rose relative to the size of the market, but the industry leaders are larger than required by scale efficiency. In addition, development of the new marketing medium of television initiated a preemption race in advertising. The national brewers won the race, and greater advertising competition led to higher sunk costs in brewing. National brewers also benefited from consumers' growing demand for the premium brands produced by the nationals. To satisfy growing demand, the national brewers built larger and more efficient plants, which also provided them with a cost advantage over other brewers. Many smaller regional brewers responded with severe price cuts to attract customers, which put further strain on the weaker firms. Brewers were thrust into a war of attrition in which many failed or were purchased by other brewers. Today, beer production is concentrated in the hands of a few surviving firms: Anheuser-Busch, Coors, and Miller.

4   The Leading Mass-Producing Brewers

[Success in brewing requires] a balanced strategy and keen knowledge of history. Both are extremely important, more today than ever before.

—Robert S. Weinberg, *Modern Brewery Age*, March 17, 1997: 33

In chapter 3 we explained why most U.S. brewing companies were under extreme financial stress from 1950 to 2000. The ability to advertise on television gave a marketing advantage to large national producers and forced brewers to compete in a preemption race in advertising. In addition, changes in technology forced them to compete in a war of attrition in which only a few firms were destined to survive. Although these were important causes of firm failure in brewing, the behavior of individual firms, especially the industry leaders, also played a role in their struggle to survive.

This chapter describes the unique character of each of the leading beer companies. Market forces and company history are discussed, with an eye toward identifying events and firm actions that contributed to the rise or fall of a firm.

In chapter 3, the mass-producing beer companies were classified into three groups or tiers. The first and second tiers consist of the brewers that had an important influence on the evolution and structure of the industry. The third tier includes all other local and small regional firms. This chapter focuses on the 13 prominent brewers that were members of the first and second tiers from 1950 through 2000: Anheuser-Busch, Ballantine, Carling, Coors, Falstaff, Genesee, Hamm, Heileman, Miller, Pabst, Schaefer, Schlitz, and Stroh.[1] One can see from table 4.1 that they occupied the top five spots for most of the period 1950–2002.[2]

The information presented below relies on public and private sources. Most companies in existence during the second half of the

Table 4.1
A history of the five largest brewing firms, 1950–2002. Italic type indicates the highest rank a firm has achieved. Source: Office of R. S. Weinberg.

	Years in size class
Largest	
Anheuser-Busch	1953–54, 1957–2002
Schlitz	1950–1952, 1955–56
Second-largest	
Anheuser-Busch	1950–1952, 1955–56
Miller	1977–2002
Schlitz	1953–54, 1957–1976
Third-largest	
Ballantine	1950, 1954–1956
Coors	1990–2002
Falstaff	1957–1960
Miller	1976
Pabst	1951–1953, 1961–1975, 1980
Schlitz	1977–1979, 1981
Stroh	1982–1989
Fourth-largest	
Ballantine	1951–1953, 1957–58
Carling	1959–60, 1962–63
Coors	1969–1974, 1988–89
Falstaff	1955–56, 1961, 1964–1968
Heileman	1981–1987
Miller	1975
Pabst	1950, 1954, 1976–1979, 1999–2002
Schlitz	1980
Stroh	1990–1998
Fifth-largest	
Ballantine	1959–60
Boston	2000–2002
Carling	1958, 1961, 1964–1967
Coors	1968, 1975–1980, 1983–1987
Falstaff	1962–63, 1969, 1972
Genesee	1999
Hamm	1956–57
Heileman	1988–1995
Miller	1952, 1973–74
Pabst	1955, 1981–82, 1996–1998
Rheingold	1950–51, 1953–54
Schaefer	1970–71

Table 4.2
Domestic market shares of leading U.S. beer producers, 1950–1959. Here and in tables 4.3–4.7, CR_L is the concentration ratio of the leading brewers and CR_4 is the four-firm concentration ratio. CR_L and CR_4 may not equal the sums from the table entries due to rounding errors. Sources for 1950–2001: Office of R. S. Weinberg; 2002, *Modern Brewery Age* (March 31, 2003).

	1950	1951	1952	1953	1954	1955	1956	1957	1958	1959
Anheuser-Busch	5.83	6.44	6.99	7.67	6.90	6.54	6.83	7.18	8.20	9.13
Ballantine	5.22	4.69	4.68	4.44	4.40	4.60	4.62	4.68	4.74	4.90
Carling	0.60	0.79	1.04	1.25	1.73	3.09	3.49	3.70	4.12	5.00
Coors	0.80	0.78	0.88	0.93	1.09	1.21	1.27	1.35	1.66	1.87
Falstaff	2.73	2.70	2.64	3.33	3.89	4.25	4.51	5.04	5.29	5.38
Genesee	0.81	0.86	0.91	0.93	0.96	0.92	0.93	0.94	0.92	0.91
Hamm	1.26	1.35	1.61	1.98	2.66	3.58	3.88	3.96	3.99	4.02
Heileman	0.51	0.44	0.44	0.57	0.56	0.58	0.54	0.45	0.44	0.45
Miller	2.51	3.07	3.53	2.44	2.48	2.55	2.62	2.61	2.61	2.67
Pabst	4.90	5.33	5.33	4.86	4.14	3.81	3.63	3.17	2.99	4.87
Schaefer	3.16	3.06	2.88	2.90	3.18	3.38	3.17	3.45	3.28	3.37
Schlitz	6.08	6.72	7.36	6.00	6.40	6.73	6.92	7.07	6.92	6.64
Stroh	0.61	0.75	0.95	1.31	1.72	2.51	3.16	3.03	2.26	2.39
CR_L	35.02	36.96	39.23	38.61	40.11	43.74	45.58	46.64	47.41	51.58
CR_4	22.03	23.18	24.36	22.96	21.84	22.12	22.89	23.97	25.14	26.15

twentieth century are described by Downard (1980), Robertson (1984), Barnett and Wilsted (1988), Hernon and Ganey (1991), Apps (1992), Burgess (1993), Certo and Peter (1993), and Baum (2001), and much of the discussion in this chapter derives from these sources. *Brewers Digest, Buyer's Guide and Brewery Directory* (an annual) lists the brands and production capacities of each brewer in the United States. For the interested reader, the March 26, 2001 issue of *Modern Brewery Age* provides a brief description of several local brewers that have survived into the twenty-first century: Hudepohl-Schoenling Brewing, Jacob Leinenkugel Brewing, Minnesota, Pittsburgh, August Schell, Straub, and D. J. Yuengling & Sons. Industry expert Robert Weinberg provides annual sales data for the 100 largest brewers in the United States from 1947 to 2000. Some economic data are available for 34 U.S. brewing companies. These companies and their important characteristics are listed in appendix A.

Tables 4.2–4.7 document the annual market share by decade of each of the leading firms from 1950 through 2002. Market share, defined as

Table 4.3
Domestic market shares of leading U.S. beer producers, 1960–1969.

	1960	1961	1962	1963	1964	1965	1966	1967	1968	1969
Anheuser-Busch	9.56	9.47	9.82	9.93	10.42	11.66	12.81	14.22	16.11	15.71
Ballantine	4.97	5.02	4.93	4.73	4.39	4.18	3.56	3.42	2.03	1.85
Carling	5.44	5.62	5.83	6.01	5.80	5.18	4.84	4.50	4.27	4.23
Coors	2.15	2.56	3.02	3.23	3.44	3.51	3.77	4.23	4.71	5.33
Falstaff	5.54	5.71	5.77	5.86	5.85	6.24	6.61	6.07	5.51	5.20
Genesee	0.91	0.98	1.05	1.16	1.23	1.29	1.32	1.32	1.26	1.30
Hamm	4.41	4.13	4.05	4.04	3.75	3.78	3.97	3.95	3.62	3.52
Heileman	0.70	0.67	0.80	0.74	0.90	0.93	0.92	1.20	1.42	1.65
Miller	2.68	3.01	3.05	2.99	3.30	3.61	3.91	4.19	4.26	4.36
Pabst	4.96	5.81	6.35	7.05	7.48	8.10	8.54	9.27	9.56	8.59
Schaefer	3.46	3.63	3.86	4.02	4.21	4.21	4.24	4.32	4.42	4.56
Schlitz	6.42	6.42	7.47	8.28	8.30	8.48	8.93	9.50	10.43	11.51
Stroh	2.34	2.26	2.22	2.16	2.37	2.37	2.26	2.28	2.22	2.47
CR_L	53.56	55.31	58.22	60.22	61.42	63.55	65.69	68.47	69.82	70.28
CR_4	26.97	27.41	29.48	31.27	32.04	34.48	36.89	39.07	41.61	41.14

firm output divided by domestic industry output (in percent), can provide insight into the economic viability of a firm in brewing, since sales growth results from marketing success and enables the average brewer to reach MES and produce at full capacity. The remainder of this chapter provides a brief description of the industry leaders. Surviving industry leaders are discussed first, followed by failed national brewers and then failed regional brewers.

4.1   Today's Industry Leaders

Only five of the leading mass-producing beer companies survived into the twenty-first century. Anheuser-Busch continues as the dominant firm, followed by Miller and Coors. Despite their prominence, Miller and Coors have experienced little growth since the 1980s. Pabst, the dominant firm as recently as 1949, has seen its fortunes wane. Today, Pabst operates as a beer company but not a brewer, since all of its beer is made under contract by Miller. Genesee, once a leading regional brewer in the Northeast, stayed afloat despite losses in market share from 1980 to 2002. Genesee now focuses on the production of domestic specialty beer. By 2010, Anheuser-Busch, Miller, and Coors probably will account for as much as 95 percent of domestic beer sales.

Table 4.4
Domestic market shares of leading U.S. beer producers, 1970–1979.

	1970	1971	1972	1973	1974	1975	1976	1977	1978	1979
Anheuser-Busch	17.83	18.74	19.86	21.29	23.13	23.40	19.07	23.01	25.16	27.06
Ballantine	1.78	1.72	0.22	—	—	—	—	—	—	—
Carling	3.96	3.50	3.00	2.71	2.56	3.28	2.93	2.73	2.08	0.40
Coors	5.84	6.57	7.32	7.79	8.37	7.89	8.96	8.02	7.48	7.56
Falstaff	4.33	3.96	4.62	4.28	3.93	3.06	2.62	1.93	1.45	0.91
Genesee	1.18	1.21	1.29	1.32	1.37	1.46	1.64	1.76	1.81	1.99
Hamm	3.14	2.92	2.94	2.35	1.97	0.32	—	—	—	—
Heileman	2.41	2.17	2.73	3.15	2.94	3.01	3.42	3.92	4.30	6.53
Miller	4.13	4.01	3.94	4.93	6.15	8.55	12.08	15.18	18.91	20.96
Pabst	8.45	9.10	9.44	9.35	9.70	10.42	11.22	10.05	9.29	8.85
Schaefer	4.62	4.32	4.14	3.95	3.87	3.91	3.45	2.93	2.38	2.07
Schlitz	12.15	12.88	14.16	15.20	15.37	15.48	15.86	13.90	11.84	9.84
Stroh	2.66	2.71	3.17	3.31	2.96	3.41	3.78	3.84	3.82	3.52
CR_L	72.46	73.80	76.82	79.60	82.33	84.20	85.02	87.28	88.52	89.70
CR_4	44.26	47.29	50.77	53.62	56.57	57.84	58.19	62.15	65.20	66.72

Table 4.5
Domestic market shares of leading U.S. beer producers, 1980–1989.

	1980	1981	1982	1983	1984	1985	1986	1987	1988	1989
Anheuser-Busch	28.42	30.38	33.07	33.61	35.96	38.20	39.82	41.97	43.21	44.00
Ballantine	—	—	—	—	—	—	—	—	—	—
Carling	—	—	—	—	—	—	—	—	—	—
Coors	7.81	7.40	6.66	7.62	7.41	8.27	8.39	8.64	9.10	9.65
Falstaff	0.91	0.82	0.68	0.60	0.54	0.52	0.39	0.33	0.30	0.28
Genesee	2.04	2.02	1.90	1.78	1.66	1.64	1.57	1.46	1.35	1.22
Hamm	—	—	—	—	—	—	—	—	—	—
Heileman	7.52	7.79	8.11	9.74	9.41	9.07	8.84	8.83	8.39	6.57
Miller	21.13	22.48	21.95	20.82	21.07	20.83	21.31	21.66	22.22	22.79
Pabst	8.55	7.51	6.87	7.11	6.49	5.00	3.91	3.40	3.27	3.60
Schaefer	2.02	1.62	—	—	—	—	—	—	—	—
Schlitz	8.47	7.98	—	—	—	—	—	—	—	—
Stroh	3.49	3.41	12.77	13.49	13.41	12.99	12.55	11.74	11.10	10.04
CR_L	90.36	91.41	92.00	94.75	95.96	96.51	96.78	98.01	98.95	98.16
CR_4	66.57	68.62	75.84	77.65	79.85	81.07	82.29	84.19	85.64	86.48

Table 4.6
Domestic market shares of leading U.S. beer producers, 1990–1999.

	1990	1991	1992	1993	1994	1995	1996	1997	1998	1999
Anheuser-Busch	45.81	46.32	47.07	47.23	47.56	47.65	49.39	50.01	51.77	52.92
Ballantine	—	—	—	—	—	—	—	—	—	—
Carling	—	—	—	—	—	—	—	—	—	—
Coors	10.23	10.52	10.61	10.73	10.99	11.07	10.89	11.28	11.65	12.01
Falstaff	0.21	0.20	0.18	0.16	0.13	0.08	0.07	0.06	0.05	0.05
Genesee	1.16	1.19	1.16	1.08	0.98	0.98	0.66	0.93	0.82	0.74
Hamm	—	—	—	—	—	—	—	—	—	—
Heileman	5.78	5.05	4.95	4.84	4.49	4.16	—	—	—	—
Miller	22.97	23.38	22.77	23.09	23.05	23.22	22.50	22.61	21.13	22.92
Pabst	3.55	3.60	3.74	3.79	3.58	3.57	3.05	2.63	2.30	7.36
Schaefer	—	—	—	—	—	—	—	—	—	—
Schlitz	—	—	—	—	—	—	—	—	—	—
Stroh	8.59	7.97	7.59	6.83	6.40	5.88	9.29	8.04	7.48	—
CR_L	98.30	98.23	98.08	97.76	97.19	96.62	95.84	95.56	96.21	96.01
CR_4	87.60	88.19	88.05	87.89	88.01	87.82	92.06	91.94	93.03	95.22

Table 4.7
Domestic market shares of leading U.S. beer producers, 2000–2002.

	2000	2001	2002
Anheuser-Busch	54.04	54.79	55.10
Ballantine	—	—	—
Carling	—	—	—
Coors	12.64	12.53	12.28
Falstaff	0.04	—	—
Genesee	0.63	0.56	0.49
Hamm	—	—	—
Heileman	—	—	—
Miller	22.25	21.75	21.47
Pabst	5.89	5.16	4.60
Schaefer	—	—	—
Schlitz	—	—	—
Stroh	—	—	—
CR_L	95.50	94.79	93.90
CR_4	94.83	94.22	93.45

Firms are discussed below in order of their size and their importance to the industry.

Anheuser-Busch Incorporated (St. Louis), 1852–Present

The roots of Anheuser-Busch can be traced to the Bavarian Brewery of St. Louis, a company started in 1852. When Bavarian failed in 1857, the company was purchased and managed by Eberhard Anheuser. Adolphus Busch, Anheuser's son-in-law, later joined the company and became president after Anheuser's retirement in 1877. The company's name was changed to Anheuser-Busch Brewing Association in 1879.

Adolphus Busch is credited with the company's early success. He pioneered the use of refrigerated rail cars in 1877, fostered the development of a new pasteurization process, and introduced new merchandising techniques. As a result, the company's annual sales reached a million barrels by 1900, ranking just behind Pabst.

August A. Busch succeeded his father as president in 1913. During Prohibition, the company survived by producing a near-beer called Bevo, malt syrup, corn sugar, yeast, ice cream, commercial refrigeration units and truck bodies, and non-alcoholic beverages. In 1933, to celebrate the repeal of Prohibition, the company acquired a team of Clydesdale horses.

Adolphus Busch III became president in 1934. His brother, August Busch II, was president from 1946 to 1974, a period in which the company prospered. By 1957, Anheuser-Busch was the world's largest brewer. It has maintained that position to this day. Under August II, the company diversified into other industries, adding amusement parks, can manufacturing, and the St. Louis Cardinals baseball franchise. In 1974, August II was replaced by his son, August A. Busch III.[3] The company continued to grow and prosper under August III's leadership.

As the tables document, Anheuser-Busch has been the largest brewer since 1957, when it ousted Schlitz from the number 1 spot. From the beginning of the August III era until today, the company's domestic share of the market increased from about 23 percent to more than 55 percent. Labor strikes have been the only major impediment to growth at Anheuser-Busch. Relatively minor strikes occurred in 1951 and 1969 (*Business Week*, November 3, 1951; *Forbes*, April 15, 1970). A 95-day strike in 1976 depleted the company's market share by almost 19 percent (*Wall Street Journal*, June 7, 1976).

Anheuser-Busch diversified into snack foods in 1979 with its Eagle Snacks division. Eagle Snacks proved unprofitable and eventually closed in 1996, allowing the company to become more focused on brewing (*Business Week*, March 4, 1996).[4]

The St. Louis plant once supplied the entire United States. Eventually, however, to reduce transportation costs and satisfy the increasing demand, Anheuser-Busch established several new breweries. The first of these, in Newark, New Jersey, was built in 1951. Others were added as follows: Van Nuys, California (1954); Tampa, Florida (1959); Houston, Texas (1966); Columbus, Ohio (1968); Jacksonville, Florida (1969); Merrimack, New Hampshire (1970); Williamsburg, Virginia (1972); Fairfield, California (1976); Baldwinsville, New York (1979, purchased from Schlitz); Fort Collins, Colorado (1988). In 2002, Anheuser-Busch had an annual brewing capacity of 107.5 million barrels.

Anheuser-Busch growth in production capacity has come from internal expansion rather than from horizontal mergers or acquisitions due to strict enforcement of the anti-trust laws. The company attempted a horizontal acquisition in 1958 when it purchased the American Brewing Company of Miami, Florida. The merger was successfully challenged by the U.S. Department of Justice, which forced Anheuser-Busch to divest of American Brewing and to refrain from acquiring another brewery for the next 5 years without court approval.[5] After this experience, Anheuser-Busch did not make another horizontal acquisition until it purchased the Baldwinsville plant from Schlitz in 1979 (*Advertising Age*, April 28, 1980). The Department of Justice allowed the acquisition because Schlitz was failing and Anheuser-Busch was the only firm large enough to absorb a plant of such size.[6]

Today, Anheuser-Busch produces some of the leading brands in the industry. Of the top ten brands in 2001, five are produced by Anheuser-Busch: Budweiser, Bud Light, Busch, Busch Light, and Natural Light. The Budweiser label is the leading seller around the world, fulfilling its "King of Beers" marketing theme. Budweiser, Bud Light, Michelob, and Busch lead their respective categories in sales.

Anheuser-Busch also competes in the specialty beer market. In 1994 it introduced the Elk Mountain specialty brands, which met with little success (*Modern Brewery Age, Weekly News Edition*, November 7, 1994). In the same year, however, Anheuser-Busch obtained a 25 percent interest in a successful Northwest microbrewery, the Redhook Ale Brewery of Seattle. By agreement, Redhook retained control of marketing and production and gained access to the Anheuser-Busch net-work of distributors.[7] This distribution advantage enabled Redhook to increase its sales from 93.7 million to 226 million barrels of beer between 1994 and 2002. In 1997, Anheuser-Busch purchased a 30.9 percent interest in another Northwest microbrewery, Widmer Brothers Brewing of Portland, Oregon (*Oregonian*, April 18, 1997; *Beverage Industry*, June 1998). Widmer's sales increased by 20.4 percent from 1997 to 2002.

In May of 2002, 64-year-old August A. Busch III retired from the position of company president. He was replaced by Pat Stokes, former president of the company's beer division. This marks the first time since 1857 that the president of Anheuser-Busch has not been a family member. A smooth transition is expected, however, as Stokes has been with the company since 1969 and August III remains as company chairman. Industry experts contend that the president position will return to a family member in a few years when August A. Busch IV, now vice-president of marketing, is ready for the post (*Business Week*, March 23, 1992 and November 11, 2002; *Modern Brewery Age, Weekly News Edition*, May 6, 2002).

Anheuser-Busch is the lone constant in the industry, as it has remained the dominant brewer in the United States since 1957. There are several reasons for its continued success. First, it was one of the first brewers to market and sell its beer nationally and to use national television advertising effectively. Second, it was the first national producer to offer a diversified line of brands. By 1957, for example, it marketed super-premium Michelob, premium Budweiser, and popular-priced Busch. Anheuser-Busch could thus compete effectively with popular-priced regional brands and with other national premium brands. Third, it was the first major brewer to invest in marketing research. Fourth, it has low production costs, since it is large enough to attain economies of scale and its brewing facilities are modern. In addition, production in multiple locations across the country cuts transportation costs. Finally, it has avoided many of the strategic mistakes of its competitors. For these reasons, Anheuser-Busch has become the "paragon of the industry" (*Modern Brewery Age Weekly News Edition*, January 20, 2003).

Miller Brewing Company (Milwaukee), 1853–Present

Pabst and Miller share a common beginning with the Best Brewing Company of Milwaukee. In 1844, Jacob Best Sr. established a small brewery in Milwaukee. After he retired in 1853, his four sons owned and operated the business. By 1860, only one son, Philip Best, remained with the company, which later became the Pabst Brewing Company. Soon after 1853, two of Philip's sons, Charles and Lorenz, left Best and started the Menomonee Valley Brewery, which was sold to Frederick Miller in 1855. This company was incorporated in 1888, and its name was changed to Frederick Miller Brewing Company. Miller died that year, and his son-in-law Carl Miller (who coincidentally had the same surname) and his sons Ernest, Frederick A., and Emil owned and managed the company. After Ernest's death in 1922, his brother Frederick A. Miller became president. During Prohibition, Miller produced cereal, beverages, soft drinks, and malt-related products.

In 1947, Frederick A. Miller was succeeded as president by his nephew, Frederick C. Miller. After he died in a 1954 plane crash, Norman Klug became president. By 1950, Miller was in the second tier and was the eighth-largest brewer in the United States. Miller, now a national producer, grew steadily from 1953 into the 1960s, entering the first tier. Expansion continued with the purchase of the A. Gettelman Brewing Company of Milwaukee (1961) and two plants in 1966, one in Azusa, California from the General Brewing Company and the other in Fort Worth, Texas from the Carling Brewing Company. Klug died in 1966, and Charles Miller (not a member of the Miller family) served as president until Philip Morris purchased 53 percent of Miller stock in 1969.

In 1970, Philip Morris bought the remaining 47 percent of Miller and inducted John A. Murphy, a Philip Morris executive, as head of the company. This event is said to have sparked the great "beer wars" of the 1970s. Philip Morris expanded production capacity, increased advertising spending, and initiated a brand-proliferation strategy at Miller, a strategy it had successfully used in the cigarette market. In the early 1970s, when most brewers marketed fewer than four brands of beer, Miller introduced four new brands: Miller Ale, Miller Malt Liquor, Löwenbräu, and Miller Lite. The other leading brewers responded by introducing their own new brands and by increasing capacity and advertising spending.

Of the four new Miller brands, only Miller Lite was a major success. In fact, it was so successful that it established the light-beer category, the most popular beer category since 1992. Although other brewers had marketed low-calorie or light beers in the past, Miller Lite succeeded where others failed by avoiding the "diet beer" connotation. Lite was promoted as a great-tasting beer that was less filling, implying that one could drink more of it. Lite was the most successful new brand introduced since Prohibition, selling 3.1 million barrels in its first year of national distribution (1975). In 1978, by which time every major brewer had its own light beer, 8.9 million barrels of Miller Lite were sold, for a 57.3 percent share of the light-beer category.

The success of Miller Lite facilitated a shift in market share to Miller from many of its competitors. Miller was the seventh-largest brewer in 1970 but ranked second by 1977, surpassing Coors, Falstaff, Pabst, Schaefer, and Schlitz. During this period, Miller's share of the market increased from 4.13 percent to 15.18 percent. Anheuser-Busch was the only brewer with a larger share, and there was considerable speculation that Miller would soon be number 1 (*Forbes*, August 7, 1978). Rivalry was so keen that John Murphy kept a voodoo doll on his desk that he called Augie, after Anheuser-Busch president August Busch III, and a rug under his desk with Anheuser-Busch's trademark emblem. Murphy conveyed his ill will toward Anheuser-Busch by pricking the doll and stomping on the rug (*Forbes*, August 7, 1978).

Miller never caught Anheuser-Busch, however. By 1981, Miller's market share was more than 22 percent, but Anheuser-Busch's was nearly 30 percent. Since 1981, Miller's share has remained fairly constant, and the company still ranks number 2 in size. The success of the light beers produced by Anheuser-Busch and Coors kept Miller out of the number 1 slot. Continued price discounting of its flagship brand, Miller High Life, may have tarnished the company's image and impeded its long-term growth potential.

To ignite stalled sales, Miller hired the former vice-president of marketing at Anheuser-Busch, Jack MacDonough, to head the company in 1992. MacDonough introduced several "phantom" specialty brands that did not bear the Miller name on their labels. The only one of these to succeed was Icehouse, an ice beer that Miller marketed under the Plank Road Brewery name (*Fortune*, September 5, 1994).

In 1999, Miller, Pabst, and D. G. Yuengling & Sons were involved in a complex acquisition of the failing Stroh Brewing Company (*Beverage Industry*, March 1999; *Modern Brewery Age*, March 27, 2000). Miller purchased the Olde English 800 Malt Liquor and Hamm brands from Stroh. As part of the deal, Miller also purchased the Tumwater, Washington (Olympia) brewery, the Mickey's Malt Liquor brand, and the Henry Weinhard brands from Pabst.[8]

Today Miller sells more than 20 brands of beer, and several are among the industry leaders. In 2001, Icehouse ranked number 1 in the ice-beer category, Miller High Life and Milwaukee's Best ranked second and third, respectively, in the popular-priced category, and Miller Lite and Coors Light continued to battle for second in the light-beer category. With an interest in refocusing on the cigarette market, and perhaps because of Miller's languishing growth, Philip Morris sold Miller to South African Breweries (SAB) in 2001.[9] SAB is a London-based international beer producer that owns brands in 30 countries and plans to market its Pilsner Urquell brand in the United States through Miller distributors and to promote Miller Genuine Draft internationally. Miller's new name is SAB-Miller.

Adolf Coors Company (Golden, Colorado), 1873–Present

Adolph Herman Joseph Coors, a German immigrant, and Jacob Schueler, a Denver businessman, founded the Golden Brewery in 1873.[10] Coors and Schueler chose to build their brewery in Golden, Colorado, a site with access to underground springs and a railroad line that served several towns to the west. In 1880, Adolph bought out Schueler's interest in the brewery and renamed it the Coors Golden Brewery. The company was incorporated in 1913. The Coors family continued to control the company. Adolph's grandsons, William (Bill) and Joseph (Joe) Coors, led the company as it expanded in the period after World War II.[11] In 2002, when William Coors retired, Peter Coors, Adolph's great grandson, became chairman.

Colorado was the first state to outlaw alcohol consumption (in 1916), and the Coors Brewing Company had to endure 17 years of prohibition. During that time, the company produced near-beer, dairy products, and malt products, becoming the country's third-largest producer of malt products (*Modern Brewery Age*, September-October 1983). Coors also developed a process for producing cement and porcelain.

From the repeal of national prohibition to the late 1970s, Coors followed a different strategy than other successful brewers. The company emphasized engineering inventiveness and product quality over marketing. In the 1950s, Bill Coors and his staff invented the first aluminum beverage can and became the first company to put the invention into practice (in 1959). This invention earned Bill "man of the year" honors by *Modern Metals* magazine. In the same year, Coors developed a cold-filtration system that enabled it to become the first major beer company to brew and ship unpasteurized (or draft) beer in cans and bottles (Baum 2001). To exploit scale economies at the plant level, Coors produced just one brand of beer, Coors Banquet, and produced it all in a single brewery. The company exhibited continued growth during this period, despite lower advertising spending per barrel than any other major brewer.

The tables document the company's market share and show that it experienced rapid growth in share during the late 1960s and the early 1970s. The company moved from the third tier to the second by leading the market in nine of the eleven states it served (Barnett and Wilsted 1988c). Since Coors invested so little in advertising at this time, there is considerable speculation concerning the source of the success of the Coors Banquet brand. The company's leaders attributed it to the superior quality of its beer.

Producing Coors beer entailed a particularly elaborate process, with a lengthy brewing time (70 days), cold filtration rather than pasteurization, and constant refrigeration of packaged beer. In addition, distributors were required to pull cans off the shelf after just 30 days (*Wall Street Journal*, October 26, 1973; *Advertising Age*, June 23, 1975; *Forbes*, June 1, 1976). As a result, Coors was one of the most expensively brewed beers in the world (*Wall Street Journal*, October 26, 1973).

An alternative explanation discussed in the literature is that Coors beer developed a mystique or cult following (*Business Week*, May 8, 1978; *Forbes*, October 16, 1978 and July 19, 1982; *Barrons*, May 12, 1980; Barnett and Wilsted 1988c; Van Munching 1997; Baum 2001). The mystique may have been linked to the belief that Coors was of superior quality or to the fact that Easterners could not buy Coors (except at very high prices). In addition, it was well known that President Gerald Ford had Coors flown to Washington on Air Force One and that Paul Newman and Clint Eastwood were regular Coors drinkers.

Perhaps Coors beer was simply right for the times. During the 1960s and the early 1970s, consumers desired lighter beers. Coors Banquet fit the bill, as it was the lightest of all major brands. Marketed as "America's fine light beer," it had the lowest alcohol and the fewest calories of the leading American brands (*Modern Brewery Age*, December 30, 1991: 3).[12]

Coors's success did not last, however. The company's market share fell from 1976 to 1979. There are several reasons for the decline. First, the company's anti-union stance and a brewery strike in 1977 led to a 10-year boycott by the AFL-CIO. Second, company actions motivated additional boycotts by homosexual, racial minority, and women's groups that continued through the mid 1980s. The conservative views of vice president Joe Coors, the company requirement that job applicants submit to a lie-detector test, and alleged racist comments by president Bill Coors alienated liberal and minority groups. A third contributing factor was Coors's slow response to the intense advertising and brand-proliferation strategies of Miller during the early 1970s. For example, Miller's successful Lite brand was first marketed nationally in 1975, but Coors did not market its own version of light beer until 1978.[13]

By the mid 1980s, Coors's behavior began to mirror that of the other leading brewers. From the mid 1970s to the mid 1980s, Coors hired more women and minorities and invested heavily in advertising. The company's advertising spending per barrel was only about 15 percent of Anheuser-Busch's expenditures in 1976, but by 1985 Coors outspent Anheuser-Busch on advertising per barrel by about 12 percent. Coors also introduced several brands in test markets and then regionally during this period: Coors Light (1978), Herman Joseph's Super-Premium (1980), Killian's Irish Red Ale (1980), and Coors Golden Lager (1983) (Barnett and Wilsted 1988c). The company's market share began a steady incline by the mid 1980s, promoting Coors to first-tier status.

Part of this growth came from expansion into new regions of the country. From 1948 until 1976, Coors sold its beer only in eleven western states (*Forbes*, February 1, 1969; *Forbes*, June 1, 1976). In 1979, Coors served 17 states by adding Montana in 1976, Iowa, Missouri, Nebraska, and Washington in 1978, and Arkansas in 1979 (*Forbes*, June 1, 1976; *Wall Street Journal*, October 2, 1979). The number of states served totaled 21 in 1980 (Barnett and Wilsted 1988c), 44 in 1985 (*Business Week*, April 15, 1985) and 47 in 1987 (*Advertising Age*, November 3, 1986; *Business Week*, August 21, 1989). Coors served every state but Indiana in 1988 (*Modern Brewery Age*, March 13, 1989) and every state by 1991 (correspondence with the Coors Consumer Relations Representative, December 20, 2002).

Eastward expansion induced Coors to build a packaging plant in Elkton, Virginia.[14] Coors brewed a dehydrated version of its beer in Colorado and then shipped it to the Elkton plant, where Virginia water was added and packaging took place (*New York Times*, August 14, 1992). This marked a dramatic shift in company policy and caused a major marketing problem for Coors: the company's 60-year-old theme, "brewed with pure Rocky Mountain spring water," was instantly rendered obsolete. After a complaint from Anheuser-Busch in 1991, the U.S. Bureau of Alcohol, Tobacco, and Firearms urged Coors to discontinue its "Rocky Mountain" slogan. Coors agreed to replace it with "Original Coors is brewed with all natural ingredients for a clean smooth fresh-from-the-Rockies taste" (*Advertising Age*, March 18, 1991).

For the first time in modern company history, accounting profits were negative in 1992–1993. Coors broke from a century-old tradition and hired its first president from outside the Coors family. President Leo Kiely cut costs and generated positive profits by 1994. The slow but steady growth in profitability and market share speaks to Kiely's managerial acumen.

Today Coors is the third-largest brewer in the United States. In 2002 its market share was more than 12 percent. In 1989, Coors purchased Stroh's Memphis plant but abandoned an attempted acquisition of Stroh because of a potential anti-trust challenge. Coors now has brewing facilities in Golden, Memphis, and Elkton. With a capacity of 23.5 million barrels, the Golden plant is the largest brewing facility in the world. In 2001, Coors marketed nine brands of malt beverages. In addition to the flagship Coors brand, other notable brands are Coors Light, which is battling Miller Lite for second place in the light-beer category, and Zima, which pioneered the malt-alternative class of alcoholic beverages.

Pabst Brewing Company (San Antonio, formerly Milwaukee), 1844–Present

As discussed above, the Best Brewing Company of Milwaukee, founded by Jacob Best Sr. in 1844, spawned both Miller and Pabst. In 1853, Jacob retired and left the firm in the hands of his four sons. Two sons left Best to form Miller, and one son, Philip Best, remained with Best Brewing and became sole proprietor in 1860. Philip's daughter married Captain Frederick Pabst in 1862, and Pabst became a partner in the brewery in 1865. When Philip retired in 1866, he left the brewery to his sons-in-law, Frederic Pabst and Emil Schandein.

Captain Pabst had a talent for business, and the brewery grew rapidly under his leadership. In 1873, the company was incorporated as the Philip Best Brewing Company. Soon it became an industry leader. When production reached half a million barrels in 1889, a year after Schandein's death, stockholders voted to change the name to Pabst Brewing Company in recognition of Captain Pabst's exceptional leadership. By the late 1880s, Pabst was the largest U.S. brewer. In 1892 it was the first brewer to produce a million barrels in a year. Captain

Pabst died in 1904. The company was run by his son Gustav until 1921, then by another son, Fred Pabst Jr.

Pabst was an early innovator in the brewing industry. The company brewed the first lager beer in Milwaukee in 1851. Pabst installed a refrigeration system in 1878 and was the first to use a pipeline to connect the brewery to the bottling house. In recognition of quality, Pabst beer was named America's best at the Chicago World's Columbian Exposition in 1893. Controversy erupted, Anheuser-Busch filing a complaint and Pabst filing a counter complaint concerning judging improprieties. In the end, Pabst won the competition, with a score of 95 to Anheuser-Busch's score of just under 95 points. Because of this award, the Pabst brand was named Pabst Blue Ribbon. During Prohibition, Pabst survived by producing near-beer, soft drinks, malt syrup, and cheese.

After Prohibition, Pabst continued to innovate. In July of 1935, Pabst became the first major brewer to sell beer in steel cans. It was also the first major brewer to produce beer at more than one plant. In 1934, Pabst purchased a brewery in Peoria Heights, Illinois. Building a new brewery in Newark in 1945 and buying the Los Angeles Brewing Company in 1948 established Pabst as the first coast-to-coast brewer (*Newsweek*, November 30, 1953). In 1949, Pabst led the industry in sales in the United States, but by 1957 it slipped to number 9.

In need of new leadership, Pabst purchased the Blatz Brewing Company in 1958, and James C. Windham, former Blatz chief executive officer, stepped in as president of Pabst (*Newsweek*, August 11, 1958). New management revitalized the company, and by 1961 Pabst advanced to the number 3 position behind Anheuser-Busch and Schlitz. Unfortunately, the large size of Pabst-Blatz motivated the Department of Justice to challenge the merger. The court ruled against Pabst, ordering divestiture of Blatz in 1969. Heileman then purchased the Blatz brands. (The Blatz plant had been closed since 1960.).

Pabst began to falter during the beer wars of the mid 1970s. In 1976, market share reached its peak; it declined steadily thereafter. Recognizing the importance of firm size to success, Pabst initiated a number of horizontal acquisitions during this period, purchasing the Burgermeister brand from the Hamm Brewing Company in 1975, the Blitz-Weinhard Brewing Company of Portland, Oregon in 1979, and the Olympia Brewing Company of Olympia, Washington in 1982. The company also attempted to purchase Schlitz in 1981, but the merger was successfully challenged by the Department of Justice.

During much of 1982, Heileman, the C. Schmidt Brewing Company, Irwin L. Jacobs (a Minneapolis entrepreneur and former owner of Grain Belt Breweries), Paul Kalmanovitz (owner of several regional breweries), and William F. Smith (chief executive officer at Pabst) battled for control of Pabst.[15] On February 2, 1982, C. Schmidt made the first offer for Pabst at $16 per share. Bidding escalated until Heileman's offer of $32 per share was accepted at the end of the year. To get the approval of the Department of Justice, Pabst-Olympia was spun off as an independent brewer with plants in Tampa, in Newark, in Olympia, Washington, and in Milwaukee. Heileman retained the Pabst brewing facilities in Pabst, Georgia; in Portland, Oregon (Blitz-Weinhard); and in San Antonio (Lone Star). Heileman also retained the following former Pabst brands: Blitz-Weinhard, Henry Weinhard, Red-White-&-Blue, Burgermeister, Lone Star, and Buckhorn. August U. Pabst, great-grandson of Captain Pabst, resigned as executive vice president and severed the company's link to the Pabst family. The Pabst Brewing Company maintained independence but at a great cost in lost brewing capacity and number of brand offerings. The distribution of Pabst beer contracted from national to regional, and Pabst dropped to the second tier.

As the market share of the restructured Pabst continued to slide, there was renewed interest in buying the company, with Heileman and Paul Kalmanovitz as the main suitors. In December of 1985, Heileman offered to buy Pabst for about $291.5 million. With a total capacity of 14.7 million barrels, the bid amounted to almost $20 per barrel of capacity. Stroh and Schmidt filed anti-trust suits to block the Heileman offer, and the federal district court granted a preliminary injunction preventing the merger. In February of 1986, Pabst accepted an offer of $265 from Paul Kalmanovitz's S&P Company (Mill Valley, California).[16]

Kalmanovitz pioneered the harvest or devolution strategy to take advantage of the war of attrition in brewing. Use of the devolution strategy began in the 1970s when S&P purchased several regional brewers that were having financial difficulties. After a purchase, S&P slashed advertising and other overhead costs, closed inefficient plants, and cut prices in an effort to appeal to price-conscious consumers. Even without advertising, S&P could retain those customers still loyal to the regional labels. Existing capital equipment and product goodwill were allowed to depreciate, which enabled the company to harvest profit in spite of shrinking market share. Use of this strategy only postpones the inevitable, however, as the company will exit the industry once its physical capital wears out or the price falls below average variable cost (McAfee 2002: 103). True to form, immediately after purchasing Pabst, Kalmanovitz cut overhead expenses as Pabst's executive officers and directors were ousted.

After Kalmanovitz's death in 1988, Lutz Issleib took over as chairman and president of Pabst. Issleib's goal was to reverse the slide at Pabst by spending more on advertising and improving quality control (*Advertising Age*, June 27, 1988). As the tables indicate, Issleib's strategy generated market share gains of more than 16 percent from 1988 to 1993. Success was short lived, however, as Pabst lost market share thereafter.

In 1999, Pabst purchased one plant and several brands of the failing Stroh Brewing Company. Although this acquisition bolstered Pabst's market share, sales continued to slide. In 2001, Pabst abandoned all of its production facilities, closing the San Antonio (Pearl) plant (*Modern Brewery Age*, March 26, 2001) and selling the Lehigh Valley (F. & M. Schaefer) plant to Guinness UDV (*Modern Brewery Age*, May 19, 2003). Pabst is now a "virtual" or contract brewer. Although Pabst employs about 200 workers in management and marketing in San Antonio, all Pabst beer is brewed under contract by Miller. Even though Pabst ranked fourth in sales in 2002, its prognosis is grim. Pabst continues to harvest the remaining value of its portfolio of declining brands. Advertising support is the smallest in the industry (at $0.04 per barrel in 2001, compared to an industry average of $4.80 per barrel), and market share continues to erode.

Genesee Brewing Company (Rochester, New York), 1878–present

The Genesee brewery originated in 1878 and sold Leibotschaner beer in the western part of New York State. The brewery was purchased by the Bartholomay Brewing Company in 1889, taking on the Bartholomay name. After Prohibition, Louis A. Wehle reorganized the company and renamed it the Genesee Brewing Company, as it was located on the Genesee River.

Genesee was a successful regional brewer, remaining in the second tier from the mid 1970s through the early 1980s. In 1980 it was the tenth-largest brewer in the country. Genesee's success derived in part from the strategy of brewing darker, heavier beer in line with Northeastern tastes, temporarily bucking the national trend for lighter beer. As well as marketing a full-bodied Genesee beer (with 5.03 percent alcohol by volume and 153 calories), Genesee marketed a bock beer and two types of ale. The company made one horizontal acquisition, purchasing a local competitor, the Fred Koch Brewery (Dunkirk, New York), in 1986.

Genesee's market share has slipped continuously since the early 1980s, forcing change at Genesee. In December 2000, Thomas Hubbard and John Henderson headed a management-led buyout from the Wehle family, and the company is now named the High Falls Brewing Company (*Modern Brewery Age*, May 19, 2003). Today, High Falls engages in contract brewing, continues to produce its traditional Genesee and Koch brands, and produces craft-style beer and ale that compete with microbreweries. This behavior is consistent with the hypothesis that marginal firms are more likely to seek out and serve niche markets (McAfee 1992: 980).

4.2   Leading National Brewers That Failed

The next two companies, Schlitz and Stroh, became linked by merger and are the only national firms to have failed in brewing. Schlitz (in 1950–51 and 1955–56) was the only brewer other than Anheuser-Busch to hold the number 1 spot in brewing during the period 1950–2002. Schlitz retained the number 2 position from 1957 through 1976 and appeared to have had the competence and the resources to vie for the number 1 position through the 1970s. However, sales plunged by the late 1970s. The Schlitz case is of particular interest because it shows how management error and bad luck can cause a once successful and dominant firm to fail. Even after exiting the industry, the Schlitz saga continued as Stroh purchased Schlitz in 1982, a merger that gave Stroh temporary national status. Without a true premium brand, however, Stroh never became a successful national brewer and continued a steady decline after the Schlitz merger. Both Schlitz and Stroh became the losers of the preemption race in advertising, as they fell behind in the race to maintain a premium image for their flagship brands. Thus, this section focuses on the rise and fall of Schlitz and Stroh.

Joseph Schlitz Brewing Company (Milwaukee), 1849–1982

The original founder of the Schlitz Brewing Company was a German immigrant named August Krug. In 1849, Krug built a small brewhouse in the basement of his Chestnut Street restaurant in Milwaukee to serve restaurant patrons. When he died in 1856, he was succeeded by the company bookkeeper, Joseph Schlitz. In 1874, Joseph changed the company name to the Schlitz Brewing Company. The following year, Joseph drowned in a shipwreck during a visit to relatives in Mainz, Germany. As a result, ownership of the company was willed to Joseph's nephews, August, Henry, Edward, and Alfred Uihlein with the stipulation that the name of the company remain unchanged. Members of the Uihlein family held a controlling interest in the company until it was sold to the Stroh Brewing Company in 1982.

An early turning point for Schlitz came in 1871, when the Chicago Fire made Chicago-produced beer scarce. Schlitz shipped beer to Chicago and saw its sales nearly double. In 1872, Schlitz introduced the slogan "the beer that made Milwaukee famous." The Chicago experience encouraged the company to ship beer to distant markets. Schlitz was the tenth-largest U.S. brewer in 1877 (producing about 78,000 barrels) and the third-largest brewer, behind Anheuser-Busch and Pabst, in 1895 (producing about 650,000 barrels). August's son, Joseph Uihlein Sr., assumed control of the company in 1906 and kept the company in operation during Prohibition by selling candy, yeast, and malt syrups. Erwin C. Uihlein, August's youngest son, became president in 1933, a position he held until his nephew, Robert A. Uihlein, became president in 1961.

The company prospered after Prohibition, becoming the nation's largest brewer in the early 1950s. Schlitz made four important horizontal acquisitions: Ehret of Brooklyn in 1949, Muehlbach of Kansas City in 1956, Burgermeister of San Francisco in 1961, and Primo of Honolulu in 1964. Because Schlitz was the second-largest brewer in the nation and Burgermeister was the third-largest brewer in California at the time of the Schlitz-Burgermeister merger, the Supreme Court ordered Schlitz to divest of Burgermeister in 1966 and constrained Schlitz from purchasing another brewer without court approval for 10 years. As a result, the company's remaining growth occurred through internal expansion.

Schlitz had been the industry leader but lost the number 1 position in 1953 following a Milwaukee strike (*Business Week*, November 19, 1955). Schlitz regained the top spot from 1955 to 1956 but then slipped to number two in 1957, a position it held through the mid 1970s. Schlitz's market share increased from 6.08 percent to 15.86 percent from 1950 to 1976. During that time, the Schlitz brand was second only to Budweiser. In 1965, Schlitz introduced its successful Schlitz Malt

Liquor. Old Milwaukee, a popular-priced brand, was marketed nationally beginning in 1975.[17]

In spite of the considerable success of Schlitz through the mid 1970s, the brewer fell victim to errors of strategic planning and the escalating beer wars of the 1970s. The company's market share fell by almost 50 percent from 1976 to 1981, slipping from the second to the third-largest brewer behind Anheuser-Busch and Miller. In 1982, Schlitz was purchased by Stroh for $335.6 million (*Advertising Age*, April 26, 1982).

A series of poor management decisions and unlucky events contributed to the descent of the once successful Schlitz.[18] Problems began when the company implemented a new brewing process it called "accelerated-batch fermentation." According to Schlitz, this shortened brewing time from 25 to 21 days and substantially improved product shelf life (*Forbes*, December 15, 1972). Competitors argued that Schlitz also cut corners by replacing natural hops and malted barley with cheaper hop pellets and corn syrup and by further reducing its brewing time, from 15–20 days compared to Anheuser-Busch's 32–40 days (*Forbes*, June 1, 1974). Because beer is consumed at very cold temperatures in the United States, executives at Schlitz believed that consumers would not notice small changes in beer quality. The company's 1973 annual report (pp. 4–5) claims that Schlitz had the most efficient breweries in the world and, because of recent success, the company was undertaking a rapid expansion of production capacity. Figures 4.1 and 4.2 indicate that the company's profit-to-sales ratio and its capacity utilization rate (production divided by capacity) were substantially above industry average levels during the early 1970s. The firm's capacity expansion program coupled with greater competition from Miller and Anheuser-Busch soon forced Schlitz to engage in prolonged price reductions of its flagship brand in order to sell more beer (*Business Week*, November 8, 1976).

The company's pricing and cost-cutting strategies proved successful at first, as the company's market share continued to increase and its profits and capacity utilization rate remained high throughout the mid 1970s. The company's market share progressed at a faster rate than that of Anheuser-Busch and Miller from 1970 to 1973. The image of Schlitz beer was eventually tarnished, however, as competitors spread the word that "Schlitz was making green [inadequately aged] beer" (*Advertising Age*, April 13, 1981: 64). The initial response from Schlitz was to simply change the name of its new brewing process to "accurate balanced fermentation."

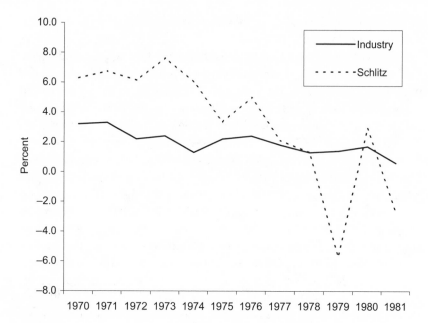

Figure 4.1
Profit-to-sales ratio for the industry and Schlitz, 1970–1981. Sources: See appendix A.

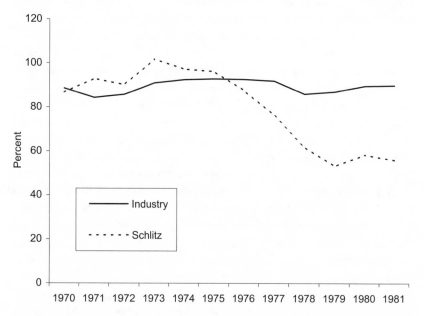

Figure 4.2
Capacity utilization rate for the industry and Schlitz, 1970–1981. Source: See appendix A.

The company's strategy of cutting brewing costs at the expense of quality and product image also appears in the handling of its Primo brand in Hawaii (*Business Week*, January 20, 1975). In the early 1970s, Schlitz discontinued brewing Primo in Hawaii and began brewing wort (the basic mixture of grains, hops, and water) for Primo in Los Angeles. The wort was then dehydrated and shipped to Hawaii, where it was rehydrated, fermented, aged, and packaged. Islanders claimed that Primo's taste had been altered, and its market share in the state of Hawaii plunged from 70 percent to 20 percent between 1971 and 1975. To correct this mistake, Schlitz discontinued the practice in 1975, and Primo returned to being a totally Hawaiian product. Sales of Primo never rebounded to their earlier levels, however.

Schlitz faced another strategic problem during the 1970s. It was the only national producer without a brand in the profitable and fast-growing super-premium category (*Fortune*, April 24, 1978). During the 1972 Olympics, Miller outbid Schlitz for the right to market Germany's Löwenbräu as a super-premium brand in the United States. Schlitz finally entered the super-premium category with its Erlanger brand in 1980, but it was too late to be successful. The market share of super-premium beer grew from 1.1 percent in 1970 to a peak of 5.6 percent in 1980 but declined thereafter. At the same time, the popular-priced and premium categories where Schlitz had its strongest brands experienced a decline in total share from 95 percent to 74 percent. Schlitz was the first major brewer to respond to Miller Lite, however, introducing Schlitz Light in late 1975. In spite of the tremendous growth in popularity of light beer in the late 1970s, Schlitz Light was an instant failure, likely because of a poor formulation or growing image problems with the Schlitz name.

The Schlitz image further deteriorated in 1976 when it experienced problems with quality control. Schlitz expected the U.S. Food and Drug Administration to implement labeling laws requiring brewers to list all ingredients in their products. Schlitz anticipated that consumers would be less inclined to buy beer if they knew it contained unnatural ingredients. In three of its seven plants in early 1976, Schlitz responded by substituting a beer stabilizer called Chill-garde for silica gel. Unlike silica gel, Chill-garde filters out of the beer before packaging and need not be listed on the label. Unfortunately, Chill-garde interacted with the foam stabilizer used by Schlitz, Kelcoloid, causing tiny flakes to develop as the product sat on the shelf. Schlitz brewmasters did not immediately understand the problem, and many Schlitz beer drinkers bought "flaky beer" for the first half of 1976. Once the problem was finally understood in the summer of 1976, Schlitz discontinued the use of Kelcoloid, but then the beer went flat. An outside lab finally solved the problem in the fall of 1976, but not before Schlitz ordered a secret recall at a cost of $1.4 million.

As if this were not enough, two additional setbacks occurred in 1976. First, the SEC investigated questionable sales practices at Schlitz and other major brewers of offering illegal kickbacks to retailers for carrying their beer exclusively. Unlike its competitors, however, Schlitz denied any wrongdoing, inducing further investigation and the suspension of the company's top four marketing executives in August of 1976 (*Business Week*, September 6, 1976; *Fortune*, April 24, 1978; *New York Times*, March 16, 1978). Second, Robert Uihlein, company chairman, became suddenly ill in late October and died on November 12, 1976. Those who rose to power in late 1976 had no marketing experience. Eugene Peters, an accountant who had been vice president of finance, became president, and Daniel McKeithan, a geologist and former husband of an important Uihlein stockholder, was elected chairman. Their first action in December of 1976 was to fire the company's four marketing executives who had been suspended in August.

During the first half of 1977, Peters and McKeithan pressured an inexperienced marketing division to abandon the previously successful "Go for the Gusto" advertising theme. In the words of McKeithan (*Advertising Age*, April 20, 1981: 52), "We're not going to spend time selling image." Instead, they directed the marketing department to create a new "high-impact" theme. The new campaign hit the air in October 1977, featuring a formidable boxer and Schlitz drinker. When asked by an off camera voice to give up his Schlitz for another brand, he glared at the camera and aggressively asked, "You want to take away my gusto?" The ads were meant to be humorous, but most viewers found them "menacing." As a result, the industry came to call this the "drink Schlitz or I'll kill you" campaign (*Fortune*, April 24, 1978: 78), and the ads were quickly taken off the air.[19]

At the same time, Miller and Anheuser-Busch were expanding their marketing efforts. As figure 4.3 shows, Schlitz kept pace with the advertising spending of Anheuser-Busch and Miller through 1977 but lost the advertising race thereafter. With falling sales and a failed advertising campaign, Schlitz's marketing efforts declined sharply after 1977. Goldfarb (2000) hypothesizes that the decision at Schlitz to cut corners in order to heighten short-term profits may have been

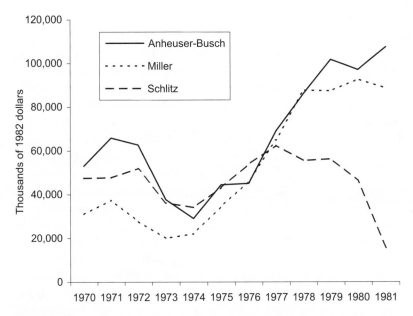

Figure 4.3
Real advertising expenditures of Anheuser-Busch, Miller, and Schlitz, 1970–1981. Source:
See appendix A.

a rational response to the increased competition from Miller and
Anheuser-Busch. Goldfarb's simulation results and statements made
by company officials support this hypothesis. In the 1970s, Robert
Uihlein and members of the Uihlein family, who owned 75 percent of
the Schlitz stock, indicated that short-term profits were more important than catching Anheuser-Busch (*Wall Street Journal*, January 3, 1975;
Fortune, April 24, 1978). According to one company official (*Advertising
Age*, April 13, 1981: 64), "the time between investment and payback
was too long for that board, which wanted nothing less than an immediate return." Thus, when faced with marketing problems and stiff
competition from Anheuser-Busch and Miller, it appears that Schlitz
stockholders conceded defeat and were willing to put the company's
long-term future at risk in order to maintain higher short-term profits.

In the long term, problems with quality control, a poor product
image, and a failed marketing campaign set the stage for the rapid
slide at Schlitz. Figures 4.1 and 4.2 and the tables show that the company's decline began around 1977, as its profit rate, capacity utilization
rate, and market share began to fall. Part of Schlitz's success in 1976 is

due to the 95-day strike at Anheuser-Busch, but by the end of 1977, it became evident that Schlitz was in severe trouble. Robert Weinberg estimates that Schlitz needed a capacity utilization rate of about 60 percent in the late 1970s to break even, and his estimate is confirmed by the data.[20] The company's capacity utilization rate dropped to below 60 percent, and the company operated in the red after 1978.

Eugene Peters resigned as president, after only 11 months on the job, and he was quickly replaced by Frank J. Sellinger in November of 1977 (*Business Week*, November 21, 1977). Sellinger, former executive vice president and brewmaster at Anheuser-Busch, changed advertising agencies, settled with the SEC concerning illegal kickbacks (*Wall Street Journal*, July 10, 1978 and November 2, 1978), and returned to traditional brewing techniques. With an improved product, Sellinger became the spokesperson for Schlitz and aired commercials with blind taste tests to convince consumers to try the new Schlitz beer. None of these efforts were effective, however. Schlitz's market share and profits continued to slip until the company was absorbed by its competitors. Its Syracuse brewery, with a capacity of 4.4 million barrels, was sold to Anheuser-Busch in 1979. The remainder of the company was sold to Stroh in 1982.

Estimates by Aaker (1991: 82) indicate that the Schlitz brand lost almost 91 percent of its market value from 1974 to 1982. The lesson from this case is that a brewer's reputation is critical to its long-term success and survivability. Firms that sacrifice product quality and reputation for short-term profits will not remain viable in the long run.[21] This view is best expressed by Ted Rosenak, former advertising manager at Schlitz (*Advertising Age*, April 20, 1981: 52): "In the beer business, if a company loses its resources and money, but retains its reputation, it can always be rebuilt. But if it loses its reputation, no amount of money and resources will bring it back." The episode of cutting product quality at Schlitz is so infamous in brewing that it has come to be called the "Schlitz mistake" (Baum 2001: 343–344).

Stroh Brewing Company (Detroit), 1850–1999

In 1850, Bernhard Stroh established the Lion Brewery in Detroit. The name was changed to the B. Stroh Brewing Company in 1882 and then to the Stroh Brewing Company in 1909, but the Stroh label continued to use the lion crest of the Lion Brewing Company. Upon the death of Bernhard in 1882, the company was managed by his son, Bernhard Jr.

Bernhard's brother, Julius, became president in 1908. The company survived Prohibition by marketing ice, ice cream, soft drinks, near-beer, and malt extract.

Julius Stroh is credited with implementing the company's "fire-brewed" process in 1912, by which beer is brewed in relatively small copper kettles directly over a flame instead of in steam-heated steel vats (*Fortune*, May 31, 1982). Through the 1990s, the Stroh flagship brand continued to be fire-brewed. The process enhances flavor and distinguishes Stroh as "America's only fire-brewed beer." When Julius died in 1939, his sons Gari and John managed the company until 1967, when John W. Shenefield was named president. In 1968, control returned to the Stroh family when Peter W. Stroh, Gari's son, became president.

Stroh grew rapidly from the late 1960s through the 1970s, when it moved into the second tier. In 1964, Stroh purchased and marketed the brands of the Goebel Brewing Company of Detroit. Acquisitions of Schaefer in 1980 and Schlitz in 1982 converted Stroh from a Midwest regional to a national brewer in the top tier. During this time, the company tried to reinvigorate the failing Schlitz brand and reposition its Stroh brand from a popular-priced regional to a premium national brand.

The strategy failed, however. Stroh's market share fell steadily after the Schlitz merger, and the company slid back to the second tier by 1987. While in decline, Stroh purchased the failing Heileman Brewing Company in 1996 for an estimated $290 million (*Wall Street Journal*, July 2, 1996). Stroh then produced the popular Heileman and Stroh brands in its most efficient plants, employing the devolution strategy and forestalling failure for a short time. As the share of the Stroh, Schlitz, and Heileman brands diminished from 1996 to 1998, Stroh's market share decreased by more than 31 percent until parts of the firm were sold to four firms in 1999. Pabst purchased Stroh's Lehigh Valley plant, assumed Stroh's contract brewing for the Boston Beer Company, and purchased the following brands: Ballantine, Falstaff, Lone Star, Old Style, Olympia, Rainier, Schmidt, and Special Export. Miller purchased the Hamm and Old English 800 brands. As part of the agreement, Miller also acquired the Tumwater, Washington (Olympia) plant and the Mickey's Malt Liquor brand and the Henry Weinhard brands from Pabst. Yuengling purchased Stroh's Tampa plant. Platinum Holdings purchased the La Crosse (Heileman) plant, which is now the City Brewing Company (Heileman's original company name). The remaining Stroh plants closed: Longview, Texas (Lone Star); Portland, Oregon (Blitz-Weinhard); Seattle (Rainier); and Winston-Salem (Schlitz).

There is no simple explanation for the demise of Stroh. It was able to reach national status temporarily, but only by purchasing Schlitz, a national brewer with a tarnished image. The company never produced a true premium brand, which put it at a great disadvantage in the pre-emption race in advertising among the national brewers. As will be seen in the examples below, brewers that focus on popular-priced brands perished from the industry as consumers switched from popular-priced to premium brands of beer.

4.3 Leading Regional Brewers That Failed

Once among the leading regional brewers during the second half of the twentieth century, the remaining six firms languished and eventually exited the industry. Although the failure of an individual firm may be due to systematic management errors, many firms fell victim to the war of attrition in brewing and either exited rather quickly or resorted to the devolution strategy that allowed them to exit gradually with the depreciation of assets and product goodwill. Discussion in this section focuses on company history and the events that contributed to a firm's demise. Firms in this group are discussed in alphabetical order.

P. Ballantine & Sons (Newark), 1833–1972

Peter Ballantine opened his first brewery in Albany, New York in 1833. In 1840 the business was moved to Newark, New Jersey. By the 1870s, P. Ballantine & Sons was the fourth-largest brewer in the United States.

In 1950, the regionally successful company was the third-largest brewer in the United States. Ballantine's regional success is attributed in part to its sponsorship of radio broadcasts of New York Yankees baseball games in the 1940s and the 1950s. Ballantine's three-ring logo (in the style of a Venn diagram) was widely recognized during this period. In the early 1970s, the company marketed several brands: Ballantine Premium, Ballantine XXX Ale, Ballantine India Pale Ale, Ballantine Bock, and Munich.

From 1950 through 1962, the company's market share was fairly constant at about 5 percent. During this period, Ballantine placed in the second tier. Thereafter, the company fell into the third tier as its market share and influence on the industry declined. In an effort to boost its image, Ballantine purchased the Boston Celtics basketball franchise in 1968, but market share continued to deteriorate (*Forbes*, September 15, 1968). Company marketing executives resigned in 1970, and Ballantine brands went unadvertised in early 1971 (*Advertising Age*, February 22, 1971). In 1972, Ballantine was purchased by Falstaff.

One explanation for Ballantine's fall is the fact that it continued to produce some of the darkest and heaviest beers and ales in a period when more and more consumers were switching to lighter beers. For example, Ballantine India Pale Ale had an alcohol content of 6.39 percent (by volume) and 192 calories in a 12-ounce can and Ballantine beer had a 4.85 percent alcohol content and 153 calories. In contrast, the three successful brands during the period were lighter in alcohol and calorie content: Budweiser (4.65 percent alcohol and 142 calories), Coors (4.55 percent alcohol and 137 calories), and Schlitz (4.58 percent alcohol and 145 calories). The company's inability to meet the growing demand for lighter beer and to compete in advertising with the national brewers are the likely reasons why Ballantine, like many other regional brewers, declined and eventually exited the market.

Carling National Breweries, Inc. (Baltimore), 1840–1979

Thomas Carling founded his original brewery in Canada in 1840. The company moved to the United States in 1933 with its first U.S. plant located in Cleveland. Formally known as the Brewing Corporation of America, it was renamed the Carling Brewing Company in 1954.

In the mid 1950s, with Ian R. Dowrie as president, Carling undertook an extensive expansion program. It purchased the Griesedieck Western brewery in Belleville, Illinois in 1954, the International Breweries plant in Frankenmuth, Illinois in 1956, the Heidelberg brewery in Tacoma in 1959, and the Arizona Brewing Company in Phoenix in 1964.[22] New plants were built in Natick, Massachusetts (1956), in Atlanta (1958), and in Baltimore (1961). Carling advanced from being the number-62 brewer in the United States to being the number-4 between 1949 and 1960. During that time, Carling established a famous advertising line for its Carling Black Label brand. As a young man watches television, he yells to a woman working in the kitchen "Hey Mabel, Black Label" (*Printers' Ink*, March 12, 1965). Carling changed its name to Carling National when it merged with the National Brewing Company in 1975.

Carling marketed a number of popular regional brands. In addition to its Carling Black Label and Original Red Cap Ale brands, Carling marketed Stag Beer (Griesedieck Western), Heidelberg Beer, and National's brands (e.g., National Premium, National Bohemian, Colt 45 Malt Liquor, and Altes Lager). Under license from Denmark's United Breweries, Carling produced Tuborg Beer·beginning in 1972 (*Advertising Age*, July 17, 1972). This strategy went against the light-beer trend, as Tuborg is a European-style beer with a heartier flavor than regular beer.

Carling was a successful regional brewer in the 1950s, when it was classified as a member of the second tier. By the mid 1960s, however, the company experienced a dramatic decline in market share and fell to the third tier. Between 1963 and 1977, its market share declined from 6.01 to 2.73 percent. Like many failing regional companies at the time, Carling National was eventually purchased by a more successful competitor. After anti-trust concerns halted Pabst's attempt to purchase Carling in 1978 (*Advertising Age*, September 18, 1978), Carling was purchased by Heileman in 1979. Like Ballantine, Carling's decline may be due, in part, to an incongruence between its brands and consumers' tastes, as Carling's brands were heavier and none had a premium image. Another factor was Carling's overly aggressive expansion program which led to excess capacity and eventually put a strain on firm profitability. (See chapter 8.)

Falstaff Brewing Company (St. Louis), 1917–1975

The Falstaff Brewing Company has roots in two other breweries, Forest Park and William J. Lemp. Joe Griesedieck purchased the Forest Park Brewing Company of St. Louis in 1917 and the Falstaff name from the William J. Lemp Brewing Company in 1933, the year the company changed its name to the Falstaff Brewing Company. Falstaff survived Prohibition by making near-beer, soda pop, and smoked hams.

Falstaff was one of the first brewers to expand by means of merger. Falstaff purchased the Fred Krug Brewery in Omaha in 1935, the National Brewery of New Orleans in 1937, the Berghoff Brewing Company of Fort Wayne, Indiana in 1954, the Galveston-Houston Brewing Company of Galveston in 1956, the Mitchell Brewing Company of El Paso in 1956, the Narragansett Brewery of Cranston, Rhode Island in 1965, and Ballantine in 1972. During this period of expansion, Falstaff became a leading regional producer and ranked in the second tier from

1950 to the early 1970s. In 1960, Falstaff was the third-largest brewer in the United States. During the early 1970s, Falstaff marketed Falstaff, Narragansett, Narragansett Ale, Krueger, Krueger Ale, Haffenreffer, Croft Ale, Hanley, Ballantine, and Ballantine Ale.

Like other regional brewers that sold popular-priced beer, however, Falstaff experienced a steady decline in market share beginning in the late 1960s. From 1967 to 1975, Falstaff's market share fell by more than 54 percent. In 1975, the S&P Company (Mill Valley, California) purchased Falstaff (*Wall Street Journal*, August 12, 1975).[23] S&P was owned by Paul Kalmanovitz, a San Francisco entrepreneur who also owned the General and Pearl Brewing Companies. Kalmanovitz applied his devolution strategy (see Pabst) at Falstaff by firing experienced company employees and closing several plants: the original St. Louis brewery in 1977, the New Orleans brewery in 1979, and the Cranston and Galveston breweries in 1982.[24] Falstaff operated as an independent brewer again after S&P purchased Pabst in 1986. By the mid 1990s, however, Pabst took over the production and distribution of all Falstaff brands.

Theodore Hamm Brewing Company (St. Paul), 1884–1975

In 1884, A. F. Keller built a brewery in St. Paul. He sold it to Theodore Hamm in 1895. It was incorporated as the Theodore Hamm Brewing Company in 1896. Hamm's beer was popular in the 1950s and known for its advertising spokesperson, the Hamm's Bear cartoon character, and its advertising theme: "born in the land of sky blue waters." In 1959, the Hamm's Bear commercial won several awards and was chosen as one of the top 100 ads of all time (Ronnenberg 1998).

Hamm belonged to the second tier in the 1950s, when it grew to become the fifth-largest U.S. brewer in 1957. The company made an unsuccessful attempt to market its beer on the West Coast in the mid 1950s. Hamm purchased the Gunther Brewing Company of Baltimore in 1960 but sold the Gunther plant to Schaefer in 1963 when sales declined. Hamm was purchased by Heublein Incorporated in 1965, but the conglomerate merger had little effect on the shrinking market share of Hamm's beer. In an effort to boost sales, the company revived the Hamm's Bear commercials in the early 1970s (*Advertising Age*, February 28, 1972 and July 31, 1972). The re-emergence of the Hamm's Bear failed to reverse the downward trend in market share. Hamm's was finally purchased by the Olympia Brewing Company in 1975.

Little is written about the Hamm Brewing Company and why it failed. Robertson (1984: 101) indicates that Olympia changed the Hamm formula after its merger. Since the current version of Hamm's beer is relatively light with 142 calories (per 12-ounce can) and an alcohol content of 4.4 percent, the original version may have been too heavy to have mass appeal in an era when consumers demanded lighter beer.

G. Heileman Brewing Company (La Crosse, Wisconsin), 1858–1996

In 1858, Gottlieb Heileman and John Gund formed a partnership in the City Brewery of La Crosse. Heileman retained ownership after Gund retired in 1872. When Heileman died in 1878, his widow, Johanna, became company president and ran the business successfully until her death in 1917. Johanna Heileman was the first female executive officer of a major U.S. brewing company. The firm was incorporated as the Heileman Brewing Company in 1890, and the company obtained a copyright for its flagship brand, Old Style Lager, in 1902. Like other brewers, the firm survived Prohibition by selling near-beer.

Heileman remained a small regional brewer until the early 1960s, when it began an aggressive horizontal acquisition campaign. Because of strict enforcement of the anti-trust laws, the major brewers could not acquire failing breweries during the period. Consequently, firms like Heileman were able to buy failing brewers and used equipment at very low cost. From 1961 to 1987, Heileman made 18 horizontal or market extension acquisitions. The firm then marketed various brands tied to different regions of the country. It was in the second tier from the mid 1960s to the mid 1990s. Heileman's strategy was to buy failing brewers, close the most inefficient facilities, and use the customer base of the newly acquired brands to keep production high at its most efficient production facilities. In 1980, it operated breweries in Phoenix (Carling), in Belleville, Illinois (Carling), in Newport, Kentucky (Wiedemann), and in La Crosse, Wisconsin. Some of the notable brands produced by Heileman include Old Style, Special Export, Henry Weinhard's Private Reserve, Schmidt, Lone Star, Colt 45, Mickey's Malt Liquor, Rainier, Carling Black Label, National Bohemian, Wiedemann, and Tuborg Gold. Heileman's acquisition strategy was very effective initially, as the firm climbed from number 32 to number 6 in production from 1959 to 1980.

As Heileman grew, anti-trust policy began to limit Heileman's ability to use this growth by merger strategy (*Fortune*, June 18, 1979), and its market share began to fall in the mid 1980s. Furthermore, the price wars of the late 1980s and the early 1990s exacerbated Heileman's descent. In 1986, Heileman was purchased by a multinational corporation, the Bond Holding Company, for $1.2 billion.[25] In an effort to increase Heileman's market share, Bond's management hiked up advertising spending (*Business Week*, October 5, 1987; *Beverage World*, January 18, 1988; *Advertising Age*, February 13, 1989). The tactic proved unsuccessful, however, and Heileman filed for bankruptcy in 1991 (*New York Times*, January 25, 1991). In another conglomerate merger, Heileman was sold to Hicks, Muse, and Company for $300 million in 1993, just 9 years after Bond paid $1.2 billion for the company (*Modern Brewery Age*, March 14, 1988 and March 26, 2001). Like other regional brewers of mostly popular-priced beer, Heileman continued to decline until it was finally purchased by the Stroh Brewing Company in 1996 and discontinued operating as an independent brewer (*Wall Street Journal*, July 2, 1996).

F. & M. Schaefer Brewing Company (Allentown, Pennsylvania), 1842–1980

Frederick and Maximilian Schaefer, immigrants from Wetzlar, Russia, founded the F. & M. Schaefer Brewing Company in 1842 when they purchased the Sommers Brewery. After several moves, they located their brewery near Grand Central Station in New York. Maximilian's son, Rudolph, was named president in 1912 and moved the company to Brooklyn in 1915. During Prohibition, the company sold near-beer and manufactured ice. When Rudolph Schaefer died in 1923, his sons, Frederick M. E. and Rudolph J., took over the company.

Schaefer grew during the 1960s and ranked fifth in the United States in 1970. Schaefer was a regional producer, serving the Northeast. Sponsorship of sporting events in New York contributed to Schaefer's success. Schaefer also employed a growth-by-merger strategy, acquiring the Standard brewery of Cleveland in 1961 and the Gunther brewery of Baltimore from Hamm in 1963. Schaefer purchased the Piel and Trommer brands from Associated in 1972. From the mid 1960s to the mid 1970s, Schaefer is classified as a member of the second tier. During the "beer wars" of the 1970s and the 1980s, however, Schaefer's market share fell like that of many other popular-priced beer producers. As a result, Schaefer closed its Brooklyn plant in 1977, and the company was sold to Stroh in 1980 for $23 million (*Fortune*, May 31, 1982).

4.4   Conclusion

The 13 most influential companies in the U.S. brewing industry originated in the mid 1800s, survived Prohibition, and succeeded as large regional or national producers through 1971. Thereafter, most of the leading brewers failed. Technological change increased minimum efficient scale (MES) relative to the size of the market, and greater emphasis was placed on advertising, creating an environment where fewer and fewer firms could operate profitably. The regional brewers were especially vulnerable, since they could not undertake national advertising campaigns, were too small to reach MES, and generally produced darker and popular-priced brands that were falling out of favor among consumers. National producers did not go unscathed, however. The failure of Schlitz, a national producer and once the leading brewer in the United States, demonstrates that maintaining a reputation for quality is crucial for survival in brewing.

Brewers employed several strategies in their struggle to survive. Successful national brewers built efficient plants throughout the country and undertook advertising and other strategies to maintain a premium image for their products. The survivors in this group are the ultimate winners of the preemption race in advertising and the war of attrition: Anheuser-Busch, Coors, and Miller. Smaller regional brewers that survive have specialized by serving a small niche market.[26] Examples of regional-niche producers are Genesee and the Stevens Point Brewery (Stevens Point, Wisconsin). Genesee produces beer for other companies by contract brewing, and both Genesee and Stevens Point brew craft-style beer. Besides Genesee, the largest of the other niche producers reside in the state of Pennsylvania: D. G. Yuengling & Son of Pottsville, the Latrobe Brewing Company, and the Pittsburgh Brewing Company.[27] Brewers that failed were generally inefficiently small, made strategic blunders, and produced beer styles that fell out of favor among consumers. Those that hung on the longest applied the devolution strategy of slashing overhead costs and cutting price until physical capital and product goodwill were depleted.

A declining market share appears to be a good predictor of firm exit among the leading brewers. Of the 13 brewers discussed here, eight exited the industry from 1950 to 2000: Ballantine (in 1972), Falstaff (1975), Hamm (1975), Carling (1979), Schaefer (1980), Schlitz (1982), Heileman (1996), and Stroh (1999). In general, these firms experienced a substantial drop in market share before their demise. An important exception occurs when a declining brewer buys another firm. For example, Carling's acquisition of National in 1975 boosted its market share temporarily, but the firm's share soon fell again until Carling was purchased by Heileman in 1979. Likewise, Stroh experienced an increase in share in 1996 when it purchased Heileman, but its market share diminished thereafter until Stroh was sold in 1999. The issue of firm failure and success will be discussed further in chapter 8.

Barring strategic blunders, the future looks bright for the leading three brewers, especially the industry leader, Anheuser-Busch. Pabst will likely exit the industry in the near future. Small niche brewers are unlikely to challenge the leaders but will continue to survive as long as they cater to unique regional tastes and avoid local price wars. If market demand continues to stagnate, the remaining brewers will compete in a zero-sum game and must fight among themselves for growth. At the same time, cooperation may be more likely with only three remaining mass-producing beer companies, an issue that will be discussed in chapter 9.

Imports and Domestic Specialty Brewers

I will make it a felony to drink small beer.[1]

—William Shakespeare, *King Henry the Sixth* (1591)

The microbrewery invasion of the brewing industry in the midst of the war of attrition among the mass producers presents a quandary. Equally puzzling is a parallel influx of imported brands into the U.S. beer market. In this chapter, the reasons for the relative popularity of the micros and imports in recent decades are explored. To reiterate: There are three distinct groups of firms that supply beer to the U.S. market. The first embodies the traditional, "macro," or mass producers that entered or re-entered the market just after Prohibition and produce regular lager beer. The second group of brewers—domestic microbreweries and brew pubs—entered the market more recently and began producing on a very small scale. They distinguish themselves from the mass producers by brewing darker "craft-style" beers and ales and are often called "craft" or "domestic specialty" brewers. The third group includes international brewers that supply imported beer to the U.S. market.

Figure 5.1 shows how the market shares of the import and domestic specialty categories have changed. Import and specialty brewers had very little effect on the U.S. market until the 1970s. Microbreweries became increasing more popular in the late 1980s but growth began to level off in 1996 and has been flat thereafter. By 1980 there were ten specialty brewers, a number that grew to 170 in 1990 and 1,368 in 2000. The market share of imports was only 0.04 percent just after Prohibition and 0.11 percent in 1950 (*Modern Brewery Age*, September-October 1983: MS-31). Demand for imports began to grow at a more rapid rate

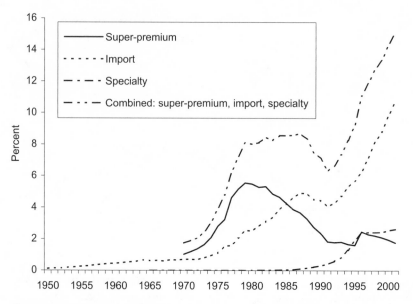

Figure 5.1
Market shares of super-premium, specialty, and imported beer in the United States,
1950–2001. Source: See appendix A.

in the 1970s, dipped in the late 1980s, and has risen markedly since the
early 1990s. Today, the United States imports more beer than any other
country in the world (*American Brewer* 2003). By 2001, the combined
market share of imports and specialty beer reached just under 13.4
percent, exceeding that of the Coors Brewing Company, the third-
largest domestic brewer.

Import and domestic specialty brands are classified into a separate
group because they are imperfect substitutes for the regular beer produced by the mass-producing beer companies (*Modern Brewery Age*,
July 10, 1989; May 14, 1990; May 13, 1991; May 18, 1998). Most import
and specialty beers appear darker in color and have a heartier flavor.
For example, few consumers consider Coors Light a close substitute for
Guinness Foreign Extra Stout, as Coors Light is mild and contains 4.36
percent alcohol, while Guinness is a rich, dark beer that is 7.5 percent
alcohol.[2] On the other hand, import and domestic specialty beers are
considered close substitutes for one another. For example, John Barnett,
president of Molson Breweries in Canada, stated that the specialty
brewers were "clearly a competitive threat" to the imports (*Modern
Brewery Age*, July 13, 1992: 7). The one exception is super-premium

Table 5.1
Percent of consumers who purchase various brands of beer, by gender, race, income, and region, fall 2001. Source: Mediamark Research Inc. as reported in *Beer Industry Update: A Review of Recent Developments* (2002).

	Bud-weiser	Coors Light	Michelob Light	Corona	Guin-ness	Samuel Adams	Sierra Nevada
Male	70.3	57.5	62.2	57.0	73.0	70.7	68.8
Female	29.7	42.5	37.8	43.0	27.0	29.3	31.2
Age							
21–24	10.6	10.3	9.0	10.8	12.9	12.4[a]	16.3[a]
25–34	23.1	23.0	26.1	29.4	29.9	27.9	38.5
35–44	25.0	25.8	27.9	27.2	23.0	27.1	28.1
45–54	17.7	19.7	17.9	15.6	15.0	20.1	11.5
55–64	7.4	7.6	8.0	4.5	5.3	6.6	4.1
65+	8.0	6.6	6.3	2.6	5.1	5.9	1.5
Race							
White	80.8	89.1	87.3	85.4	88.4	92.4	86.8
Af.-Am.	15.3	6.2	8.7	9.8	7.2	1.3	5.2
Income (×$1,000)							
75+	30.2	38.9	40.0	44.2	47.2	55.5	57.1
60–<75	10.2	15.6	13.0	13.7	12.4	13.9	10.5
50–<60	7.8	12.1	7.8	8.0	9.6	8.4	7.7
40–<50	11.4	9.0	9.0	9.7	10.2	6.4	7.7
30–<40	10.7	9.5	10.9	7.2	7.4	5.7	4.7
20–<30	13.0	7.3	9.7	6.9	5.1	5.4	2.4
10–<20	10.4	4.5	3.8	6.1	5.1	2.2	6.2
−10	6.3	2.9	5.8	4.2	2.9	2.5	3.7
Region							
Northwest	22.7	29.5	16.3	16.4	23.2	34.4	19.9
South	33.3	30.6	36.9	30.5	20.8	21.6	13.3
N. Central	21.8	19.0	33.4	21.5	23.5	24.1	11.4
West	22.3	20.9	13.4	31.6	32.4	19.9	55.4

a. The "21–24" age group includes consumers aged 18–24 for Samuel Adams and Sierra Nevada.

Table 5.2
Average retail price per case (nominal dollars) by beer category. Source: *Beer Industry Update: A Review of Recent Developments* (1996: 137; 2002: 139).

	1999	2000	2001
Import	$22.77	$23.53	$23.94
Micro	$24.41	$24.85	$25.49
Regional specialty	$20.51	$21.73	$23.87
Super-premium	$16.74	$17.08	$17.62
Premium	$14.81	$15.15	$15.62

beer (e.g., Michelob) marketed by the mass producers as an upscale product competing with import and domestic specialty beers.

Income and demographic differences among consumers of the leading regular, domestic specialty, and imported brands are displayed in table 5.1. The brands sampled include Budweiser (domestic premium regular), Coors Light (domestic premium light), Michelob Light (domestic super-premium light), Corona (imported light), Guinness (imported dark), Samuel Adams (domestic craft), and Sierra Nevada (domestic craft). Table 5.2 lists the average price per case for the import, microbrewery, regional specialty, super-premium, and premium categories. It shows that the import, microbrewery, and regional specialty (i.e., large microbrewery) beers sell for a substantially higher price than premium beers and that the prices of super-premium beers fall between those of specialty and premium beers.[3] Consistent with Veblen effects and an image of quality, table 5.1 demonstrates that the higher-priced beers appeal to the more affluent consumer. In fact, industry analysts typically identify super-premium, domestic specialty, and imported beers as "prestige brands" (*Modern Brewery Age*, May 13, 1991; *Forbes*, October 15, 1997; *American Brewer*, winter 2003: 23).

Consumers of the regular and prestige brands differ in other ways too. As table 5.1 shows, women and consumers in warmer climates are more likely to drink the lighter brands (e.g., Coors Light, Michelob Light, Corona). Consumers in the Northeast and in the West have a stronger preference for darker import and craft beer (Guinness, Samuel Adams, Sierra Nevada). Location differences can be quite pronounced —for example, the percent of beer drinkers favoring specialty beer exceeded 22 percent in San Francisco but was less than 1 percent in the state of Georgia in 2001 (*Beer Industry Update: A Review of Recent Developments* 2002).

To better understand the import and specialty segments of the beer market, the remainder of the chapter documents their evolution and growth. Motives for change since the 1970s and the performance of the leading firms and brands will also be discussed. Of particular interest are the strategic interactions among the import, specialty, and mass-producing beer companies.

5.1   Imports

The entry of imports into the domestic market predates the entry of the specialty brands. Like domestic craft beer, most imported brands are darker, more bitter in flavor, and higher in alcohol and calories than regular domestic beer (*Consumer Reports*, August 2001). Imported brands are generally shipped longer distances, which also increases their cost and reduces their freshness.[4]

Both demand and supply factors have contributed to the rapid escalation of import beer consumption in the United States since the 1970s. Part of the explanation is the growing mass appeal of lighter beer, which drove most of the domestic brewers of dark beer out of business. In 1961 this trend induced Anheuser-Busch to reformulate Michelob (the leading super-premium brand) to give it a lighter and milder flavor (Robertson 1984: 49–50). This created a void in the market for heartier beers. Foreign brewers were in a perfect position to fill this void, as they already produced quality brands of darker beer for consumption in their homelands in large enough quantities to realize scale efficiency.

While domestic beer became lighter and more uniform, continued economic prosperity in the United States led to an increase in demand for variety and for high-status products (Silberberg 1985; Veblen 1899). Imports came in a variety of styles and sold for a price premium, fulfilling the new desires of U.S. beer consumers. Figure 5.1 shows that all of the high-priced categories (super-premium, imported, and specialty beer) gained market share in the 1970s. Growth of their total or combined share stalled from 1979 to 1987 and declined in the late 1980s and the early 1990s, when the economy went into recession. Then, their total market share grew rapidly again during the economic expansion of the 1990s. For most of the period, the major beneficiaries of this heightened demand for high-priced beer were the imports.

The claim that a higher price indicates higher quality for specialty and imported beer provokes debate. The traditional domestic brands obtain their lighter flavor by replacing malted barley with corn or rice adjuncts. Regular domestic beer typically contains 25–65 percent adjuncts, while the proportion of adjuncts used by European brewers ranges from 0 to 30 percent (Goldammer 1999). Because adjuncts are cheaper than malted barley, many foreign and specialty brewers are proud to boast that they produce "all-malt" beverages.

The belief that beer is superior when made with malt instead of adjuncts dates back to Germany's beer purity law, the Reinheitsgebot (meaning "commandment for purity").[5] Duke William IV of Bavaria introduced this law in 1516 to prevent the use of cheap adjuncts and sugars in the brewing process. It required that beer be brewed from just three ingredients: malt, hops, and water. (Yeast's role in fermentation was not understood at the time. Yeast is now permitted.) The law eventually spread to all parts of Germany and later served to bar lower-priced foreign beers from entering the German market. In the twentieth century, German brewers and trade journals advertised that their all-malt brands were of superior quality, a marketing strategy that created the impression that beers made with adjuncts were impure and inferior. The Court of Justice of the European Communities in Luxembourg settled the issue in 1987, ruling that the Reinheitsgebot did not ensure quality or purity but was an illegal barrier to free trade. Today most German beer made for homeland consumption continues under the Reinheitsgebot, a valued marketing claim as this traditional style of brewing is still preferred by German beer drinkers. German brands made for export sometimes use cheaper adjuncts and sugars, however.

Many beer connoisseurs in the United States also contend that regular domestic beer lacks flavor and that import and craft beers are of superior quality. Greer (2002: 41) argues that specialty brewers make superior beer because they use costlier ingredients (e.g., more malted barley) and greater care when brewing. Scherer (1996: 401) states that "U.S. premium beers are crafted for people who do not appreciate the taste of beer." Weinberg agrees, arguing that regular domestic beer is designed for the majority of Americans who drink beer at social gatherings but do not like the taste of beer (*New Brewer*, January-February 1996: 14). Others contend that domestic light beer and low-carbohydrate Michelob Ultra are successful because they appeal to the growing number of health-conscious and physically active beer drinkers (*Fortune*, October 28, 2002; *Newsweek*, December 9, 2002). Aside from differences in calories and carbohydrates, *Consumer Reports*

(June 1996: 15) identifies two objective characteristics that distinguish craft from light beer: bitterness and maltiness. Relative to craft beer, domestic light beer is low in bitterness and has little malt flavor. Because some consumers prefer all-malt beer and others prefer lighter beer, the use of adjuncts in place of malt appears to create horizontal differentiation rather than vertical differentiation.[6] Much as some dinner guests prefer white wine to red, some beer drinkers prefer light beer to dark. In the end, *de gustibus non est disputandum*.

The distinction between domestic and imported beers is no longer sharp. Michelob, for example, is brewed in the United States but is made with imported hops. Foreign direct investment enables many foreign products to be produced in the United States. Licensing agreements—contracts that give a domestic firm permission to produce and market a foreign brand—are more common in brewing. In the 1970s, for example, Carling brewed the Danish Tuborg and Miller brewed the German Löwenbräu for consumption in the United States (Robertson 1984). In 1993, Anheuser-Busch and the Kirin Brewing Company of Japan formed an agreement, with Kirin brewing and distributing Budweiser in Japan and Anheuser-Busch brewing and distributing several Kirin brands in the United States (*Brewers Digest*, January 1997). At the same time, many European companies established brewing facilities in Canada for shipment to the United States (*Modern Brewery Age*, March 13, 1995 and July 15, 1996).

Such licensing agreements generate social benefits and costs. On the plus side, transportation costs fall and imported brands reach consumers more quickly, an important concern when freshness is an issue. On the other hand, product characteristics are not always preserved under such agreements (*Forbes*, October 15, 1977; *Advertising Age*, June 26, 1978; *Wall Street Journal*, March 14, 1979). This strategy also denigrates the "import identity" of the brand, a factor that some consumers value.[7]

Import identity is less of an issue in brewing, since most foreign brands are brewed and packaged outside the United States. The primary countries that ship beer to the United States are Canada, Germany, Ireland, Mexico, Netherlands, and the United Kingdom. From 1950 to 2001, these countries sold 88 percent to 96 percent of all imported beer consumed in the United States. Table 5.3 lists the leading 25 import brands for 2001, with a share of total imports at more than 88 percent for that year. Twenty-three of the top 25 brands were supplied by the leading six countries. Although these countries have continued to supply the majority of foreign beer to the United States,

Table 5.3
Import shares of the top 25 imported brands, 1980–2001. Here brands are ordered by 2001 rank in market share. Sources: for 1980 and 1985, *Beer Industry Update: A Review of Recent Developments* (1983 and 1988); for 1990, 1995, 2000, and 2001, *Modern Brewery Age* (July 15, 1991: 10; July 15, 1996: 9; July 23, 2001: 9; July 22, 2002: 6).

	1980	1985	1990	1995	2000	2001
1. Corona (Mexico)	—	4.7	11.4	14.6	27.8	28.5
2. Heineken (Netherlands)	37.0	32.5	26.5	22.2	19.6	18.3
3. Labatt (Canada)	4.9	4.0	6.5	6.6	5.2	5.3
4. Tecate (Mexico)	1.5	1.8	2.7	3.0	4.1	4.0
5. Guinness (Ireland)	—	—	2.0	2.9	3.7	3.2
6. Foster's (Australia)	1.6	1.4	3.1	3.0	3.2	3.1
7. Amstel (Netherlands)	—	2.2	3.7	3.4	2.6	2.8
8. Beck's (Germany)	5.1	8.7	9.5	5.6	3.2	2.8
9. Bass Ale (UK)	—	—	2.0	2.8	2.7	2.6
10. Modelo Especial (Mexico)	—	—	—	1.3	1.9	2.2
11. Corona Light (Mexico)	—	—	—	—	1.5	1.9
12. Dos Equis (Mexico)	5.4	2.7	2.4	1.4	1.6	1.7
13. Molson Ice (Canada)	—	—	—	—	2.3	1.7
14. Labatt Light (Canada)	—	—	—	—	1.2	1.4
15. Newcastle (UK)	—	—	—	0.8	1.3	1.3
16. Pacifico (Mexico)	—	—	—	0.5	1.9	1.1
17. Molson (Canada)	21.9	12.2	11.9	12.6	1.4	1.1
18. Molson Canadian (Canada)	—	—	—	—	1.0	0.9
19. Harp (Ireland)	—	—	0.7	0.6	1.0	0.8
20. St. Pauli Girl (Germany)	1.8	4.1	2.4	1.2	0.9	0.7
21. Moosehead (Canada)	4.0	5.3	4.9	1.9	0.7	0.7
22. Negra Modelo (Mexico)	—	—	—	—	0.5	0.6
23. Grolsch (Netherlands)	—	0.9	0.9	0.5	0.7	0.5
24. Warsteiner (Germany)	—	—	—	—	0.5	0.5
25. Sapporo (Japan)	—	0.7	1.1	0.9	0.6	0.5
Total	83.2	81.2	91.7	85.8	91.1	88.2

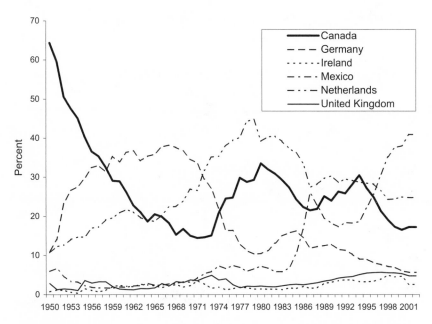

Figure 5.2
Import market share by country of origin for the six leading countries, 1950-2002. Source: *Beer Industry Update: A Review of Recent Developments* (various issues) and *Brewers Almanac* (various issues).

figure 5.2 shows that each country except Ireland and the United Kingdom experienced striking variability in market share from 1950 to 2001.

The changes in the market shares of the leading import brands from 1980 to 2001 are also of interest. Table 5.3 reveals the impressive success of Corona, a brand with an import market share of only 0.9 percent in 1983 that grew to more than 28 percent by 2001. Corona not only ranked number 1 among imports but also ranked seventh among all brands of beer sold in the United States in 2001. Corona is a relatively light import and may have grown by drawing consumers away from domestic super-premium brands and other light imported brands (e.g., Heineken). The trend toward variety is consistent with the moderate growth of the darker imports (Guinness, Bass Ale, Harp) and the decline in share of the leading imported brands. For example, the top four imported brands accounted for 69.4 percent of import sales in 1980 and only 56.1 percent in 2001.

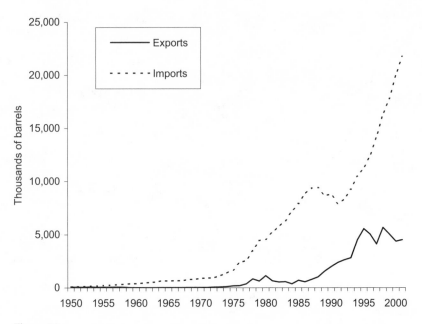

Figure 5.3
Beer exports and imports in the United States, 1950–2001. Source: See appendix A.

The United States runs a trade deficit in beer. Figure 5.3 shows that total U.S. imports and exports of beer were negligible until the early 1970s but that trade activity began to pick up by the mid 1970s. One way to characterize the level of trade within an industry is with an intra-industry trade index (ITI), defined here as $(IM - EX)/(IM + EX)$, where IM measures imports and EX measures exports in barrels (Karrenbrock 1990; Thompson 2001, chapter 7). $ITI = -1$ when a product is only exported; $ITI = 1$ when it is only imported. Intra-industry trade is said to be perfect or balanced when imports equal exports (i.e., when $ITI = 0$). Figure 5.4 plots the index for U.S. brewing for each year from 1950 through 2001. ITI is always positive, as imports exceed exports in every year. The index is close to 0 in the early 1950s, a time of little trade activity. ITI rose dramatically from 1950 before leveling off at about 0.9 in the early 1960s. Trade flows became unstable during the 1970s and the early 1980s, dropped sharply, and then rebounded from 1995 on. The intra-industry trade index for the leading beer importing countries (table 5.4) varies considerably by country. In every country except Japan, imports exceed exports.

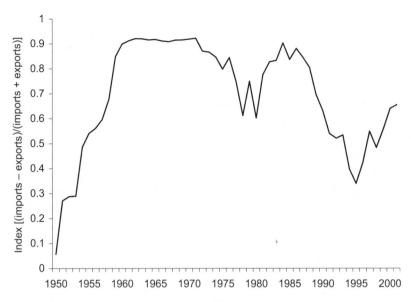

Figure 5.4
Index of intra-industry trade for U.S. beer, 1950–2001. Source: See appendix A.

Table 5.4
U.S. brewing industry trade statistics for major importing countries, 1991, 1995, and 2001.
Imports and exports are measured in thousands of barrels. Intra-industry trade index
equals (Imports − Exports)/(Imports + Exports). Sources: *Beer Industry Update: A Review
of Recent Developments*, 2002; *Brewers Almanac*, 1998.

	U.S. Imports			U.S. Exports			Intra-industry trade index		
	1991	1995	2001	1991	1995	2001	1991	1995	2001
Canada	2,085	3,052	3,754	434	394	410	0.66	0.77	0.80
Germany	862	952	1,231	—	8.0	37	—	0.98	0.94
Ireland	521	357	565	3.5	84	14	0.97	0.61	0.95
Japan	162	105	144	557	151	246	−0.55	−0.18	−0.26
Mexico	1,372	2,488	8,800	161	176	450	0.79	0.86	0.90
Netherlands	2,262	3,189	5,368	7.9	23	17	0.99	0.99	0.99
U.K.	329	603	1,038	82	174	83	0.60	0.55	0.85

Both imports and exports flowed more freely when transportation costs declined after World War II. The homogenization of domestically produced beer and growing wealth also contributed to the growing demand for imported beer. These forces caused ITI to rise in the 1950s and are consistent with the comparative advantage theory for international trade, with domestic brewers specializing in light beer and foreign brewers specializing in dark beer and ale. American brewers began cultivating foreign markets in the 1970s (*Business Week*, July 12, 1982). This, in conjunction with substantial scale economies and increased world demand for variety, led to more balanced trade from the 1970s through the 1990s.

Sales growth of imported beer limited the growth of domestic specialty brewing and came at the expense of the super-premium brands. Weinberg argues that the decline of the super-premium brands is due to the stiff competition from Corona and other brands from Mexico and Canada (*Modern Brewery Age*, July 22, 2002: 17). Corona and most of the Mexican and Canadian imports are relatively light and serve as close substitutes for the domestic super-premium brands. Owing to their close proximity to the United States, these brewers have relatively low transportation costs, and their products are priced more competitively than other imported brands. Success may also stem from the substantial investment in advertising dollars for imported brands. From 1990 to 2001, imported brands generally outspent specialty and super-premium brands on advertising per barrel. (See figure 5.5.) The domestic super-premium brands might rebound, however, if domestic brewers invest in advertising that improves the image of their brands.

5.2   Domestic Brew-Pub, Micro, and Regional Specialty Brewers

As the mass producers continued to consolidate in the 1960s and the 1970s, a "micro" or "boutique" brewing renaissance began. Disagreement over who initiated the microbrewery movement centers on one's definition of a microbrewery.[8] One could argue that Fritz Maytag, the Maytag appliance heir, launched the movement when he purchased the failing Anchor Brewing Company of San Francisco in 1965. In that year, Anchor had the capacity to brew 50,000 barrels of beer but sold only 1,000 barrels. To revitalize the company, Maytag reverted to traditional brewing methods and began producing all-malt beer with no adjuncts or preservatives. Robertson (1984) describes Anchor Steam as a European-style beer that is more full-bodied, complex, and flavorful

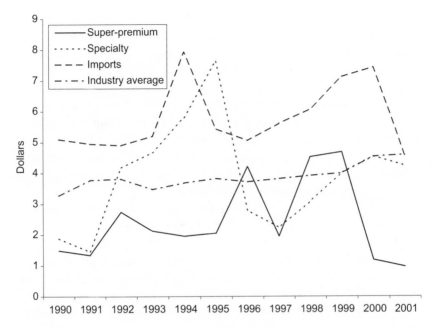

Figure 5.5
Advertising expenditures per barrel of production, 1990–2001. Source: See appendix A.

than regular beer. Anchor gained success in the San Francisco area, earning its first profit in 1975 when sales reached 7,500 barrels. Sales swelled to 20,000 in 1980 and 28,000 by 1982. In the early 1980s, owners of new microbreweries attributed their decisions to enter the business to Anchor's success (*Wall Street Journal*, March 15, 1983; Rhodes 1995). By 1983, more than 100 people had contacted Maytag for advice about opening up a microbrewery (*Barron's*, May 9, 1983: 41).

Johnson (1993) argues that Maytag is not the rightful founder of the microbrewery movement since Anchor was not a new establishment but a revitalized brewery dating back to 1896. Johnson claims that John McAuliffe founded the first true microbrewery in the United States. When stationed in Scotland while serving in the U.S. Navy, McAuliffe developed a taste for English and Scottish ales. After returning to the United States, he began brewing beer at home, trying to replicate the beers and ales he drank overseas. McAuliffe's home-brewed ale and stout were so well received by friends that he and two partners opened the first U.S. microbrewery that was built from scratch in the summer of 1977. His New Albion Brewing Company of Sonoma, California first appeared in *Brewers Digest, Buyer's Guide and Brewery Directory* in 1978 and had a brewing capacity of 200 barrels. New Albion operated successfully for a time but failed in 1982, and the company's brewing equipment was sold to the Mendocino Brewing Company of Hopland, California. McAuliffe also went to work for Mendocino at that time.

The microbrewery movement took off in the 1980s, initially on the West Coast along the "Interstate 5 corridor" from San Francisco to Seattle. Notable early entrants include the Debakker Brewing Company of Marin County, California (started in 1979), the Cartwright Brewing Company of Portland, Oregon (1980), Sierra Nevada of Chico, California (1980), and the Redhook Ale Brewery of Seattle (1982). The first brew pub (i.e., restaurant-brewery) also originated in the West when Bert Grant founded the Yakima Brewing & Malting Company of Yakima, Washington in 1982.

As several new entrants became successful, many grew beyond micro in size and some firm restructuring occurred. Those that outgrew the micro definition are now called "regional specialty brewers." All brewers with micro beginnings are designated domestic craft or specialty brewers, including microbrewers, brew pubs, regional specialty brewers, and craft contract brewers. In 1999, Full Sail Brewing of Hood River, Oregon became employee owned. Several specialty brewers took advantage of widespread excess capacity in the industry by outsourcing production to other brewers. Thus, these contract brewers focus primarily on marketing and strategic decision making.[9]

The main differences between specialty and mass-producing brewers are that specialty brewers are recent entrants and brew craft-style beers and ales. The mass producers make beer with a high concentration of adjuncts, yielding a paler and lighter-flavored beer. Specialty brewers follow Belgian, British, or German brewing traditions, generally following Germany's Reinheitsgebot. In some cases, however, malted wheat, malted rye, fruit, herbs, and other spices are used to add distinctive flavors.[10] As a result, craft beer is darker, heartier, and more flavorful, much like the beer found in Europe. The terms "micro," "specialty," and "craft" are used loosely in the popular press. The terms used in the industry are defined in table 5.5. According to the Association of Brewers, about 60 percent of craft beer was produced by regional specialty brewers, 18 percent by contract brewers, 12 percent by microbrewers, and 10 percent by brew pubs in 2002.

Many entrepreneurs were attracted to the niche market for craft-style beer. Figure 5.6 plots the number of specialty brewers from 1965

Table 5.5
Terms for types of brewers used in the industry. Sources: www.beertown.org; *Modern Brewery Age, Weekly News Edition,* December 30, 1996; *Modern Brewery Age,* May 13, 1991 and May 20, 1996.

Microbrewer A brewer with over 50 percent of its sales off site that produces less than 15,000 barrels of beer per year. Microbreweries produce craft-style beers and ales.[a]

Brew pub A restaurant-brewery that sells at least 50 percent of its craft-style beer on site and less than 15,000 barrels of beer per year. Those with over 50 percent of its sales off site are classified as microbrewers.

Contract brewer A business that identifies a beer recipe, designs a marketing plan, and then hires another brewer for production. A contract brewer may market craft-style or traditional-style beer.

Craft brewer This category includes all micro, brewpub, and contract brewers that produce less than 15,000 barrels of craft-style beer and ale per year. The term "craft" sometimes refers to all brewers of craft-style beer and ale.

Regional specialty brewer A brewer that produces between 15,000 and 2 million barrels of craft-style beer and ale. These are microbreweries that have outgrown the 15,000 barrel annual production limit.[b]

Specialty brewer This category includes all craft and regional specialty brewers of craft-style beer and ale.

Regional macro brewer A brewer that produces between 15,000 and 2 million barrels of traditional or regular lager beer per year. These are sometimes referred to as "mass-producers."

National macro brewer A brewer that produces over 2 million barrels of traditional or regular lager beer per year. These are sometimes referred to as "mass-producers."

a. Initially the upper limit for a microbrewery was 10,000 barrels of annual production (*Barron's,* May 9, 1983; *Business Week,* January 20, 1986). The Cascade Brewers Guild (www.cascadebrewersguild.org) sets the upper limit for a microbrewery at 75,000 barrels.
b. According to *Beer Industry Update: A Review of Recent Developments* (2002: 257), a regional specialty brewer is a firm that produces between 15,000 and 500,000 barrels per year and whose flagship brand is a craft-style beer or ale.

to 2001 and reveals four distinct periods.[11] Similar to the output trends of specialty beer found in figure 5.1, the number of firms grew slowly from 1977 through 1986 and increased at a faster rate through 1993. Rates of entry escalated even more rapidly from 1993 to 1998, when the number of specialty brewers soared from 461 to 1,631. A shakeout occurred thereafter, with the number of specialty brewers falling to 1,401 by 2001. Discussion of the forces driving entry and exit for the specialty brewers follows below.

There are several reasons why the specialty segment of the market began to take off in the 1980s. The uniformity of mass-produced beer and the income effects (augmented by Veblen effects) have already been discussed in the section on imports. With growing income, many

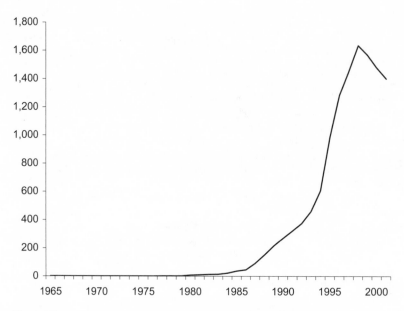

Figure 5.6
Number of specialty brewers, 1965–2001. Source: See appendix A.

consumers revealed a preference for specialty and import brands with a reputation for quality and status. Microbreweries responded by emulating the boutique wineries in California: they offered high-priced products produced in small batches (*New York Times*, April 29, 1979). Second, specialty brewers have a location advantage over imports, allowing cost savings on transportation and delivery of a fresher product. Third, the continued success of Anchor and the imports through the mid 1980s appears to have signaled the presence of economic profits and encouraged entrepreneurs to enter the market with a variety of craft-style beers (*Barron's*, May 9, 1983: 16; *Wall Street Journal*, March 15, 1983: 1).

Changes in government policy also benefited the micro brewers. In February 1977, with smaller mass producers exiting the industry at an alarming rate, the government cut taxes for smaller brewers. Before the cut, all brewers paid a federal excise tax of $9 per barrel. Under the new law, brewers selling less than 2 million barrels annually paid an excise tax rate of $7 per barrel on the first 60,000 barrels sold and $9 per barrel on additional sales. All brewers with more than 2 million barrels in sales paid an excise tax rate of $9 on every barrel sold. All of the new specialty brewers benefited from the tax break, since they all began with an annual capacity below 60,000. The first microbreweries built from scratch went into business just after the law took effect. The tax advantage for small brewers was enlarged in 1991. The federal excise tax rate doubled from $9 to $18 per barrel, but brewers with annual sales of less than 2 million barrels continued to pay only $7 per barrel on the first 60,000 barrels sold annually. The effect on firm costs is striking. In a subsample of firms, the excise tax accounted for approximately 5 percent of the cost of goods sold for small specialty brewers but about 29 percent of costs for the mass-producing brewers in 2001.[12]

Other legislation that encouraged craft brewing includes the legalization of home brewing and brew pubs. To give home brewers the same legal rights as home winemakers, Senator Alan Cranston of California introduced a federal bill to legalize home brewing. The bill was signed into law by President Carter and became effective on February 1, 1979.[13] The legalization of home brewing likely stimulated microbrewery entrepreneurship. Johnson (1993: 10) argues that "some of the early home brewers later became pioneers in the microbrewery revolution." Beginning in the 1980s, changes in state laws lifted prohibitions on brew pubs. In 1984, only six states allowed brew pubs. Two years later, four more states legalized on-premises brewing in restaurants. By 1990, brew pubs were legal in 30 states. The remaining states quickly fell in line, and by 1995 all but two of the states allowed brew pubs. In 1999, Mississippi became the fiftieth state to legalize brew pubs.[14]

Not all government legislation benefited microbreweries, however. In the late 1990s, a change in Hawaii's tax code penalized brewers for bottling beer within the state. Not only was Hawaii's regular excise tax well above the average of all states (at $28.83 per barrel compared to $7.96 for all states), but Hawaii also levied a tax of 50 cents per case on all empty beer bottles shipped to Hawaii. However, brewers that packaged and shipped beer in bottles from the mainland avoided the bottle tax and paid only the state's beer excise tax. Because Hawaii does not manufacture beer bottles, brewers that bottled beer in Hawaii were forced to pay both the excise tax and the empty bottle tax.

The increase in the effective tax rate for Hawaiian brewers was substantial and discouraged microbrewery production within the state. The added tax increased bottling costs by almost 24 percent, and brewing capacity fell dramatically after the law was imposed. Microbrewery capacity was 12,000 barrels in 1996, just before the law was passed, and fell to 7,000 barrels by 2002 (*Brewers Digest, Buyer's Guide and Brewery Directory* 1996 and 2002). The Kona Brewing Company has been the only microbrewery in Hawaii to prosper in this environment. Kona continued brewing keg beer in Hawaii but avoided the bottle tax by contracting with two Oregon beer companies to brew and bottle its Kona brands for consumption in Hawaii. Other microbreweries in Hawaii did not follow this strategy, however, and either went out of business (e.g., Maui Kine Brewing) or lost a considerable share to Kona (e.g., Gordon Biersch Brewing). With few potential buyers for used beer equipment in Hawaii, Kona was able to purchase nearly new brewing equipment from failing brewers at about 25 percent of replacement value.[15] Recall the evidence from chapter 3 indicating that sunk costs in brewing are generally about 50 percent, two-thirds of the rate experienced by failing brewers due the Hawaiian legislation. This experience demonstrates the power of a tax to affect sunk costs, firm value, and industry structure.

On the mainland, the specialty sector flourished and a handful of microbreweries experienced substantial growth and success. Table 5.6 lists the largest regional specialty and micro brewers in 2001. Although early data are limited, table 5.7 lists the output of the leading brewers in the regional specialty, micro, and brew pub segments of the market for several years from 1985 to 2001. Early entrants appear to hold a competitive advantage. All but one of the leading regional specialty brewers in 2001 entered the market before 1989. Anchor, arguably the first microbrewery, more than doubled sales from 1985 to 2001 and ranks among the leading ten domestic specialty brewers.

Two companies, Boston and Sierra Nevada, now dominate the specialty category. In 2001, they produced more than 27 percent of all domestic specialty beer. Sierra Nevada began as a small microbrewery in 1980 and has expanded markedly since that time. It has followed a traditional strategy of brewing all of its beer in one location. In contrast, the Boston Beer Company started later and became the largest specialty brewer by contracting with traditional regional firms to brew its Samuel Adams brands of beer.[16] Contract brewing appears to have worked well for Boston but has also benefited the traditional regional brewers with excess capacity. Boston's beer has been produced under contract with the Blitz-Weinhard Brewing Company in Portland, the High Falls (Genesee) Brewing Company in Rochester, the Hudepohl-Schoenling Brewing Company in Cincinnati, and the Pittsburgh Brewing Company.[17]

Table 5.6
Leading regional specialty and micro brewers, 2001.

Year brewer started	Brewer and location
Regional Specialty Brewers	
1986	Alaskan Brewing Co., Juneau
1965[a]	Anchor Brewing Co., San Francisco
1985	Boston Beer Co., Boston
1988	Deschutes Brewing Co., Bend, Oregon
1987	Full Sail Brewing Co., Hood River, Oregon
1986	Harpoon Brewery, Boston[b]
1983	Mendocino Brewing Co., Hopland, California
1992	New Belgium Brewing Co., Fort Collins, Colorado
1985	Pete's Brewing Co., Palo Alto, California
1986	Portland Brewing Co., Portland, Oregon
1984	Pyramid Brewing Co., Kalama, Washington
1982	Redhook Ale Brewing Co., Seattle
1980	Sierra Nevada Brewing Co., Chico, California
1984	Widmer Bros. Brewing Co., Portland, Oregon
Microbreweries	
1986	Capital Brewery, Middleton, Wisconsin
1993	Carolina Beer & Beverage, Mooresville, North Carolina
1983	Hale's Ales, Seattle
1987	James Page Brewing Co., Minneapolis
1988	North Coast Brewing Co., Fort Bragg, California
1996	Stone Brewing Co., San Marcos, California
1987	Stoudt's Brewing Co., Adamstown, Pennsylvania
1994	Tabernash/Left Hand Brewing Co., Longmont, Colorado[c]
1993	Uinta Brewing Co., Salt Lake City
1996	Victory Brewing Co., Downington, Pennsylvania

a. Anchor Brewing had its early beginnings in 1896. It was converted to a specialty brewer in 1965.
b. Formerly the Massachusetts Brewing Co.
c. Tabernash and Left Hand opened in 1994. They merged in 1998.

Table 5.7
Output of the leading domestic specialty brewers in selected years (thousands of barrels).
Source: Office of R. S. Weinberg.

	1985	1990	1995	2000	2001
Domestic Specialty Brewers					
Boston	—	113	948	1,241	1,175
Sierra Nevada	5.0	31.0	200	499	541
New Belgium	—	—	32.0	165	229
Redhook	4.0	24.0	155	213	223
Pete's	—	12.0	348	152	143
Widmer Bros.	—	12.0	69.0	127	128
Pyramid	1.0	8.0	123	119	111
Deschutes	—	2.0	32.0	95.2	103
Anchor	38.0	68.0	103	93.3	85.9
Alaskan	—	—	22.0	81.8	82.2
Harpoon (Massachusetts)	—	4.0	18.0	63.3	65.0
Full Sail	—	15.0	72.0	65.5	60.8
Portland	—	4.0	62.0	68.2	60.0
Mendocino	1.0	9.0	15.0	49.3	58.2
Microbreweries					
North Coast	—	—	—	14.639	14.650
Capital	—	—	13.0	13.369	13.866
Uinta	—	—	—	13.749	13.780
Stone	—	—	—	9.400	12.779
Hale's Ales	—	—	9.0	13.220	11.500
Carolina Beer & Beverage	—	—	—	9.578	9.718
James Page	—	—	—	9.800	9.525
Victory	—	—	—	7.800	9.500
Stoudt's	—	—	7.8	9.000	9.200
Tabernash/Left Hand	—	—	—	8.000	8.736
Independent brew pubs					
Red Oak	—	—	—	5.000	5.700
McMenamin's Edgefield	—	—	—	5.105	4.901
Bear Republic	—	—	—	4.800	3.800
Four Peaks	—	—	—	2.600	3.707
BJ's	—	—	—	2.822	3.427
Total	84	623	3,796	5,178	5,341

Another strategy of specialty brewers and macrobrewers is to offer a wide variety of products and brands. Table 5.8 records all brands offered by a sample of specialty brewers for 1990, 1995, and 2002. Each firm markets a wide selection of brands and product types of ale, bock, stout, porter, wheat, and lager beer. The larger specialty brewers, including Boston, Pyramid, and Sierra Nevada, have developed flagship brands that have been offered continually. At the other extreme, none of the brands offered by the Portland Brewing Company in 1990 can be purchased today.

As was noted in the section on imports, another distinguishing feature of specialty brands is high price. Craft brands compete with the high-status imported and super-premium brands, and craft beer is more expensive to produce than regular domestic beer. Higher production costs result from using more expensive malted barley and from producing beer in small batches. Table 5.9 lists the 1996 cost breakdown for a six-pack of mass-produced, non-contract craft, and contract-craft beer. The cost of ingredients is higher for both craft and contract-craft brewers, and craft brewers have substantially higher labor and production costs than the mass producers.

Specialty brewers are too small to take advantage of economies of scale in brewing. The empirical evidence discussed in chapter 2 indicates that not even a single producer of specialty beer could brew enough beer to reach minimum efficient scale today. The evidence in figure 2.10 also indicates that a specialty brewer producing less than 100,000 barrels of beer annually will incur a substantially higher unit cost of production than larger brewers. The three specialty brewers sampled produced less than 100,000 barrels per year, with an average unit cost of $145 per barrel. In contrast, Redhook, a specialty brewer with annual sales of more than 200,000 barrels, had an average production cost of $120, and Boston, a contract brewer whose beer was brewed by other large-scale brewers, had an average production cost of only $70.[18] This exaggerates the full cost difference between Boston and other specialty brewers, however, since Boston spends much more than the microbrewers on advertising. Boston spends about $1.35 per six-pack of beer on advertising and management, while craft brewers spend only $0.54. Although the financial reports of Redhook and other publicly owned microbreweries do not list advertising expenses, Boston's average cost jumps to $139 per barrel when advertising is included. This illustrates important strategic differences between the microbrewers and some of the larger domestic specialty brewers.

124

Chapter 5

Table 5.8
Brands offered in 1990, 1995, and 2002 by the leading domestic specialty brewers. Source:
Brewers Digest, Buyer's Guide and Brewery Directory, various issues.

	1990	1995	2002
Boston Beer Company			
Samuel Adams Boston Lager	×	×	×
Samuel Adams Boston Lightship	×	×	×
Samuel Adams Boston Ale	×	×	×
Samuel Adams Double Bock	×	×	×
Samuel Adams Octoberfest	×	×	×
Samuel Adams Winter Lager	×	×	×
Samuel Adams Cranberry Lambic		×	×
Samuel Adams Cream Stout		×	×
Samuel Adams Summer Wheat		×	
Samuel Adams Dark Wheat		×	
Samuel Adams Triple Bock		×	×
Samuel Adams Honey Porter		×	
Samuel Adams Summer Ale			×
Samuel Adams Pale Ale			×
Samuel Adams Golden Pilsner			×
Samuel Adams Cherry Wheat			×
Samuel Adams Old Fezziwig Ale			×
Full Sail Brewing Company			
Full Sale Amber Ale	×	×	×
Full Sale IPA	×		×
Full Sail Pale Ale	×		×
Full Sail Golden Ale		×	
Full Sail Brown Ale		×	
Full Sail Pilsner		×	
Pete's Brewing Company			
Pete's Wicked Ale	×	×	×
Pete's Pacific Dry	×		
Pete's Gold Coast Lager	×		
Pete's Wicked Lager		×	
Pete's Wicked Red		×	
Pete's Wicked Winter		×	
Pete's Helles Lager			×
Pete's Summer Brew			×
Pete's Winter Brew			×
Pete's Strawberry Blonde			×
Pete's Octoberfest			×
Pete's Wicked Red Rush			×

Table 5.8
(continued)

	1990	1995	2002
Portland Brewing Company			
Portland Ale	×	×	
Timberline Classic Ale	×		
Oregon Dry Beer	×		
Grant's Scottish Ale	×		
Grant's Imperial Stout	×		
Grant's Winter Ale	×		
Oregon Honey Beer		×	×
Winter Ale		×	
Portland Porter		×	
Mt. Hood Beer		×	
Portland Stout		×	
MacTarnahan's Scottish Ale		×	×
MacTarnahan's Blackwatch Cream Porter			×
MacTarnahan's Highland Pale Ale			×
Woodstock IPA			×
Uncle Weiss Beer			×
Uncle Otto's Octoberfest Maerzen			×
Saxer Bock			×
Saxer Lemon Lager			×
Nor-wester Hefeweizen			×
Pyramid Brewing Company			
Pyramid Pale Ale	×	×	×
Pyramid Wheaten Ale	×	×	×
Pacific Crest Ale	×		
Snowcap Ale	×	×	×
Sphinx Stout	×	×	
Pyramid Wheaten Bock		×	
Pyramid Hefeweizen		×	×
Pyramid Amber Wheaten		×	×
Pyramid Best Brown		×	×
Espresso Stout		×	×
Pyramid Apricot Ale		×	×
Anniversary Ale		×	
Pyramid Porter		×	×
Redhook Ale Brewing Company			
Redhook Ale	×	×	
Blackhook Porter	×	×	×
Ballard Bitter	×	×	

Table 5.8
(continued)

	1990	1995	2002
Winterhook Christmas Ale		×	×
Wheathook		×	
Redhook ESB		×	×
Redhook Hefeweizen			×
Redhook IPA			×
Doublebock Stout			×
Redhook Blond Ale			×
Redhook Nut Brown Ale			×
Sierra Nevada Brewing Company			
Sierra Nevada Ale	×	×	
Sierra Nevada Porter	×	×	×
Sierra Nevada Stout	×	×	×
Celebration Ale	×	×	×
Sierra Nevada Bigfoot Barley-Wine, Ale	×	×	×
Sierra Nevada Draught Ale	×	×	
Sierra Nevada Summerfest Beer		×	×
Sierra Nevada Pale Bock		×	×
Sierra Nevada Pale Ale			×
Sierra Nevada Draft-Style Pale Ale			×

Table 5.9
Cost breakdown of mass-produced, craft, and contract-craft beers, 1996. Costs and prices are measured in dollars, and % abbreviates the percent of the total price devoted to each category. Source: *Consumer Reports*, June 1996.

	Mass-produced		Craft		Contract-craft	
	Cost per six-pack	%	Cost per six-pack	%	Cost per six-pack	%
Ingredients	.16	4	.25	4	.27	4
Labor and production	.47	12	1.06	16	.47	7
Packaging	.66	16	.83	13	.71	11
Advertising and management	.33	8	.54	8	1.35	21
Brewer profit	.24	6	.67	10	.53	8
Retail and distributor markup	1.46	36	2.48	38	2.50	38
Taxes and shipping	.69	17	.62	10	.69	11
Price	4.01		6.45		6.52	

Microbreweries produce on a small scale but require little advertising to support sales. Some became large, in part, because of intensive advertising campaigns. Thus, they are more scale efficient, but they experience high marketing costs.

In spite of higher unit costs, small specialty brewers have several advantages over larger domestic and import producers. First, flexible production facilities allow quick responses to changes in local demand (*Modern Brewery Age*, May 16, 1994). In addition, small specialty brewers benefit from the strong preferences of some consumers who favor small local producers over national or multinational corporations (Carroll and Swaminathan 2000). Consumers of craft beer may shun advertised products and may believe that a true microbrewery produces a higher-quality, hand-crafted product. To placate these customers, many microbreweries are reluctant to advertise, contract-craft brewers are secretive about where their products are brewed, and mass producers often conceal the corporate identity of their own specialty brands.[19] Paul Shipman, president of Redhook, echoes this belief: "... what offends the real brewers is when the contract brewers portray themselves as charming entrepreneurs who diligently brew their beers. In reality, they are pure marketing entities." (*Wall Street Journal*, April 15, 1996)

Many smaller brewers spend little on advertising, yet the marketing practices of specialty brewers vary considerably. In the beginning, most brew pubs and microbrewers sell draft beer in restaurants and bars. The primary marketing challenge is to convince drinking establishments to carry their beer in place of another brand. Once a brand proves successful and attains name recognition, it can be introduced in bottles. At this point, sales efforts focus on acquiring shelf space in local supermarkets. In general, traditional advertising is "something almost unheard-of among tiny [micro] brewers" (*Barron's*, May 9, 1983). Even the number 2 specialty brewer, Sierra Nevada, refuses to engage in traditional marketing activities (*Brandweek*, January 17, 2000). Instead, promotions target local customers with displays in bars, giveaways (e.g., glassware, hats, coasters, samples at bars), and sponsorship of local community events (*Business Week*, January 20, 1986; Barndt 2002).

In sharp contrast, the Boston Beer Company invested heavily in advertising during the 1990s and pursued provocative marketing practices. In the mid 1980s, Boston Beer Company president Jim Koch informed the public that Boston's Samuel Adams Lager met Germany's strict Reinheitsgebot law, whereas most regular domestic brands and several imported brands, including Heineken and St. Pauli Girl, did not. This campaign generated notoriety for Samuel Adams and embarrassed Heineken and St. Pauli Girl, so much so that they began shipping all-malt versions of their brands to the United States within 12 months.[20] Koch also questioned the quality of regular domestic beer, arguing for the classification of domestic craft and imported beer into a single category he calls "better beer" (*American Brewer*, winter 2003). Owners of small specialty breweries use the same tactic when talking about craft beer, normally referring to it as "real beer" (*Brandweek*, March 31, 1997). Smaller and failing firms commonly initiate nontraditional advertising ploys, a topic that will be discussed further in chapters 6 and 7.

Advertising expenditures per barrel for the leading domestic, import, and specialty brands are listed in table 5.10. Many of the premium, super-premium, and imported brands are advertised intensively, perhaps in an effort to preserve and enhance their high-status image. The limited data on the specialty brewers reveal that Pete's spends relatively little on advertising and that the amount has declined since 1998. Perhaps the company is unwilling to promote brands whose sales are slipping. (See table 5.7.) Until 2001, Boston advertised heavily and behaved more like an import supplier than a microbrewer. The cutback in advertising spending in 2001 may be an aberration or a turning point in Boston's strategy.

The sustained success of the micro and imported brands eventually induced a strong response from the national macrobrewers. First, Anheuser-Busch, Coors, and Miller chose to branch into microbrewing. Miller acquired the Leinenkugel Brewing Company in 1988 and partial interest in the Celis Brewing Company and the Shipyard Brewing Company in 1995 (*Modern Brewery Age*, March 25, 1996). Similarly, Anheuser-Busch purchased a 25 percent interest in the Redhook Brewing Company in 1994 (Barndt 2002) and a 30.9 percent interest in the Widmer Brothers Brewing Company in 1997 (*Oregonian*, April 18, 1997; *Beverage Industry*, June 1998). In 1995, Coors opened its own microbrewery, the Sandlot Brewery at Coors Field in Denver, with an annual capacity of 4,000 barrels. The macro linked microbreweries obtained access to the wider distribution channels of the national brewers and allowed the national brewers to play a more prominent role in the spe-

Table 5.10
Advertising expenditures per barrel of leading domestic and imported brands, 1993–2001. Source: TNS Media Intelligence/CMR as reported in *Beer Industry Update: A Review of Recent Developments* (various issues).

	1993	1994	1995	1996	1997	1998	1999	2000	2001
Domestic premium									
Budweiser	2.52	2.38	2.68	3.42	3.73	3.41	3.86	4.57	3.94
Coors	1.56	2.72	4.30	10.95	14.77	15.22	15.71	23.25	20.98
Miller Genuine Draft	11.28	7.26	6.68	3.82	11.51	9.10	5.18	4.70	9.69
Domestic light									
Bud Light	4.36	3.94	3.79	3.35	2.51	4.98	3.69	3.42	2.75
Coors Light	4.76	4.84	4.86	5.87	6.76	5.40	6.39	7.21	7.80
Miller Lite	5.31	3.94	5.60	6.41	9.34	6.03	5.12	5.61	6.45
Domestic super-premium									
Killian's	—	—	—	—	—	9.34	20.66	16.90	19.60
Michelob	1.29	1.14	2.11	6.58	1.89	5.00	6.95	7.96	9.16
Domestic specialty									
Boston	14.03	18.62	11.85	5.06	6.36	8.91	9.46	11.90	4.42
Pete's	—	—	—	—	—	2.27	0.12	1.18	0.38
Import									
Corona	1.85	2.12	1.70	2.05	4.40	4.65	7.11	6.57	5.33
Guinness-Bass	0.53	0.11	0.09	0.06	0.09	11.13	6.47	5.87	14.71
Heineken	10.65	9.99	6.47	6.22	5.62	5.07	10.62	12.48	14.44
Industry average	4.04	3.83	3.87	3.72	3.76	3.90	4.01	4.54	4.80

cialty sector. Second, the national brewers began to mimic the micros in the mid 1990s by introducing mass-produced versions of specialty beer—Anheuser-Busch under the names Elk Mountain and Red Wolf, Coors under the name Blue Moon, and Miller under the names Red Dog and Plank Road. To maintain the micro illusion, many of these macro brands omitted the controlling company's name on the packaging. Hence, these brands are sometimes called "phantom," "stealth," "faux," or "microclone" brands of specialty beer (*Fortune*, September 19, 1994; USA *Today*, October 21–23, 1994; *Business Week*, April 24, 1995; *Wall Street Journal*, April 15, 1996; Carroll and Swaminathan 2000; Greer 2002). Third, in the mid 1990s Anheuser-Busch and Miller started financial incentive programs that encouraged distributors to exclusively carry their own regular and specialty brands in an effort to squeeze out rival craft and contract products (*Beverage World*,

September 1996; *Modern Brewery Age, Weekly News Edition*, June 10, 1996; *Modern Brewery Age*, May 12, 1997). The national brewers also made efforts to revive their failing super-premium brands. Anheuser-Busch increased its advertising spending on Michelob (see table 5.10) and recently expanded its Michelob line, adding Michelob Ale, Bock, Black and Tan, Malt, and Ultra (*Advertising Age*, November 13, 2002). Coors added Killian's Brown, stepped up advertising of the Killian's label, and reintroduced its super-premium Herman Joseph's brand (*Modern Brewery Age*, March 25, 1996). Miller reintroduced its super-premium Löwenbräu labels. These efforts had only limited success, however, because many of the phantom brands were relatively light versions of traditional craft beer and because growth in the specialty sector was beginning to wane when they entered the market.

In spite of warnings from a few industry experts, the downturn of the small specialty sector took many brewers by surprise.[21] Figures 5.1 and 5.6 confirm that market growth of specialty beer slowed in late 1996. The number of specialty brewers peaked in 1998 at 1,636, then declined by 235 from 1998 to 2001.

A number of events contributed to the pattern of entry and exit in the specialty sector. In the early 1980s, the success of Anchor and a handful of new entrants drew others into microbrewing. In the 1980s and the early 1990s, strong growth further enticed entrepreneurs until the market could no longer support excessive entry. By the mid 1990s, the market was saturated with hundreds of brands—many of them named after fish or animals, and many flavored (with everything from berries to pumpkins)—and it was difficult for a consumer to form loyalty to a particular brand. Distribution became a serious bottleneck, and new entrants could not find retail distributors, restaurants, and bars willing to market one more brand of craft beer. At the same time, import suppliers stepped up advertising spending. The macrobrewers introduced their own specialty products, prodded their distributors to squeeze out competitors' products, and boosted advertising spending on their super-premium brands. This led to swelling inventories, quality variability, and heightened price competition in the specialty sector. All of these forces led to the specialty brewer shakeout of the late 1990s.[22]

Financial data on specialty brewers are limited, but the data that are available reveal that firm profit rates declined for most companies by the mid 1990s. The March 16, 1998 issue of *Business Week* indicates that poor profit performance triggered the sharp drop in the stock value of

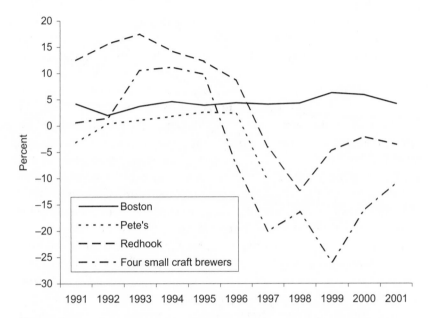

Figure 5.7
Profit-to-sales ratios of leading specialty brewers, 1991–2001. Source: See appendix A.

several publicly traded microbreweries from 1995 to 1998. During this time, Pyramid's stock value fell from $19 to $3 a share, Pete's from $18 to $4, Redhook's from $17 to $6, and Boston's from $20 to $9. By comparison, the stock value of a share of Anheuser-Busch went from about $14 to about $26 during the same period. Figure 5.7 plots the profit-to-sales ratios for Boston (1991–2001), Redhook (1991–2001), Pete's (1991–1997), and the average of four small specialty brewers: Frederick, Nor'Wester, Portland, and Pyramid (1991–2001). As might be expected, Pete's, Redhook, and the four smaller brewers experienced a substantial drop in profit beginning in 1996. Boston is the lone exception, as its profit rate remained relatively stable during the period. Boston's aggressive advertising strategy appears to have paid off. Boston's relative success is consistent with comments from industry experts who claim that experienced specialty brewers with established brands were most likely to maintain market share and survive the shakeout (*Modern Brewery Age*, May 10, 1999).

The evolution of the specialty sector of the beer industry exemplifies a theory proposed by Horvath et al. (2001). Entrepreneurs are slow to enter a new market when profitability is uncertain. Proven success of a few new firms triggers a wave of entrants. The lags involved with building new plants and observing adjustments in profitability result in excessive entry and then a mass exit of the most inexperienced firms.

At this point, the domestic specialty sector appears to be stabilizing. The most recent data show that firms are still exiting but that market share for the sector is up and profitability is negative but rising. The number of firms will likely bottom out shortly, and the spectacular growth of the early 1990s will probably not recur. With about 1,400 local brew pubs, microbreweries, and regional specialty brewers in the United States, consumers in every region of the country can find one or more brands of locally brewed craft beer. Thus, new entry and growth will be more difficult and will depend on local levels of competition. Specialty brewers and regional niche brewers with a quality product, strong marketing, and sufficient scale could distribute nationally and compete successfully with the leading imported brands, including Corona, Heineken, Guinness, and Bass. Boston and Sierra Nevada are situated to undertake this strategy and will continue to be successful if they can maintain quality and effectively combat the countermeasures of the macro and import brewers. Such efforts are required if the domestic specialty brewers want to capture market share from the imports.

5.3 Conclusion

This chapter has traced the emergence and course of the import and domestic specialty sectors of the U.S. brewing industry. Since the mid 1970s, import and specialty brands have become an integral part of the market. The domestic specialty sector originated in 1965 and experienced remarkable growth during the microbrewery revolution of the 1980s and the early 1990s. Since the mid 1990s, the market share of the domestic specialty sector has leveled off and excessive entry has exerted downward pressure on profits, causing many specialty brewers to close their doors. The import segment has grown rapidly since the early 1970s, with the exception of the recession of the late 1980s and the early 1990s. Much of the success of domestic specialty and imported beer came at the expense of the super-premium brands produced by the mass-producing brewers. By 2001, the market share of the super-premium category was 1.76 percent, that of domestic specialty was 2.63 percent, and that of imports was 10.73 percent.

Changes in technology, in consumer demand, and in the structure of the domestic brewing industry benefited the import and specialty sectors. Through the 1970s, the beers brewed by the mass producers became more homogeneous. They were typically light in flavor, in color, in calories, and in alcohol content. At the same time, consumers' income rose, stimulating demand for variety and high-status goods. Import and specialty brewers offered a diverse array of full-bodied products and high-status labels, appealing to consumers' desires. Tax breaks and other government policies also contributed to the entry of the new specialty brewers.

Each type of brewer brings different strengths and weaknesses to the market. Import brewers have several competitive advantages, including sufficient size, established brands with reputations for quality, and experience with successful marketing in the U.S. Brewery location is a drawback, however, since transportation costs are high and imported products may not be as fresh as locally brewed beer. Imports from Mexico and Canada suffer less from these difficulties than imports from overseas, which may explain why several of their brands are so popular in the United States. Domestic specialty brewers face the import situation in reverse, delivering a fresh product but incurring high production costs arising from small-scale production. The mass producers have responded with their own versions of craft beer, but their specialty products are bland since their plants are geared more for large-scale production than for small-scale craft brewing. The consumer has been the beneficiary of import and specialty competition, as the variety of different ale, porter, stout, and lager beer found in the United States has never been greater.

Domestic brewers are concerned that most of the market for high-priced beer has recently been won by the import producers. The domestic super-premium brands have lost considerable market share and the demand for domestic specialty beer has leveled off in recent years. In addition, attempts by the mass producers to introduce their own specialty brands have met with limited success. In the future, it is expected that strategically located brew pubs that cater to local markets will continue to be successful, but their total effect on the U.S. brewing industry will remain small. To regain share lost to the import brewers, individual domestic specialty brewers will have to produce enough beer to attain scale efficiency and to market their brands in a way that attracts import beer drinkers. At this point, only Boston and Sierra Nevada are in a position to pursue these strategies. In this arena, the mass producers will likely stick with mass-produced beer and develop super-premium brands to compete with the lighter of the successful imports, including Corona and Heineken, and to target affluent and status-conscious consumers in marketing campaigns. Anheuser-Busch appears to be following this strategy with the recent introduction of the Michelob Ultra brand of super-premium beer (*Modern Brewery Age, Weekly News Edition*, September 1, 2003).

6   Product and Brand Proliferation

The key to success [in brewing] is ... the introduction of new products.
—Robert S. Weinberg, *New York Times*, August 14, 1992

The invention of a new product can augment an existing market or create a new one. Whether originating from a new firm or an existing one, it constitutes an important form of entry that may stimulate competition and threaten the profits of rival firms. Entry from existing firms serves a particularly important role in promoting competition in the mass-producing segment of the brewing industry, a segment which no new firm has entered since the industry was reestablished after Prohibition.[1]

In an established market, product development and entry can occur within an existing product category or by creating a new and differentiated product category. For our purposes, a product category is defined as a type of beer (for example, light beer, premium beer, malt liquor, or ale), and a brand is defined as a distinctive name or label that identifies a particular firm's offering within the general classification of malt beverages. For example, Anheuser-Busch produces a number of brands of beer, including two in the light-beer category (Bud Light and Natural Light) and one in the premium-beer category (Budweiser).

In order to avoid direct price competition, a firm may decide to differentiate its product along objective, subjective, horizontal, or vertical dimensions. Important objective characteristics of beer include alcohol content, calories, color, and bitterness. These features clearly distinguish light beer from ale, for example, ale being darker, more bitter, and higher in alcohol and calories. When consumers believe that physically identical products differ, product differentiation is subjective. For example, *Consumer Reports* (1996, 2001) rates the Stroh and Budweiser brands to be of like quality. Yet consumers generally favor the higher-priced Budweiser over Stroh. In 1999, Budweiser's U.S. market share was 19.0 percent, while Stroh's was 0.05 percent.

Modern Brewery Age (October 1961) and Greer (1981, 1998, 2002) argue that persuasive and image-enhancing forms of advertising play important roles in the creation of subjective differentiation in brewing. This is supported by Allison and Uhl (1964), who find that most consumers cannot distinguish one brand of regular beer from another in blind taste tests. In addition, when consumers compare the same brand of beer in a labeled bottle and an unlabeled one, consumers generally prefer the labeled product. This suggests that advertising influences a consumer's choice by inflating the subjective valuation of the advertised brand.

Products can also be distinguished vertically and horizontally. On the assumption that brands differ with respect to a single characteristic, differentiation is said to be vertical if all consumers favor the brand with the greatest amount of that characteristic, *ceteris paribus*. A characteristic is said to produce horizontal differentiation when consumers disagree about the attribute's desirability. For example, a car's gas mileage is a vertical attribute; its color is a horizontal attribute. In brewing, all consumers prefer a fresh product, so freshness is a vertical characteristic. Lightness is a horizontal characteristic: some consumers prefer a light beer, others a dark one.

New brands with characteristics that appeal to consumers, particularly when supported by effective advertising, can reap profits for firms. Brand proliferation, then, is a strategy that brewers might pursue. This chapter describes the history of product and brand proliferation and explains why brewers continue to develop new products and brands during the battle for supremacy in the industry today.

6.1   The History of Product and Brand Proliferation in Brewing

Only recently did beer producers begin to introduce new products and brands. After Prohibition, about 700 brewers entered the industry, and most produced a single pilsner beer in a local or a regional market. A few produced ale or dark beer, but these categories had meager sales. Ale accounted for less than 0.7 percent of all malt beverage consumption in the United States in 1968 (*Marketing/Communications*, January 1969). Table 6.1 documents the share of the leading beer categories from 1970 to 2001 and shows that the market share of ale never surpassed 1.0 percent in those years. Anheuser-Busch pioneered the super-premium category with Michelob. Developed in 1896 as a "draft beer for connoisseurs" (Certo and Peter 1993), Michelob was the only super-premium brand produced by a major brewery until the mid 1950s.

Before World War II, several brewers began to ship their brands long distances. The most successful were Anheuser-Busch, Miller, Pabst, and Schlitz, brewers with a production advantage because of their access to cheap ice in Milwaukee and deep caves in Missouri, which provided the cool temperatures needed to brew lager beer. These firms came to be called "shipping brewers" because their production capacity exceeded the size of their local markets, enabling them to ship to distant locations (*Brewers Digest*, June 1945; *Business Week*, August 27, 1949; *Fortune*, November 1972; McGahan 1991). To recover the cost of shipping, they charged a premium price and promoted the superior quality of their products. For example, in 1954, Anheuser-Busch's Budweiser brand sold for a premium of 25.6 percent in New York and 29.7 percent in Los Angeles over the price paid in St. Louis, where it was brewed and packaged (*Federal Trade Commission v. Anheuser-Busch Inc.*, 363 U.S. 536 (1960), note 4). By the 1950s, these firms marketed their premium-priced brands nationally.

Industry experts offer several explanations for the continued success of the shipping or national brewers. First, they were the primary suppliers of beer to the U.S. armed forces during World War II (*Business Week*, November 24, 1945; Weinberg 1978a; Baum 2001), promoting consumption and potential brand loyalty among a large number of young beer drinkers. Second, the national brands appear to have had a marketing advantage, as they were the first brands of beer to be advertised on billboards, in magazines, and on television (Porter 1979; Tremblay 1985b; McGahan 1991). An advantage in television advertising in particular gave the national brewers a competitive advantage, as was discussed in chapter 3. In addition, the ability of the national brewer to reap returns from a premium image was enhanced by the acceptance of packaged beer (*Business Week*, July 17, 1948; Cochran 1948, 384; *Fortune*, April 1950; *Business Week*, April 19, 1952; *Beverage World*, December 1991). Before Prohibition, about 25 percent of beer was sold in bottles or cans, but this rose to almost 72 percent by 1950 (*Modern Brewery Age*, April 1955; *Brewers Almanac* 1998). After all, one is better able to impress one's neighbors at a restaurant or a bar by

Table 6.1
Market shares (percentages) of leading product categories. Excluded categories include imports, specialty products, non-alcoholic beer, and malt alternatives. Source: *Beer Industry Update: A Review of Recent Developments*, various issues.

	Popular	Premium	Super-premium	Ale	Malt liquor	Light	Low-alcohol	Dry	Ice
1970	58.8	36.2	1.1	0.8	2.4	—	—	—	—
1971	56.6	38.4	1.2	0.7	2.4	—	—	—	—
1972	52.7	42.2	1.4	0.6	2.4	—	—	—	—
1973	48.1	46.9	1.7	0.7	2.3	—	—	—	—
1974	44.4	48.5	2.1	0.7	2.3	0.3	—	—	—
1975	42.6	48.6	2.8	0.8	2.4	1.1	—	—	—
1976	39.6	48.4	3.3	0.8	2.7	1.7	—	—	—
1977	33.3	50.8	4.6	0.9	2.4	6.0	—	—	—
1978	29.8	50.8	5.1	1.0	2.8	9.2	—	—	—
1979	25.2	51.4	5.5	1.0	2.8	11.2	—	—	—
1980	20.7	52.9	5.6	0.6	2.9	13.0	—	—	—
1981	21.0	52.9	5.3	0.5	3.0	14.8	—	—	—
1982	21.0	49.4	5.4	0.4	3.2	17.9	—	—	—
1983	21.9	47.4	4.9	0.4	3.2	18.7	—	—	—
1984	21.3	45.7	4.7	0.4	3.1	20.6	0.2	—	—
1985	21.9	43.7	4.3	0.3	3.1	22.1	0.2	—	—
1986	22.0	42.2	3.9	0.3	3.1	23.5	0.1	—	—
1987	21.5	41.4	3.7	0.3	3.0	24.9	0.1	—	—
1988	20.6	41.1	3.4	0.3	2.9	26.4	0.02	0.1	—
1989	20.4	39.5	2.8	0.3	2.9	28.3	0.02	0.9	—
1990	19.4	37.0	2.4	0.3	3.2	30.8	0.01	2.1	—

Year									
1991	19.0	35.1	1.9	0.3	3.6	33.1	—	2.0	—
1992	18.0	33.6	1.8	0.3	4.3	34.4	—	1.9	—
1993	19.1	30.2	1.9	0.4	4.7	35.5	—	1.4	0.3
1994	17.9	27.8	1.8	0.4	4.7	35.1	—	0.8	2.6
1995	16.8	26.5	1.7	0.4	4.7	36.1	—	0.5	1.6
1996	15.3	25.7	2.6	0.3	4.6	36.6	—	0.4	2.8
1997	14.5	24.3	2.3	0.3	4.3	38.2	—	0.3	3.1
1998	13.4	23.5	2.3	0.3	3.9	39.8	—	0.2	3.6
1999	12.4	22.4	2.1	0.2	3.3	41.4	—	0.2	3.7
2000	11.3	21.6	2.0	0.2	2.9	43.0	—	0.1	3.7
2001	10.4	20.6	1.8	—	2.7	44.0	—	—	3.5

drinking premium beer in a labeled can than in an unlabeled pitcher or glass.

With growing demand and developments in refrigeration technology after World War II, the national brewers began to build new brewing facilities throughout the country.[2] In spite of the resulting decline in transportation costs, they were able to retain a price premium for their flagship brands: Budweiser, Miller High Life, Pabst Blue Ribbon, and Schlitz.[3] This resulted in regular beer being split into three categories: super-premium and premium-priced beer (sold primarily by the national producers) and popular-priced beer (sold mostly by local and regional firms). Thus, by 1950 there were five product categories: ale, dark beer, super-premium, premium, and popular-priced beer. One can see from the information in table 6.1 that the market share of the popular-priced category fell in absolute terms and relative to the premium category from 1970 through 2001, a pattern consistent with the relative success of national brewers over regional ones.

From 1950 to 2001, five categories of new products evolved in brewing. Table 6.2 documents the introduction of the major brands into every category except the premium and popular-priced categories. Firms are identified by their tier status as discussed in chapter 3. The first new category in this period was malt liquor, a beer that normally has about 20 percent more alcohol than regular beer. Metropolis pioneered malt liquor with the introduction of the Champale brand in 1952.[4] Subsequent entry occurred by third-tier producers through the 1960s and later by first-tier firms beginning in 1965.

Light beer was developed in the 1960s as a reduced-calorie product for diet-conscious consumers. Diet or light beer is brewed with more water relative to grains and hops and with an enzyme called amylogucosidase, which is added during fermentation (Robertson 1984: 34). This produces a milder beer with less alcohol, calories, and carbohydrates. Miller Lite, for example, has one-third fewer carbohydrates than regular beer. In a June 1996 *Consumer Reports* survey of major brands, light beer had an average of 26 percent fewer calories and 16 percent less alcohol than regular beer. Light beer was first introduced by Piel in 1961, with its Trommer's Red Label brand (*Advertising Age*, September 11, 1961; *Printers' Ink*, January 19, 1962), followed by Rheingold's Gablinger brand in 1967 and Meister Brau's Lite in 1968 (*Advertising Age*, March 30, 1970: 62; *Business Week*, August 22, 1970:

Table 6.2
Leading entrants into a new product category, 1950–2000. In parentheses: the company's brand name and the year the product was introduced.

Tier		
First	Second	Third
Super-premium beer		
Anheuser-Busch (Michelob, 1896)	Hamm (Waldech, 1982)	Heileman (Special Export, 1953)
Pabst (Andeker, 1957)	Coors (Herman Joseph, 1982)	
Miller (Löwenbräu, 1977)		
Schlitz (Erlanger, 1980)		
Stroh (Signature, 1982)		
Ale[a]		
Pabst (Old Tankard, 1957)	Carling (Red Cap, 1950)	Many firms (pre-1950)
Miller (Miller, 1974–75)	Ballantine (Ballantine, 1952)	C. Schaefer (Schaefer, 1953)
Anheuser-Busch (Elk, 1995; Michelob, 1996)	Heileman (20 Grand, 1973)	National (Sportsman, 1955)
	Coors (G. Killian, 1982)	Goebel (Goebel, 1958)
		Duquesne (Duke, 1960)
		Associated (Pfeiffer, 1961)
		Falstaff (Croft, 1966)
		Rainier (Rainier, 1970)
		Pittsburgh (Robin Hood, 1975)
Dark beer[b]		
Pabst (Pabst, 1970)	Heileman (H. Weinhard, 1987)	Schmidt (Schmidt bock, 1954)
Miller (Löwenbräu, 1977)		Ruppert (Ruppert dark, 1958)
Anheuser-Busch (Michelob, 1985)		Carling (Tuborg, 1973)
Coors (Winterfest, 1989)		Peter Hand (Old Chicago, 1975)
		Schaefer (Schaefer bock, 1979)
		General (Luck bock, 1983)
		Pittsburgh (Iron City dark, 1984)
		Genesee (Genesee bock, 1994)

Table 6.2
(continued)

Tier

First	Second	Third
Malt liquor		
Schlitz (Schlitz, 1965)	Schaefer (Malta, 1973)	Metropolis (Champale, 1952)
Miller (University Club, 1967–68, Miller, 1972–1975, Magnum, 1986)		Goetz (Country Club, 1956)
Anheuser-Busch (Bud, 1972–73, King Cobra 1984)		Heileman (Special Export, 1959)
Pabst (Iceman, 1985)		Blitz-Weinhard (Olde English 800, 1964)
Coors (Turbo 1000, 1988)		National (Colt 45, 1964)
Stroh (Silver Thunder, 1993)		Pittsburgh (Mustang, 1964)
		Carling (Calgary, 1965)
		Associated (Michey's, 1965)
		Hamm (Velvet Glove, 1969)
Premium light beer		
Miller (Miller Lite, 1975)	Heileman (Old Style, 1977)	Piel (Trommers RL, 1961)
Schlitz (Schlitz, 1975)		Rheingold (Gablinger, 1967)
Pabst (Pabst Extra, 1976)		Meister Brau (Meister Brau, 1968)
Anheuser-Busch (Natural, 1977; Bud, 1981)[c]		
Coors (Coors, 1978)		
Stroh (Stroh, 1981)		
Popular-priced light beer		
Pabst (Burgie, 1978)	Genesee (Fyfe & Drum, 1976)	Pearl (Pearl, 1974)
Schlitz (Old Milwaukee, 1981)	Heileman (Heileman, 1977)	Schmidt (Schmidt, 1975)
Anheuser-Busch (Natural, 1983; Busch, 1990)[c]		General (Lucky, 1978)
Stroh (Old Milwaukee, 1980)		Schaefer (Piel, 1978)
Coors (Keystone, 1990)		Pittsburgh (Iron City, 1979)
Miller (Milwaukee's Best, 1986)		Olympia (Olympia, 1980)
		Falstaff (Falstaff, 1986)
Super-premium light beer		
Miller (Löwenbräu 1977)		Heileman (Special Export, 1988)
Anheuser-Busch (Michelob, 1978)		
Coors (H. Joseph, 1989)		

Table 6.2
(continued)

Tier		
First	Second	Third
Low-alcohol beer		
Anheuser-Busch (LA, 1985–1990)	Heileman (Blatz LA, 1985–1988)	Hudepohl (Pace Pilsner, 1983–1989)
Stroh[d] (Schaefer LA, 1986)		
Dry beer		
Anheuser-Busch (Michelob Dry, 1988; Bud Dry, 1989)	Heileman (Old Style, Ranier, 1988)	Pittsburgh (Iron City Dry, 1989)
Coors (Coors Dry, 1991; Keystone Dry, 1992)	Pabst (Olympia, 1988)	Jones (Esquire Dry, 1989)
Ice beer		
Anheuser-Busch (Bud Ice, 1993)	Stroh (Schlitz Ice, 1993; Old Milwaukee Ice, 1993)	Genesee (Genesee Ice, 1994)
Miller (High Life Ice, 1993; Icehouse, 1994)		
Coors (Coors Ice, 1993)		

a. For example, the following third-tier brewers sold ale in 1948: Drewery, Genesee (12 Horse Ale), Grain Belt, Harvard, Narragansett (Banquet), Rheingold, Ruppert, and C. Schmidt (Tiger Head). No first- or second-tier firms appear to have produced ale between Prohibition and 1948.
b. At least one third-tier firm produced a dark beer by 1950: Harvard (Harvard Porter, 1948).
c. Natural Light was repositioned from the premium to the popular-priced light category in 1983.
d. The source for Schaefer LA is *Business Today* (spring 1986, 23–24).

60). Diet beer was never accepted by consumers, however, and these early brands failed miserably. For example, Rheingold spent almost $6 million on advertising in 1967 to introduce Gablinger, but it generated only about 200,000 barrels in sales, for an advertising cost of $27 per barrel (*Advertising Age*, April 1, 1968; *Business Week*, August 22, 1970). This is substantially above the $2.32 per barrel that was spent on advertising at the industry level in 1967.

The success of the light-beer category is attributed to the acceptance of the Miller Lite brand.[5] In 1972, Miller bought the rights to Meister Brau's Lite. In developing its version of light beer, Miller reformulated the product so that it tested well against its targeted brand, Coors. Coors beer was noticeably milder than other brands, with about 9 percent fewer calories than regular beer, and was successfully marketed as

"America's fine light beer." Miller also developed a bold marketing plan. When reviewing Meister Brau Lite's history, Miller discovered that it sold well in the blue-collar town of Anderson, Indiana. This suggested that light beer could appeal to drinkers of regular beer. Instead of pitching it as a diet beer, Miller Lite was marketed as "a great-tasting premium beer that is less filling," which implied that one could drink more Lite at a sitting. The slogan was right for the 1970s, when consumers were becoming more health conscious. Miller Lite was introduced nationally in February 1975 and sold more than 5 million barrels within a year. Schlitz offered its version of light beer by November of 1975, and most brewers marketed one or more brands of light beer by 1978. Light beer has been a great success ever since and is currently the most popular beer category in the United States.

Although Miller successfully established the light-beer category with Miller Lite, consumers' demand for lighter beer dates back much further. Articles in *Fortune* (April 1950), in *Business Week* (July 14, 1951 and April 19, 1952), and in *Modern Brewery Age* (June 1954) indicate that the average consumer in the early 1950s demanded alcoholic beverages that were more mild, light, dry, and bland, a trend that induced many brewers to discontinue production of dark beer and reformulate their flagship brands. Coors switched to a lighter formulation in 1951 (Baum 2001), and available evidence indicates that other brands became lighter during the 1950s through the 1970s (*Business Week*, July 14, 1951 and September 29, 1980; *Printers' Ink*, November 29, 1963; *New York Times*, May 12, 1982). For example, Michelob was brewed with malted barley and no adjuncts from 1896 until 1961, when rice was added to make it a lighter beer (Robertson 1984: 49–50). The average 12-ounce can of regular lager beer had 163 calories in 1946 but only 146 calories in 1996.[6] About 99 percent of brands contained 6 percent alcohol before World War II, but by 1996 the average brand of regular beer contained only 4.9 percent alcohol (*Consumer Reports* 1996; *Modern Brewery Age*, September 13, 1999: 9; Baum 2001: 21).

The trend toward lighter and milder beer was taken to its final extreme in the 1980s with the introduction of low-alcohol (LA) beer, a product category that some analysts expected to account for up to 10 percent of the beer market (*Adweek*, August 19, 1985). LA had half the alcohol of regular beer and was first introduced by Hudepohl in 1983 under the name Pace Pilsner. Anheuser-Busch offered the first low-alcohol brand nationally with the introduction of its LA brand in 1984. Several other brewers soon followed. As seen in table 6.1, demand for low-alcohol beer was limited, however. No major brewer marketed a low-alcohol beer by 1991 (*Adweek*, August 19, 1985; *Business Week*, May 2, 1988; *Beer Industry Update: A Review of Recent Developments* 1992).

Asahi Breweries Ltd. of Tokyo developed dry beer, a product that is fermented longer to yield 10 percent more alcohol, the same calorie content, and a drier (less sweet) taste than regular beer (*New York Times*, July 10, 1988; *Advertising Age*, March 27, 1989; *Modern Brewery Age*, March 13, 1989). In 1985, Asahi Dry was introduced to the Japanese market, where it was a big hit. After gaining almost 40 percent of the Japanese market, three Japanese brewers (Asahi, Kirin, and Sapporo) began exporting versions of dry beer to the United States by the middle of 1988. In response, Anheuser-Busch introduced Michelob Dry in November 1988, and other U.S. brewers sold a number of new brands of dry beer in 1989.

The last major product category, ice beer, originated in Canada (*Advertising Age*, November 29, 1993; *Modern Brewery Age*, March 21, 1994 and March 13, 1995; *Business Week*, February 12, 1996).[7] Like dry beer, ice beer has about 10 percent more alcohol than regular beer. The Niagara Falls Brewing Company of Canada first introduced Ice Bock beer to the United States in the early 1990s. In response, all of the major brewers began marketing their version of ice beer in 1993–94. According to *Fortune* (September 19, 1994), 40 new brands of ice beer entered the market in 1994.

Table 6.1 documents the growing popularity of light beer, with a market share that has surpassed the combined share of popular, premium, and super-premium beer since 1998. Ale and malt liquor command small shares that have declined since the mid 1990s. Low-alcohol beer experienced a short life, with all of the major producers abandoning this category by 1991. Although more successful than low-alcohol beer, dry beer appears to be destined for extinction. On the other hand, the consumption of ice beer has grown. Ice beer currently has a larger market share than malt liquor.

Tables 6.3–6.9 document the output levels of the leading brands in the seven major beer categories for the years 1974–2001. Budweiser, the "king of beers," was the best-selling brand in the United States until being overtaken by Bud Light in 2001. Budweiser sales have slipped continuously since 1989, in keeping with the general decline in the premium category. Table 6.3 shows that all premium brands have experienced declining sales before the end of the sample period. The sales of most popular-priced brands have also declined. (See table 6.4.)

Table 6.3
Outputs of leading brands in the premium category, 1974–2001 (thousands of barrels). Company ownership of each brand predates any merger with another brewer. Source: *Beer Industry Update: A Review of Recent Developments*, various issues.

	Total	Budweiser	Coors	Miller High Life	Miller Genuine Draft[a]	Schlitz[b]
1974	71,180	26,000	9,066	7,800	—	17,900
1975	73,040	26,200	11,875	9,200	—	16,800
1976	74,010	21,100	13,650	13,500	—	15,900
1977	80,940	25,000	12,824	16,900	—	14,750
1978	84,470	27,400	12,066	21,700	—	12,600
1979	88,650	31,100	11,312	23,800	—	9,600
1980	94,090	34,600	11,279	23,500	—	7,325
1981	95,370	39,100	10,050	23,500	—	5,800
1982	89,250	40,700	8,525	20,600	—	4,420
1983	87,160	43,100	9,694	17,500	—	2,550
1984	83,420	43,840	8,350	14,240	—	1,740
1985	80,010	45,080	8,550	12,210	—	1,360
1986	79,190	47,130	7,900	10,240	1,490	870
1987	77,480	48,460	7,060	8,970	2,530	560
1988	77,110	49,300	6,200	8,040	3,650	630
1989	74,270	48,720	5,030	7,280	4,560	830
1990	71,490	48,460	4,230	6,200	5,720	980
1991	66,370	45,750	3,440	5,320	6,280	1,140
1992	62,830	44,010	2,890	4,320	6,520	1,370
1993	56,870	41,740	2,550	4,900	7,100	1,270
1994	51,920	39,340	2,200	4,730	6,620	1,050
1995	49,140	37,440	1,960	4,580	6,360	950
1996	49,505	36,500	1,925	4,680	5,600	700
1997	47,075	36,250	1,900	5,000	5,550	450
1998	45,840	35,800	1,850	5,050	5,450	370
1999	44,630	34,800	1,775	5,350	5,425	320
2000	43,300	34,050	1,710	5,225	5,200	270
2001	41,700	32,975	1,610	5,300	5,100	225

a. Miller Genuine Draft was introduced in 1986.
b. Schlitz became a popular-priced brand in the early 1980s.

Pabst Blue Ribbon, once a premium brand, experienced the most dramatic loss in sales. Although Blue Ribbon dominated the popular-priced category from 1977 to 1983, sales nearly vanished by 2001. On the other hand, Anheuser-Busch's Busch brand fared well from 1979 to 1991.

Consistent with the growth in the light-beer category overall, most of the major light-beer brands experienced a sales increase from 1974 to 2001. (See table 6.5.) Miller Lite, the first successful light beer, had a commanding lead over all competing brands until 1994, when Bud Light captured the lead. The data also show that Coors Light is a notable competitor, with sales approaching those of Miller Lite.

As was discussed in chapter 5 and as table 6.6 shows, total consumption of super-premium beer has declined since 1980. Only Killian's and Rolling Rock, both of which were re-classified as super-premium in the mid 1990s, experienced sales growth in that decade. Although the overall market for malt liquor has remained rather stable, there is no dominant brand in that category. (See table 6.7.) Schlitz Malt Liquor, once a leading brand, has lost sales since 1983, probably because of the image problems of the Schlitz premium brand. As table 6.8 shows, dry beer had a short life. As table 6.9 indicates, ice beer grew steadily from 1993 to 1999. Miller's Icehouse leads the ice-beer category, but Anheuser-Busch sells two successful ice brands, Bud Ice and Natural Ice.

In general, the surviving brewers entered most of these beer categories, sometimes with more than one label or brand. Figure 6.1 plots the number of brands sold by today's industry leaders (Anheuser-Busch, Coors, and Miller) and the average number of brands of the remaining 31 brewers sampled. (See appendix A.) The average firm marketed fewer than six brands until the mid 1970s. Anheuser-Busch offered only premium Budweiser and super-premium Michelob until it introduced its popular-priced Busch brand in 1957. Anheuser-Busch entered the malt liquor market with Bud Malt Liquor in 1972, but discontinued it in 1973 (*Advertising Age*, August 6, 1973). Miller produced just one brand until it purchased the Gettelman Brewery in 1961, enabling it to enter the popular-priced category with the Milwaukee's Best brand. Early on, Coors followed a focused strategy by marketing just one brand until 1978, when it began producing Coors Light in response to the success of other light beers. Since then, Coors has continued to develop new brands. Figure 6.1 illustrates that brand proliferation was the norm by the 1990s, with the average brewer and all of the leading brewers marketing more than ten different brands of

Table 6.4
Outputs of leading brands in the popular-priced category, 1974–2001 (thousands of barrels). Source: *Beer Industry Update: A Review of Recent Developments*, various issues. Here and in subsequent tables, "A-B" stands for Anheuser-Busch.

	Total	Busch (A-B)	Milwaukee's Best (Miller)	Old Milwaukee (Stroh)	Pabst	Schaefer	Stroh[a]
1974	65,130	4,600	—	3,900	—	—	—
1975	64,040	4,800	—	5,200	—	—	—
1976	60,470	3,000	—	5,500	—	—	—
1977	53,160	3,300	—	4,375	15,200	—	—
1978	49,440	3,500	—	4,125	13,900	—	—
1979	43,430	2,935	—	4,360	12,380	—	—
1980	40,140	2,930	—	4,595	11,375	—	—
1981	38,260	3,100	—	5,100	9,663	2,315	5,415
1982	38,230	3,400	—	6,450	8,683	1,900	5,100
1983	40,290	3,500	—	7,375	7,548	3,350	5,150
1984	38,900	5,070	2,100	7,000	6,340	2,570	5,270
1985	40,010	6,060	3,100	7,300	4,690	2,700	4,590
1986	41,310	7,270	4,600	7,400	3,630	2,650	4,090
1987	40,180	8,170	5,100	7,150	3,110	2,630	3,670
1988	38,740	8,990	6,000	7,100	3,040	2,370	3,170
1989	38,380	9,100	6,700	6,950	2,830	2,150	1,760
1990	37,570	9,500	7,000	6,230	2,440	1,590	1,170
1991	35,860	9,800	7,000	5,630	2,390	1,280	1,050
1992	33,780	9,500	6,550	4,810	2,350	920	970
1993	35,940	9,100	6,450	4,330	2,410	760	800

1994	33,430	8,500	5,100	3,730	2,600	620	720
1995	31,200	8,100	4,600	3,440	2,640	490	670
1996	29,410	8,200	4,070	3,135	2,180	385	595
1997	28,115	7,850	3,900	3,095	1,700	275	430
1998	26,170	7,450	3,600	2,750	1,450	225	300
1999	24,675	8,000	3,350	2,270	1,000	200	100
2000	22,715	7,750	3,100	2,050	800	160	—
2001	20,930	7,500	2,750	1,850	700	125	—

a. Stroh was marketed as a premium-priced beer for part of the 1980s.

Table 6.5
Outputs of leading brands in the light beer category, 1974–2001 (thousands of barrels).
Source: *Beer Industry Update: A Review of Recent Developments*, various issues.

	Total	Budweiser (A-B)	Busch (A-B)	Coors	Michelob (A-B)	Miller	Natural (A-B)
1974	1,580	—	—	—	—	400	—
1975	2,570	—	—	—	—	3,100	—
1976	5,580	—	—	—	—	4,600	—
1977	10,634	—	—	—	—	6,800	1,540
1978	15,520	—	—	500	1,000	8,900	2,400
1979	19,700	—	—	1,600	1,700	11,200	2,450
1980	23,030	—	—	2,500	2,150	12,900	2,222
1981	26,930	185	—	3,100	2,450	15,500	1,900
1982	32,700	3,850	—	3,200	2,550	17,100	1,300
1983	34,390	3,925	—	3,850	2,400	18,000	975
1984	37,710	4,250	—	4,570	2,370	17,930	1,090
1985	40,510	5,460	—	6,020	2,510	18,380	1,380
1986	44,090	6,750	—	7,200	2,540	18,670	1,680
1987	46,610	8,070	—	7,900	2,600	18,710	1,990
1988	49,480	9,540	—	8,880	2,550	18,810	2,190
1989	53,240	10,730	—	10,450	2,350	19,150	2,490
1990	59,440	11,480	2,000	11,510	2,140	19,290	3,110
1991	62,620	12,020	2,900	11,930	1,990	18,340	4,270
1992	64,450	13,190	3,500	12,220	1,970	17,150	5,100
1993	66,820	14,650	4,000	12,290	2,020	16,560	6,650
1994	65,590	15,690	4,100	12,260	2,050	14,760	6,680
1995	67,130	17,390	4,300	12,590	2,220	14,890	6,620
1996	70,485	19,805	4,600	13,100	2,480	15,700	6,620
1997	73,880	22,300	4,600	13,700	2,500	16,000	6,850
1998	77,725	25,300	4,975	14,200	2,625	15,800	7,200
1999	82,410	28,200	5,150	14,850	2,725	16,175	7,700
2000	86,220	31,350	5,275	15,425	2,825	16,075	8,000
2001	88,850	33,850	5,500	15,525	2,875	15,950	8,200

Table 6.6
Outputs of leading brands in the super-premium category, 1974–2001 (thousands of barrels). Source: *Beer Industry Update: A Review of Recent Developments*, various issues.

	Total	Killian's[a] (Coors)	Löwenbräu (Miller)	Michelob[b] (A-B)	Rolling Rock[a] (Latrobe)	Special Export (Heileman)
1974	3,090	—	—	3,100	—	—
1975	4,270	—	—	4,200	—	—
1976	4,990	—	100	5,000	—	—
1977	7,470	—	500	6,400	—	260
1978	8,672	—	700	7,310	—	300
1979	9,687	—	800	8,025	—	350
1980	9,930	—	900	8,250	—	400
1981	9,750	—	1,200	7,750	—	450
1982	9,840	—	1,500	7,350	—	475
1983	9,060	—	1,450	6,600	—	475
1984	8,640	—	1,290	6,210	—	450
1985	7,940	—	1,190	5,980	—	210
1986	7,380	—	1,140	5,460	—	220
1987	7,010	—	1,000	5,100	—	240
1988	6,310	—	1,000	4,450	—	260
1989	5,280	—	700	3,790	—	280
1990	4,680	170	650	3,340	—	250
1991	3,550	220	550	2,740	160	200
1992	3,460	350	500	2,590	220	200
1993	3,530	480	450	2,550	310	200
1994	3,290	550	400	2,530	360	190
1995	3,160	650	400	2,490	400	150
1996	4,920	625	400	2,725	970	140
1997	4,520	600	410	2,420	970	100
1998	4,410	640	420	2,260	1,000	75
1999	4,235	670	300	2,145	1,050	50
2000	3,950	725	—	2,095	1,075	30
2001	3,570	700	—	1,875	970	—

a. First listed as a super-premium beer in *Beer Industry Update: A Review of Recent Developments* in the mid 1990s.
b. All Michelob labels.

Table 6.7
Outputs of leading brands in the malt liquor category, 1974–2001 (thousands of barrels).
Source: *Beer Industry Update: A Review of Recent Developments*, various issues.

	Total	Colt 45 (Heileman)	King Cobra (A-B)	Magnum (Miller)	Olde English 800 (Pabst)	Schlitz
1974	3,410	—	—	—	—	800
1975	3,550	—	—	—	—	1,000
1976	4,050	—	—	—	—	1,300
1977	3,935	1,250	—	—	350	1,485
1978	4,645	1,200	—	—	475	1,800
1979	4,920	1,100	—	—	725	2,050
1980	5,160	1,150	—	—	1,250	2,150
1981	5,480	1,350	—	—	1,086	2,240
1982	5,750	1,450	—	—	993	2,305
1983	5,860	1,600	—	—	939	2,325
1984	5,700	1,660	80	—	850	2,100
1985	5,650	1,790	100	—	850	1,900
1986	5,850	1,990	80	—	850	1,930
1987	5,660	2,000	80	—	860	1,870
1988	5,400	2,000	80	—	860	1,850
1989	5,480	1,950	160	—	950	1,880
1990	6,090	1,600	200	400	1,270	1,880
1991	6,750	1,430	550	700	1,650	1,650
1992	8,030	1,770	730	850	1,790	1,830
1993	8,910	1,960	880	1,000	1,970	1,880
1994	8,830	1,780	950	1,000	1,750	1,970
1995	8,750	1,780	950	900	1,780	1,980
1996	8,930	1,650	1,000	900	1,670	1,900
1997	8,375	1,500	1,000	900	1,500	1,700
1998	7,615	1,400	1,025	800	1,380	1,470
1999	6,500	1,350	950	725	1,170	1,100
2000	5,900	1,200	975	600	1,025	900
2001	5,500	1,050	1,000	525	975	875

Product and Brand Proliferation

Table 6.8
Outputs of leading brands in the dry beer category, 1988–2000 (thousands of barrels).
Source: *Beer Industry Update: A Review of Recent Developments*, various issues.

	Total	Budweiser (A-B)	Coors	Michelob (A-B)
1988	260	—	—	—
1989	1,740	—	—	—
1990	3,980	—	—	—
1991	3,790	2,820	160	700
1992	3,650	2,510	220	620
1993	2,650	1,930	110	390
1994	1,550	1,140	50	190
1995	890	690	—	140
1996	790	—	—	—
1997	575	—	—	—
1998	360	—	—	—
1999	300	—	—	—
2000	200	—	—	—

Table 6.9
Outputs of leading brands in the ice beer category, 1993–2001 (thousands of barrels).
Source: *Beer Industry Update: A Review of Recent Developments*, various issues.

	Total	Budweiser (A-B)	Icehouse (Miller)	Lite (Miller)	Milwaukee's Best (Miller)	Natural (A-B)
1993	480	480	—	—	—	—
1994	4,840	2,340	—	1,420	—	—
1995	3,030	1,610	—	840	—	—
1996	5,415	1,795	1,600	470	425	900
1997	5,925	1,600	1,800	350	725	1,300
1998	6,975	1,750	2,050	225	900	1,625
1999	7,440	1,650	2,275	165	1,000	1,900
2000	7,400	1,550	2,175	80	1,025	2,150
2001	7,000	1,300	2,000	50	1,075	2,250

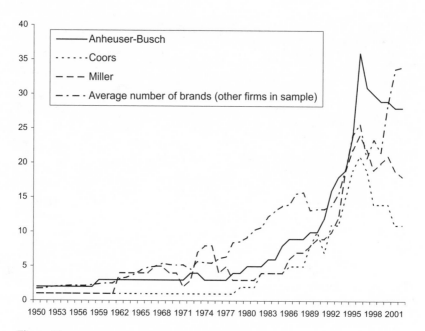

Figure 6.1
Number of brands (labels) marketed by average and leading brewers, 1950–2002. Source:
See appendix A.

beer. Chapter 5 reports a similar result among the domestic specialty
brewers. From 1992 to 2002, the total number of brands produced by
the average U.S. brewer nearly tripled. Today the specialty and mass-
producing brewers market more than 2,800 brands of beer in the
United States (Beer Institute 2002–2003).

Some industry experts attribute the trend toward brand proliferation
in brewing to the purchase of Miller by Philip Morris in 1970 (Mueller
1978; *Business Week*, November 8, 1976; *Advertising Age*, January 9,
1978). After the merger, Philip Morris applied the same strategy at
Miller that had been successful in the cigarette industry: market segmentation, brand and product proliferation, and heavy advertising.
Indeed, according to industry expert Robert Weinberg, "two words
have changed this industry completely—Philip Morris" (*Business Week*,
November 8, 1976: 59). Figure 6.1 provides evidence to support this
argument. As early as 1963, however, the beer industry had been criticized for offering a limited variety of products compared to the cigarette, soft-drink, and hard-liquor industries (*Printers' Ink*, November
29, 1963). Thus, brewers may have offered new brands in response to

consumer demand for variety and media pressure even without the influence of Philip Morris. The continued exit of the mass producers may also have eventually induced surviving firms to fill up the vacated product space with new brands of their own.

6.2   The Causes of Product and Brand Proliferation in Brewing

Demand, cost, and strategic considerations motivate a firm to diversify its portfolio of brands.[8] Regarding costs, the presence of economies of scope generates efficiency gains from multi-product production. New technologies that increase economies of scope would induce firms to expand their product lines and would encourage mergers between firms with complementary products. On the demand side, economic prosperity may stimulate brand proliferation, as the demand for variety appears to be a normal good (Silberberg 1985). In addition, an unexpected decline in the demand for one brand may motivate brand diversification to reduce risk and avoid excess capacity. Demand interdependencies among existing brands and a potential new offering may also influence a firm's decision to diversify. A firm would be discouraged from introducing a new brand if it were expected to substantially cannibalize sales of existing brands but would be encouraged to do so if the reputation of existing brands facilitated consumers' acceptance of the new brand.

When markets are imperfectly competitive, strategic factors may also play a role. For example, dominant firms may brand proliferate in an effort to deter entry. By filling up the characteristic space and the shelf space in supermarkets, dominant firms foreclose the entry opportunities of other firms, a strategy that is more likely when products are differentiated horizontally (Schmalensee 1978; Brander and Eaton 1984; Gilbert and Matutes 1993). In addition, if a brand's reputation benefits from a "first mover advantage," then firms would race to develop new product categories (Schmalensee 1982).

Diversification strategies may differ for successful and unsuccessful firms. With imperfect capital markets, it may be cheaper for a successful firm to finance the cost of developing and introducing a new brand or product. As will be discussed in chapter 7, the introduction of a new brand takes a substantial investment in marketing. On the other hand, Aron and Lazear (1990) show that an unsuccessful firm may take a desperate action such as pioneering a new brand or product to avoid failure.[9] That is, a radical action would be optimal if it leads to a sufficient increase in the variance of success since only the upside risk matters when a traditional strategy will lead to almost certain failure. This is sometimes called a "Hail Mary" strategy, in reference to a trailing football team that throws long passes at the end of the game, hoping for a miracle touchdown that will win the game.[10] The Aron-Lazear model also predicts that if new products can be copied quickly then the best response for successful rivals is to take a wait-and-see approach.[11] A successful firm will follow into a new product category only after rival brands prove profitable. In this setting, unsuccessful firms will be more likely than successful ones to launch new brands and products.

We analyzed these issues empirically in Tremblay and Tremblay 1996. Table 6.2 here updates table I in that article and shows that new products are generally introduced by the leading national producers in the first tier and by the relatively unsuccessful brewers in the third tier. Of the first five brands to enter each of the product categories in table 6.2, 40 percent were introduced by first-tier firms, 10 percent by second-tier firms, and 50 percent by third-tier firms.[12] Of the eight product categories, first-tier firms were first to enter the super-premium and super-premium light categories. Third-tier firms were first to enter the dark, malt liquor, premium light, and popular-priced light categories. The dry and ice categories were developed outside the United States, but first-tier and second-tier firms were the first domestic producers in these categories.[13]

In Tremblay and Tremblay 1996 we test several hypotheses regarding firm motives for product introductions in brewing. Their empirical results confirm that entry is more likely to occur from national brewers and unsuccessful firms. The results also show that entry increases with consumers' income. There is little evidence of economies of scope in brewing, and no evidence that economies of scope affect a firm's decision to introduce a new brand. Finally, the results indicate that a firm's excess capacity and other market variables have no significant effect on a firm's decision to enter a new product category.

6.3   Empirical Analysis of the Introduction of New Products

This section updates Tremblay and Tremblay 1996. The 1996 sample of 389 annual firm-level observations from 1950 through 1988 is extended through 2000 and includes 611 observations. The model specifies the number of new product categories a firm enters (NEWPROD) as a

Table 6.10
Poisson regression estimates of the determinants of new product introductions, with absolute values of t-statistics in parentheses.

Variable	Regression model		
	6.1	6.2	6.3
Constant	-4.863^a	-4.298^a	-2.191^a
	(6.763)	(9.024)	(13.98)
π ($\times 10^2$)	-5.629^a	-4.934^a	-5.444^a
	(3.139)	(2.827)	(2.812)
DN	0.516^c	0.599^b	1.081^a
	(1.879)	(2.207)	(4.552)
Inc ($\times 10^4$)	2.593^a	2.569^a	—
	(4.892)	(4.907)	
CUR ($\times 10^2$)	0.743	—	—
	(1.083)		
Likelihood ratio	47.031^a	45.710^a	21.475^a
Number of observations	603	611	611

a. Significant at 0.01 level (two-tailed test).
b. Significant at 0.05 level (two-tailed test).
c. Significant at 0.10 level (two-tailed test).

function of consumer income (Inc) and firm characteristics: the profit-to-sales ratio (π), a dummy variable that equals 1 when the firm is a national producer and 0 otherwise (DN), and the capacity utilization rate (CUR), defined as the firm's production divided by its capacity (in percent). The regressors are lagged one period because of the time delay between planned and actual entry.[14] The dependent variable, NEWPROD, is assumed to be drawn from a Poisson distribution (Greene 2003: 740–747), since it always takes non-negative integer values. To be consistent with a Poisson model, the variance of the dependent variable must equal its mean, a condition that could not be rejected by an overdispersion test (Cameron and Trivedi 1990).

The parameter estimates of the Poisson model are reported in table 6.10. All parameter estimates are significant, except for the capacity utilization rate. The results imply that higher consumer income induces firms to enter new product categories, suggesting that demand for variety in the beer market is a normal good. In addition, national brewers and firms with lower profit rates are more likely to enter new product categories. National producers may use this strategy to fill up product niches and maintain their dominant position. They are also in a better position to market and finance new brand introductions. On the other hand, the negative coefficient on profit-to-sales may indicate that less successful brewers introduce new products in a desperate attempt to survive, a result that supports the "Hail Mary" hypothesis of Aron and Lazear. These new results are consistent with the 1996 study and with the evidence presented earlier in the chapter.

6.4   Conclusion

During the period 1950–2000, U.S. brewers developed a number of new products. Malt liquor was introduced in the early 1950s and has been modestly successful. Light beer originated in the early 1960s but did not become popular until Miller Lite arrived in 1975. Lite's success is a tribute to Miller's advertising campaign that was aimed at convincing regular beer drinkers that Lite was not a diet product but a beer that tasted great and was less filling. Light beer has become more and more popular, even surpassing the premium category in sales in 1992. Light beer continues to be the best-selling type of beer in the United States. Low-alcohol beer and dry beer came to the market in the 1980s, but performed poorly. On the other hand, ice beer has grown in popularity since its inception in the early 1990s and currently outsells malt liquor.

Beginning in the mid 1970s, the average U.S. beer producer substantially expanded its brand offerings. In the early 1950s, most firms produced a single brand of beer. By the late 1990s, each major brewer produced more than ten brands. It appears that firms introduce new brands in response to consumer demand for variety, a factor that was especially important for the specialty brewers. The evidence also indicates that first-tier firms and unsuccessful firms have been more likely to pioneer new products and brands. National or first-tier firms introduced brands to fill up the product space so that no profitable niches remained for their rivals. A failing firm may try a new product in an attempt to stay afloat. In any event, brand and product proliferation are important features of the U.S. brewing industry today.

7   Strategic Behavior: Price, Advertising, Merger, and Other Strategies

Business is a game, the greatest game in the world if you know how to play it.
—attributed to Thomas J. Watson Sr.

In addition to brand proliferation, imperfect competition opens the door to many other strategic moves by rivals. A firm can gain an advantage over competitors by better understanding the effects of its own actions on the profits and subsequent reactions of rival firms. In this setting, game theory reveals each firm's optimal strategic path. This chapter describes important strategies used in brewing and compares them with the predictions of game theory.

Many strategies arose in response to the war of attrition. (See chapters 3 and 4.) Substantial increases in minimum efficient scale (MES) and a preemption race in advertising made it profitable for fewer and fewer firms to survive. Survival required a firm to grow in size, either internally or by merger, or find a profitable niche market. Most brewers would fail, however. Those that were declining could choose between an immediate exit or a harvesting strategy and eventual failure. In this environment, competition in price, advertising, gimmicks, and new product introductions was fierce.

This chapter outlines strategies (in addition to brand proliferation) that proved successful or at least enabled declining brewers to eke out the last bit of profit before exiting the industry. The chapter begins with a discussion of pricing strategies in brewing. Studying the actual pricing behavior of firms in an imperfectly competitive industry is important in and of itself, because oligopoly theory generates many theoretical possibilities.[1] Depending on the structure of the game (e.g., the number of players, the choice of strategic variables, the degree of product differentiation, the timing of play, and the information available to players), the Nash or subgame-perfect equilibrium price can range from monopoly to competitive. As the actual outcome depends upon so many factors, the only way to fully understand the pricing behavior in a particular setting is to conduct a detailed study of individual firms within an industry. Important examples discussed in the chapter include mixed pricing, trigger strategies, and merger strategies.

The histories of advertising behavior at the industry, firm, and brand levels are documented for the period 1950–2000. Some of the most heavily advertised products come from consumer-goods markets in imperfectly competitive industries, and a detailed study of advertising behavior in brewing may provide insights into the causes and consequences of advertising in related markets. The economics literature suggests that advertising may create subjective differentiation, provide consumers with useful information about new products and their characteristics, and signal high quality.[2] One significant conclusion is that marketing efficiency is critical to a firm's success in brewing, a conclusion that may also be true for other consumer-goods industries with similar characteristics.

The third strategic issue addressed is mergers. After reviewing the extensive merger activity in brewing from 1950 through 2002, this chapter investigates the motives for mergers in brewing. More than 200 major mergers and acquisitions occurred during this period, making the brewing industry an excellent candidate for a case study of merger activity. Evidence from chapter 3 shows that mergers in brewing have had little effect on industry concentration, and evidence from this chapter indicates that most mergers have promoted efficiency because of strict enforcement of the anti-trust laws.

Several other strategies are discussed, such as exclusive dealing contracts with drinking establishments and wholesalers. This chapter also documents several "Hail Mary" strategies used by small and failing firms as they struggled to avert failure.

7.1   Pricing Strategies

Owing to laws in many states prohibiting vertical integration, the brewing industry is organized into a three-tier distribution system. That is, mass-producing brewers sell their beer to wholesalers, who then sell to retailers. In general, a brewer sets the wholesale price at the

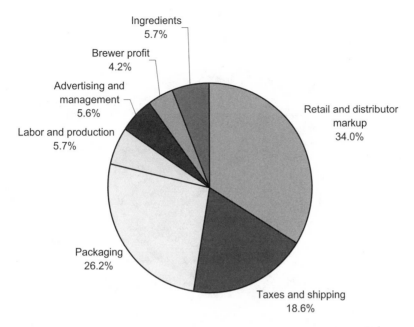

Figure 7.1
Price-cost breakdown of mass-produced beer in 1976. Source: R.S. Weinberg and Associates, "The Economics of the Malt Beverage Production/Distribution System, 1976," August 8, 1978.

brewery (freight on board, f.o.b.) but may vary price by region of the country in response to differences in demand and levels of competition. Wholesalers or distributors are responsible for storing the product and delivering it to retailers. In many cases, they are also responsible for stocking retailer shelves and setting up attractive retail displays.

Weinberg (1978b) and *Consumer Reports* (1996) provide a price-cost breakdown among profits and various cost components for a typical six-pack of domestic beer. This information is reproduced in figures 7.1 and 7.2 and shows that the product itself accounts for a small portion of the consumer price. Ingredients, labor, and production costs account for less than 12 percent of the consumer price in 1976 and about 16 percent in 1996. Brewer profit ranges from 4.2 percent to 6 percent, and tax and shipping expenses account for about 18 percent of the price of beer.[3]

Table 7.1 presents the average price of a case of 12-ounce cans for the major categories of beer in 1993, 1995, and 2000. The data indicate that import, specialty, and super-premium products sell for the highest

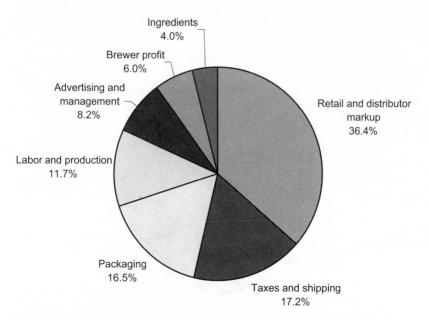

Figure 7.2
Price-cost breakdown of mass-produced beer in 1996. Source: *Consumer Reports* (1996).

Table 7.1
Average retail price per case by product category (nominal dollars per case of 24 12-ounce cans). Source: *Beer Industry Update: A Review of Recent Developments*, 1996, 2001.

	1993	1995	2000
Super premium	15.78	18.40	17.08
Premium	13.98	13.77	15.15
Popular	11.33	10.64	11.25
Light beer	12.45	12.51	14.13
Malt liquor	—	11.24	11.91
Ice beer	15.27	13.44	12.79
Dry beer	13.90	13.18	—
Specialty	—	—	24.85
Import	20.99	20.68	23.53

prices and malt liquor and popular-priced beer sell for the lowest prices. Changes in relative prices are consistent with changes in consumer demand. Relative to the price of premium beer, the prices of light and imported beer rose as they gained share during the period (see table 6.1), and the prices of malt liquor, ice beer, and popular-priced beer fell as they lost share.

Price, Quality, and Image

As was discussed in the previous chapter, the shipping or national brewers initially charged a premium price for their flagship brands to cover additional transportation costs. Remarkably, the price premium persisted after the national brewers built new plants around the country which eliminated the transportation-cost differential.

The ability of a premium brand to command a higher price relies on consumers' beliefs that premium beer is of superior quality. Product image plays a role, as premium and popular-priced beer are of like quality and have similar production costs. For example, in 1972 a 12-ounce container of premium Budweiser cost less than half a cent more than one of popular-priced Busch to produce, yet the price of the container of Budweiser was 15 cents higher (*Fortune*, November 1972). On the consumption side, blind taste tests reveal that consumers generally cannot distinguish between the national and regional brands of domestic lager beer and cannot identify their favorite brand.[4] In a series of taste tests by experts at *Consumer Reports* (1983, 1996, 2001), the evaluation of a particular brand is not always consistent across judges, and popular-priced brands often outperform premium-priced brands.[5]

When consumers are uncertain about product quality, some may use price as a signal of quality (Milgrom and Roberts 1986). After all, one would expect a higher-quality product to cost more. McConnell (1968) finds that a firm's pricing strategy does influence consumers' perceptions of product quality. McConnell asks a sample of consumers to evaluate the quality of three different bottles of beer over 2 months. Each bottle contains the same beer but is labeled as brand L, M, or P. Consumers are falsely told that the labels contain different brands of beer that sell for $0.99, $1.20, and $1.30 per six-pack, respectively. After repeated taste tests, consumers evaluated the highest-priced brand to be of highest quality by a wide margin. In a similar study where one brand of beer was falsely labeled as four different brands, Ackoff and

Emshoff (1975b, 12) conclude that "all the subjects believed that the brands were different and that they could tell the differences between them" and that most of the 250 subjects "felt that at least one of the four brands was not fit for human consumption." The evidence has prompted Elzinga (1971: 206) to conclude that the price differential between premium and popular-priced beer is "in part due to customers' tastes and [is] subjective for there are no important differences in the cost of labor or materials for the various grades of beer."

One possible motive for the price differential is the Veblen effect. As was discussed in chapter 2, some consumers may prefer to purchase high-priced brands, as they signal to others that the buyer is wealthy and appreciates quality. Even if brands of beer are physically identical, status-conscious consumers will prefer markets with high-priced and low-priced brands and will support the "premium" brand that sells for a higher price. Those with more limited incomes or who are less concerned with status will buy the cheaper popular-priced brands. Thus, it may be profitable for firms to market both premium and popular-priced brands, a game-theoretic strategy that allows the firm to price discriminate between those affected and those unaffected by Veblen effects (Wolinsky 1987).

Another possible reason for the price differential is that risk-averse consumers may be willing to pay a higher price for a premium brand if they believe that a premium label ensures a lower variance in quality (McGahan 1991). Unwanted bacteria and contaminants can produce a bad batch of beer.[6] Further, the quality of packaged beer deteriorates over time.[7] If national brands are more uniform in quality, then a price premium is warranted. Klein and Leffler (1981) argue that large national producers who invest heavily in advertising will have a greater incentive to maintain high quality standards. Since most advertising costs are sunk, heavy advertisers simply have more to lose from the deterioration of product quality.

There is evidence to support the hypothesis that national brewers generally maintain high quality standards, at least if they want to maintain their premium status. For example, trade journals and industry experts attribute Anheuser-Busch's success to its devotion to product quality and its ability to avoid mistakes (*Modern Brewery Age*, March 27, 2000). As a rival brewing executive puts it, "... whatever the Anheuser-Busch people do they do better than the rest of us" (*Forbes*, March 1, 1968: 30). Since 1996, Anheuser-Busch has publicized its commitment to quality and freshness by printing the packaging date on every bottle and can (*Fortune*, January 13, 1997).

The "Schlitz mistake" that was discussed in chapter 4 illustrates how a premium image can be ruined by failing to maintain consistent quality. Recall that because executives at Schlitz believed that consumers could not distinguish one brand of beer from another, Schlitz took a series of actions to cut production costs in the mid 1970s. The company lowered the aging time of its flagship brand, substituted adjuncts for malted barley, and compromised quality control. Even though most consumers could not tell the difference, the Schlitz image was tarnished and the company's market share plummeted as consumers became aware of the cost-cutting measures. To rescue its reputation, Schlitz returned to traditional brewing practices and launched several bold marketing campaigns. In spite of these efforts, Schlitz's market share continued to decline, and the brand quickly lost premium status.

Other national brewers that failed to maintain a premium price and image for their flagship brands saw them slip into the popular-priced category. Beginning in January of 1961, Pabst began discounting its Blue Ribbon brand in select regions of the country. In the New York area, the price of Blue Ribbon was cut from its premium price of $1.25 to a popular price of $1.05 per six-pack (*Advertising Age*, January 30, 1961). In the short term, the company's theme of marketing a "premium beer at popular prices" increased market share, but it eventually tarnished Blue Ribbon's premium image and led to a decline in market share (*Advertising Age*, March 29, 1982: M39; *Forbes*, January 16, 1984). The company has never been able to return Blue Ribbon to its premium status.[8] Similarly, in 1993 Miller started discounting Miller High Life in response to declining sales, and it is now categorized as a popular-priced brand.[9]

Several brewers have attempted to reposition their flagship brands into the premium category. Coors's focus on product quality enabled it to charge a premium price for its flagship brand as early as 1972 and to achieve national status by 1991 (*Fortune*, November 1972: 106; *Wall Street Journal*, October 26, 1973; *Forbes*, June 1, 1976; *Business Week*, September 29, 1980). Another regionally distributed beer advancing a premium image is Rolling Rock, a brand of the Latrobe Brewing Company (*Advertising Age*, May 16, 1977; *Modern Brewery Age*, March 16, 1992). With the depreciation of the High Life brand, Miller introduced Miller Genuine Draft as a premium brand in 1986 (*Forbes*, June 30,

1986). In contrast, Stroh attained national distribution by purchasing Schlitz in 1982 and made an unsuccessful attempt to reposition its Stroh brand from a popular-priced to a premium beer.

With the lion's share of premium beer being produced by the national brewers, the price differential between popular-priced and premium beer gauges the degree of price competition between national and regional producers as well as the relative status of premium beer.[10] Although a premium image benefits from a high price, competition for the lowest price is more common for generic or popular-priced brands. Marketing research shows that some consumers will always purchase the cheapest brand, fueling fierce competition in the popular-priced category as these brands compete on price alone (*Economist* 1992; Foxall and Goldsmith 1994). In addition, competition in the popular-priced category is exacerbated by a decrease in the price of the premium brands.

Table 7.2 indicates that the differential between premium and popular-priced brands, defined as the average price of premium beer divided by the average price of popular-priced beer, reached its lowest point in 1970 and its highest point in 2001.[11] In all likelihood, the low price differential in the 1970s results from the beer wars that are discussed in chapter 3, a period of intense competition when national producers expanded production capacity and market share. To sell more beer, national producers introduced new brands, increased advertising spending, and cut prices. These actions narrowed the price gap and squeezed many regional brewers out of the market. Since 1980, the observed price differential exceeded 20 percent; in 2001 it exceeded 40 percent. This may be attributable to the relative growth in demand for premium beer (see chapters 2 and 6) and weak price competition following the exodus of most regional producers from the market.

Mixed Strategy in Prices

Brewers appear to use a mixed strategy to market their premium brands.[12] These brands generally sell at a regular price but are discounted occasionally for short periods of time (*Beverage World*, January 1977: 18; Keithahn 1978). To compete effectively in this setting, each firm must identify a premium price, a discount price, and a probability of setting a discount price on the basis of the expected behavior of rivals.

Table 7.2
The price differential between premium and popular-priced beer. All prices are in nominal dollars and reflect the price of a six-pack of 12-ounce cans. The differential is defined as the price of premium beer divided by the price of popular-priced beer. Mean differential: 1.245.

	Price			
	Premium	Popular	Differential	Source
1953	1.46	1.17	1.25	Brooks 1970[a]
1956			1.27	Keithahn 1978: 96
1960			1.13	Keithahn 1978: 96
1961	1.25	1.05	1.19	*Advertising Age*, January 30, 1961: 3
1965			1.24	Keithahn 1978: 96
1970			1.03	Keithahn 1978: 96
1972	1.35	1.15	1.17	*Fortune*, November 1972
1980	2.38	1.89	1.26	Weinberg 1980: 33[a]
1983	2.58	1.89	1.36	*Consumer Reports*, July 1983[b]
1993			1.23	*Beer Industry Update*, 1996: 137
1995			1.29	*Beer Industry Update*, 1996: 137
2000			1.32	*Beer Industry Update*, 2001: 139
2001	4.57	3.17	1.44	*Consumer Reports*, August 2001[c]

a. Prices in St. Louis area only.
b. The premium beer sample includes Budweiser, Miller High Life, Schlitz, and Coors. The popular-price sample includes Old Milwaukee, Schmidt, Blatz, and Pabst.
c. The premium beer sample includes Budweiser, Coors Original, and Miller Genuine Draft. The popular-price sample includes Stroh, Pabst, Miller High Life, Busch, and Old Milwaukee.

Mixed pricing means that sometimes a firm will set a high price but at other times (e.g., when the product goes "on sale") it will set a low price. Demand asymmetries render a mixed-pricing strategy more common for premium than for popular-priced brands. Consumers of premium brands are more brand loyal than consumers of popular-priced brands. As a result, a temporary price cut of a premium brand will attract more customers away from popular-priced brands than a price cut of a popular-priced brand will attract customers away from premium brands.

In brewing, industry leader Anheuser-Busch pioneered the mixed-pricing strategy by offering temporary discounts on its premium Budweiser brand (*Fortune*, November 1972). The price cuts occur at random, making a rival response more difficult. Random play and unpredictability are major elements of a successful mixed strategy

(Gibbons 1992; Fudenberg and Tirole 1992). Brewers discount prices judiciously, however, since excessive discounting can signal an inferior product, tarnish a brand's image, and knock it out of the premium-priced category. Aware of this potential risk, "Coors insisted that its wholesalers not cut prices, so as to protect its image" in the early 1970s (*Fortune*, November 1972: 105). The experiences of Pabst Blue Ribbon and Miller High Life discussed above attest to the dangers of prolonged discounts.

Trigger Strategy

Game-theory models indicate that noncompetitive pricing can result from the effective use of a trigger strategy (Gibbons 1992; Vives 1999; Symeonidis 2002). Consider an imperfectly competitive market where products are homogeneous and firms compete in prices over an infinite time horizon. A trigger strategy is defined as follows: each firm sets price equal to the monopoly price (p_m) in the current period if rivals set price at p_m in the previous period; otherwise, each firm pursues a more competitive or "grim strategy" (e.g., the stage-game Nash-equilibrium price). By punishing non-cooperative behavior, a trigger strategy encourages cooperation as long as the penalty is sufficient to make the present value of discounted future profits greater for cooperative than for non-cooperative behavior. In a repeated Bertrand-type game where firms have perfect and complete information, for example, it is optimal for each firm to cooperate on price if the future is not discounted too heavily and if the number of competitors is sufficiently low.[13] If cooperation is optimal in this setting, then a trigger strategy will support collusion forever and punishment will never be observed. When firms have incomplete information or make mistakes, however, a punishment phase may occur.

Anheuser-Busch has used and threatened to use substantial price reductions to punish rivals for behaving non-cooperatively. Several sources indicate that Anheuser-Busch is the clear price leader in brewing, using a "statesmanlike pricing position" to maintain high prices in brewing (*Business Week*, March 24, 1973: 45).[14] In 1974 the chairman of Schlitz, Robert Uihlein, said "a price increase is needed, but it will take Anheuser-Busch to do it" (*Fortune*, November 1975: 92). When competitors substantially discounted or failed to follow an Anheuser-Busch price increase, a harsh response was common. For example, after an increase in costs that followed a union wage agreement in the

Table 7.3
Beer prices in the St. Louis market (prices per case of 24 12-ounce containers). A-B represents Anheuser-Busch. Rivals' price equals the average price of beer sold by Falstaff, Griesedieck Western, and Griesedieck Brothers in the market. The differential is defined as the price of Anheuser-Busch's Budweiser brand divided by the rivals' price. Source: Brooks 1970, 733.

	A-B's price	Rivals' price	Differential
Fall 1953 (after wage increase)	$2.93	$2.35	1.25
January 4, 1954 (after first A-B price cut)	$2.68	$2.35	1.14
June 21, 1954 (after second A-B price cut)	$2.35	$2.35	1.00
February 16, 1955 (after A-B price increase)	$2.80	$2.50	1.12

fall of 1953, Anheuser-Busch raised the price of Budweiser. Although many regional and local brewers followed, several Midwest rivals (Griesedieck Western, Griesedieck Brothers, and Falstaff) did not raise their prices. Between January and June of 1954, Anheuser-Busch responded by completely eliminating the price premium between Budweiser and the renegade brands in the St. Louis region.[15] This put a severe strain on its rivals, as Anheuser-Busch's market share in St. Louis more than tripled, increasing from 12.5 percent to 39.3 percent. On February 16, 1955, Anheuser-Busch marked up the price of Budweiser once again, and this time its Midwest rivals responded with their own price increase. These events and price changes are summarized in table 7.3.

Although Anheuser-Busch's behavior was unsuccessfully challenged by the Federal Trade Commission for price discrimination under the Robinson-Patman Act (1936), concerns raised by the hearing examiner and comments by Anheuser-Busch's president strongly suggest that this is a classic case of a price leader disciplining a select group of mavericks. According to the hearing examiner, the 1954 price reductions by Anheuser-Busch "were ordered by its president for two admitted reasons: to get business away from its competitors, and to punish them for refusing to increase prices when [Anheuser-Busch] did so in the fall of 1953. Apparently the lesson was well taught and better learned, because those three St. Louis breweries promptly followed A.B. up with price increases in March 1955. . . ."[16]

A similar event occurred in 1988 when Miller and Coors discounted their premium and popular-priced brands in order to draw consumers away from their weaker rivals, Stroh and Heileman.[17] After 18 months of heavy discounting, Anheuser-Busch announced that the price of

Budweiser would be cut substantially in select regions of the country. August Busch III, then president of Anheuser-Busch, said "We don't want to start a bloodbath, but whatever the competition wants to do, we'll do." (*Fortune*, January 15, 1990: 81) Company sources state that "Anheuser's announcement was meant as a warning to its rivals that they would pay dearly if they continued the price-slashing that sent prices down by as much as 22% in some markets" (*Business Week*, December 18, 1989: 124). Rivals' price cutting abated quickly, and Anheuser-Busch backed off of its threat to cut the price of Budweiser.[18] In this case, a formal threat of a future price cut was enough to preserve less competitive behavior.

A firm that discounts the price of a premium brand to boost sales temporarily or to punish uncooperative rivals risks losing its premium image if the discounting goes on too long. Price movements of the major brewers can be seen in the average revenue data in figure 7.3.[19] The data reveal a substantial drop in the average revenue of Pabst after it purchased the popular-priced Blatz brand in 1958 and after it began discounting its premium Blue Ribbon brand in the early 1960s. One can also see that Miller had relatively high average revenue in the

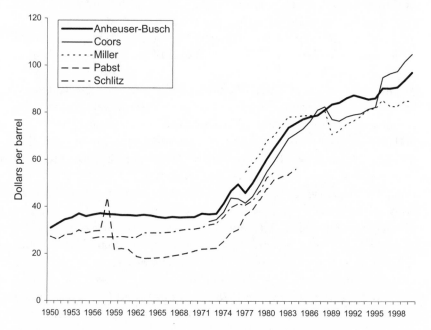

Figure 7.3
Average revenue of major beer producers, 1950–2001. Source: See appendix A.

1970s, when Miller Lite and Miller High Life were successful premium brands. The data reveal that discounting led to lower average revenues for Miller and Coors beginning in the late 1980s. Average revenues began to rise by 1990, supporting the conclusion that Anheuser-Busch's threat of punishment was effective. Today, Anheuser-Busch remains the price leader and price discounts appear less frequently (*Modern Brewery Age*, March 26, 2001).[20]

7.2 Advertising Strategies

Advertising is an important form of non-price competition in the U.S. brewing industry. In 2000, the top three brewers (Anheuser-Busch, Miller, and Coors) spent about $744 million on advertising—about $4.60 per barrel. Table 7.4 lists the ratios of advertising expenditures to

Table 7.4
Ratios of advertising expenditures to sales revenues for a sample of U.S. manufacturing industries, 2000.

	SIC code[a]	Advertising as percentage of sales
Computer and office equipment	3570	1.5
Computers	3571	1.6
Tires	3011	1.7
Dairy products	2020	2.5
Motor vehicles and car bodies	3711	2.7
Cigarettes	2111	2.9
Tobacco products	2100	4.8
Pharmaceutical preparations	2834	6.9
Beverages	2080	7.1
Beer	*2082*	*8.6*
Household furniture	2510	9.7
Games and toys	3944	10.3
Food	2000	11.0
Wine and brandy	2084	11.5
Cutlery and hardware	3420	12.0
Rubber and plastic footwear	3021	12.0
Soap and detergent	2840	12.5
Perfume and cosmetics	2844	12.8
Liquor	2085	15.2
Watches and clocks	3873	15.2

a. For a discussion of SIC codes, see Pepall et al. (2002, 100–101). Source: *Advertising Age* (www.adage.com).

sales revenues for a sample of consumer-goods industries in the year 2000. In brewing, 8.6 percent of sales are devoted to advertising; when the advertising-to-sales ratio exceeds 5 percent, Bain (1959: 390–391) argues, advertising is "significant" and "substantial." Indeed, advertising influenced the evolution of the brewing industry, as was discussed in chapter 3. Thus, a discussion of advertising theories, strategies, and themes may be enlightening.

Persuasive and Informative Advertising

For advertising to be an effective strategy, it must increase demand for the advertised brand. Advertising can influence demand by providing consumers with information about price and product characteristics, by enhancing brand loyalty and goodwill, or by creating subjective product differentiation.

Critics argue that persuasive advertising creates subjective images, changes tastes, and distorts consumers' perceptions of product quality in order to generate brand loyalty and additional demand. Chamberlin's (1933: 119–120) discussion of monopolistic competition describes persuasive advertising as "selling methods which play upon the buyer's susceptibilities, which use against him laws of psychology with which he is unfamiliar and therefore against which he cannot defend himself, which frighten or flatter or disarm him—all of these have nothing to do with his knowledge. They are not informative; they are manipulative. They create a new scheme of wants by rearranging his motives." When purely persuasive, advertising can create a premium image by inducing consumers to increase their valuation of the advertised brand.

Persuasive advertising can be more effective in markets where consumers suffer from cognitive dissonance, a state of tension that occurs when a person holds beliefs that are psychologically inconsistent (Akerlof and Dickens 1982; Aronson 1999: 182). For example, a cigarette smoker may value health and also believe that cigarette smoking causes lung cancer. In that case, one way to eliminate the dissonance is to quit smoking. Another is to accept the cigarette advertisers' portrayal of smokers as healthy and energetic individuals, which suggests that smoking is not really damaging to one's health. Advertising that exploits cognitive dissonance will raise demand if it causes fewer smokers to quit smoking or entices more people to try smoking for the first time.[21]

Since excessive beer consumption is also unhealthy, beer marketers design their ads to counteract the association of beer drinking with poor health. In most advertisements the typical spokesperson for beer is healthy, attractive, and athletic. Concern with cognitive dissonance may contribute to the close connection between beer and sports and the use of former athletes as spokespersons in beer commercials. Budweiser linked itself with athletics as early as 1909, when one of its ads was headlined "Ball Players Use Beer in Training" (*Sports Illustrated*, August 8, 1988: 71). From 1985 to 1987, in a highly successful ad campaign, Coors featured the handsome actor Mark Harmon—a former UCLA quarterback—as a spokesman (Burgess 1993: 116–120).

Advertising can also be persuasive if it generates subliminal stimulation. Interest in this form of advertising arose in the 1950s when the market researcher James Vicary performed an experiment on movie patrons (Brean 1958). Without the knowledge of moviegoers, the words "EAT POPCORN" and "DRINK COCA-COLA" flashed on the screen for a fraction of a second in the middle of a film, leading to a reported 58 percent increase in popcorn demand and an 18 percent increase in Coke demand. The Vicary result could never be replicated, however, and subsequent research shows that the effectiveness of subliminal advertising in a controlled setting is small (Sheth et al. 1991: 60–62; Rogers 1992).

A more effective form of persuasive advertising ties a desirable image to the product. Tremblay and Polasky (2002) argue that this is the strategy used in the premium cola market. Because their colas taste very much alike, Coke and Pepsi use advertising to segment the market by creating images that appeal to different consumers. Coke pursues an image of traditional family values, while Pepsi presents a more youthful and rebellious image. This strategy benefits both firms by strengthening brand loyalty and reducing price competition (that is, it helps both firms avoid the Bertrand Paradox). Research published in *Fortune* (September 19, 1994: 80) shows that beer companies employ a similar strategy, using advertising to segment their brand images along white-collar and blue-collar lines. In the *Fortune* study, 100 beer drinkers between 21 and 49 years old were shown photographs of 98 men and asked to match the picture with the brand the individual is most likely to drink: Budweiser, Coors, or Miller High Life. The results show that the Budweiser drinker is viewed as "tough, grizzled, and blue-collar." The Miller drinker has a lighter blue-collar image, and the Coors drinker has more of a white-collar or feminine image.[22]

Even if the tastes of most consumers are not easily manipulated, advertising can still boost demand by disseminating product information. For example, advertising can increase demand by informing consumers about price discounts and product characteristics. Newspaper and point-of-sale advertising are often cited as providing consumers with price information. For beer—an experience good whose product characteristics are difficult to evaluate before purchase—advertising can also provide consumers with indirect information by signaling quality (Nelson 1974; Milgrom and Roberts 1986). This suggests that a high price and large advertising expenditures may be used to signal premium quality.

Casual observation suggests that beer advertisements have elements of both persuasion and information. Bauer and Greyser (1968) interviewed 1,846 consumers about their beliefs concerning the advertising of 78 different product groups during the 1960s, a time when beer advertising profoundly affected the industry. The results reproduced here in table 7.5 show that consumers view print advertising as more informative than broadcast advertising, as Leong et al. (1998) confirmed. In addition, the informative content of the advertising for alcoholic beverages is much lower than the mean for all products sampled and for non-alcoholic beverages. Consumers felt that only 4 percent of beer advertising contains useful information.

Table 7.5
Percent of advertising classified as informative. Based on a survey of 1,846 consumers who evaluated 9,325 advertisements for 78 types of products. Source: Bauer and Greyser 1968: 243, 292–294.

Media	
Newspapers	59
Magazines	48
Radio	40
Television	31
All	36
Beverages	
Wine	2
Beer	4
Liquor	8
Soft drinks	11
Coffee, tea, cocoa	22
Fruit and vegetable juice	24
Mean of 78 products	35

Two conclusions emerge regarding the relationship between the advertising of beer and the demand for it. First, the predominately persuasive nature of beer advertising suggests that it will lead to higher prices.[23] Tremblay and Tremblay (1995) confirm that a marginal increase in advertising leads to higher equilibrium prices in brewing. One could attribute the price effect to pure persuasion or to growing demand for premium products that are heavily advertised.[24] Second, the brewing industry is well established and the qualities of regular domestic beer are well known. In this setting, one would expect advertising to attract few new customers to the market and to have little effect on market demand. The empirical evidence discussed in chapter 2 supports this expectation, indicating that beer advertising is used to capture market share from competitors but has little or no effect on the size of the market. To be effective in this setting, advertising must catch the attention of consumers and convince them to switch brands.

Results from a study by Video Storybook Tests, a New York research firm, show that some of the most persuasive beer ads use humor, real-life situations, and pets (*Fortune*, June 9, 1997), and that some of the least successful ones compare brands, focus on a musical theme, or feature the company's president or chief executive officer. For example, in the late 1970s and the early 1980s, Schlitz CEO Frank Sellinger appeared in television commercials for the failing Schlitz brand. Schlitz also used brand comparisons in the winter of 1980–81, when it spent $4 million on five "blind taste test" commercials aired during the professional football playoffs and the Super Bowl. The Super Bowl commercial alone cost about $1.7 million. The tests were live, with 100 regular drinkers of a competing brand (Budweiser or Miller High Life) comparing their favorite brand to Schlitz. In the first test, 46 percent of Budweiser drinkers stated that they preferred the taste of Schlitz to that of Budweiser. That sounds impressive,[25] but the ads failed to improve Schlitz's sales (perhaps because of previous quality-control problems). Heileman also had little success with taste tests promoting its Blatz brand in the mid 1970s (*Beverage World*, January 1977). In 1991, comparative advertising by Coors asserted that 58 percent of Budweiser drinkers preferred Coors Extra Gold (*Forbes*, March 4, 1991). Sales of Coors Extra Gold continued to decline, however. More recently, the High Falls Brewing Company conducted blind taste tests in an effort to revitalize Genny Light beer (*Modern Brewing Age*, May 19, 2003). The outcome of this effort is not yet known.

Table 7.6
A sample of brand advertising themes used by major brewers.

Budweiser (*Advertising Age*, May 7, 1973): "Somebody cares about quality ...
Budweiser."

Coors (Burgess, 1993): "Made with pure Rocky Mountain spring water."

Coors Light (*Advertising Age*, December 18, 1978): "Real taste of Coors in a light beer."

Hamm (*Newsweek*, July 22, 1957): "From the land of sky-blue waters."

Michelob (*Advertising Age*, February 13, 1978): "Weekends are made for Michelob."

Michelob Light (*Wall Street Journal*, February 13, 1978): "Good taste runs in the family."

Miller High Life (*Advertising Age*, February 1, 1971): "The champagne of bottled beers."

Miller Lite (*Advertising Age*, January 9, 1978): "Everything you always wanted in a beer,
and less."

Old Style (*Barrons*, April 24, 1961): "Aged longer than any other beer."

Olympia (*Advertising Age*, March 22, 1965): "It's the water."

Pabst (*Advertising Age*, June 23, 1958): "Pabst makes it perfect."

Schlitz (*Printers' Ink*, February 7, 1958): "Move up to quality ... move up to Schlitz."

Schlitz (*Fortune*, October 1964): "Real gusto in a great light beer."

Schlitz Light (*Advertising Age*, October 20, 1975): "It took Schlitz to bring the taste to
light."

Stroh (*Advertising Age*, March 21, 1977): "The art of brewing is not to turn beer into
water but water into beer."

Advertising Themes and the Quality of Advertising in Brewing

Historical records indicate that most advertising themes in brewing emphasize the lightness and quality of the product. Table 7.6 provides prominent examples for leading brands.

Marketing success can be affected by a brewer's own actions and by the actions of rivals. For example, the great success of Miller Lite in the mid 1970s made the marketing theme of Coors beer, "America's fine light beer," instantly outdated (Burgess 1993: 16). In addition, after more than 100 years of advertising that Coors beer is "brewed with pure Rocky Mountain spring water," the firm had to discontinue this claim when it began using Virginia water at a new plant to make Coors beer in the early 1990s.[26]

Considerable criticism of the general quality of beer advertising was aired during the 1950s and the early 1960s. At that time, most advertising themes were similar, repetitive, and uncreative (*Printers' Ink*, November 29, 1963). "In the 50s and 60s," according to Robert Weinberg (*Sports Illustrated*, August 8, 1988: 73), "most of the beer ad campaigns on television were either silly comic things ... or they were deadly serious ego trips for the brewer that pontificated about excellence and fineness and quality."

Anheuser-Busch was the first brewer to invest heavily in marketing research (*Forbes*, March 1, 1968; *Business Week*, March 24, 1973; Ackoff and Emshoff 1975a,b). This research began in 1961 when president August A. Busch Jr. questioned a proposal by the vice president of marketing to increase Budweiser's advertising by 8 percent. The vice president defended the proposal on the grounds that it would increase sales. Mr. Busch responded, "Is there any way I can find out at the end of the year whether I got what I paid for?" (Ackoff and Emshoff 1975a: 2). To address this question, Anheuser-Busch hired Russell Ackoff, a professor of management and behavioral science at the University of Pennsylvania, to investigate the effect of advertising on Budweiser sales. By experimenting with advertising spending in different media and in different regions of the country, Ackoff found that advertising is more effective when a variety of media are used and when it is conveyed intermittently, an outcome that is consistent with a mixed strategy in advertising. He also found that television was the most effective advertising medium for generating sales. Further, Ackoff's research showed that outdoor advertising had no effect on sales, a surprising result insofar as Anheuser-Busch devoted 20 percent of its advertising budget to outdoor advertising and insofar as the brewing industry as a whole ranked first in outdoor advertising in the mid 1950s (*Modern Brewery Age*, March 1956). Ackoff also found that different brands appeal to different personality segments of the beer-drinking population, and that advertising is more effective if targeted to the personality segment most likely to appreciate the advertised brands. As a result of this research, Anheuser-Busch adjusted its advertising tactics. Sales nearly doubled from 1963 to 1968, while advertising expenditures fell from $1.89 to $0.80 per barrel.

In 1970, Philip Morris brought sophisticated marketing to the industry after purchasing Miller. Using techniques that had been successful in the cigarette market, Philip Morris emphasized market segmentation, target marketing, and image advertising (*Business Week*, November 8, 1976; *Advertising Age*, January 9, 1978; *Sports Illustrated*, August 8, 1988). This strategy provoked a marketing war among leading brewers during the 1970s and the 1980s.

The evidence discussed in chapter 2 from Kelton and Kelton (1982) and Färe et al. (2004) confirms that the industry leaders, Anheuser-Busch and Miller, have had a marketing advantage over other brewers. Both studies suggest that once a firm is large enough to reach scale efficiency, overall success depends critically on marketing efficiency. Some industry experts claim that marketing is even more important than production efficiency in brewing (Scherer et al. 1975: 258).

Advertising Spending of the Leading Brewers

Figure 7.4 shows how the leading brewers' advertising intensity (advertising expenditures per barrel) changed from 1950 to 2000.[27] Miller behaved predictably until it was purchased by Philip Morris in late 1969 (see figure 3.3). With an injection of funds from its parent company, Miller began to introduce new brands and increased advertising spending. Miller's advertising intensity rose sharply after 1969, and Miller was the most intensively advertised beer through the mid 1970s. The success of Miller's advertising and of its new Lite brand (introduced nationally in 1975) caused sales to rise markedly. By 1977, Miller's advertising intensity was in line with those of the other major brewers. It has remained so.

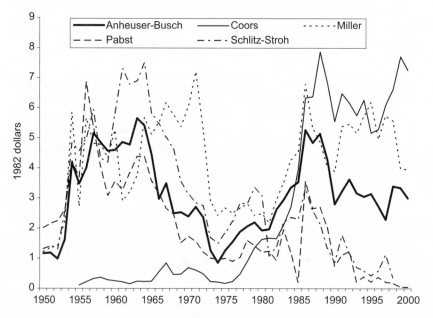

Figure 7.4
Real advertising expenditures per barrel of leading brewers, 1950–2000. Source: See appendix A.

Anheuser-Busch's advertising intensity fell during the period of Ackoff's research (1963–1974), but so did the advertising intensities of the other leading brewers. As was discussed in chapter 3, this was a period when advertising spending fell and profits rose at the industry level. From 1974 through the mid 1980s, in response to Miller's increased advertising and brand proliferation, Anheuser-Busch increased its advertising intensity dramatically. Then its advertising spending per barrel dropped. In the 1990s it leveled off at about $3 per barrel.

Until the late 1970s, Coors followed a relatively conservative strategy, marketing a single brand of beer produced in a single brewery. Coors emphasized production efficiency and product quality over marketing, and from 1950 to 1978 it spent less on advertising per barrel than any other leading brewer. As was noted in chapter 4, there are several reasons why Coors was successful in spite of so little advertising. First, Coors had been the first to produce a lighter beer, and it flourished with the light-beer trend. Its flagship brand had about 9 percent fewer calories and 9 percent less alcohol than other premium brands in the 1950s through the mid 1970s, and it was marketed as "America's fine light beer." In addition, Coors emphasized the quality of its beer, the only major brand that was cold filtered rather than pasteurized. According to Coors, "pasteurization involves heat, which changes the flavor" (*Forbes*, February 1, 1969). This emphasis on quality may have reinforced a mystique that became associated with Coors beer and substantially boosted its sales during the early 1970s. But the company's image problems and the 1975 introduction of Miller Lite, a product formulated to taste like Coors, eroded Coors's market share in the mid 1970s. Coors responded by putting more emphasis on marketing. By the late 1980s, Coors was spending more on advertising per barrel than any other leading brewer.

The advertising spending of Pabst and Schlitz rose and fell with that of other major brewers from 1950 until the late 1970s.[28] By the mid 1970s, Schlitz suffered from production and marketing problems. In addition, both Pabst and Schlitz were under pressure from the continued success of Anheuser-Busch and the later success of Miller. Schlitz increased advertising intensity in 1979 and 1980 in an unsuccessful attempt to revitalize the company. Stroh purchased Schlitz in 1982, but the merged company languished. Advertising intensity fell dramatically from the mid 1980s until the company was purchased by four other brewers in 1999. (See chapter 4.) Pabst experienced similar problems and has reduced advertising intensity substantially since the mid 1980s. This evidence suggests that the national brewers Anheuser-Busch, Coors, and Miller preempted Pabst, Schlitz, Stroh, and other regional brewers in the advertising race.

Advertising Spending of the Leading Brands

Table 7.7 reveals several interesting facts about the advertising intensity of the leading brands from 1977 to 2001. First, most premium-priced, popular-priced, and malt liquor brands have an advertising intensity that is less than the industry average. In the case of premium beer, advertising per barrel is low because so many barrels are sold. With the decline in share of the premium category, however, the advertising intensity of most premium brands rose and actually exceeded the industry average by the mid 1990s.[29] The low advertising intensity of popular-priced beer is consistent with its generic nature, as popular-priced brands compete on price more than on image and advertising. Research at Miller suggests that the typical malt liquor drinker is a young male who will eventually switch to regular beer (Van Munching 1997). Advertising cannot effectively induce brand loyalty in such a consumer, so firms are left to compete on price and alcohol content instead of advertising in the malt liquor category.

   Table 7.7 also shows that most premium and super-premium brands have higher advertising intensities than popular-priced brands. The few exceptions include episodes when a brand is being repositioned up or down the premium spectrum. For example, the Stroh brand was advertised more intensively in the mid 1980s, when the company was attempting to reposition it from the popular-priced to the premium category. Production and image problems at Schlitz caused the Schlitz brand to fall out of the premium category by the mid 1980s. (See chapter 4.) Similar problems downgraded Miller High Life from the premium to the popular-priced category in the early 1990s. As a result, the advertising intensities of Schlitz and Miller High Life fell. This evidence supports the hypothesis that advertising serves to signal a premium image if not premium quality.

   Another interesting fact revealed by table 7.7 is that many of the newer brands and categories (i.e., dry and ice) have above-average advertising intensities. New brands, especially those that pioneer new product categories, have low initial sales and require a great deal of advertising to inform consumers, to convince them to try something new, and to create a desirable image. For example, note the relatively high advertising intensities of the light brands in the 1970s and the 1980s, when the product category was new and sales were relatively low. As consumers become aware of the new product, advertising spending generally falls and sales generally rise, causing a decline in advertising expenditures per barrel.

Table 7.8 provides convincing evidence that new brands are heavily advertised. Of the 15 new brands for which data are available, each has an advertising intensity above the industry average in its introductory year, and the average new brand has an advertising intensity more than 7 times the industry average. The extreme cases are also of interest. In 1985, Anheuser-Busch made an unsuccessful attempt to develop the low-alcohol category, spending more than 19 times the industry's average advertising intensity to generate only 200,000 barrels in sales. At the other extreme, Coors was able to successfully market Coors Light with modest advertising spending—behavior that is consistent with Coors's emphasis on production over marketing. Another factor may be the fact that Coors Light entered the market 3 years after Miller informed consumers of the merits of light beer. The variation in advertising intensity across new brands is due in part to their relative success. For example, the low sales from Gablinger's advertising campaign produced a high advertising intensity, while the rapid success of Coors Light produced a low advertising intensity.[30] The evidence from brewing is similar to findings from the marketing literature that the advertising differential between new brands and established ones is normally greater than 4 times (Kotler and Armstrong 1998).

Because dry beer was unsuccessful, the advertising intensities of brands in this category are of particular interest. As table 6.8 showed, the category grew rapidly at first, peaked in 1990 with total sales of 3.98 million barrels, declined rapidly thereafter, and is now vanishing. When new brands of dry beer (Bud Dry, Coors Dry, and Michelob Dry) were introduced, in the late 1980s, they were advertised heavily. Anheuser-Busch and Coors, speculating that dry beer would be a big success, initially spent more than 5 times the industry average on advertising per barrel (*New York Times*, July 10, 1988). As the evidence mounted that dry beer would not live up to expectations, advertising spending fell dramatically. The decline began in 1993, and advertising spending essentially dried up by 1995. The experiences of both LA and dry beers confirm that heavy advertising does not guarantee the success of a new product or a new brand.

Table 7.7
Advertising expenditures per barrel for leading brands of beer, 1977–2001. Sources: TNS Media Intelligence/CMR as reported in *Beer Industry Update: A Review of Recent Developments* (various issues); *Brewers Almanac* (various issues).

	1977	1978	1979	1980	1981
Premium					
Budweiser	0.91	0.90	0.95	0.93	1.09
Coors	0.31	0.56	0.99	1.21	1.42
Miller High Life	0.87	1.12	1.25	1.56	1.60
Miller Genuine Draft	—	—	—	—	—
Schlitz	1.29	1.81	2.66	2.68	3.04
Popular					
Busch	0.91	1.56	2.79	3.56	2.50
Old Milwaukee	1.35	0.88	1.30	1.20	1.11
Pabst	0.64	0.83	0.81	1.17	1.19
Stroh	—	—	—	—	1.72
Light					
Bud	—	—	—	—	12.61
Busch	—	—	—	—	—
Coors	—	2.66	2.30	2.81	2.27
Michelob	—	6.48	9.58	7.96	8.82
Miller	2.39	2.62	2.47	2.52	2.20
Natural	5.98	6.16	6.89	8.52	9.50
Super premium					
Löwenbräu	22.57	23.36	21.21	21.11	16.24
Michelob	1.56	1.60	1.92	1.64	2.36
Malt liquor					
Colt 45	—	—	1.78	2.13	1.46
King Cobra	—	—	—	—	—
Olde English 800	—	—	—	—	—
Dry					
Bud	—	—	—	—	—
Coors	—	—	—	—	—
Michelob	—	—	—	—	—
Ice					
Bud	—	—	—	—	—
Icehouse	—	—	—	—	—
Miller Lite Ice	—	—	—	—	—
Industry average	1.63	2.08	2.18	3.20	2.38

1982	1983	1984	1985	1986	1987	1988	1989
1.15	1.38	1.60	1.64	2.28	2.26	2.68	2.30
1.53	1.83	2.79	4.13	5.13	4.40	4.56	6.28
2.35	2.95	3.87	4.90	6.44	2.75	4.73	4.52
—	—	—	—	25.28	22.28	16.43	12.40
1.71	1.15	0.88	0.47	—	—	—	—
2.35	1.95	1.71	3.80	4.03	3.75	3.73	3.35
1.06	1.68	1.94	1.43	0.03	0.12	0.32	0.46
0.77	2.15	0.60	0.23	—	2.23	2.07	3.09
1.40	3.85	6.04	4.99	5.15	3.55	2.20	4.54
9.37	12.57	12.84	8.47	9.22	7.89	7.32	5.09
2.35	1.95	1.72	3.70	—	3.75	3.73	7.21
1.82	2.80	2.80	3.43	4.57	4.63	6.45	5.48
8.42	10.23	10.18	9.61	12.78	12.05	7.05	0.89
2.60	2.80	3.67	3.72	4.53	4.28	4.09	3.76
12.78	5.93	2.17	1.81	2.41	1.59	1.30	1.08
15.08	14.35	14.09	14.32	4.53	15.73	5.82	4.86
3.63	5.22	5.78	6.40	9.59	10.80	14.30	7.17
2.02	2.00	1.08	—	2.74	3.14	4.92	3.12
—	—	—	—	62.53	49.69	31.20	1.73
—	—	—	—	—	2.18	3.04	1.78
—	—	—	—	—	—	—	22.47
—	—	—	—	—	—	—	—
—	—	—	—	—	—	—	38.33
—	—	—	—	—	—	—	—
—	—	—	—	—	—	—	—
—	—	—	—	—	—	—	—
2.83	3.13	4.16	4.48	5.12	5.07	5.46	4.01

Table 7.7
(continued)

	1990	1991	1992	1993	1994
Premium					
Budweiser	1.52	1.81	2.52	2.52	2.38
Coors	5.01	4.40	1.37	1.56	2.72
Miller High Life	3.92	3.19	1.41	0.33	0.54
Miller Genuine Draft	9.98	8.70	9.91	11.28	7.26
Schlitz	—	—	—	—	—
Popular					
Busch	1.95	0.43	0.51	0.64	1.04
Old Milwaukee	0.40	0.52	0.82	0.95	0.13
Pabst	1.05	1.46	2.39	0.50	0.56
Stroh	3.09	1.63	3.30	1.68	1.85
Light					
Bud	3.82	4.83	4.69	4.36	3.94
Busch	2.80	0.49	0.87	1.08	0.89
Coors	5.86	5.55	5.02	4.76	4.84
Michelob	0.32	2.31	0.55	0.36	0.34
Miller	3.56	5.15	4.82	5.31	3.94
Natural	0.64	0.44	0.19	0.01	0.01
Super premium					
Löwenbräu	3.55	3.24	2.99	2.92	5.18
Michelob	0.54	0.91	0.82	1.29	1.14
Malt liquor					
Colt 45	1.29	5.06	2.91	3.57	2.08
King Cobra	0.34	0.48	0.43	0.22	0.23
Olde English 800	1.31	1.34	1.09	0.13	0.69
Dry					
Bud	11.48	16.92	16.00	9.47	2.42
Coors	—	22.13	48.60	0.99	—
Michelob	39.68	6.43	0.33	—	—
Ice					
Bud	—	—	—	10.42	13.62
Icehouse	—	—	—		7.81
Miller Lite Ice	—	—	—	—	19.95
Industry average	3.84	3.76	4.48	4.08	3.83

1995	1996	1997	1998	1999	2000	2001
2.68	3.42	3.73	3.41	3.86	4.57	3.94
4.30	10.95	14.77	15.22	15.71	23.25	20.98
0.70	0.31	0	2.83	2.65	1.90	3.19
6.68	3.82	11.51	9.10	5.18	4.70	9.69
—	—	—	—	—	—	—
1.30	1.06	0.31	0.23	0.89	2.34	1.22
0.14	1.31	2.33	0.25	0.01	0.03	—
0.28	0.29	0.31	0.25	0.13	0.21	—
1.75	1.93	4.68	0.40	0.40	0.02	—
3.79	3.35	2.51	4.98	3.69	3.42	2.75
1.03	0.76	0.04	0	0.01	0.01	0.01
4.86	5.87	6.76	5.40	6.39	7.21	7.80
2.14	1.32	0.25	5.55	8.28	12.99	13.74
5.60	6.41	9.34	6.03	5.12	5.61	6.45
0.01	0.02	0.02	0	0.02	0.01	0.02
3.55	0.41	0.61	0	—	—	—
2.11	6.58	1.89	5.29	6.04	0.63	1.31
0.56	0.16	0.72	0.10	0.01	0.08	—
0.20	0.15	0	—	—	—	—
0.33	1.02	0.05	0.17	0.02	0	—
—	0.12	0.06	0.04	0.02	0.08	—
—	—	—	—	—	—	—
—	—	—	—	—	—	—
13.89	8.22	7.33	5.60	0.05	0.10	0.09
16.79	3.44	1.64	3.55	3.68	3.93	0.63
33.25	0.36	0.08	0	0.18	1.79	0.88
3.87	3.72	3.76	3.90	4.01	4.54	4.80

Table 7.8
Intensity of advertising of new brands (dollars per barrel) and differential (brand advertising spending divided by industry advertising spending per barrel). Sources: same as for table 7.7.

Brand (year of introduction[a])	Intensity of advertising		
	By brand	By industry	Differential
Gablinger Light (1967)	$27.00	$2.05	13.17
Löwenbräu (1977)	22.57	1.63	13.85
Natural Light (1977)	5.98	1.63	3.67
Coors Light (1978)	2.66	2.08	1.28
Michelob (1978)	6.48	2.08	3.12
Bud Light (1981)	12.61	2.38	5.30
Anheuser-Busch LA (1985)	85.26	4.48	19.16
King Cobra (1986)	62.53	5.12	12.21
Miller Genuine Draft (1986)	25.28	5.12	4.94
Bud Dry (1989)	22.47	4.01	5.60
Michelob Dry (1989)	38.33	4.01	9.56
Coors Dry (1991)	22.13	3.76	5.89
Bud Ice (1994)	13.62	3.83	3.57
Miller Ice Lite (1994)	19.95	3.83	5.21
Icehouse (1995)	16.79	3.87	4.34
Mean			7.39

a. Except for the Gablinger brand (which was marketed regionally), year of introduction is the year in which the brand was first marketed nationally.

Several conclusions can be drawn from previous research and from the marketing evidence presented above. First, in brewing, advertising causes firm demand to increase but has little or no effect on market demand. Second, most beer advertising is devoted to persuasion and image enhancement. The important exception occurs when a firm introduces a new brand and must inform consumers of the brand's presence in the market and of its attributes. In this case, advertising per barrel is generally more than 7 times the industry average. Third, a marginal increase in advertising generally leads to higher beer prices. Fourth, successful beer advertisements focus on humor, emphasize the quality and lightness of the product, and feature an animal or a healthy and robust spokesperson. Finally, advertising intensities are likely to be lower for low-priced brands, for products with fickle consumers, and for brands that are well established. Thus, the general pattern is that new and premium brands receive intensive advertising support, mature products receive moderate advertising support, and more generic or declining brands are advertised very little.

7.3 Mergers and Acquisitions

In the second half of the twentieth century, the brewing industry became more and more concentrated as most of the companies exited. From 1950 to 2000, the number of independent mass-producing brewers declined from 350 to 24, the Herfindahl-Hirschman index increased from 204 to 3,612, and the four-firm concentration ratio rose from 22.03 percent to 94.82 percent.

Available evidence indicates that most of the brewers that exited the industry during this time did so by combining with another beer producer. Recall from chapter 3 that consolidation is one strategic response to the attrition war in brewing. With too many inefficiently small firms in the industry, brewers that combine can close the least efficient plants and gain an efficient size. Tremblay and Tremblay (1988) document the major attempted and actual mergers and acquisitions in the brewing industry from 1950 through 1983. Table 7.9 updates their work, listing more than 215 mergers and acquisitions from 1950 to 2002. (This table orders mergers by *acquiring* firm, whereas table C.1 in appendix C orders them by *acquired* firm.)

For several brewers, the acquisition of another firm's brands, plants, and equipment became an important means of expansion. The best example is Heileman, a company that made 17 acquisitions in the period 1961–1987. This growth-by-merger strategy transformed the company into a near-national brewer by the 1970s, as Heileman was able to establish a network of regionally distributed brands (*Fortune*, June 18, 1979). Heileman benefited from the strict enforcement of the anti-trust laws by the Department of Justice, which made it impossible for a major brewer to purchase another large brewery through the 1980s.[31] Because it was a medium-size firm and did not have to compete with the major firms for the assets of failing brewers, Heileman was able to acquire them at low cost (*Forbes*, October 1, 1977; *Fortune*, June 18, 1979).[32] Other firms that chose to grow by merger include Falstaff, Miller, Pabst, and Stroh, each of which made seven or more acquisitions of smaller brewers between 1950 and 1999. Coors followed its stated policy of single-plant operation until 1989, when it purchased Stroh's Memphis plant. Coors has made no other acquisitions.

Table 7.9
Major mergers and acquisitions, 1950–2002. An acquisition includes the purchase of brands and facilities unless otherwise noted. "Purchased brands only" means that facilities were not included in the merger or were immediately sold. Unless otherwise noted, the source is *Brewers Digest, Buyer's Guide and Brewery Directory* (various issues). *AA: Advertising Age. BW: Business Week. MBA: Modern Brewery Age. MIM: Moody's (Mergent) Industrial Manual. WSJ: Wall Street Journal.*

Acquiring firm	Acquired firm	Sources and comments
Anheuser-Busch (St. Louis)		
1958	American (Miami)[a]	Horowitz and Horowitz 1969. Purchased Regal brand and facilities. Justice Dept. issued consent decree to divest in 1960.
1979	Schlitz (Milwaukee)	Bought Syracuse plant.
1993	Tsingtao (China)	*MBA Weekly News Edition*, April 14, 2003. Purchased 4.5 percent interest in company.
1994	Redhook (Seattle)	Barndt 2002. Purchased 25 percent of company's equity.
1997	Widmer Bros. (Portland, OR)	*Oregonian*, April 18, 1997; *Beverage Industry*, June 1998. Purchased 30.9 percent interest in company.
Associated (Pfeiffer before 1962) (Detroit)		
1955	F. W. Cook (Evansville)	Robertson 1984. Closed plant.
1955	J. Schmidt (St. Paul)	*MIM*, 1955
1962	E & B (Detroit)	*MIM*, 1972
1964	Sterling (Evansville)	Robertson 1984
1965	Drewerys (South Bend)	*AA*, December 13, 1965: 1
1967	Dawson (New Bedford, MA)	Purchased brands. Plant was sold to Rheingold.
Atlantic (Chicago)		
1956	Bohemian (Boise)	
1956	Bohemian (Spokane)	
1958	Terre Haute (Terre Haute)	
1959	Ambrosia (Chicago)	
1962	American (New Orleans)	
Ballantine (Newark)		
1968	Boston Celtics	*Forbes*, September 15, 1968. Conglomerate merger.
Bond Corporation Holdings Ltd. (Australia)		
1986	Pittsburgh (Pittsburgh)	*MBA*, March 14, 1988. Conglomerate merger. Pittsburgh became an independent brewer again in 1991 (*MBA*, March 16, 1992).

Table 7.9
(continued)

Acquiring firm	Acquired firm	Sources and comments
1987	Heileman (La Crosse, WI)	*MBA* (March 14, 1988). Conglomerate merger. Purchase price: $1.2 billion (*MBA*, March 26, 2001: 20).
Boston Beer Company (Boston)		
1997	Hudepohl-Schoenling (Cincinnati)	*MBA* (March 23, 1998). Purchased Cincinnati plant only. Boston Beer Co. brews Hudepohl-Schoenling brands under contract.
Burger (Cincinnati)		
1956	Burkhardt (Akron)	
Carling (Waltham, MA)		
1954	Griesedieck-Western (Belleville, IL)	*BW*, October 2, 1954: 60. Purchased Stag brand and plant.
1956	International (Frankenmuth, MI)	Purchased brands only.
1959	Heidelberg (Tacoma)	*BW*, June 20, 1959: 45
1964	Arizona (Phoenix)	Sold to National (Baltimore) in 1966.
1975	National (Baltimore)	Robertson 1984
Chock Full o' Nuts		
1974	Rheingold (Brooklyn)	*Financial Week* (August 14, 1974: 23), from Pepsi Cola. Conglomerate merger.
Cold Spring (Cold Spring, MN; changed name to Gluek Brewing in 1997)		
1951	Mankato (Mankato, MN)	
1966	Dakota (Bismarck, ND)	
1973	Heileman (La Crosse, WI)[a]	*WSJ*, June 14, 1973. Purchased Duluth brand (Karlsbrau) and Gluek brands (Gluek and North Star) from Heileman because of Justice Dept. consent decree.
Coors (Golden, CO)		
1989	Stroh (Detroit)[a]	*WSJ*, September 26, 1989. Attempted merger opposed by Justice Dept. Coors purchased Memphis plant only.
2002	Carling (U.K.)	*MBA Weekly News Edition*, January 7, 2002; February 11, 2002. Market-extension merger.
Dakota (Bismarck, ND)		
1963	Butte (Butte, MT)	Purchased brands only.

Table 7.9
(continued)

Acquiring firm	Acquired firm	Sources and comments
Drewerys (South Bend)		
1951	Atlas (Chicago)	Robertson 1978
1951	Schoenhofen Edelweiss (Chicago)	*MIM*, 1952
1961	Hampden-Harvard (Willimansett, MA)	*Forbes* (September 15, 1962: 16)
1962	Piel Bros. (Brooklyn)	*Forbes* (September 15, 1962: 16)
1965	Atlantic (Chicago)	*AA* (June 7, 1965). Purchased brands only.
Duquesne (Pittsburgh)		
1963	Pilsener (Cleveland)	*Barrons*, September 16, 1963: 11. Purchased brands only.
Eastern (Hammonton, NJ)		
1968	Canadian Ace (Chicago)	Purchased brands only.
Esslinger (Philadelphia)		
1960	Gretz (Philadelphia)	Purchased brands only.
Evansville (Evansville)		
1988	Heileman (La Crosse, WI)	*MBA*, March 13, 1989. Purchased Evansville plant and Cook's, Sterling, Falls City, and Drewerys brands.
Falstaff (Corta Madera, CA)		
1952	Pacific (San Jose, CA)	*MIM*, 1953
1954	Berghoff (Fort Wayne)	*MIM*, 1955
1956	Galveston-Houston (Houston)	
1956	Mitchell (El Paso)	
1957	Griesedieck Brothers (St. Louis)	
1965	Narragansett (Cranston, RI)[a]	*AA*, July 26, 1965: 82; Greer 1984: 147. Purchased brands and facilities; was unsuccessfully challenged by Justice Dept.
1972	Ballantine (Newark)	*AA*, March 20, 1972: 25. Purchased brands and closed plant.
Fox Head (Waukesha, WI)		
1955	P. Fox (Chicago)	
1958	Weber Waukesha (Waukesha, WI)	
Gambrinus (San Antonio)		
1989	Spoetzl (Shiner, TX)	www.shiner.com. Conglomerate merger.
1995	Bridgeport (Portland, OR)	*Brandweek*, October 16, 1995; www.firkin.com. Conglomerate merger.

Table 7.9
(continued)

Acquiring firm	Acquired firm	Sources and comments
General (formerly Lucky) (Vancouver, WA)		
1950	Interstate (Vancouver, WA)	*MIM*, 1951
1957	Fisher (Salt Lake City)[a]	CCH Trade Cases, 1958, paragraph 69, 160. Ordered to divest in 1958.
1972	Maier (Los Angeles)	
Genesee (changed name to High Falls in 2000) (Rochester, NY)		
1986	Fred Koch (Dunkirk, NY)	
Goebel (Detroit)		
1950	Golden West (Oakland)	
W. R. Grace		
1967	Miller (Milwaukee)	*Financial World*, March 29, 1967: 13. Conglomerate merger.
Grain Belt (Minneapolis)		
1959	Kiewel (Little Falls, MN)	Leased plant. Closed plant in 1961.
1967	Storz (Omaha, NE)	Leased plant. Purchased brands and facilities in 1970.
1970	Hauenstein (New Ulm, MN)	*MIM*, 1971. Purchased brands only.
Griesedieck Western (Belleville, IL)		
1950	Hyde Park (St. Louis)	
Guinness UDV		
2001	Pabst (Milwaukee)	*WSJ*, November 27, 2001; *MBA*, May 19, 2003. Purchased Lehigh Valley plant only.
Gunther (Baltimore)		
1956	Fort Pitt (Pittsburgh)	Purchased brands only.
Hamm (St. Paul)		
1954	Rainier (Seattle)	*BW*. February 6, 1954: 12. Purchased Rainier's San Francisco plant.
1957	Rheingold (Brooklyn)	*AA*, January 16, 1961. Purchased Los Angeles plant
1960	Gunther (Baltimore)	*AA*, December 21, 1959: 6. Purchased plant only.
1963	Gulf (Houston)	*AA*, April 1, 1963: 111. Purchased plant only.
1972	Meister Brau (Chicago)	*AA*, December 20, 1971: 8. Purchased Burgermeister brand (San Francisco) and closed plant.

Table 7.9
(continued)

Acquiring firm	Acquired firm	Sources and comments
Hampden (Willimansett, MA)		
1956	Harvard (Lowell, MA)	Changed name to Hampden-Harvard and closed Lowell plant.
P. Hand (Chicago)		
1973	Old Crown (Fort Wayne)	Purchased brands only.
Heileman (La Crosse, WI)		
1961	Kingsbury (Sheboygan, WI)	*Barrons*, April 24, 1961: 12
1962	Fox Head (Waukesha, WI)	*AA*, July 9, 1962: 12. Purchased brands only.
1963	Independent Milwaukee	Purchased brands only.
1964	Gluek (Minneapolis)	*MIM*, 1965. Purchased brands only.
1966	Duluth (Duluth)	Purchased brands only.
1967	Oertel (Louisville)	*MIM*, 1968. Purchased brands only.
1967	Weidemann (Newport, KY)	Purchased brands only.
1969	Pabst (Milwaukee)	*Forbes*, September 15, 1969: 95. Purchased Blatz brand only.
1972	Associated (Detroit)[a]	*WSJ*, June 14, 1973. Purchased three plants: Fort Wayne (Drewerys), Evansville (Sterling), and St. Paul (J. Schmidt). Was forced to divest of some brands by 1974.
1975	Grain Belt (Minneapolis)	*MIM*, 1976. Purchased brands only.
1977	Rainier (Seattle)	*Forbes*, October 1, 1977: 51
1979	Falls City (Louisville)	*MIM*, 1980. Purchased brands only.
1979	Carling (Baltimore)	*Fortune*, June 18, 1979: 124
1980	Duncan (Auburndale, FL)	*MIM*, 1981. Purchased brands and facilities. Sold in 1983 to become independent firm, Florida Brewing.
1982	Pabst (Milwaukee)[a]	Barnett and Wilsted 1988d. Purchased plants in Perry, GA (Pabst), San Antonio (Lone Star), and Portland, OR (Blitz-Weinhard) and the following brands: Blitz-Weinhard, Henry Weinhard, Red-White-&-Blue, Burgermeister, Lone Star, and Buckhorn. To ensure Justice Dept. approval, remaining plants and brands of Pabst and Olympia were spun off as an independent Pabst brewer.
1986	Champale (Trenton)	*WSJ*, November 4, 1986. Purchased brands only.

Table 7.9
(continued)

Acquiring firm	Acquired firm	Sources and comments
1987	C. Schmidt (Philadelphia)	*MBA*, March 14, 1988. Purchased brands only.
Heublein		
1965	Hamm (St. Paul)	*AA*, October 18, 1965. Conglomerate merger.
Hicks, Muse, and Co.		
1993	Heileman (La Crosse, WI)	*MBA*, March 21, 1994. Conglomerate merger. Purchase price was $300 million (*MBA*, March 26, 2001: 20).
Huber (Monroe, WI)		
1972	Potosi (Potosi, WI)	Purchased brands only.
1980	P. Hand (Chicago)	Robertson 1984. Purchased brands only.
Hudepohl (Cincinnati)		
1973	Burger (Cincinnati)	www.littlekings.com. Purchased brands only.
Hudepohl-Schoenling (formerly Schoenling) (Cincinnati)		
1966	Fehr (Louisville)	www.littlekings.com. Purchased brands only.
1986	Hudepohl (Cincinnati)	www.littlekings.com. Purchased brands and facilities and closed Schoenling plant.
International (Detroit)		
1955	Frankenmuth (Frankenmuth, MI)	
1955	Iroquois (Buffalo)	
1956	Krantz (Finley, OH)	
1957	Phoenix (Buffalo)	
1959	Bavarian (Covington, KY)	
1961	Tampa Florida (Tampa)	
Investors Funding Corp.		
1968	Ballantine (Newark)	*Financial World*, June 18, 1969: 13. Conglomerate merger.
Jones (Smithton, PA)		
1957	Gunther (Baltimore)	Purchased Fort Pitt brands only.
Kingsbury (Sheboygan, WI)		
1959	Sioux City (Sioux City)	
Koch (Dunkirk, NY)		
1971	Simon of Buffalo (Buffalo)	Purchased brands only.

Table 7.9
(continued)

Acquiring firm	Acquired firm	Sources and comments
1971	International (Detroit)	Purchased Iroquois (Buffalo) brands only.
1973	William Simon (Buffalo)	http://heritage575.tripod.com. Purchased brands only.
Labatt Importers (Darien, CT)		
1988	Latrobe (Latrobe, PA)	
Leinenkugel (Chippewa Falls, WI)		
1973	Busch (Houghton, MI)	Purchased brands only.
Lion (Wilkes-Barre, PA)		
1967	Bartels (Edwardsville, PA)	Purchased brands only.
1974	Stegmaier (Wilkes-Barre, PA)	Robertson 1978. Purchased brands only.
Lone Star (San Antonio)		
1959	Progress (Oklahoma City)	*MIM*, 1960
Maier (Los Angeles)		
1962	Regal (San Francisco)	Purchased brands only.
Massachusetts Bay (Boston)		
2000	Catamount Brewing (Windson, VT)	Company web page. Company changed name to Harpoon at time of merger.
Meister Brau (Chicago)		
1966	Buckeye (Toledo)	*Barrons*, May 8, 1967: 3
1969	Schlitz (Milwaukee)	*Barrons*, July 13, 1970: 10. Purchased Burgermeister brand and San Francisco plant.
Miller (Milwaukee)		
1950	Reality	*BW*, September 8, 1951: 68. Conglomerate merger.
1961	Gettelman (Milwaukee)	*WSJ*, November 3, 1975: 19
1966	Carling (Waltham, MA)	*Printers' Ink*, February 10, 1967: 11. Purchased Fort Worth plant.
1966	General (formerly Lucky, Vancouver)	*Barrons*, May 8, 1967: 3. Purchased Azusa, CA plant.
1972	Meister Brau (Chicago)	*AA*, July 3, 1972. Purchased brands only.
1988	J. Leinenkugel (Chippewa Falls, WI)	*MBA*, March 14, 1988

Table 7.9
(continued)

Acquiring firm	Acquired firm	Sources and comments
1995	Molson (Canada)	*MBA*, March 25, 1996. International merger. Miller sold its equity interest in Molson in 1997 (*MBA*, March 23, 1998).
1995	Celis Brewing (Austin)	*MBA*, March 25, 1996. Purchased partial interest.
1995	Shipyard Brewing (Portland, ME)	*MBA*, March 25, 1996. Purchased partial interest.
1999	Stroh (Detroit)	*MBA*, March 27, 2000. Miller purchased the following brands from Stroh: Olde English 800 and Hamm. As part of the Pabst-Stroh merger, Pabst sold its Tumwater, WA (Olympia) plant and the following brands to Miller: Mickey's Malt Liquor and the Henry Weinhard brands.
Molson (Canada)		
1965	Hamm (St. Paul)[a]	Horowitz and Horowitz 1969. Successfully challenged by Justice Dept.
Narragansett (Cranston, RI)		
1952	Croft (Boston)	Purchased brands only.
1957	Hanley (Providence, RI)	Purchased brands only.
1961	Krueger (Newark)	*AA*, April 17, 1961: 12. Purchased brands only.
1964	Haffenreffer (Boston)	Robertson 1978. Purchased brands only.
National (Baltimore)		
1954	Altes (Detroit)	*BW*, October 2, 1954: 60
1956	Marlin (Orlando)	
1961	Anheuser-Busch (St. Louis)[a]	Bought Miami (American) plant and brands from Anheuser-Busch because of Justice Dept. consent decree.
1966	Carling (Waltham, MA)	Bought Phoenix (Arizona Brewing Co.) plant from Carling.
Olympia (Olympia, WA)		
1975	Hamm (St. Paul)	*AA*, March 3, 1975: 25. Purchased from Heublein.
1976	Lone Star (San Antonio)	*AA*, July 4, 1977: 25

Table 7.9
(continued)

Acquiring firm	Acquired firm	Sources and comments
H. Ortlieb (Philadelphia)		
1966	Fuhrmann and Schmidt (Shamokin, PA)	Robertson 1984
1968	Kaier (Mahanoy, PA)	Purchased brands only.
1968	Neuweiler (Allentown, PA)	Purchased brands only.
1978	C. Schmidt (Philadelphia)	Robertson 1978. Purchased McSorley Cream Ale brand.
Oshkosh (Oshkosh, WI)		
1966	Rahr (Green Bay, WI)	Purchased brands only.
Pabst (Milwaukee)		
1952	L.A. (Los Angeles)	
1958	Blatz (Milwaukee)[a]	Horowitz and Horowitz 1969. Purchased brand and closed plant. Court ordered Pabst to divest of Blatz in 1969.
1975	Hamm (St. Paul)	Robertson 1978. Purchased Burgermeister brand only.
1978	Carling (Waltham, MA)[a]	AA, September 18 and July 3, 1978; Elzinga 1982. Attempted merger stopped by Justice Dept.
1979	Blitz-Weinhard (Portland, OR)	AA, February 5, 1979: 70
1982	Olympia (Olympia, WA)	BW, June 14, 1982: 40; WSJ, March 21, 1983: 7. Part of merger with Heileman in 1982.
1982	Stroh (Detroit)[a]	Elzinga 1986. Purchased Tampa (Schlitz) plant; Pabst sold its St. Paul (Pabst, Olympia) plant to Stroh; Justice Dept. required Stroh to sell Schlitz plant.
1999	Stroh (Detroit)	MBA, March 22, 1999; Beverage Industry, March 1999. Pabst purchased Stroh's Lehigh Valley plant and the following brands: Ballantine, Falstaff, Lone Star, Old Style, Olympia, Rainier, Schmidt, and Special Export. Pabst also took over Stroh's contract brewing for the Boston Beer Company. Miller purchased the following brands from Stroh: Hamm and Olde English 800. As part of the agreement, Miller purchased the Tumwater, Washington (Olympia) plant and the

Table 7.9
(continued)

Acquiring firm	Acquired firm	Sources and comments
		Mickey's Malt Liquor and Henry Weinhard brands from Pabst. Yuengling purchased Stroh's Tampa plant. Platinum Holdings purchased the La Crosse (Heileman) plant, which later became the City Brewing Company. The following Stroh plants were closed: Longview, TX (Lone Star); Portland, Oregon (Blitz-Weinhard); Seattle (Rainier); Winston-Salem (Schlitz).
Pearl (San Antonio)		
1961	Goetz (St. Joseph, MO)	*Barrons*, June 12, 1961: 30
1965	Judson Candy (San Antonio)	*AA*, April 15, 1968: 2. Conglomerate merger.
1974	Jackson (New Orleans)	Purchased brands only.
PepsiCo (Purchase, NY)		
1972	Rheingold (Brooklyn)	*WSJ*, January 7, 1974: 9. Conglomerate merger.
Philip Morris		
1969	Miller (Milwaukee)	*AA*, June 16, 1969: 94. Conglomerate merger. Philip Morris purchased 53 percent of Miller's stock in 1969 and the remainder of Miller's stock in 1970.
Pickett (formerly Dubuque) (Dubuque)		
1972	Associated (Detroit)	Robertson 1978. Purchased Edelweiss and Champagne Velvet brands.
Pilsener (Cleveland)		
1952	Franklin (Columbus)	
Pittsburgh (Pittsburgh)		
1965	Duquesne (Pittsburgh)[a]	*CCH Trade Cases*, 1966. Justice Dept. issued consent decree to stop merger in 1966.
1967	DuBois (DuBois, PA)	Purchased brands only.
1974	Queen City (Cumberland, MD)	Purchased brands only.
1974	Wagner (Columbus)	Purchased brands only.
1997	Evansville (Evansville)	*MBA*, March 22, 1999. Plant closed. Purchased the following brands: Drewerys, Cook's, Falls City, Drummond Brothers, Lemp.

Table 7.9
(continued)

Acquiring firm	Acquired firm	Sources and comments
Platinum Holdings (New York)		
1999	Stroh (Detroit)	*MBA*, March 27, 2000. Purchased La Crosse (Heileman) plant only. Conglomerate merger. Became City Brewery Company.
1999	Genesee (Rochester, NY)	*MBA*. March 27, 2000. Attempted conglomerate merger. Genesee purchased by a New York management group; company name changed to High Falls Brewing Company.
Pub United Corp.		
1964	Rheingold (Brooklyn)	*Forbes*, November 15, 1964: 30. Conglomerate merger.
Queen City (Cumberland, MD)		
1969	Cumberland (Cumberland, MD)	Purchased brands and closed plant in 1970.
1973	American (Baltimore)	Purchased brands only.
Rainier (Seattle)		
1955	Sick's Spokane (Spokane)	
1964	Missoula (Missoula, MT)	Purchased brands only.
Rheingold (Brooklyn)		
1950	Trommer (Orange, NJ)	Robertson 1978
1954	Acme (Los Angeles)	*BW*, January 16, 1954: 128. Purchased plants in Los Angeles and San Francisco.
1965	Ruppert (New York)[a]	*WSJ*, June 5, 1968; Horowitz and Horowitz 1969. Challenged by Justice Dept. Purchased brands only.
1967	Dawson (New Bedford, MA)	Robertson 1978. Purchased plant; brands purchased by Associated (Detroit).
1969	Pepsi Cola (Santa Ana, CA)	*Barrons*, March 31, 1969. Conglomerate merger of Pepsi distributor.
1970	Grapette Co. (Camden, AK)	*Financial World*, April 7, 1971: 18. Conglomerate merger.
Ruppert (New York)		
1964	Esslinger (Philadelphia)	Purchased brands only.
S&P Co. (Mill Valley, CA)		
1973	General (San Francisco)	Conglomerate merger.

Table 7.9
(continued)

Acquiring firm	Acquired firm	Sources and comments
1975	Falstaff (St. Louis)	*WSJ*, August 12, 1975; www.americanbreweriana.org. Conglomerate merger.
1978	Pearl (San Antonio)	Robertson 1984. Conglomerate merger. Pearl is listed as subsidiary of General Brewing Company.
1986	Pabst (Milwaukee)	Conglomerate merger.
Schaefer (Brooklyn)		
1961	Standard (Cleveland)	*Printers' Ink*, January 19, 1962; Robertson 1984
1963	Hamm (St. Paul)	Purchased Baltimore (Gunther) plant from Hamm.
1973	Associated (Detroit)	*WSJ*, December 18, 1974. Purchased Piel and Trommer brands.
Schell (New Ulm, MN)		
1973	Fitger (Duluth)	Purchased brands only.
2002	Minnesota (Minneapolis)	*MBA Weekly News Edition*, August 26, 2002. Purchased Grain Belt brand only. Minnesota plant closed.
Schlitz (Milwaukee)		
1956	Muehlbach (Kansas City, MO)	*BW*, March 9, 1957: 87. Purchased facilities only.
1961	Burgermeister (San Francisco)[a]	Horowitz and Horowitz 1969. Court ordered divestment in 1966.
1964	Labatt (Canada)[a]	*AA*, February 24, 1964: 199. Labatt owned General (Vancouver, WA). Schlitz bought 39% interest in Labatt; court ordered divestment in 1966.
1964	Hawaii (Honolulu)	*Fortune*, October 1964. Purchased Primo brand and facilities.
C. Schmidt (Philadelphia)		
1955	Scheidt (Norristown, PA)	Robertson 1984
1963	Schaefer (Brooklyn)	Purchased Standard (Cleveland) brands and facilities.
1972	Duquesne (Pittsburgh)	Purchased brands only.
1976	Reading (Reading, PA)	*BW*, April 24, 1978: 31. Purchased brands only.
1977	Rheingold (Brooklyn)	*BW*, April 24, 1978: 31. Purchased only two plants.
1978	Erie (Erie, PA)	*BW*, April 24, 1978: 31. Purchased brands only.

Table 7.9
(continued)

Acquiring firm	Acquired firm	Sources and comments
1981	H. Ortlieb (Philadelphia)	*Tin International,* July 1981: 277. Purchased brands only.
South African Breweries		
2002	Miller (Milwaukee)	*MBA Weekly News Edition,* June 10, 2002. Purchased from Philip Morris by international brewer.
Standard-Rochester (Rochester, NY)		
1956	Merger of Standard and Rochester Brewing Companies	http://heritage575.tripod.com. Closed Standard plant.
1962	Haberle Congress (Syracuse)	Purchased brands only.
Stroh (Detroit)		
1964	Goebel (Detroit)	Purchased brands only.
1980	Schaefer (Brooklyn)	*BW,* July 12, 1982: 50
1982	Schlitz (Milwaukee)[a]	Aaker 1991. Justice Dept. required Stroh to sell Schlitz plant in Tampa.
1982	Pabst (Milwaukee)[a]	Elzinga 1986. Purchased St. Paul (Hamm/Olympia) plant but sold Tampa (Schlitz) plant to Pabst. Justice Dept. required Stroh to sell Schlitz plant.
1987	Pabst (Milwaukee)	*MBA,* March 14, 1988. Purchased Tampa (Schlitz) plant.
1988	Huber (Monroe, WI)	www.berghoffbeer.com/history.htm. Purchased Augsburger brand only.
1996	Heileman (La Crosse, WI)	*WSJ,* July 2, 1996
Van Merritt (Chicago)		
1958	Monarch (Chicago)	Purchased brands only.
1966	Oconto (Oconto, WI)	
Walter (Eau Claire, WI)		
1969	Bub (Winona, MN)	Robertson 1984. Purchased brands only.
1972	West Bend Lithia (West Bend, WI)	Robertson 1984. Purchased brands only.
1973	Rice Lake (Rice Lake, WI)	Robertson 1984. Purchased brands only.
Walter (Pueblo, CO)		
1954	Berghoff (Fort Wayne)	Purchased Berghoff brand. Falstaff purchased Berghoff plant.
1962	Metz (Omaha)	Purchased brands only.

Table 7.9
(continued)

Acquiring firm	Acquired firm	Sources and comments
Weber Waukesha (Waukesha, WI)		
1954	Burlington (formerly Wisconsin) (Burlington, WI)	
West End (Utica, NY)		
1959	Utica (Utica, NY)	Robertson 1978. Purchased brands only.
Yuengling (Pottsville, PA)		
1959	Lebanon (Lebanon, PA)	Purchased brands only.
1976	Mt. Carbon (Pottsville, PA)	Robertson 1984. Purchased brands only.
1999	Stroh (Detroit)	*MBA*, March 27, 2000. Purchased Tampa plant only.

a. Acquisition was challenged or investigated by U.S. Department of Justice for violation of antitrust laws.

Why all the mergers in brewing? If the profit motive is paramount, then one brewer will purchase another if the merger increases revenues or lowers costs sufficiently to raise expected profits.[33] A merger can raise revenues if it reduces competition. Since negotiating a merger is costly, however, firms involved in the merger may gain less from the merger than other remaining competitors, which reduces the market-power incentive to merge (Salant et al. 1983). Empirical evidence (Baker and Bresnahan 1985; Chalk 1988) suggests that mergers have had little effect on market power in the brewing industry.

A merger may also reduce the costs of production and marketing. For example, when multi-plant economies of scale exist and sunk costs are high, it may be cheaper to expand by purchasing a used plant than by building a new one. In addition, a merger between neighboring regional producers may expand the market for a successful brand and reduce advertising expenditures per unit. A merger can also promote efficiency if one firm owns an efficient plant but has considerable excess capacity and another firm has an inefficient plant but a successful brand. In this case, closing the inefficient plant and producing all successful brands in the efficient plant increases productivity. Efficiency gains from multi-plant operation and closure of inefficient plants appear to be the motive for many of Heileman's early acquisitions. In the 1960s and the 1970s, Heileman expanded its geographic base and brewing capacity by making market extension mergers. By the 1980s, the company marketed beer in all regions of the country and began acquiring successful brands and closing inefficient plants to reduce excess capacity.[34] This suggests that mergers in brewing may be motivated by efficiency reasons. According to Dewey (1961), mergers "are merely a civilized alternative to bankruptcy or the voluntary liquidation that transfers assets from failing to rising firms." Heileman's acquisitions appear to fit this scenario. Likewise, a merger could promote efficiency if the successful management team of one firm replaces the unsuccessful team of another firm (Manne 1965; Demsetz 1973). This appears to be the primary motivation for the Pabst-Blatz merger in 1958. According to a Pabst spokesperson, Pabst bought Blatz in order to replace its retiring president with James Windham, a former executive at Blatz (*Newsweek*, August 11, 1958; *Barrons*, March 16, 1959).

Tremblay and Tremblay (1988) formally test the Dewey hypothesis using data from the U.S. brewing industry from 1950–1983. They estimate a logit model of the probability that a firm will buy equipment and/or brands from another brewer, sell equipment and/or brands to another brewer, or neither buy nor sell. Two main results emerge from their study. First, the anti-trust laws have constrained the largest brewers from growing by merger. Second, successful brewers that are not constrained by anti-trust concerns buy failing ones, a result consistent with the Dewey hypothesis.

Evidence from more recent mergers in brewing continues to support the Dewey hypothesis. In the period 1984–2002, every major acquisition involved a failing firm.

Heileman purchased the brands of the C. Schmidt Brewing Company in 1987. Schmidt was failing badly in the mid 1980s, experiencing a 78 percent decline in production from 1984 to 1987. In 1996, Stroh purchased Heileman, which had filed for bankruptcy in 1991 (*New York Times*, January 25, 1991). A complex merger occurred in 1999, when Miller, Pabst, Yuengling, and Platinum Holdings purchased the failing Stroh Brewing Company. Miller purchased the Olde English 800 and Hamm's brands from Stroh. Miller also purchased the Tumwater plant and the Mickey's Malt Liquor and Henry Weinhard brands from Pabst. Pabst purchased all the remaining brands and the Lehigh Valley plant from Stroh. Yuengling purchased Stroh's Tampa plant. Platinum Holdings purchased the La Crosse (Heileman) plant, which later became the City Brewing Company. The remaining Stroh plants were closed. In each of these cases, a relatively successful firm purchased a declining firm.[35]

7.4 Exclusive Dealing Contracts

As is common in many industries, brewers have engaged in exclusive dealing contracts to attain a competitive advantage over rivals. In theory, it is unclear how such contracts will affect society. An exclusive dealing contract between a producer and its distributors can be efficient if it encourages distributors to maintain product quality and enables the producer to receive a return on general training provided to distributors. On the other hand, such a contract can be inefficient if it impedes competition.[36]

Several types of exclusive dealing contracts have been used in brewing. First, from 1967 to 1976 the major brewers offered illegal kickbacks to bars and restaurants in exchange for exclusively selling their brands. Subsequent government litigation appears to have eliminated such illegal contracts (*Advertising Age*, March 20, 1978; *Wall Street Journal*, November 2, 1978). Second, except where illegal by state law, all of the leading brewers hold contracts that specify exclusive territories for their distributors.[37] Third, all of the leading brewers have contracts with at least some of their distributors, requiring that the distributor market no other brewer's products. Anheuser-Busch has initiated a program that provides financial incentives to distributors that carry Anheuser-Busch products exclusively (*Modern Brewery Age Weekly News Edition*, June 10, 1996; *Beverage World*, September 1996; *Wall Street Journal*, October 2, 1997 and March 9, 1998; Sass 2001). Fourth, advertising contracts with network television have clauses that allow only one brewer to advertise on a particular program. In many cases, these contracts give the current advertiser the opportunity to renew the advertising agreement ahead of its competitors (*Sports Illustrated*, August 8, 1988: 76; *Wall Street Journal*, November 3, 1988). In 1978, for example, Miller purchased all of the available advertising time for major sporting events on network television (*Forbes*, August 7, 1978). Since 1989, Anheuser-Busch has purchased the right to be the exclusive beer advertiser on the television broadcast of the Super Bowl, a contract that cost the company about $20 million in 2002 (*St. Louis Post-Dispatch*, February 3, 2002).

The little empirical work that has been done has focused on the economic effects of exclusive dealing contracts between brewers and distributors. The fact that some states require and others prohibit exclusive territory contracts makes it possible to compare prices with and without such contracts. Culbertson and Bradford (1991) find that exclusive territory mandates increased beer prices by about 4 percent from 1985 to 1987, and Sass and Saurman (1993) find that they increased beer prices by about 7 percent from 1982 to 1987.[38] This raises concerns that an exclusive territory restriction harms consumers by reducing competition. Further analysis by Sass and Saurman (1993) indicates that such restrictions may benefit consumers, however, since they raise the promotional and quality control efforts of the distributor enough to offset the negative effect of higher prices. Regarding contracts that require a distributor to exclusively market a brewer's products, Sass (2004) concludes that they serve to reduce the incentive conflicts between brewers and distributors over issues of marketing and quality control. Foreclosure and reduced competition may become more pressing concerns, however—especially as the number of brewers and distribution outlets continue to fall.

7.5   Gimmicks and "Hail Mary" Strategies

Although most of the mass-producing brewers exited the market between 1950 and 2000, few exited quietly. Many have tried a variety of gimmicks and new strategies in an effort to survive. One of the most successful of these in the short run is the use of the devolution or harvest strategy (*Beverage World*, October 1982: 32; *Modern Brewery Age*, March 22, 1999: 28). As was discussed in chapter 4, with this strategy a firm buys the brands and often the facilities of a failing firm and severely cuts overhead costs and prices, harvesting all of the remaining value of its physical assets and product image or goodwill. In most cases, advertising is eliminated and the least efficient plants are shut down. With reduced costs and some loyal customers remaining for the failing brand, this strategy can earn a profit while physical assets depreciate and the brand's image and market share deteriorate. Paul Kalmanovitz of the S&P Company initiated this strategy in brewing when he purchased Falstaff, Pearl, Lucky, Ballantine, and Pabst. (See chapter 4.) After acquisition, he immediately made drastic cuts in marketing and overhead, and then consistently undercut competitors' prices (*Business Week*, October 16, 1989).[39] Heileman began a harvest strategy in the 1980s and the early 1990s but soon went bankrupt (*Beverage World*, January 1977: 29–31, 46–48; *New York Times*, January 25,

1991). Pabst may be the last brewer to use this strategy, as it milks the remaining goodwill from the formerly successful Pabst, Heileman, Schlitz, and Stroh labels. With the supply of failing firms drying up, this strategy is no longer viable in brewing. This undoubtedly explains the demise of Heileman and Stroh in the 1990s and the continued decline of Pabst today (*Modern Brewery Age*, March 25, 2002: 17).

An alternative response to market pressure is to try a gimmick or a "Hail Mary" strategy, as was discussed in chapter 6. The evidence shows that firms under the most financial stress are more likely to implement new and sometimes desperate strategies. In the words of Robert Weinberg (*Modern Brewery Age*, March 21, 1994: 39), "there seems to be an inverse relationship between having the means to take risks, and the willingness to take them."

Gimmick strategies abound in brewing. As was noted previously, declining firms often resort to blind taste test commercials to turn around a failing brand. In addition, failing firms repeatedly introduce provocative new products and brands in search of a hit. A notable example is "generic beer," first produced by the General Brewing Company in the early 1980s.[40] This brand was marketed in bottles and cans with big black letters on a plain white label that simply read BEER. The brand had no advertising budget, but it was sold for only $1.50 a six-pack at a time when a six-pack of Budweiser was sold for about $2.50. Generic beer was one of the top-selling beers in Seattle during the recession of the early 1980s, but it eventually faded from the market.[41] Another example is Olde Frothingslosh, marketed by the Pittsburgh Brewing Company in the late 1960s and the 1970s. Olde Frothingslosh's labels bore day-glow colors and a photograph of a 300-pound dancer.[42] Slogans for Olde Frothingslosh included "the pale stale ale," "so light the foam is on the bottom," and the "only brew you can find in the dark." Another extreme example is Nude Beer, a brand marketed by the Eastern Brewing Company in the 1980s (Robertson 1984: 59; Clark 2002). Each can had a piece of foil covering a portion of the label. The foil could be scratched off to reveal a picture of a nude woman. In 1977, the Falls City Brewing Co. and Billy Carter, brother of President Jimmy Carter, developed a brand called Billy Beer. With Billy Carter as spokesperson, Billy Beer was marketed nationally. In spite of its grand introduction, Billy Beer proved to be a fad.[43] Like most gimmicks, these new brands faded from the market once their novelty wore off.

7.6 Conclusion

Brewers commonly engage in strategic behavior. Mixed pricing, predatory pricing, preemptive advertising, merger, devolution, and "Hail
Mary" strategies have been used. These actions are consistent with
game theory, as they are rational responses to a war-of-attrition game.
Prices remained competitive for most of the war; however, with only
three macro brewers expected to survive, competitive pricing may be
at risk in the future.

8   Economic Performance

While performance is good, it is far from perfect.

—F. M. Scherer (1970: 400)

An assessment of the performance of an industry requires a comparison of industry outcomes with well-defined social objectives. Most industry studies identify efficiency and technological progress as important social goals, and many traditional studies include the importance of equity and social responsibility.[1] Markets for alcoholic beverages may bear a particularly heavy burden of responsibility, insofar as excessive alcohol consumption produces negative externalities. In this chapter, the industry's performance regarding equity, social responsibility, efficiency, and technological progress will be evaluated.

8.1   Equity and Socially Responsible Behavior in Brewing

This section evaluates whether or not U.S. brewers have behaved in an equitable and socially responsible manner. The main issues relevant to brewing include treating employees fairly and using responsible marketing practices. Although it is impossible to address these normative issues without value judgments, their importance to social welfare makes them impossible to ignore. There are many examples of behavior that was unacceptable by today's standards, but one must be careful to consider the norms and practices that were acceptable at the time in society at large (Ronnenberg 1998: 207). After all, it would be unfair to criticize a brewer for using a cartoon character in its beer advertising in the 1950s, as this was a socially accepted practice at the time.

The first issue that will be addressed here is the distribution of revenue between owners and workers. When all markets are perfectly

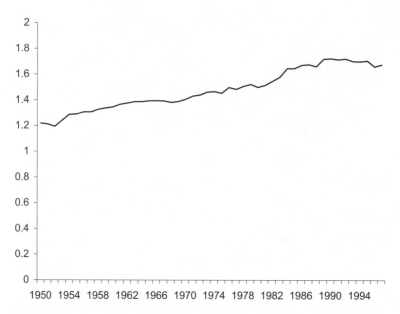

Figure 8.1
Ratio of wages in brewing to wages in U.S. manufacturing, 1950–1997. Source: See appendix A.

competitive and other regularity conditions hold, each factor of production is paid the value of its marginal product. This is a standard
benchmark in welfare economics, as it implies that each individual
receives the value of his or her marginal contribution to society (Mas-
Colell et al. 1995). But if brewers have market power, then they may
not offer fair wages to their employees. Profits remained low in brewing for most of the period 1950–2000, however, and real wages in
brewing have increased considerably since 1950. Figure 8.1 shows the
trend in the ratio of wages paid to workers in brewing relative to the
average wage paid to workers in U.S. manufacturing from 1950 to
1997. Wages in brewing exceeded wages in manufacturing as a whole,
and wages generally rose faster in brewing than in manufacturing,
especially from 1952 through 1989. The wage ratio flattened out during
the 1990s, but wages in brewing are still more than 60 percent above
the average in manufacturing. The bad news for labor is that overall
employment in brewing has fallen during this period. (See chapter 2.)
At least part of the decline is due to labor-saving technological changes
that led to the substitution of capital for labor.

Another important question in brewing is whether or not the industry promotes values and norms about alcohol consumption that are appropriate from society's perspective. One concern is that beer advertising has encouraged underage and excessive drinking. Cartoon characters, such as the Hamm's Bear of the 1950s and the 1960s, appeal to children as well as adults. In the early 1970s, Schaefer was criticized for promoting excessive drinking with the slogan "the one beer to have when you're having more than one" (*Marketing Communications*, January 1971). Although common in the past, this type of advertisement is forbidden by current advertising guidelines voluntarily adopted by the industry. (See chapter 9.)

The depiction of women as sex objects in beer commercials continues to be an issue of contention. Clark (2002: 29) reviews sexism in beer advertising from the late 1800s to 2000 and states that the marketing theme "Beer + Babes = Good Times" has "deep roots in our culture." Clark documents the use of artistic nudes and pin-ups in beer ads since the late 1800s. This is a continued marketing practice, since males between the ages of 21 and 34 are relatively heavy beer drinkers (*Beer Industry Update: A Review of Recent Developments* 2002). As was discussed in chapter 7, an extreme example is Nude Beer, marketed by the Eastern Brewing Company in the 1980s, which had a picture of a nude woman on each can.

Social change is underway to eliminate the "beer + babes" formula of marketing. For example, Stroh aired an advertisement with a "Swedish Bikini Team" (five women in blond wigs and bikinis) to market Old Milwaukee in 1991 (Ronnenberg 1998: 207). In response, a group of female employees filed a lawsuit against Stroh, claiming that the ads created a work environment that encouraged sexual harassment. Stroh responded by dropping the advertising campaign.

Clark concludes that continued social pressure has tempered the sexual imagery of beer advertising in the United States. New ads from three important brewers, Coors, Miller, and Boston, indicate otherwise, however (*Wall Street Journal*, November 6, 2002; *Advertising Age*, January 27, 2003; *Modern Brewery Age, Weekly News Edition*, February 3, 2003 and August 25, 2003).[2] Rance Crain, editor-in-chief of *Advertising Age*, has called Miller's "catfight ads" of 2002–03 "blatant sexism and exploitation of the female body" (*Modern Brewery Age, Weekly News Edition*, February 3, 2003: 3; *Advertising Age*, July 7, 2003). In addition, the leading specialty brewer, the Boston Beer Company, aired a "Sex for Sam" radio promotion of its Samuel Adams brand. The broadcasts offered to reward couples who engaged in sex in public with a free trip to a concert in Boston. Although company president James Koch formally apologized for the ads, marketing experts speculate that they were successful with many males in their twenties (*Advertising Age*, August 23, 2002 and September 3, 2002; *Modern Brewery Age Weekly News Edition*, September 9, 2002). In all fairness to brewers, Reichert (1999) notes that there has been a general increase in sexually oriented advertising in the United States overall. Thus, such ads are likely to continue as long as they are successful and remain legal.

Several of the leading brewers have also been accused of using offensive brand names and promoting high-alcohol products in minority communities. For example, in 1991 Heileman introduced PowerMaster, a high-alcohol malt liquor that was targeted at African-Americans in the Chicago area.[3] African-American leaders, the Surgeon General, and representatives of several anti-alcohol groups complained that the name PowerMaster promoted the high alcohol content of the product. As a result, the Bureau of Alcohol, Tobacco, and Firearms required that Heileman drop the PowerMaster name in late 1991. The debacle continued after Heileman renamed the product Crazy Horse Malt Liquor in 1992. Because Crazy Horse is another name for Tasunke Witko, the spiritual warrior and defender of the Lakota Sioux, some consumers objected to the use of that name for a malt liquor. In the late 1990s, Stroh, Heileman's new owner, agreed to stop using the name.[4]

Like many other U.S. industries, the brewing industry has exhibited ethnic, gender, age, and religious bias. Most of these events reflect the social norms and laws of the times. The following help-wanted ads, which appeared in *Brewers Technical Review* (July 1936: 40 and January 1944: 62, respectively), provide excellent historical examples:

WANTED
Young graduate chemist (gentile) for position in Chicago. Must have experience in regular brewing laboratory analyses. State age, nationality, education, experience in detail and salary desired. Good opportunity for right man. Write Box 275, The Brewers Technical Review, 965 Montana St. Chicago.

BREWING or CEREAL CHEMIST
Experienced in analysis of beer and brewing materials or cereal products for analytical and research work in well known commercial laboratory. State age, education, experience, nationality, draft status and salary desired. If possible, attach snapshot.

Of course these ads would be illegal under current law.[5]

Other examples illustrate more recent discrimination by brewers and their customers. In the early 1950s, racial tension flared at Falstaff after the company donated $500 to the National Association for the Advancement of Colored People (NAACP) and was granted lifetime membership in that organization (*Business Week*, December 17, 1955). The donation prompted many non-African-American Falstaff consumers to switch brands. In response, Falstaff denied responsibility for the donation, claiming that it had been made by a sales representative. A wave of protests ensued. Racial conflict also occurred in the early 1970s when minorities boycotted the Pittsburgh Brewing Company because of alleged racist hiring practices. After 11 months, the boycott ended when Pittsburgh agreed to hire more minority workers, but then white consumers boycotted Pittsburgh and hurt sales for many years.[6] Another example of racial strife centers around statements by William Coors, president of the Coors Brewing Company. Several sources indicate that William Coors made derogatory remarks about racial minorities, unions, and gay people, which led to a boycott of Coors beer in the late 1970s.[7] In 1993, there were allegations of racial harassment and discrimination at Miller's New York plant (*New York Times*, December 2, 1993).

Brewing has been a male-dominated industry. In general, women did not work in U.S. breweries until the labor shortages in World War II (Baron 1962: 335). The notable exception is Johanna Heileman, who was president of the Heileman Brewing Company from 1879 to 1917. According to Burgess (1993), the industry continued to be dominated by white males through the 1980s. The little evidence that exists supports this claim but also shows that the industry is becoming less male-dominated. Listings in *Brewers Digest, Buyer's Guide and Brewery Directory* (1972 and 2001) indicate that today's top four brewers (Anheuser-Busch, Coors, Miller, and Pabst) had no female executives in 1972. By 2001, however, about 18 percent of executives at Anheuser-Busch were women, 27 percent at Coors, 9 percent at Miller, and 11 percent at Pabst. These data indicate great progress but are still below the average for other U.S. industries, as the representation of women in all executive, administrative, and managerial positions was 20 percent in 1972 and 45 percent in 1999 (Blau et al. 2001). These data do not prove discrimination, however, since there may be fewer women interested in working in the brewing industry.

To the extent that employment discrimination exists in brewing, it will lead to x-inefficiency, a form of inefficiency that is more likely to occur in monopolistic and imperfectly competitive markets (Leibenstein 1966).[8] Because firms that behave in a biased way will face higher costs than non-discriminatory rivals, they will fail in the long run if the market is sufficiently competitive. Therefore, this form of inefficiency is most likely to occur in less competitive markets where economic profits are positive. In view of the relative competitiveness of brewing, the level of x-inefficiency is unlikely to be high. This may be less true in the future, however, as non-competitive behavior becomes more likely as concentration continues to rise. Efficiency will be discussed further in section 8.3.

8.2   Technological Change

The evidence reported in chapter 2 reveals considerable technological change in the post-World War II brewing industry. The question to ask is whether or not the industry has reached its innovation potential. One issue is that most of the technological advances in brewing originated from outside the industry.[9] For example, the brewing industry benefited from the development of faster canning lines by the canning industry, more effective foam and beer stabilizers by the chemical industry, and faster pumps and larger kettles by the steel fabrication industry.

The primary contributions from U.S. brewing are the development of new products like malt liquor and light beer, innovations that involved creativity but little research and development effort. Industry income statements published by the U.S. Treasury Department (Internal Revenue Service, Source Book) show no R&D expenditures for brewing. Even the industry leader, Anheuser-Busch, states that it "does not consider to be material the dollar amounts expended on research activities. . . . In addition, the company does not consider the number of employees engaged full time in such research activities to be material." (Certo and Peter 1993: 522) With the wide variety of beer brands and new products in brewing today, especially those developed by the craft brewers, the one area where the industry appears to be highly creative is in new brand and product development.

8.3   Efficiency in Production and Marketing

The notion of efficiency applies to the areas of exchange, production, and marketing and can be evaluated for the economy as a whole, a single industry, or a particular firm. Firm production is economically efficient, for example, when a certain level of output is produced at lowest cost. Even if every firm produces at lowest cost, however, a market may be allocatively inefficient if too much or too little output is produced from society's perspective. Ignoring for the moment the problems associated with externalities, allocative efficiency occurs when price equals long-run marginal cost in every market.[10] Under perfect competition this condition is met, as it ensures the maximization of consumer and producer surplus in every market.

Chapters 2, 3, and 7 discuss the previous work on the degree of efficiency at the firm level in brewing. The literature indicates that brewers operate with a high degree of technical efficiency but not scale efficiency. That is, many brewers became inefficiently small as changes in technology increased minimum efficient scale. Today, only the three industry leaders have sufficient size to reach scale efficiency. On the marketing side, the evidence shows that national brewers, especially the two largest firms, have had a marketing advantage over smaller regional brewers. The ability to attain scale efficiency and to market beer effectively explains the relative success of Anheuser-Busch, Miller, and Coors. Since these topics are discussed in previous chapters, this section turns to issues of profitability and allocative efficiency at the industry level.

An output market is allocatively efficient when the market price (P) equals the long-run marginal cost (MC) and is, therefore, associated with competitive markets. Firms with market power may restrict output and raise prices above marginal cost in order to increase profits. This is allocatively inefficient because it causes the social value of consuming an additional unit to exceed the social cost of producing and selling it. A common measure of monopoly power or the allocative inefficiency associated with a monopoly is the Lerner (1934) index (L):

$$L = \frac{P - \text{MC}}{P} = \frac{1}{\eta}, \tag{8.1}$$

where η is the absolute value of the price elasticity of demand. The value of L can range from 0 to 1 and equals 0 when the market operates efficiently (i.e., $P = \text{MC}$). With exerted market power, price exceeds marginal cost and L is greater than 0. The Lerner index is difficult to calculate, however, since marginal cost is generally unobservable. The one exception is when marginal cost equals average cost (AC). In this case, the Lerner index equals the price-cost margin,

$(P - AC)/P$, as well as the profit-to-sales ratio. That is, when marginal and average costs are equal the price-cost margin can be rewritten as

$$[(P - AC)Q]/PQ = \pi/TR,$$

where Q is total output, π is total profit, and TR is total revenue or sales. In this case, the profit-to-sales ratio will be positive when firms exercise market power.[11] Other common measures of profitability include the rate of return on stockholder equity and the rate of return on the value of assets.[12]

Several game-theoretic models of oligopoly predict that market power and industry profits will increase as the number of competitors declines or as industry concentration rises.[13] An early method for describing this outcome makes use of "conjectural variations."[14] To illustrate, consider a static market with n symmetric firms that produce homogeneous goods. The goal of each firm is to maximize profit with respect to output, q_i. Firm i's profit (π_i) is

$$\pi_i = P(Q)q_i - C(q_i), \tag{8.2}$$

where $P(Q)$ is the inverse market demand function, Q is the aggregate output of all firms in the industry, q_i is the output of firm i, and $C(q_i)$ is the firm's long-run total cost function. The firm's first-order condition of profit maximization is

$$\frac{\partial \pi}{\partial q_i} = P(Q) + q_i \left(\frac{\partial P}{\partial Q} \frac{\partial Q}{\partial q_i} \right) - \frac{\partial C}{\partial q_i} = 0. \tag{8.3}$$

Rearranging terms and abbreviating $P(Q)$ to P yields

$$\frac{P - MC}{P} = -\frac{q_i}{P} \frac{\partial P}{\partial Q} \Theta, \tag{8.4}$$

where $MC = \partial C / \partial q_i$, $\Theta = \partial Q / \partial q_i = 1 + \partial Q_{-i} / \partial q_i$, and Q_{-i} is the output of all firms except firm i (i.e., firm i's rivals' output). The conjectural variation is defined as $\partial Q_i / \partial q_i$. With symmetry, each firm will produce the same output in equilibrium and q_i/Q will equal $1/n$. As a result, the Lerner index in an oligopoly setting can be written as

$$L = \frac{P - MC}{P} = \frac{\Theta}{n\eta}. \tag{8.5}$$

Recall from chapter 3 that $HHI = 1/n$ when firms are symmetric. Thus, L also equals $(\Theta HHI)/\eta$.

Equation 8.5 generalizes the Lerner index for an imperfectly competitive market with n firms. When Θ and η are positive constants, market power decreases with the number of firms or as HHI falls. That is, an increase in industry concentration leads to less competitive pricing and more severe allocative inefficiency. Equation 8.5 identifies the value of L that corresponds to several important models of imperfect competition. In a monopoly setting, $\Theta = n = 1$ and $L = 1/\eta$, the standard Lerner index of monopoly power. With more than one firm, $\Theta = n$ with cartel behavior and again $L = 1/\eta$. In a Cournot setting, $\Theta = 1$ and $L = 1/(n\eta)$. In a Bertrand or competitive setting, $\Theta = 0$ and the market is allocatively efficient.[15] Thus, Θ should range from 0 to n, with a higher value representing greater market power and allocative inefficiency. For this reason, Θ is referred to as an index of market power.

Chapter 3 documents the pronounced decline in the number of brewers and the substantial increase in industry concentration from 1950 through 2000. In spite of this structural change, profit rates (shown in figure 3.6) fell between 1950 and 1989. Figure 8.2 compares the profit-to-sales ratios for brewing and all manufacturing and shows

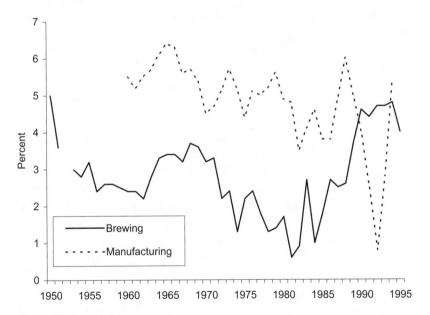

Figure 8.2
Profit-to-sales ratio in brewing and in U.S. manufacturing, 1950–1995. Source: See appendix A.

that profitability in manufacturing exceeded that of brewing through the late 1980s. Low profits coincide with the beer wars that resulted from the technologically induced overabundance of brewers. Competition in price, new product introductions, and advertising raged during this period.

Tremblay and Tremblay (1995) confirm that there was little market power in brewing through the 1980s. Using firm-level data from 1950–1988, they estimate a supply relation, a modified version of equation 8.3 above. They reject the hypothesis that beer companies are price-takers but find that the degree of exerted market power in brewing is low. Specifically, their estimates indicate that the index of market power (Θ) is close to 0, at 0.08. Thus, the market was imperfectly competitive, but the degree of competition was relatively strong.[16]

In the 1990s, however, the profit rates for the industry overall and for the industry leaders increased (*Modern Brewery Age Weekly News Edition*, November 4, 2002). Perhaps the mass exit of firms unable to attain scale economies has come to an end, as the four largest brewers account for about 95 percent of all domestic beer sales. With Pabst rapidly losing sales, there may not be enough viable competitors in brewing to support a reasonably competitive market. New empirical estimates of market power for the 1990s will be discussed at the end of this chapter.

In view of the high degree of firm heterogeneity in brewing, it may be worthwhile to review the performance of individual brewers. Profit rates may differ by firm and over time owing to changes in market power and to differences in production and marketing efficiency. Figure 8.3 begins by plotting the profit-to-sales ratios for the industry and for today's leading brewers (Anheuser-Busch, Coors, Miller, and Pabst). Consistent with the image of industry leader, Anheuser-Busch earned a profit rate well above the industry average for the entire period. Miller earned above-average profits in every year since 1977, the first year data were available. Miller's profit data may be suspect, however, as it is difficult to separate Miller's overhead costs from those of its then parent company, Philip Morris.

Coors experienced exceptional profitability in the 1970s when the Coors brand was popular in spite of meager advertising support. The firm's competitive advantage began to erode in the late 1970s, however, because of extensive marketing efforts by Anheuser-Busch and Miller and a boycott of Coors. Company profits declined rapidly into the 1980s, as the company stepped up its advertising spending (see

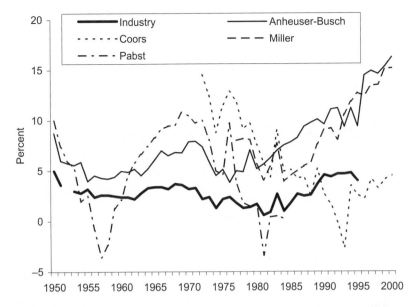

Figure 8.3
Profit-to-sales ratios for the U.S. brewing industry and for leading brewers, 1950–2000.
Source: See appendix A.

figure 7.4) and began a campaign to market Coors beer nationally. One problem with the strategy to go national was that Coors brewed all of its beer in its lone brewery in Golden, Colorado. Consequently, Coors faced higher shipping costs than its competitors, as all other national brewers operated multiple plants. In the late 1980s, Coors began shipping dehydrated beer from Colorado to its second plant in Virginia, where it was rehydrated and packaged. This reduced costs; however, it created an image and marketing problem for Coors, which could no longer claim that its beer was brewed with Rocky Mountain water. Profits continued to fall until the company began cost-cutting efforts in 1993. Since then, Coors's profit rates have approached the industry average.

Pabst, the industry leader in 1949, was successful in the early 1950s. Profits plummeted in the late 1950s, when Pabst experienced management and financial difficulties. In 1958, Pabst merged with Blatz and hired a new president, James C. Windham. Profits rebounded until the 1970s. The company had repositioned its Blue Ribbon brand from the premium to the popular-priced category in the early 1960s, just when consumers began to switch from popular-priced to premium brands.

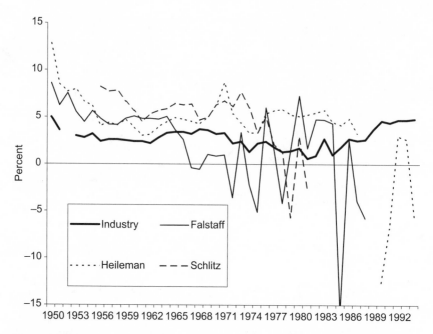

Figure 8.4
Profit-to-sales ratios for the U.S. brewing industry and for a sample of failing brewers,
1950–1994. Source: See appendix A.

This and stiff competition from Anheuser-Busch and Miller caused
profits to fall dramatically by the mid 1970s. At that time, Pabst
became a target of a hostile takeover which plagued the brewer into the
1980s. Part of the company's assets were finally acquired by Heileman
in 1982, and the remaining brands and assets were purchased by the
S&P Company in 1986.

One other brewer attained national status but eventually failed:
Schlitz. A series of management blunders tarnished the company's
image and led to the fall of Schlitz. (See chapter 4.) Most other firms
were regional or local brewers, were inefficiently small, and marketed
heartier beers at popular prices at a time when consumers were shift-
ing to lighter brands with a premium image. (See chapters 2 and 6.)
Since brewing capacity cannot be adjusted quickly, falling demand
creates excess capacity and a rise in the average cost of production for
the typical regional brewer. To remain viable, many cut their prices
and advertising spending, a strategy that eventually led to further erosion of the image of their brands and falling profits. Figure 8.4 depicts
the profit rates of three leading regional brewers just before each was

Table 8.1
Profit per barrel (1982 dollars) of failing firms in each of the five years preceding the firm's exit from the industry. The averages are calculated for firms that have data for all five years preceding failure.

	Year				
	5	4	3	2	1
Associated (1967–1971)	0.48	0.64	1.44	−12.05	—
Burgermeister (1956–1960)	5.33	3.48	3.36	3.19	—
Carling (1974–1978)	−1.66	−0.30	−2.11	1.90	−3.40
Drewerys (1960–1964)	3.46	2.47	0.64	0.49	1.00
Falstaff (1970–1974)	0.65	0.75	−2.47	1.78	−1.16
Goebel (1958–1962)	3.39	3.29	3.29	3.30	3.29
Grain Belt (1970–1974)	1.87	2.08	0.08	0.94	−0.27
Heileman (1991–1995)	−4.59	2.04	1.82	−4.39	—
Lone Star (1971–1975)	7.25	6.77	4.27	3.48	3.33
Lucky (1968–1972)	−4.13	0.03	0.29	—	—
Meister Brau (1967–1971)	−0.03	1.03	0.22	−3.75	—
Olympia (1977–1981)	0.66	1.19	1.51	0.48	−0.21
Schaefer (1975–1979)	−9.13	0.40	0.16	−21.87	−1.54
Schlitz (1977–1981)	1.31	0.76	−3.07	1.61	−1.40
Average	0.83	1.81	0.37	−0.73	−1.24

purchased by another brewer: Falstaff (purchased in 1975), Schlitz (1982), and Heileman (1996). The data reveal that their profits began to vacillate and drop below the industry average several years before being purchased by another brewer. Table 8.1 documents the accounting profits per barrel of 14 failing firms during each of the five years preceding the company's departure from the industry. Their average profit rates were well below the industry average of $2.90 (in 1982 dollars, 1950–1995). As firms approached the end, profit rates diminished and turned to losses 2 years before exit.

Market share and capacity data are available for a larger sample of 42 firms. Tables 8.2 and 8.3 record trends in the market share and capacity utilization rates [(Production/Capacity) × 100] before exiting the industry. The data support the view that failing firms generally experienced a drop in market share and an increase in excess capacity before exiting the market.[17] The average failing firm used less than 70 percent of capacity in each of the four years before exit and less than 60 percent the year immediately preceding exit.[18] These numbers are well below the averages for Anheuser-Busch, at 90 percent, and the industry

Table 8.2
Market shares of failing firms (in percent) in each of the five years preceding the firm's exit from the industry. The averages are calculated for firms that have data for all five years preceding failure.

	Year				
	5	4	3	2	1
Acme (1949–1953)	0.76	0.67	0.58	0.49	0.45
Associated (1967–1971)	3.85	3.46	3.33	3.00	1.95
Ballantine (1967–1971)	3.42	2.03	1.85	1.78	1.72
Blatz (1954–1958)	1.15	1.07	1.11	1.46	2.00
Blitz-Weinhard (1974–1978)	0.52	0.53	0.47	0.37	0.35
Burgermeister (1956–1960)	1.20	1.14	1.14	1.10	1.01
Carling (1974–1978)	2.56	3.28	2.93	2.73	2.08
Champale (1981–1985)	0.23	0.18	0.18	0.17	0.13
Drewerys (1960–1964)	1.82	1.84	2.21	2.75	2.62
Duquesne (1960–1964)	0.60	0.56	0.56	0.50	0.51
Evansville (1992–1996)	0.12	0.10	0.22	0.23	0.24
Falls City (1974–1978)	0.40	0.39	0.38	0.29	0.22
Falstaff (1970–1974)	4.33	3.96	4.62	4.28	3.93
Fort Pitt (1951–1955)	0.92	0.56	0.60	0.49	0.44
Goebel (1958–1962)	0.69	0.61	0.44	0.34	0.29
Grain Belt (1970–1974)	1.01	0.75	0.79	0.78	0.64
Griesedieck Bros. (1952–1956)	0.96	0.89	0.76	0.55	0.42
Griesedieck W. (1949–1953)	1.68	1.72	1.67	1.65	1.69
Gunther (1955–1959)	0.93	0.93	0.79	0.85	—
Hamm (1970–1974)	3.14	2.92	2.94	2.35	1.97
Harvard (1951–1955)	0.33	0.32	0.29	0.23	0.21
Heileman (1991–1995)	5.05	4.95	4.84	4.49	4.16
Hudepohl (1981–1985)	0.20	0.20	0.19	0.18	0.16
Jackson (1969–1973)	0.77	0.68	0.62	0.54	0.45
Koch (1980–1984)	0.04	0.04	0.04	0.03	0.03
Krueger (1956–1960)	0.68	0.65	0.67	0.59	0.47
Lone Star (1971–1975)	0.81	0.80	0.76	0.65	0.65
Lucky (1968–1972)	1.16	0.95	0.81	0.81	1.02
Meister Brau (1967–1971)	0.82	0.78	0.86	1.21	1.23
Narragansett (1960–1964)	1.01	1.21	1.26	1.30	1.27
National (1970–1974)	1.77	1.70	1.61	1.56	1.43
Olympia (1977–1981)	4.29	4.03	3.53	3.45	3.18
Ortlieb (1976–1980)	0.15	0.21	0.22	0.16	0.12
Pearl (1973–1977)	1.15	1.09	0.93	0.87	0.73
Piel (1957–1961)	1.69	1.67	1.71	1.67	1.51
Rainier (1972–1976)	0.62	0.60	0.59	0.59	0.61

Table 8.2
(continued)

	Year				
	5	4	3	2	1
Rheingold (1972–1976)	2.38	2.06	1.34	1.14	0.93
Ruppert (1960–1964)	1.47	1.34	1.31	1.34	1.48
Schaefer (1975–1979)	1.93	1.77	1.38	1.09	0.94
Schlitz (1977–1981)	13.90	11.84	9.84	8.47	7.98
Schmidt (1982–1986)	1.62	1.50	1.23	1.01	0.88
Stegmaier (1970–1974)	0.28	0.27	0.22	0.22	0.14
Stroh (1994–1998)	6.40	5.88	9.28	8.04	7.48
Average	1.85	1.69	1.67	1.55	1.42

as a whole, at 80 percent, for the years 1950–2000. In addition, these rates signal serious financial stress as a brewer requires a capacity utilization rate in excess of 50–65 percent to earn positive accounting profits.[19]

The few regional brewers that survive fill small but profitable niches. Most continue to produce their flagship brands, several produce craft beer under contract with a specialty brewer, and most market their own versions of craft beer. For example, Dixie added Voodoo Ale, Genesee (now High Falls Brewery) added Dundee's full-bodied lagers and dark beers, Schell added several all-malt lagers and dark beers, and Yuengling added full-bodied lagers, ales, and porters. F. X. Matt (formerly West End) took this strategy to the limit by repositioning itself as a craft brewer of its Saranac brands in 1990.

Available data indicate wide and persistent differences in profit rates among brewers. In general, the national producers have earned higher average profit rates than regional brewers (Tremblay 1993a). The evidence presented above suggests that their competitive advantage is due in part to size, which enables them to take advantage of scale economies and to make effective use of national television advertising. The national brewers also offer and promote premium brands that have grown in popularity.

The theory of "strategic groups" provides another possible explanation for a persistent difference in profit rates among groups of firms within an industry (Caves and Porter 1977; Porter 1980, 1985; Oster 1999; Ghemawat 2001). According to this theory, profit rate differences among firms can persist in the long run if barriers to entry vary for

Table 8.3
Capacity utilization rates (defined as production divided by capacity times 100) of failing firms in each of the five years preceding the firm's exit from the industry. The averages are calculated for firms that have data for all five years preceding failure.

	Year				
	5	4	3	2	1
Acme (1949–1953)	86.93	74.80	65.87	56.53	53.07
Associated (1967–1971)	68.37	64.21	64.57	60.83	41.14
Ballantine (1967–1971)	74.62	46.30	44.00	44.40	44.60
Blatz (1954–1958)	39.00	36.60	37.96	49.88	68.00
Blitz-Weinhard (1974–1978)	95.50	100.4	88.75	74.63	72.88
Burgermeister (1956–1960)	79.38	74.92	74.77	74.92	68.54
Carling (1974–1978)	91.08	118.9	72.50	79.69	63.12
Champale (1981–1985)	42.00	32.00	33.00	31.00	24.00
Drewerys (1960–1964)	89.56	82.55	90.60	92.93	93.21
Duquesne (1960–1964)	45.67	44.53	46.67	43.00	45.20
Evansville (1992–1996)	18.33	15.00	34.17	35.00	36.67
Falls City (1974–1978)	73.75	73.13	72.75	58.13	46.50
Falstaff (1970–1974)	71.81	68.47	82.24	80.11	77.33
Fort Pitt (1951–1955)	112.0	68.57	75.14	59.43	53.57
Goebel (1958–1962)	45.32	41.55	39.33	30.35	26.37
Grain Belt (1970–1974)	78.88	60.94	65.63	100.0	86.36
Griesedieck Bros. (1952–1956)	91.67	86.44	71.56	52.22	40.00
Griesedieck W. (1949–1953)	143.6	144.2	76.65	74.95	74.15
Gunther (1955–1959)	80.00	80.00	67.30	72.00	—
Hamm (1970–1974)	83.96	81.51	84.45	70.90	64.44
Harvard (1951–1955)	69.50	69.00	63.50	49.25	45.75
Heileman (1991–1995)	72.69	70.80	69.30	83.15	76.30
Hudepohl (1981–1985)	35.00	36.00	34.00	31.50	28.00
Jackson (1969–1973)	68.30	62.96	59.63	53.33	46.59
Koch (1980–1984)	60.95	71.43	66.67	57.14	78.57
Krueger (1956–1960)	58.40	55.00	56.70	52.50	51.88
Lone Star (1971–1975)	69.67	71.20	71.07	64.00	65.53
Lucky (1968–1972)	103.3	88.67	80.00	81.07	97.13
Meister Brau (1967–1971)	112.1	74.17	75.56	65.17	68.09
Narragansett (1960–1964)	74.50	75.24	80.07	84.55	84.27
National (1970–1974)	76.46	76.46	74.79	76.25	90.64
Olympia (1977–1981)	80.36	78.38	70.93	71.66	67.16
Ortlieb (1976–1980)	38.33	55.00	60.00	46.67	35.00
Pearl (1973–1977)	54.80	61.54	53.85	50.69	68.82
Piel (1957–1961)	65.23	64.55	68.68	67.32	61.82
Rainier (1972–1976)	82.50	83.80	87.60	88.70	92.70

Table 8.3
(continued)

	Year				
	5	4	3	2	1
Rheingold (1972–1976)	60.50	55.03	37.62	52.12	42.73
Ruppert (1960–1964)	52.00	48.00	48.36	50.76	58.80
Schaefer (1975–1979)	81.92	76.27	61.86	45.00	40.00
Schlitz (1977–1981)	76.31	61.96	53.18	58.41	55.88
Schmidt (1982–1986)	81.92	76.27	61.86	45.00	40.00
Stegmaier (1970–1974)	44.25	43.13	37.50	38.75	26.00
Stroh (1994–1998)	62.37	56.74	77.66	66.68	61.80
Average	71.73	67.30	63.59	60.66	58.63

different groups within an industry. Work by Tremblay (1985b, 1993a) supports the hypothesis that the national brewers have a marketing advantage, which may explain why they earn a higher profit rate than regional brewers.[20] A simple national/regional distinction is less relevant today, however, as Schlitz (once a leading national brewer) has exited the market, Coors has successfully moved from the regional to the national group, few traditional regional brewers remain, and a new group of domestic specialty brewers have entered the market. Since most specialty brewers are privately owned, further research into their financial success is limited by a lack of data. Frequent entry and exit is expected in the specialty and import groups, but entry into the national and regional groups is unlikely in view of the high sunk costs and scale economies associated with entry at this level.

An alternative explanation derives from Demsetz (1973), who argues that firms with superior production and marketing programs will be more profitable, grow in size, and displace less successful firms. The process of competition for supremacy would be especially important in brewing as only a few firms will be able to ultimately reach scale and marketing efficiency. Consistent with this viewpoint is Anheuser-Busch, the dominant firm in the industry with superior production facilities and a successful marketing program. Anheuser-Busch gained a production advantage by producing beer in eleven large, low-cost breweries that are strategically located to minimize transportation costs. It was also the first brewer to market popular, premium, and super-premium brands and to conduct extensive marketing research in order to improve its marketing efficiency. Miller's success during the

1970s is attributed to brand proliferation and heightened advertising spending, strategies employed successfully by its parent company, Philip Morris, in the cigarette market. Success at Coors in the 1970s derives partially from mystique, but Coors was also the first brewer to market a lighter beer, Coors Banquet. Previous evidence about the failing brewers also supports Demsetz's position, since many were not only inefficiently small but were unresponsive to consumer demand for lighter beer. Thus, individual firm effects also played a role in the evolution of the U.S. brewing industry.[21]

The recent rise in industry profits may be due to survival of the most efficient firms as well as diminished competition at the end of the attrition war. One would expect low industry profits during the beer wars as firms battle for survival. Until the least successful firms exit the industry, they will drag down industry profit rates. Once the industry reaches equilibrium, profits would be higher since the least efficient brewers are gone. With a handful of competitors remaining, positive economic profits may persist.

In summary, high concentration in the U.S. brewing industry had little effect on allocative efficiency from 1950 through 1989. During this period, the Lerner index was low and industry profits fell below those of the manufacturing sector as a whole. Changes in technology and marketing opportunities forced brewers into an attrition war. High costs and tough competition held profit rates down from 1950 through 1989, since most brewers were too small to reach scale efficiency. Industry profits began to rise in the 1990s. New market-power estimates for this period will be discussed at the end of the chapter.

8.4 Externalities and Beer Consumption

Externalities also play an important role in assessing the economic performance of alcoholic beverage industries. An externality exists when the action of one economic agent affects the welfare of others but without compensation (Mas-Colell 1995). Externalities are present and generate inefficiencies when private costs differ from social costs and/or private benefits differ from social benefits. Social costs (benefits) are defined as private costs (benefits) plus any additional or external costs incurred by others. Negative (positive) externalities exist when one party imposes uncompensated costs (benefits) on others. Alcoholic beverage consumption can generate both positive and negative externalities.

The negative externalities associated with alcohol consumption are well documented. For example, alcohol abuse can increase the risk of developing cirrhosis of the liver, cardiovascular problems, and certain forms of cancer.[22] Alcohol is also a factor in about 41 percent of all fatal motor vehicle crashes, and about 31 percent of those alcohol-related deaths involve people other than the intoxicated driver.[23] Furthermore, an increase in alcohol consumption and abuse correlates with a general increase in sexually transmitted diseases, violent crimes, and a deterioration in the academic performance of college students (Phelps 1997; Markowitz and Grossman 1998; Chesson et al. 2000; Wolaver 2002).[24]

Harwood et al. (1998) and Harwood (2000) provide the most recent estimates of the costs of alcohol abuse in the United States. These costs are divided into three categories: medical, productivity, and other (motor vehicle crashes, crime, and fire) costs. Unfortunately, their cost estimates include private as well as external costs and are calculated for total alcohol consumption (i.e., beer, wine, and spirits).

To identify the purely external cost of beer consumption in the United States, several assumptions are made. First, because ethanol consumption is the direct source of the externality, the proportion of costs attributed to beer is assumed to equal 58 percent, the fraction of all U.S. ethanol consumed in the form of beer in the 1990s (*Beer Industry Update: A Review of the Evidence* 2000). The next step is to determine the proportion of costs that are truly external to the beer drinker. Regarding the external medical costs associated with alcohol consumption, the estimate by Levitt et al. (1994) that 44 percent of all health-care expenditures in the United States are paid by federal, state, and local governments is adopted. The productivity adjustment is assumed to equal 25 percent, the estimated fraction of lost productivity from alcohol-induced premature deaths that is external to the drinker (Phelps 1997). The external cost from the "other" category is assumed to be 38.5 percent, since this is the percent of people killed in alcohol-related car accidents other than the alcohol-abusing driver.

Estimates of the total external cost and the external cost per six-pack of 12-ounce containers of beer are listed in table 8.4. The estimated external cost of beer consumption per six-pack is substantial, ranging from $2.73 for 1992 to $3.49 for 1998. These estimates are in line with estimates from other studies: $1.74 (Pogue and Sgontz 1989), $4.67 (Miller and Blincoe 1994), and $3.63 (Kenkel 1996).[25]

Although alcohol consumption produces large social costs, there is growing evidence that moderate consumption of alcoholic beverages

Table 8.4
Estimates of external cost of beer consumption in the U.S. Total cost (Total) is measured in billions of dollars. Cost per six-pack (Six-pack) is for 12-ounce containers and is measured in dollars. The sum of the cost components in each column may differ slightly from total cost figures due to rounding errors. Sources: Harwood et al. (1998) and Harwood (2000) provide estimates of the total cost of alcohol abuse. The cost associated with beer is total costs multiplied by 0.58, the proportion of ethanol consumed in the form of beer (*Beer Industry Update: A Review of Recent Developments*, 2001). The external health care costs are then multiplied by 0.44, the fraction of health-care costs incurred by federal, state, and local governments (Levitt et al. 1994). Productivity losses due to death and illness are multiplied by 0.25, the proportion of losses from premature death that are external to the alcohol abuser (Phelps 1997). The other category includes the cost of automobile crashes and fires due to alcohol abuse. These figures are multiplied by 0.385, the ratio of others (those other than the alcohol abusing driver) to all people killed in alcohol related accidents in 2000 (National Highway Traffic Safety Administration 2000).

	1992		1995		1998	
	Total	Six-pack	Total	Six-pack	Total	Six-pack
Health-care costs	$4.8	$0.46	$5.7	$0.56	$6.7	$0.65
Lost productivity						
Death, illness	$14.6	$1.41	$16.3	$1.58	$18.0	$1.75
Crime	$3.8	$0.37	$4.2	$0.41	$5.9	$0.57
Other impacts	$5.0	$0.48	$5.5	$0.54	$5.3	$0.52
Total costs	$28.1	$2.73	$31.7	$3.08	$36.0	$3.49

generates positive externalities.[26] Recent evidence indicates that moderate beer drinkers have a lower incidence of cardiovascular disease, strokes, hypertension, cataracts, and arteriosclerosis.[27] These results should be interpreted with caution, however, since it is still not clear if beer is the direct cause of these health benefits or if moderate beer drinkers are generally healthier by nature or by choice of lifestyle than others. Another issue is the lack of reliable estimates of the possible monetary value of the health benefits from moderate beer or alcohol consumption. The possible benefits could be important, however, since the total cost of cardiovascular disease alone was about $286.5 billion in 1999.[28] If, for example, an increase in moderate beer consumption reduces cardiovascular medical costs by 10 percent (and assuming that 44 percent of the health-care savings are external), the external benefits would be $12.6 billion. With this single added benefit, the estimated range of the net external cost of beer consumption would be $1.52–$2.28 per six-pack ($0.45–$0.67 per ounce of absolute alcohol). Even with benefits of this magnitude, the net external cost of beer consumption still exceeds the (federal and average state) excise tax rate of $0.47

per six-pack. This suggests that beer taxes are too low and that beer consumption is too high from society's perspective, issues that will be addressed further in chapter 9.

8.5   Advertising and Social Welfare

U.S. brewers spend a great deal of money on advertising each year (more than \$1 billion in 2002), yet the evidence from chapter 2 indicates that advertising has little or no effect on market demand. Firms advertise to battle for market share, but intense advertising competition may eat away firm and industry profits. The opportunity cost associated with the sheer amount of advertising spending along with socially undesirable advertising themes, particularly those targeted at young people, brings into question the social value of beer advertising.

The social desirability of advertising is mired in controversy. Ignoring the externality issue for the moment, Dixit and Norman (1978) show that advertising will be socially excessive if it changes consumers' tastes and leads to higher market prices. Advertising may be socially optimal or undersupplied, however, if advertising does not alter tastes, if advertising supports television and radio programming, if the price is regulated, or if advertising lowers consumer search costs.[29]

To analyze the social welfare effect of advertising, consider a general model in the spirit of Becker and Murphy 1993. The model extends the Becker-Murphy framework by expanding the number of firms from 1 to n and admitting negative as well as positive externalities.[30] Assume social welfare (SW) is a function of the money value of consumer surplus (V), producer surplus (Π), and other effects that are external to the industry (E). The social welfare function can then be written as

$$SW = V(A, P) + \Pi(A, P) + E(A, P), \tag{8.6}$$

where A is the industry level of advertising and P is the price of output. Assuming SW is twice continuously differentiable and concave, one can determine whether advertising raises or lowers welfare by totally differentiating equation 8.6 with respect to A.

$$\frac{dSW}{dA} = \frac{\partial V}{\partial A} + \frac{\partial V}{\partial P}\frac{\partial P}{\partial A} + \frac{d\Pi}{dA} + \frac{dE}{dA}. \tag{8.7}$$

Note that dE/dA is the change in the equilibrium level of externalities associated with a change in A; if advertising increases consumption

and the increased consumption generates additional negative externalities, then $dE/dA < 0$. The term $d\Pi/dA$ is the change in the equilibrium
level of industry profits with respect to a change in advertising.

The Dixit-Norman (1978) and Becker-Murphy (1993) specifications
are special cases of equation 8.7. The simple version of the Dixit-
Norman model assumes a profit-maximizing monopolist, advertising
that changes tastes, and no externalities. The monopolist's first-order
condition of profit maximization requires that $d\Pi/dA = 0$. With no
externalities, $dE/dA = 0$. When advertising changes tastes, Dixit and
Norman argue that the resulting increase in consumer surplus gen-
erates no real value to society, implying that $\partial V/\partial A = 0$. In this limiting case, equation 8.7 becomes

$$\frac{d\text{SW}}{dA} = \frac{\partial V}{\partial P}\frac{\partial P}{\partial A}. \tag{8.8}$$

If the commodity is an economic good (i.e., $\partial V/\partial P < 0$), the socially
optimal amount of advertising is supplied when a marginal change in
advertising has no effect on the equilibrium price (i.e., social welfare is
maximized when $d\text{SW}/dA = 0$). Advertising that increases the market
price lowers social welfare. When advertising does not change tastes
but subsidizes programming, as Becker and Murphy claim, then
$\partial V/\partial A + dE/dA > 0$. In this case, advertising need not reduce social
welfare when it boosts price, and advertising will unambiguously raise
social welfare when it lowers price.

The analysis is more complex when the market is imperfectly competitive, as $d\Pi/dA$ will generally not equal zero. When advertising
increases firm but not market demand, an expansion of one firm's
advertising expenditures enables the firm to capture sales from rivals.
If each firm ignores the negative effect of its own advertising on competitors, then the Nash-equilibrium level of advertising will exceed the
level that maximizes joint profits and $d\Pi/dA$ will be negative. Alternatively, if firm advertising increases the demand for both own and
rival products, the Nash-equilibrium level of advertising will be less
than the level that maximizes joint profits and $d\Pi/dA$ will be positive
(Tremblay 2003).

In the U.S. brewing industry, the market is imperfectly competitive
and externalities are important. In this case, each term in equation 8.7
will be nonzero. Survey evidence discussed in chapter 7 indicates that
beer advertising is both persuasive and informative, implying that
$\partial V/\partial A$ does not equal zero. Tremblay and Tremblay (1995) find that a

marginal increase in advertising leads to higher prices in brewing. This implies that the second term on the right hand side of equation 8.7 is negative. Most of the studies in chapter 2 agree that beer advertising affects firm but not market demand, implying that industry costs rise more than revenues, so that $d\Pi/dA < 0$. Saffer (2002) concludes that advertising encourages alcohol abuse, and, therefore, creates negative externalities. At the same time, advertising expenditures that subsidize radio and television programming generate positive externalities. Thus, the signs of dE/dA and dSW/dA are ambiguous on theoretical grounds.

Taking an empirical approach, Tremblay and Tremblay (1995) esti-mate the magnitude of each component in equation 8.7 for the brewing industry. They account for the effect of advertising on consumer and producer surplus, possible subsidies to television and radio program-ming, and the externalities associated with beer consumption. Accord-ing to their results, the market level of beer advertising is excessive from society's point of view, indicating a potential role for advertising restrictions. Their study fails to account for the benefits of moderate drinking and fails to identify the effect of advertising on alcohol abuse, however. Those issues will be discussed further in chapter 9.

8.6 Estimation of Market Power in Brewing

The traditional way to assess the degree of market power in an indus-try is to estimate a supply relation (Appelbaum 1979, 1982; Bresnahan 1989). Because Anheuser-Busch is the largest firm and the price leader in the industry, a supply relation is estimated for Anheuser-Busch and for the industry as a whole.

The specification of the industry supply relation follows Denney et al. (2002). It derives from the representative firm's first-order condi-tion in equation 8.3 and can be rearranged as

$$P = MC(w, K, T) + \lambda q_i, \qquad (8.9)$$

where w is a vector of variable input prices, K is the quantity of the fixed input, capital, and T controls for technological conditions. The output or market-power parameter, $\lambda = -(\partial P/\partial Q)\Theta$, will be positive when market power is present.[31] Under certain regularity conditions, individual firm supply relations can be aggregated into an industry supply relation.[32] For empirical implementation, let the marginal cost function take a Generalized Leontief functional form (Diewert 1974) and include an additive error term, $e_{t,S}$. In this case, the industry supply relation at time t becomes

$$P_t = \alpha_0 + \alpha_1 w_t^L + \alpha_2 w_t^M + \alpha_3 (w_t^L w_t^M)^{1/2} + \alpha_4 K_t + \alpha_5 T_t$$

$$+ \alpha_6 \tau_t^f + \alpha_7 \tau_t^s + \lambda Q_t + e_{t,S}, \qquad (8.10)$$

where w^L is the price of labor, w^M is the price of materials, K is the quantity of capital (measured as industry capacity), T is a time trend representing technological change, τ^f is the federal excise tax rate, and τ^s is the average state excise tax rate. Because the price and output of beer are determined simultaneously, equation 8.10 is estimated jointly with the market demand function in chapter 2 using two-stage least squares.[33]

Table 8.5 summarizes the results of Denny et al. (2002) using annual data for the years 1953–1995. All the parameter estimates have the expected signs and all are significant except the state excise tax parameter.[34] Coefficient estimates indicate that technology has changed. Consistent with previous work, the index of market power (Θ) is close to 0, at 0.06, indicating that the industry has been reasonably competitive. Once a new equilibrium with fewer firms emerges, brewers will be in a better position to exploit market power, but data limitations make it impossible to determine if market power has increased since 1995.

Table 8.5
Supply relation parameter estimates for U.S. brewing industry. Adjusted $R^2 = 0.994$; $F = 908.9$[a].

Variable	Parameter estimate	$|t\text{-statistic}|$
Intercept ($\times 10^2$)	1.040[a]	16.186
w^L	3.537[a]	4.295
w^M ($\times 10^{-2}$)	32.315[a]	4.100
$(w^L w^M)^{1/2}$ ($\times 10^{-2}$)	−2.213[a]	4.240
K	−0.074[b]	2.514
T	−1.193[a]	8.230
τ^f	1.070[a]	8.419
τ^s	0.306	0.722
Q ($\times 10^3$)	0.160[b]	2.565

a. Significant at 0.01 level (two-tailed test).
b. Significant at 0.05 level (two-tailed test).
c. Significant at 0.10 level (two-tailed test).

Fortunately, data are available from 1950 through 2001 for the industry leader, Anheuser-Busch. Estimates of the firm's supply relation and market power can provide insight into the extent of market power in the industry. Because Anheuser-Busch is the dominant firm in the industry, a low estimate of the firm's market power during the 1990s would suggest that market power is also low for the industry. The company's supply relation and demand function are estimated simultaneously. The estimation procedure and demand results are discussed in chapter 2. Specification of the supply relation follows equation 8.9, except that marginal cost is approximated by average cost because of data limitations.[35] In order to determine how market power has changed, the supply relation allows the market-power parameter to vary over the five regimes identified in chapter 3. Market-power estimates are low and highly insignificant for the first three periods. Much like the industry as a whole, this evidence suggests that Anheuser-Busch had no market power from 1950 through 1986. Consequently, the market-power parameter is set to 0 for the years 1950–1986, and allowed to vary for the last two regimes: 1987–1996 and 1997–2001.

Parameter estimates are provided in table 8.6. As expected, the marginal cost parameter is highly significant and close to one. In addition, both of the market-power parameter estimates (on output) are positive and significantly different from 0. In addition, the market-power parameter is rising, and the difference between the 1987–1996 and the 1997–2001 parameters is significant at better than 1 percent. The evidence indicates that Anheuser-Busch has exerted market power since the late 1980s, providing evidence that market power has risen as the number of competitors has diminished.[36]

Table 8.6
Supply relation parameter estimates for Anheuser-Busch. Adjusted $R^2 = 0.999$; $F = 21057$[a].

Variable	Parameter estimate	$|t\text{-statistic}|$
Intercept	0.004	0.26
Marginal cost	1.053[a]	64.25
Output, 1987–1996 ($\times 10^6$)	0.722[a]	3.72
Output, 1997–2001 ($\times 10^6$)	0.817[a]	6.15

a. Significant at 0.01 level (two-tailed test).
b. Significant at 0.05 level (two-tailed test).
c. Significant at 0.10 level (two-tailed test).

8.7   Conclusion

The performance of the U.S. brewing industry is good but not perfect. Episodes of racial and gender discrimination and irresponsible advertising occurred in brewing as well as in society at large. Price and advertising competition kept a lid on industry profits until the late 1980s, when profits began to rise and Anheuser-Busch gained market power. At the same time, Anheuser-Busch's success is due at least in part to superior production facilities and superior marketing, and industry profits have been enhanced by gains in productive efficiency that have resulted from the exit of inefficient firms during the beer wars.

Success in marketing appears to be more elusive than success in production. The leading national producers have a strategic advantage not only because they are scale efficient but also because they can televise advertisements nationally. An unresolved question is whether advertising creates a premium image or simply informs consumers of the identity of superior brands. In any case, evidence and testimony from industry experts indicate that a brewer must be an effective marketer to have long-term success.

An important concern is the extent to which brewers' actions contribute to excessive alcohol consumption and abuse. Recent estimates indicate that excessive beer consumption imposes substantial costs on society. Government policies to reduce these social costs, such as advertising restrictions and higher excise taxes, will be addressed in the next chapter.

9   Public Policy Issues

The law is the last result of human wisdom acting upon human experience for
the benefit of the public.

—Samuel Johnson

The previous chapter identifies a number of issues of social concern
regarding the U.S. brewing industry. Few mass producers survived
the attrition war, and less competitive behavior became evident in the
1990s. Industry critics also question the social desirability of marketing
practices in brewing. Perhaps the most challenging issue facing policy
makers is to design policies that will discourage alcohol abuse and
underage drinking.

When a market fails to achieve desirable performance standards,
the government may use one or more policy measures to encourage
socially desirable outcomes. Examples include taxes, tariffs, and direct
government intervention, such as restrictions on advertising and
merger activity.

It is common to judge a policy's effectiveness by evaluating its costs
and benefits. Although this approach is widely used by economists, it
has several limitations. For example, data on the potential costs and
benefits of a policy are often lacking. A new government regulation
may impose direct costs on a firm that are easy to measure, but it may
also impose indirect costs that are unobservable or even concealed
from the public, like firm expenditures to resist and influence policy
actions. Measurement issues also plague the benefit side, since a policy
may generate benefits that cannot be measured monetarily—e.g.,
improved health or a reduction in violent crime. This is even more
problematic when a policy generates several types of unmeasurable benefits. If this is the case, normative decisions must be made

regarding the value of each unmeasurable benefit. Another difficulty is that cost-benefit analysis often requires intertemporal comparisons, as most policy decisions produce benefits and costs in the future as well as the present. In this case, one must forecast the value of future costs and benefits and decide the extent to which future values should be discounted. In light of these difficulties, many scholars who use cost-benefit analysis produce ranges of estimates, depending on different discount rates, benefit and cost estimates, and the weights given to the various unmeasurable benefits. Another approach is the "use of multiple perspectives, theories, and methods" in order to gain a broader and more complete understanding of the issues involved (Dunn 1993: 6).[1] In this chapter, these approaches are used to review policy concerns, to assess alternative remedies, and to make policy recommendations. Anti-trust, alcohol abuse, and advertising policies as they apply to the brewing industry are considered.

9.1   Anti-Trust Policy

The anti-trust laws of the United States promote competition in at least four ways.[2] The first addresses concerns with high industry concentration by breaking up large corporations. The second outlaws collusive business practices. The third attacks vertical contracts and arrangements that create market power. And the last challenges mergers that increase concentration and the probability of collusion. This section discusses the anti-trust issues most relevant to the brewing industry: horizontal and market extension mergers and other anti-competitive business practices. With only three major mass-producing beer companies remaining, collusive behavior is a growing concern.

Mergers

In order to understand the anti-trust response to merger activity in brewing during the second half of the twentieth century, one must understand how the anti-merger laws and relevant court precedents have evolved. In 1950, the Celler-Kefauver Act amended section 7 of the Clayton Act (1914), making all mergers illegal when the effect "may be substantially to lessen competition, or tend to create a monopoly." The new law was motivated by a concern in Congress that mergers were increasing concentration in many U.S. industries. Officials at the Department of Justice and at the Federal Trade Commission became more vigilant, issuing an unprecedented number of anti-merger complaints. The court took a "hard line" against horizontal mergers as well (Scherer 1980: 544–558).

One concern with the law and early court precedents was that they did not clearly identify what was legal and illegal. During this discussion, Stigler (1955: 182) recommended that the government establish a clearly defined set of anti-merger rules that "would serve the double purpose of giving the business community some advanced knowledge of public policy toward mergers and of achieving the important goals of the legislature." Later, Bok (1960: 299) argued that "there is much to be said for a simple standard which can at least be fairly and inexpensively administered in a fashion that is understandable to the businessman contemplating merger." Legal ambiguity was also at issue in a *Fortune* editorial (February 1965: 228) which said that the business community does not want to "make present laws less restrictive on mergers [but] would simply codify them in such a way that businessmen know what they can and can't do." In response, the Department of Justice (1968) established a set of "Merger Guidelines" to inform the business community of the government's position on mergers. The Merger Guidelines define criteria that are generally consistent with the law and major legal precedents. For example, the standards are tougher on mergers between firms in highly concentrated industries, where the four-firm concentration ratio (CR_4) exceeds 75 percent. The Merger Guidelines also indicate that a stricter standard applies in markets where concentration is increasing, and a more lenient standard is applied when one of the firms is clearly failing. An efficiency defense is possible, but only in exceptional circumstances. The important enforcement policies of the 1968 Merger Guidelines are outlined in table 9.1.

Anti-trust experts agree that the main problem with the 1968 Guidelines was that they failed to clearly define the relevant market. In all fairness to the Department of Justice, however, the law and the courts provided little guidance regarding how product and geographic markets should be defined. For example, the Celler-Kefauver Act outlaws a merger if it reduces competition in "any section of the country." In specific cases, the Court has often used inconsistent definitions of the market. In *Brown Shoe Co. v. U.S.* (370 U.S. 294, 1962), for example, the Court held that the geographic market was a single city when considering the effect of a merger on horizontal markets but was national when considering the vertical effect of the merger. Regarding the product market, the Court used a narrow definition in *U.S. v. Aluminum Co.*

Table 9.1
Summary of Horizontal Merger Guidelines, 1968. Source: U.S. Department of Justice, *Merger Guidelines*, May 30, 1968.

1. The Guidelines focus on the following standard:

A. Where the four-firm concentration ratio is 75 percent or more, the market is defined as highly concentrated and the government "will ordinarily challenge" mergers between firms with the following market shares:

Acquiring Firm	Acquired Firm
4%	4% or more
10%	2% or more
15% or more	1% or more

B. Where the four-firm concentration ratio is less than 75 percent, the government "will ordinarily challenge" mergers between firms with the following market shares:

Acquiring Firm	Acquired Firm
5%	5% or more
10%	4% or more
15%	3% or more
20%	2% or more
25%	1% or more

2. The Guidelines also list several "exceptional circumstances or additional factors" that may require a departure from the structural standard above. Important examples include the following.

A. The structural standards may be ignored for industries being significantly transformed (by technological change, for example), since market boundaries may be uncertain.

B. A stricter standard will be applied to markets where there is a significant trend toward concentration.

C. The government will not allow the acquisition of an important (disturbing, disruptive, or unusually competitive) rival in the market.

D. The government will allow the acquisition of a failing firm if the failing firm does not have a reasonable prospect for survival and there are no other buyers that would better promote competition.

E. An efficiency defense will be accepted but only in exceptional circumstances.

F. A more lenient standard will be applied for market extension mergers (i.e., firms selling similar products in different regions of the country).

of America [374 U.S. 321, 358, 361, 1963) and a broad definition in *U.S. v. Continental Can Co.* (378 U.S. 441, 1964). Thus, it would be impossible for the Department of Justice to provide a clear definition of a market based on the original law and early court precedents.[3]

To facilitate coordination between business and government, the Hart-Scott-Rodino Act was enacted in 1976 and required firms of appreciable size to notify the Department of Justice and the Federal Trade Commission of their intentions to merge and to wait 30 days before completing mergers. The waiting period allows the government time to study the evidence and decide whether to file suit. Although the Act had no direct effect on merger law, it did encourage the government to work with the parties involved to eliminate the anti-competitive aspects of the merger before the merger actually took place. Government agencies gained discretionary power and effectively became anti-merger regulators. As a result, the Hart-Scott-Rodino Act caused a dramatic drop in anti-merger litigation (Beuttenmuller 1979; Johnson and Smith 1987).

A 1982 revision of the Merger Guidelines incorporated major changes (U.S. Department of Justice 1982). First, the merits of the Herfindahl-Hirschman index (HHI) were not lost on the Department of Justice representatives. The HHI replaced CR_4 as a measure of industry concentration. Under the new Guidelines, an industry is classified as highly concentrated when the HHI is above 1,800, moderately concentrated when the HHI is between 1,000 and 1,800, and unconcentrated when the HHI is less than 1,000.[4] In a moderately concentrated industry like brewing in the 1970s, a merger will generally be challenged if it raises the HHI by 100 points or more.[5] Second, the new Guidelines provide a precise definition of the market, based on the "five-percent test." A firm's competitors include (1) all suppliers that buyers would switch to if the firm raised its price by 5 percent and (2) all potential competitors that would be expected to enter the market within one year if all existing firms raised their prices by 5 percent. Like the 1968 Guidelines, the 1982 Guidelines consider other factors when investigating a merger. The important criteria of the 1982 Guidelines are described in more detail in table 9.2.

A 1984 revision provided a clarification of the 1982 Guidelines regarding the efficiency defense. Although the 1982 Guidelines (at 28,502) indicate that the government will allow firms to "achieve efficiencies through mergers," the 1984 Guidelines give more weight to the efficiency defense. According to the 1984 Guidelines (at 26,834):

Table 9.2
Summary of Horizontal Merger Guidelines, 1982 and 1984. Source: U.S. Department of Justice, *Merger Guidelines*, Washington, D.C., June 30, 1982 and June 29, 1984.

1. The 1982 and 1984 Guidelines continue to use a structural standard but replace the four-firm concentration ratio with the Herfindahl-Hirschman Index (HHI). Under the 1982 and 1984 Guidelines, the following structural standard is used.

A. Where the post-merger HHI is above 1,800, the market is defined as highly concentrated and a merger will generally be challenged if the resulting merger causes HHI to rise by 50 points or more.[a]

B. Where the post-merger HHI ranges from 1,000 to 1,800, the market is defined as moderately concentrated and a merger will generally be challenged if the resulting merger causes HHI to rise by 100 points or more.

C. Where the post-merger HHI is less than 1,000 points, the market is defined as unconcentrated and the government will not generally challenge a merger between firms in this market.

2. The 1982 and 1984 Guidelines propose a "5 percent test" to define a market. That is, if a hypothetical firm increases its price by 5 percent, the market is defined to include all existing competitors that consumers would turn to for supplies within one year and all new competitors that would enter the market within one year if all existing firms increased their prices by 5 percent.

3. Like the 1968 Guidelines, the 1982 and 1984 Guidelines consider other factors, such as the rate of technological change, the rate of industry growth, and the ease of entry. The 1982 and 1984 Guidelines also provide for a failing firm and an efficiency defense.

4. The 1984 Guidelines revise the 1982 Guidelines by elaborating on the efficiency defense and making it clear that greater weight is given to the efficiency defense.

a. HHI is calculated with market share measured in percent. The increase in HHI due to a merger can be derived by doubling the product of the market shares of the merging firms. For example, a market of 12 firms with market shares of 30 percent, 20 percent, and 5 percent for the 10 remaining firms has an HHI of 1,550 and is defined as moderately concentrated. If two of the smallest firms merge, this will increase HHI by 50 points and is, therefore, unlikely to be challenged. A merger between the largest and smallest firms will raise HHI by 300 points, however, falling outside the acceptable structural standard.

"The primary benefit of mergers to the economy is their efficiency-enhancing potential, which can increase the competitiveness of firms and result in lower prices to consumers.... The Guidelines will allow firms to achieve available efficiencies through mergers without interference from the Department." This clarification emphasizes that both the 1982 and the 1984 Guidelines allow U.S. corporations to benefit from the efficiency gains of mergers.

In 1992, the Department of Justice and the Federal Trade Commission worked together to further refine the Merger Guidelines. Although the structural standard was unaffected, the revision elabo-

Table 9.3
Summary of Horizontal Merger Guidelines, 1992 and 1997. Source: U.S. Department of Justice and Federal Trade Commission, *Horizontal Merger Guidelines*, Washington, D.C., April 2, 1992 and April 8, 1997.

1. The 1992 and 1997 Guidelines use the same structural standard as the 1982 and 1984 Guidelines.

A. Where the post-merger HHI is above 1,800, the market is defined as *highly concentrated* and a merger will generally be challenged if the resulting merger causes HHI to rise by 50 points or more.

B. Where the post-merger HHI ranges from 1,000 to 1,800, the market is defined as *moderately concentrated* and a merger will generally be challenged if the resulting merger causes HHI to rise by 100 points or more.

C. Where the post-merger HHI is less than 1,000 points, the market is defined as *unconcentrated* and the government will not generally challenge a merger between firms in this market.

2. The 1992 and 1997 Guidelines define a market using the rule of a "small but significant and nontransitory" increase in price. Like the 1982 and 1984 Guidelines, this will be a 5 percent increase in price in most cases. If a hypothetical firm increases its price by 5 percent, the market is defined to include all existing competitors that consumers would turn to for supplies within one year. The 1992 and 1997 Guidelines also offer a more detailed discussion on how entry conditions will be considered when defining the market.

3. The 1992 and 1997 Guidelines elaborate on how a merger may diminish competition and how the government will evaluate the potential harm that may result from a merger.

4. Like the 1982 and 1984 Guidelines, the 1992 and 1997 Guidelines provide for an efficiency defense and a failing firm defense.

5. The 1997 Guidelines revise the 1992 Guidelines regarding the efficiency defense. The revision makes clear that efficiency gains can be an important justification for a merger but more clearly defines what evidence is necessary to substantiate such a defense.

rates on how the government will evaluate entry conditions and on the potentially harmful effects of a horizontal merger. A minor addition to the Merger Guidelines in 1997 included a more detailed description of the evidence required to justify an efficiency defense. The important details of the 1992–1997 revisions are listed in table 9.3.

The 1982–1997 versions of the Merger Guidelines are clearly more lenient than the 1968 version. Later versions place greater emphasis on the efficiency defense, which relaxes the anti-merger constraint and conflicts with previous court cases. In *Federal Trade Commission v. Procter and Gamble Company* (386 U.S. 568, 580 (1967), for example, the court held that "possible economies cannot be used as a defense to illegality." As a result, the National Association of Attorneys General

Antitrust Enforcement (1987) does not endorse the efficiency defense. Second, Tollison (1983) and Tremblay (1993) show that the new structural standard is generally more lenient. Further, Fisher and Lande (1983: 1,683) argue that the 5 percent test in the newer Merger Guidelines yields a broader market definition and "probably loosened merger enforcement standards far more than the change due to the different numerical [structural] standards."

Many experts allege that the Reagan administration is responsible for the more lenient 1982 Merger Guidelines, citing President Ronald Reagan's deregulation agenda and the appointment of William Baxter to head the anti-trust division of the Department of Justice (*Fortune*, October 5, 1981; Adams and Brock 1988; Krattenmaker and Pitofsky 1988). Scherer (1980: 554, and 1996: 421) and Waldman (1986: 97–99) argue, however, that this trend began in the mid 1970s with the appointment of new, more conservative Supreme Court Justices. Supreme Court approval of an important horizontal merger (*U.S. v. General Dynamics Company*, 415 U.S. 486, 1974) broke with court precedent by using a broad definition of the market. In the words of Waldman (1986: 99), "the General Dynamics decision signaled that a more conservative Supreme Court would no longer automatically side with the government in all section 7 cases [of the Clayton Act]. . . ."

The brewing industry played an important role in the development of U.S. anti-trust case law on horizontal mergers. The trend toward higher concentration in the industry motivated close scrutiny of all mergers in brewing by the Department of Justice, and some of the earliest court cases based on the Celler-Kefauver Act involved horizontal mergers in brewing. Table 9.4 lists 14 important mergers that were investigated or challenged by the Department of Justice in the period 1957–1989. Table 9.5 describes the structural characteristics of the firms that were involved.

The Lucky (later General) Brewing Company (San Francisco) purchased the Fisher Brewing Company (Salt Lake City) in 1957. Their combined share of the national market was less than 2.2 percent. Recall that the market was regional until the 1960s, however, so that the national data for market share and concentration do not apply in this case. In the state of Utah, which was more relevant, Lucky's market share was 36.1 percent and Fisher's was 3.1 percent in 1961, the closest year for which data are available (Keithahn 1978: 170). In 1958, the U.S. District Court ruled that the merger was illegal, and Lucky was ordered to divest of Fisher and to refrain from acquiring another brewer for the next 5 years without court approval. This sent a strong signal to the

Table 9.4
Mergers and anti-trust actions in the brewing industry.

	Buyer	Seller	References and outcomes
1957	Lucky (General)	Fisher	*U.S. v. Lucky Lager* (1958); *CCH Trade Cases*, para. 69160; Elzinga 1969. Lucky was ordered to divest of Fisher.
1958	Anheuser-Busch	American	*U.S. v. Anheuser-Busch* (1960); *CCH Trade Cases*, para. 69,599; Elzinga 1982. Anheuser-Busch was ordered to divest of American and refrain for 5 years from buying another brewery without court approval.
1958	Pabst	Blatz	*U.S. v. Pabst* (1964) 233 F. Supp. 475 and (1966) 384 U.S. 546; Elzinga 1982. Pabst was ordered to divest of Blatz.
1961	Schlitz	Burgermeister	*U.S. v. Jos. Schlitz* (1966) 385 U.S. 37 (1966); Elzinga 1982. Schlitz was ordered to divest of Burgermeister.
1964	Schlitz	General	*Fortune*, October 1964. Dept. of Justice objected to and stopped Schlitz purchase of a 39% share of John Labatt Ltd, which owns a large interest in Lucky.
1965	Falstaff	Narragansett	*U.S. v. Falstaff* (1973) 410 U.S. 526; Waldman 1986. Supreme Court ruled that the merger was legal.
1965	Rheingold	Ruppert	*Wall Street Journal*, June 5, 1968. Department of Justice dropped suit because of changing market conditions. Merger approved.
1965	Pittsburgh	Duquesne	*U.S. v. Pittsburgh* (1966); *CCH Trade Cases*, para. 71,751. Merger dropped after Dept. of Justice challenge.
1972	Heileman	Associated	*U.S. v. Heileman* (1972); *CCH Trade Cases*, para. 74,080; *Wall Street Journal*, June 14, 1973. Merger approved but Heileman ordered to divest of several brands with at least 400,000 barrels of production in 1972.
1978	Pabst	Carling	*Advertising Age*, July 3 and September 18, 1978; Elzinga 1982. Merger dropped after Dept. of Justice challenge.
1982	Heileman	Pabst	Elzinga 1986. Merger dropped after Dept. of Justice challenge.
1982	Heileman	Schlitz	Elzinga 1986. Merger dropped after Dept. of Justice challenge.
1982	Stroh	Schlitz	Elzinga 1986. Approved merger but only after Stroh agreed to sell Schlitz Tampa plant to Pabst in exchange for Pabst St. Paul plant.
1989	Coors	Stroh	*Wall Street Journal*, September 26, 1989. Merger dropped over concern with possible Dept. of Justice challenge.

Table 9.5
Structural characteristics of horizontal mergers challenged by the Department of Justice. MS_B is the market share of the buyer, MS_S is the market share of seller, ΔHHI is the change in the Herfindahl-Hirschman index, FF indicates whether or not one of the firms was failing, Brands indicates whether or not brands and no facilities were purchased, and ME indicates a market-extension merger. Asterisk indicates that a merger was successfully challenged by the Department of Justice or abandoned due to antitrust concerns.

Buyer	Seller	Year	MS_B	MS_S	CR_4	HHI	ΔHHI	FF	Brands	ME
*Lucky	Fisher[a]	1957	2.02	0.11	24.0	272	0.4	Yes	No	No
*A-B	American	1958	8.20	0.22	25.1	293	3.6	No	No	No
*Pabst	Blatz	1958	2.99	2.00	25.1	293	12.0	No	Yes	No
*Schlitz	Burgermeister	1961	6.42	0.81	27.4	359	10.4	No	No	No
*Schlitz	Lucky[b]	1964	8.30	1.77	32.0	432	29.4	No	No	No
Falstaff	Narragansett	1965	6.23	0.76	34.5	487	9.5	No	No	Yes
Rheingold	Ruppert	1965	4.17	0.79	34.5	487	6.6	No	Yes	No
*Pittsburgh	Duquesne	1965	0.88	0.68	34.5	487	1.2	No	No	No
Heileman	Associated	1972	2.73	1.89	50.8	857	10.3	Yes	No	No
*Pabst	Carling	1978	9.29	2.01	65.2	1,345	37.4	Yes	No	No
*Heileman	Pabst	1982	8.11	6.87	75.8	1,909	111.4	Yes	No	No
*Heileman	Schlitz[c]	1982	8.11	7.98	75.8	1,909	129.4	Yes	No	No
Stroh	Schlitz[c]	1982	3.41	7.89	75.8	1,909	53.8	Yes	No	No
*Coors	Stroh	1989	9.65	10.04	86.5	2,707	193.8	No	No	No

a. The market share for Fisher is for 1958, the closest year to the merger for which data are available.
b. Schlitz purchased a 39 percent interest in John Labatt Ltd. (the third-largest brewer in Canada), which holds a large interest in Lucky [*Fortune* (October 1964)].
c. The market share of Schlitz is for 1981, the closest year to the merger for which data are available.

business community that the government would challenge horizontal mergers that may affect competition in a small region of the country.

The vigorous enforcement of the anti-merger laws against the three largest national producers made it clear that large brewers would be unable to grow by merger. In 1958, the industry leader, Anheuser-Busch, purchased the American Brewing Company (Miami). Although American was very small, the Department of Justice successfully argued that the merger would reduce competition in Florida. Anheuser-Busch was ordered to sell American and to refrain from purchasing another brewery for the next 5 years. American was sold to the National Brewing Company in 1961. Likewise, the Pabst acquisition of the Blatz Brewing Company (Milwaukee) in 1958 was successfully challenged by the government. Although the merged company had a national market share of less than 5 percent, the court ruled that the merger was illegal because of its effect on the Wisconsin market, of which Pabst had a 11.1 percent share and Blatz had a 12.8 percent share. Schlitz faced similar difficulties when it purchased the Burgermeister Brewing Company (San Francisco) in 1961 and an interest in Lucky in 1964. The combined market share of Schlitz, Burgermeister, and Lucky was 23.4 percent in California in 1964 (Keithahn 1978). The government successfully forced Schlitz to divest of these two firms and to refrain from purchasing another brewer without court approval for the next 10 years.

The cases against the national brewers demonstrated that the court would stand firm against horizontal mergers in brewing and would narrowly define geographic markets. In the early 1960s, the appropriate geographic market for beer may not have been the nation as a whole, but it was certainly broader than a single state. During this time, the national four-firm concentration ratio was less than 35 percent; none of the mergers involved a buyer with a national market share greater than 9 percent and a seller with a market share above 2 percent. Scherer (1980: 554) speculates that the courts simply defined a market in a way that would win the case and preserve competition in any section of the country.

With the leading brewers effectively constrained from merger activity, the next three cases involved mergers between smaller regional brewers. First, Falstaff purchased the Narragansett Brewing Company (Cranston, Rhode Island) in 1965. At the time, Falstaff was the fourth-largest brewer, with a national market share of 6.23 percent. A strong regional producer, Falstaff sold beer in 32 states but did not have a presence in the Northeast. Narragansett was a prominent regional brewer with a market share of 20 percent in the New England market. This was clearly a market extension merger, but the government argued that Falstaff was a potential competitor in the Northeast. The court ultimately ruled in favor of the merger but not until 1973. One factor that may have influenced the decision was the rapid deterioration of Falstaff's competitive position between 1965 and 1973, when its market share fell from 6.23 percent to 4.28 percent. Declining market share also played a role in the second case, the 1965 merger between the Rheingold Brewing Company and the Jacob Ruppert Brewing Company. Although Rheingold and Ruppert were competitors in the New York City area, the Department of Justice dropped its suit in 1968 because market conditions were changing (*Wall Street Journal*, June 5, 1968). Both firms had substantial excess capacity (see table 8.2), and the market share of the combined firm declined from 4.17 to 2.90 between 1965 and 1968. The Pittsburgh and Duquesne brewing companies, vigorous competitors in western Pennsylvania, discontinued their 1965 merger proceedings after the Department of Justice filed suit.

Merger cases in brewing illustrate that the establishment of the 1968 Merger Guidelines encouraged the Department of Justice to act more as a regulator long before the passage of the Hart-Scott-Rodino Act in 1976. This regulatory approach proved to be more efficient because it is far less costly to rectify an anti-competitive merger before the merger has taken place. For example, Lucky was finally forced to divest of Fisher, but there were no subsequent buyers for the Fisher plant and it was never restored to a fully independent company (Elzinga 1969). Similarly, Pabst bought Blatz in 1958, but the court did not force Pabst to divest of Blatz until 1969. By that time the Blatz plant had been closed and all that remained was the Blatz trademark, 32 trucks, and the Blatz marching band (Scherer 1996: 420). Elzinga (1969) shows that the inability of the courts to restore competition after a merger took place was a general problem with anti-merger enforcement at the time. Elzinga calls these early court cases "Pyrrhic victories," since they were costly to litigate and usually failed to restore the firms back into two independent enterprises.

In the remaining merger cases, the Department of Justice worked closely with the firms involved to define a set of provisions that would make the merger acceptable to the government. For example, the Department ruled that Heileman could purchase the Associated Brewing Company (Detroit) in 1972 but only if Heileman divested of several brands that accounted for at least 400,000 barrels of total production and at least one brand that produced at least 100,000 barrels per year (*Wall Street Journal*, June 14, 1973). Heileman accepted these provisions and sold its Karlsbrau, Gluek, and North Star brands to the Cold Spring Brewing Company (Cold Spring, Minnesota) in 1973. To make the 1982 Stroh-Schlitz merger acceptable, Stroh was required to divest of a brewery in the Southeast. Stroh met this condition by selling the Schlitz brewery in Tampa to Pabst in exchange for a Pabst plant in St. Paul (Elzinga 1986). The remaining four merger attempts listed in table 9.5 were abandoned after the Department of Justice indicated that they would be challenged in court.[6]

Empirical evidence (Tremblay 1993) indicates that the Merger Guidelines give the business community a good indication of the mergers that are likely to be challenged, at least in the U.S. brewing industry. Tremblay estimates a logit model to determine the accuracy of the structural standards found in the Merger Guidelines at predicting the probability that a merger would be challenged in the U.S. brewing industry from 1950 to 1983. The results indicate that the probability of litigation goes up with the market shares of the firms involved and with industry concentration and goes down with the likelihood that the selling firm will fail.

Tremblay's results also indicate that the anti-merger laws have been more leniently applied over time. Consider the proposed merger of Coors and Stroh in 1989. The model predicts that the probability that the Coors-Stroh merger would be challenged is 99 percent for the years 1950–1967, 92 percent under the 1968 Merger Guidelines (1968–1981), and 53 percent under the 1982 Merger Guidelines (1982–1983). This trend is evident in table 9.5. It is unlikely that many of the mergers that were challenged before 1968 would have been challenged under the 1982–1984 Merger Guidelines, since none of the mergers would have increased the HHI by more than 30 points. Likewise, the merger between Schlitz and Stroh would have undoubtedly been challenged if it had occurred in the early 1960s. In 1962, for example, the national market shares of Schlitz and Stroh were 7.47 and 2.22 percent, respectively. In addition, Stroh was the number-one brewer in Michigan, with a 22.1 percent share of the market, while Schlitz ranked fifth in Michigan with a 3.7 percent share (Keithahn 1978: 154). Just as Schlitz was forced to divest of Burgermeister in 1961, Stroh would have certainly been forced to divest of Schlitz had the merger occurred in the early 1960s.

In hindsight, it is clear that the anti-merger laws were too stringently applied in brewing during the 1950s and the 1960s. Increasing economies of scale and growing consumer demand for premium brands pushed many of the traditional regional brewers into financial difficulty and even failure. As was shown in chapter 7, most mergers that were permitted by the Department of Justice promoted efficiency, with successful brewers buying failing ones. The continued trend toward industry concentration appears to have had a negligible effect on the degree of price competition, at least until the late 1980s. If this outcome had been understood at the time, social welfare would have been better served by encouraging mergers among all but the national producers. Mergers among the largest regional brewers may have allowed some of them to become viable competitors today.

One might argue that it is inappropriate to criticize the government, since the causes and economic consequences of increasing concentration in brewing were poorly understood in the 1950s and the 1960s. However, there were early rumblings among academic economists and in the business community that the anti-merger policy was hampering competition rather than promoting it (Elzinga 1969; Scherer 1970, chapter 20). A 1966 editorial in *Printers' Ink* (February 11: 22) actually forecasts the state of the industry today: "If the government has its way, the net effect of preventing brewer mergers will be to strengthen the competitive position of Anheuser-Busch and create a GM type situation in brewing, with one company dominating the major portion of the market and the survivors fighting for the remains."

The most damaging piece of evidence comes from government-sponsored research. In a Federal Trade Commission study, Keithahn (1978: 65–66) criticized the strict anti-merger constraint imposed on smaller brewers, arguing that it "prevented them from achieving some economies in production and marketing that might have preserved their competitive influence and slowed or arrested the industry's trend toward greater concentration." Keithahn concluded (ibid.: 1, 123) that, despite the substantial increase in concentration, "the weight of the evidence supports the view that the industry has actually become more competitive," and that the "industry will continue to behave competitively, despite the higher level of concentration." Keithahn's conclusions are supported by the later work of Baker and Bresnahan (1985), who find that a merger between all but the largest brewers would have little or no effect on market power. In addition, Chalk (1988) uses event-study analysis to show that the proposed 1982 merger between Heileman and Schlitz would have promoted efficiency rather than market power.

In view of these results, the greater emphasis placed on an efficiency defense in the 1982–84 Merger Guidelines, and the continued financial problems of Carling, Pabst, Schlitz, and Stroh, it seems clear that the Department of Justice was overzealous in its opposition to the attempted mergers between Pabst and Carling in 1978, Heileman and Pabst in 1982, Heileman and Schlitz in 1982, and Coors and Stroh in 1989.[7] Today, the only potential mergers with anti-trust implications would involve Anheuser-Busch, Miller, Coors, and Pabst. A merger between any two of these would undoubtedly be challenged unless one firm was clearly failing.

Price Discrimination

Another policy concern in brewing is the use of price discrimination by some of the leading brewers. "Price discrimination" refers to the practice of charging different prices to different groups of customers for the same commodity when the price difference is not proportional to the difference in marginal cost.[8] Constitutional law makes discrimination illegal when people are segmented along racial or religious lines, and other federal, state, and local laws prohibit some forms of age and gender discrimination. Even when these laws are not violated, however, the anti-trust laws outlaw price discrimination when it reduces competition.

Current law is based on section 2(a) of the Robinson-Patman Act of 1936, which makes it illegal to "discriminate in price between different purchasers of commodities of like grade and quality ... where the effect of such price discrimination may be substantially to lessen competition or tend to create a monopoly in any line of commerce." The law allows three exceptions: (1) when disposing of perishable or obsolete goods, (2) when price differences reflect differences in costs, and (3) when price discrimination results "in good faith to meet an equally low price of a competitor."

In brewing, there have been several complaints that national producers selectively cut prices to drive regional brewers out of business. For example, the Grain Belt Brewing Company (Minneapolis) settled a price-fixing suit with Schlitz for $315,000 and filed a similar suit against Anheuser-Busch (*Wall Street Journal*, June 27, 1975). The Canadian Ace Brewing Company (Chicago) sought $15 million in damages against Anheuser-Busch for price cutting and other illegal activities that put Canadian out of business (*Wall Street Journal*, November 14, 1977). Three San Francisco brewers (General, Falstaff, and S&P) filed suit against Miller and Schlitz for illegal discounting that began in 1965 and substantially harmed competition (*Wall Street Journal*, December 12, 1977).

The most dramatic case occurred in 1955 when the Federal Trade Commission accused Anheuser-Busch of using price discrimination to harm competition in the St. Louis area. Recall from chapter 7 that Anheuser-Busch cut price to discipline regional producers that failed to follow an Anheuser-Busch price increase. The market share of the regional producers subsequently plummeted. The court indicated that this form of geographic price discrimination would come under the jurisdiction of the Robinson-Patman Act if it resulted in harm to competition. The court ruled in favor of Anheuser-Busch, however, for lack of proof that Anheuser-Busch subsidized the price cut in St. Louis with profit from another region. The court also found that the Federal Trade Commission failed to show that these price cuts caused any "actual injury to competition." The court overlooked the intention behind the actions of Anheuser-Busch to encourage cooperative pricing. Although this action falls short of a conspiracy to fix prices, behavior designed to raise prices in concert violates the Sherman Act (1890).

Exclusive Dealing Contracts

Another common institution in brewing is the exclusive dealing contract, with brewers forming such contracts with retailers, advertisers, and drinking establishments. Section 3 of the Clayton Act (1914) prohibits exclusive dealing contracts when the effect "may be to substantially lessen competition or tend to create a monopoly."

At the same time, these contracts may enhance efficiency, and the courts have generally used a "rule of reason" when deciding the legality of exclusive dealing contracts (Scherer 1980; Waldman 1986; Sass 2004). That is, the legality of an exclusive dealing contract depends on the extent to which it enhances market power relative to efficiency. Efficiency gains can result if such a contract reduces transaction costs and generates gains from specialization. Manufacturers of high quality goods may also benefit if such an arrangement encourages retailers to maintain quality and to maximize marketing effort (Marvel 1982). Anti-competitive effects can arise, however, if these contracts foreclose the market to existing and potential competitors. The anti-competitive effect would depend critically upon the fraction of the market covered by such contracts. Closer scrutiny is generally paid to large firms that have an exclusive dealing policy.

As was discussed in chapter 7, brewers have contracts with television stations for exclusive advertising rights to a particular television program. Leading brewers have also developed contracts with their distributors that specify an exclusive territory for each distributor (when allowed by state law). In general, these contracts have not been challenged by the government—an appropriate outcome in view of the evidence that exclusive dealing contracts between brewers and distributors have not hampered competition (Sass and Saurman 1993; *Wall Street Journal*, October 2, 1997 and March 9, 1998; Sass 2004).

In contrast, exclusive dealing contracts with restaurants and bars have attracted considerable attention from the government. From 1967 to 1976, several major brewers were accused of offering rebates or side payments to drinking establishments in exchange for exclusively selling their brands of beer. (See chapter 7.) According to William Coors, "you can't be in the brewing industry and not know that this type of thing has been going on for years" (*Business Week*, September 6, 1976: 20). As well as blocking off an important segment of the market to many regional brewers, such rebates and exclusivity clauses are illegal "per se" under the Federal Alcohol Administration Act of 1935.

Several firms have been accused of violating this federal law. For example, the Securities and Exchange Commission charged Anheuser-Busch with distributing an estimated $2.7 million in illegal rebates from 1971 to 1973. The company negotiated an out-of-court settlement, paying a fine of $750,000 (*Wall Street Journal*, September 3, 1976; *Advertising Age*, April 3, 1978). In 1973, Coors was ordered by the Federal Trade Commission to stop using exclusive dealing contracts (*Wall Street Journal*, June 6, 1974). Later, Falstaff, Olympia, Rainier, and Schaefer voluntarily informed the government of similar rebate activity and discontinued the practice (*Advertising Age*, January 10, 1977 and March 27, 1978). Finally, the Securities and Exchange Commission accused Schlitz of offering at least $3 million in rebates after the Bureau of Alcohol, Tobacco, and Firearms ordered Schlitz to stop in 1973 (*Wall Street Journal*, April 8, 1977, March 16, 1978, and November 2, 1978; *Advertising Age*, March 20, 1978 and November 6, 1978). Because the money was often "laundered" through advertising agencies and other third parties, Schlitz was charged with tax fraud. Unlike other brewers,

Schlitz denied the charges. If convicted, Schlitz would have been forced to cease operating in several states that have laws prohibiting production and sales of alcoholic beverages by corporations with felony convictions. Schlitz eventually agreed to an out-of-court settlement of $761,000 in exchange for a dismissal of all felony charges. Prohibiting these business practices is appropriate, and government action appears to have deterred the illegal rebate activity; there has been no subsequent litigation under the Federal Alcohol Administration Act in the brewing industry.

Market Power

Changes in industry structure and other evidence presented in previous chapters suggest that non-competitive behavior may have become problematic by the 1990s. Market demand is relatively inelastic, concentration has increased sharply, and the industry is classified as highly concentrated. In addition, Anheuser-Busch has become the dominant firm and the price leader, with more than 55 percent of the domestic market.

From 1950 through the 1980s, the U.S. beer industry was relatively competitive. Estimates of market power are low and the profit rate in brewing has been below par for U.S. manufacturing as a whole. There is also little evidence of price fixing in brewing during this period. The only legal action involving a true price-fixing agreement occurred in 1973–1974 when Schlitz and several distributors were indicted for setting prices at noncompetitive levels in the state of Hawaii (*Wall Street Journal*, June 9, 1977).[9] In addition, there has been a high degree of turnover among the leading brewers, and high turnover is consistent with a competitive market. Table 9.6 lists the five largest brewers in five-year intervals from 1950 to 2000. Except for the continued dominance of Anheuser-Busch, there has been a high degree of turnover among the leading five brewers from 1950 to 1990.

Evidence from more recent years suggests, however, that competition in brewing has subsided. First, profit rates for the industry and the leading brewers have risen in the 1990s. (See figures 8.2 and 8.3.) Second, Anheuser-Busch appears to have exercised market power since about 1987, according to supply relation estimates (table 8.6). Recently, Anheuser-Busch instigated a price increase that was followed by Miller and Coors (*Advertising* Age, October 24, 2002; *Modern Brewery Age, Weekly News Edition*, September 16, November 4, and November 18,

Table 9.6
The dominant five firms.

	First	Second	Third	Fourth	Fifth
1950	Schlitz	Anheuser-Busch	Ballantine	Pabst	Rheingold
1955	Schlitz	Anheuser-Busch	Ballantine	Falstaff	Pabst
1960	Anheuser-Busch	Schlitz	Falstaff	Carling	Ballantine
1965	Anheuser-Busch	Schlitz	Pabst	Falstaff	Carling
1970	Anheuser-Busch	Schlitz	Pabst	Coors	Schaefer
1975	Anheuser-Busch	Schlitz	Pabst	Miller	Coors
1980	Anheuser-Busch	Miller	Pabst	Schlitz	Coors
1985	Anheuser-Busch	Miller	Stroh[a]	Heileman	Coors
1990	Anheuser-Busch	Miller	Coors	Stroh	Heileman
1995	Anheuser-Busch	Miller	Coors	Stroh	Heileman
2000	Anheuser-Busch	Miller	Coors	Pabst	Boston

a. Stroh purchased Schlitz in 1982.

2002). With the exit of Heileman and Stroh and the continued decline of Pabst, the industry will soon be dominated by Anheuser-Busch, Miller, and Coors. Cooperative behavior is more likely with just three major firms, and the Department of Justice and the Federal Trade Commission should challenge any major merger attempt and closely monitor the behavior of firms.[10]

Growth of the specialty and import sectors of the market mitigates some of the concerns about increasing concentration in brewing. As the number of mass-producing brewers plunged during the 1960s and the 1970s, domestic specialty brewers entered the market in droves. Today, import and domestic specialty brewers produce more than 13 percent of all beer consumed in the United States. The influence of these brewers on price competition may be limited to the super-premium category, however, since most specialty and imported brands of beer are not in direct competition with regular domestic beer.

9.2 Public Health Policy and Alcohol Abuse

The consumption of alcoholic beverages is embedded in American culture. A 2000 Gallup poll reports that about 64 percent of adults drink alcoholic beverages. Of those who drink, more than 91 percent do so in moderation. The National Institute on Alcohol Abuse and Alcoholism defines moderate drinking as no more than two drinks per day for adult men under the age of 66 and no more than one per day for adult women and for men over the age of 65.[11] In 1981, the Surgeon General recommended that all pregnant women abstain from alcohol consumption, because even moderate drinking may lower infant birth weight and cause health problems in the unborn child. Recent evidence discussed in chapter 8 suggests that moderate drinking may be beneficial, as moderate drinkers have a lower incidence of cardiovascular disease, stroke, hypertension, cataracts, and arteriosclerosis.

At the same time, evidence presented in chapter 8 indicates that heavy drinking, alcohol abuse, and binge drinking can cause a number of health problems, including increased risk of cirrhosis, heart disease, several forms of cancer, and automobile and other accidents. In addition, several studies find an association between alcohol consumption and such undesirable outcomes as sexually transmitted diseases, violent crimes, and poor student performance in college. Even if one accounts for fairly generous benefits that result from moderate alcohol consumption, the estimated social cost of alcohol consumption ranges from $0.45 to $0.67 per ounce of ethanol, or about $1.52–$2.28 per six-pack of beer.

The magnitude of these external costs has motivated public health officials to recommend laws and regulations designed to curb alcohol consumption and abuse. Policies include efforts to inform the public about the risks associated with alcohol consumption, to raise the cost of underage drinking and drunk driving, to boost excise taxes, and to restrict alcohol advertising.

Public Health Information

For individuals to make rational decisions about alcohol consumption, they must have accurate and complete information about health consequences. Survey results indicate that the average person is aware that heavy drinking can cause cirrhosis of the liver but is unaware that it can also cause cancer of the throat and mouth (Kenkel 1996). More important, only 19 percent of heavy drinkers are fully informed about the health risks of alcohol consumption. This suggests that the negative consequences of alcohol consumption could be mitigated by eliminating this information gap.

There are a number of strategies for disseminating information to consumers about the relationship between alcohol and health. First, children in junior and senior high school can learn about alcohol-related health problems in their health education classes. Health experts agree that a comprehensive health education program should discuss the issue of alcohol abuse (American Medical Association, May 8, 2002; American School Health Association 1994).[12] Second, counter advertising campaigns and warning signs displayed wherever alcoholic beverages are sold can bring greater public awareness. Third, health information can be printed directly on the containers of alcoholic beverages. Since the passage of the Alcoholic Beverage Labeling Act of 1988, the following warning must appear on the label of each alcoholic beverage sold in the United States (Bureau of Alcohol, Tobacco, and Firearms, Notice 917, May 22, 2001):

GOVERNMENT WARNING: (1) According to the Surgeon General, women should not drink alcoholic beverages during pregnancy because of the risk of birth defects. (2) Consumption of alcoholic beverages impairs your ability to drive a car or operate machinery, and may cause health problems.

The evidence suggests that education programs may temper risky behavior. For example, Tremblay and Ling (2003) find that young people who studied AIDS education in school are more likely to use condoms. In addition, anti-smoking information and advertising campaigns have reduced the demand for cigarettes in the United States (Hamilton 1972; Wallace and DeJong 1995; Farr et al. 2001). Prugh (1986) finds that warning signs in New York increased public awareness of the health risks associated with alcohol consumption.

Research on the effect of health information on the demand for alcoholic beverages is limited, however. Regarding warning labels, a survey by the Center for Science in the Public Interest (May 25, 2001) revealed that few people read or notice them. Of alcohol drinkers, 63 percent said they never noticed the warning statement even though the labeling law has been in effect since November of 1989. Labeling may be ineffective because the print is difficult to read and is usually printed vertically on the label. As a result, more than 100 public health organizations and consumer groups petitioned the Bureau of Alcohol, Tobacco, and Firearms to make the following changes (Center for Science in the Public Interest, May 25, 2001):

• The health warning must appear in a prominent place on the front of the container and in a horizontal position.

• The warning statement must appear in red or black type on a white background and be surrounded by a lined border.

• The "government warning" statement must appear in capital letters and bold type that is at least 15 percent larger than the remaining text, which should be written in a font that maximizes legibility.

• The warning statement must appear with a red icon, a triangle with an exclamation mark inside.

There is little justification for opposing these changes, as they can only broaden consumer awareness and discourage excessive consumption.

Some groups fear that information on alcohol content may encourage certain consumers to seek out the strongest beers. Fearful that such "strength wars" would result if brewers were allowed to list alcohol content on packaging, section 5(e)(2) of the Federal Alcohol Administration Act of 1935 prohibited displaying alcohol content on beer labels.[13] In 1995, the Supreme Court ruled that this portion of the law violates freedom of speech (*Rubin, Secretary of the Treasury v. Coors Brewing Co.*, April 19, 1995; *Oregonian*, April 20, 1995). Writing for the court, Justice Clarence Thomas said that the law was "more extensive than necessary" and that less intrusive alternatives, such as limiting the ban to malt liquors where strength wars are more likely, are available. The ruling is sensible as it allows health-conscious consumers to identify low-alcohol products and fortuitously has not triggered a strength war.

Table 9.7 lists the alcohol and calorie content of the major brands in the leading categories of beer that were sold in the United States in 1991.[14] Domestic regular and light beer rank the lowest in both calories and alcohol content. On the other hand, malt liquor ranks highest in alcohol content of all beer categories. Potency, low price (see table 7.1), and marketing to minority communities have prompted considerable social concern about malt liquor in recent years.

As a final informational issue, Kenkel (1996) discovers that more complete health information about the risks of alcohol consumption is associated with a more price elastic demand function for alcoholic beverages. In this case, an excise tax increase will be more effective at curtailing demand. It is more likely, however, that heavy drinkers do not respond to price changes or information about health risks because they are addicted to alcohol and/or suffer from cognitive dissonance (Akerlof and Dickens 1982; Aronson 1999: 182). In the Manning et al. (1995) study, for example, the hypothesis that very heavy drinkers (i.e., the top 5 percent in terms of ethanol consumption) have perfectly inelastic demands cannot be rejected. If true, more accurate informa-

Table 9.7
Alcohol and calorie contents of leading brands of beer, 1991 and 2002. "Alcohol" represents alcohol content by volume. "Calories" represents total calories per 12 ounces. n.a.: not available. "Regular beer" includes popular, premium, and super-premium brands. Sources: Connecticut Agricultural Experiment Station, as reported in *Modern Brewery Age* (December 30, 1991, 3); firm documents.

| | Owning brewer | | | |
	1991	2002	Alcohol	Calories
Regular beer				
Andeker	Pabst	Pabst	4.71	n.a.
Ballantine	Falstaff	Pabst	4.82	153
Blatz	Heileman	Pabst	4.86	153
Budweiser	Anheuser-Busch	Anheuser-Busch	4.65	142
Busch	Anheuser-Busch	Anheuser-Busch	4.72	153
Carling Black Label	Heileman	—	4.46	149
Coors Banquet	Coors	Coors	4.55	137
Genesee	Genesee	High Falls	5.03	153
Hamm's	Pabst	Miller	4.40	142
Keystone	Coors	Coors	4.74	121
Knickerbocker	Heileman	—	4.46	136
Löwenbräu Special	Miller	—	4.93	158
Meisterbrau	Miller	Miller	4.57	141
Michelob	Anheuser-Busch	Anheuser-Busch	4.80	152
Michelob Golden Draft	Anheuser-Busch	Anheuser-Busch	4.80	152
Miller Genuine Draft	Miller	Miller	4.67	147
Miller High Life	Miller	Miller	4.67	147
Miller Reserve	Miller	—	4.71	133
Milwaukee's Best	Miller	Miller	4.34	133
Old Milwaukee	Stroh	Pabst	4.53	145
Olympia Lager	Pabst	Pabst	4.80	146
Pabst Blue Ribbon	Pabst	Pabst	4.78	149
Piels Draft-Style	Stroh	Pabst	4.54	146
Red, White & Blue	Pabst	—	4.79	149
Rheingold	Heileman	—	4.46	136
Rolling Rock Extra Pale	Latrobe	Latrobe	4.64	142
Schaefer	Stroh	Pabst	4.31	138
Schlitz	Stroh	Pabst	4.58	145
Signature	Stroh	—	4.84	153
Stroh's	Stroh	Pabst	4.39	140

Table 9.7
(continued)

	Owning brewer		Alcohol	Calories
	1991	2002		
Utica Club Lager	F. X. Matt	Matt	4.82	96
Yuengling Premium	Yuengling	Yuengling	4.38	138
Mean			4.66	143.3
Light beer				
Natural Light	Anheuser-Busch	Anheuser-Busch	4.26	114
Bud Light	Anheuser-Busch	Anheuser-Busch	4.16	114
Coors Light	Coors	Coors	4.36	107
Genesee Light	Genesee	High Falls	3.55	96
Henry Weinhard's Light	Pabst	Miller	n.a.	118
Keystone Lite	Coors	Coors	4.17	100
Löwenbräu Light	Miller	—	4.18	98
Meisterbrau Light	Miller	—	4.18	98
Michelob Light	Anheuser-Busch	Anheuser-Busch	4.23	134
Michelob Golden Draft Light	Anheuser-Busch	Anheuser-Busch	4.20	110
Michelob Ultra[a]	—	Anheuser-Busch	4.10	95
Miller Genuine Draft Light	Miller	—	4.18	98
Miller Lite	Miller	Miller	4.18	96
Miller Ultra Light	Miller	—	3.40	77
Miller Reserve Light	Miller	—	4.18	106
Milwaukee's Best Light	Miller	Miller	4.18	98
Old Milwaukee Light	Stroh	Pabst	3.82	114
Olympia Gold Light	Heileman	Pabst	n.a.	70
Pabst Extra Light	Pabst	Pabst	2.51	67
Piels Light	Stroh	Pabst	4.49	142
Rheingold Extra Light	Heileman	—	4.32	96
Schaefer Light	Stroh	Pabst	4.07	121
Schlitz Light	Stroh	Pabst	4.28	110
Stroh's Light	Stroh	Pabst	4.24	115
Mean			4.05	104.3
Malt liquor				
Colt 45	Heileman	Pabst	5.59	156

Table 9.7
(continued)

	Owning brewer		Alcohol	Calories
	1991	2002		
Haffenreffer	Falstaff	—	6.62	178
King Cobra	Anheuser-Busch	Anheuser-Busch	5.90	180
Magnum	Miller	Anheuser-Busch	5.92	160
Mickey's	Heileman	Miller	5.71	160
Olde English 800	Pabst	Miller	5.96	167
Schlitz	Stroh	Pabst	5.90	177
Mean			5.94	168.3
Ale and traditional dark beer				
Ballantine India Pale Ale	Falstaff	—	6.39	192
Ballantine XXX Ale	Falstaff	Pabst	5.38	170
Black Horse Ale	Genesee	—	4.74	160
Genesee 12-Horse Ale	Genesee	High Falls	4.87	160
Genesee Cream Ale	Genesee	High Falls	4.84	153
George Killian's Red	Coors	Coors	5.00	161
Lord Chesterfield Ale	Yuengling	Yuengling	5.49	131
Löwenbräu Special Dark	Miller	—	4.93	158
Michelob Classic Dark	Anheuser-Busch	—	4.80	154
Yuengling Pottsville Porter	Yuengling	Yuengling	4.13	142
Mean			5.06	157.8
Dry beer				
Bud Dry	Anheuser-Busch	Anheuser-Busch	4.80	130
Michelob	Anheuser-Busch	Anheuser-Busch	4.80	130
Mean			4.80	130.0
Ice beer				
Bud Ice	—	Anheuser-Busch	5.5	148
Icehouse	—	Miller	5.5	149
Milwaukee's Best Ice	—	Miller	5.5	132
Mean			5.50	143.0

Table 9.7
(continued)

	Owning brewer			
	1991	2002	Alcohol	Calories
Craft beer				
Anchor Porter	Anchor	Anchor	5.66	209
Anchor Steam	Anchor	Anchor	4.63	153
Boulder Porter	Boulder	—	6.07	188
Liberty Ale	Anchor	Anchor	6.12	188
Obsidian Stout	—	Deschures	6.7	220
Samuel Adams Lager	Boston Beer	Boston Beer	4.76	167
Sierra Nevada Pale Ale	Sierra Nevada	Sierra Nevada	4.82	160
Sierra Nevada Porter	Sierra Nevada	Sierra Nevada	5.34	170
Sierra Nevada Stout	Sierra Nevada	Sierra Nevada	5.11	199
Mean			5.37	183.8
Imported beer				
Bass Pale Ale (U.K.)			4.83	146
Beck's (Germany)			5.13	153
Corona Extra (Mexico)			4.84	160
Dos Equis Special (Mexico)			4.96	156
Foster's (Australia)			5.16	153
Guinness Extra Stout (Ireland)			4.27	153
Heineken Lager (Netherlands)			5.00	160
Kirin (Japan)			6.06	170
Molson's Golden Ale (Canada)			5.20	153
Pilsner Urquell (Czech Republic)			4.25	160
St. Pauli Girl (Germany)			4.91	160
Mean			5.46	172

a. Michelob Ultra is marketed as a low-carbohydrate light beer. It has 2.6 grams of carbohydrates, compared to 10.6 for Budweiser and 6.6 for Bud Light.

tion and a higher excise tax will have the smallest effect on those who abuse alcohol the most.

Alcohol and Motor Vehicle Accidents

The United States has made substantial progress in reducing alcohol-related motor vehicle collisions and fatalities. The total number of traffic fatalities associated with alcohol fell from 24,045 in 1986 to 17,126 in 2000 (National Highway Traffic Safety Administration 2000). In addition, underage drinking among junior and senior high school students has declined over the last decade, and the alcohol-related fatality rate of automobile crashes involving youth fell almost 55 percent from 1982 to 2000 (National Highway Traffic Safety Administration 2000; *Beer Industry Update: A Review of Recent Developments* 2002). In spite of these improvements, alcohol still contributed to about 40 percent of all fatalities from motor vehicle accidents in 2002, and of these alcohol-related fatalities, more than 77 percent involved those who were legally intoxicated. Evidence presented in the previous chapter makes it clear that driving while under the influence of alcohol imposes tremendous costs on society, much of which are external to the alcohol user.

One way to discourage alcohol-related motor vehicle accidents is to lower the legal limit on the amount of alcohol ingested before driving. In the area of traffic safety, this limit is expressed as a level of blood alcohol concentration (BAC), the proportion of alcohol to blood in the body.[15] In the last several years, most states have changed their BAC limit from 0.10 percent to 0.08 percent. Tables 9.8 and 9.9 list BAC levels by the number of standard-size drinks consumed after a particular time period for a male and female with average absorption rates. For example, a 180-pound male and a 120-pound female would have BAC levels of 0.12 percent if they drank seven and four cans of beer, respectively, in 2 hours. This BAC level exceeds the legal limit to drive in every state. (Appendix D gives BAC-level estimates for individuals of different body weights.)

Stricter BAC limits appear to reduce the cost of drunk driving.[16] After the National Highway Traffic Safety Administration (2000) estimated that decreasing the BAC limit from 0.10 percent to 0.08 percent would reduce the number of alcohol-related motor vehicle fatalities by 13.7 percent, Congress set 0.08 percent as the national standard. Effective October 1, 2003, states with BAC limits exceeding 0.08 percent lose 2 percent of their annual federal highway funds. As of the October 1

Table 9.8
Blood alcohol concentration for 180-pound male. Bold type indicates BAC values in excess of 0.10 percent. Underlined and bold values exceed BAC of 0.08 percent. A drink contains 0.6 ounce of pure alcohol. This corresponds to a 12-ounce container of beer (5 percent alcohol by volume), a 6-ounce glass of wine (10 percent alcohol by volume), or a 1.5-ounce shot of spirits (80 proof; 40 percent alcohol by volume). See appendix D for sources and further discussion.

	Hours since drinks were consumed							
Drinks	1	2	3	4	5	6	7	8
0	0	0	0	0	0	0	0	0
1	0.005	0	0	0	0	0	0	0
2	0.025	0.010	0	0	0	0	0	0
3	0.045	0.030	0.015	0	0	0	0	0
4	0.065	0.050	0.035	0.020	0.005	0	0	0
5	<u>0.085</u>	0.070	0.055	0.040	0.025	0.010	0	0
6	**0.105**	<u>**0.090**</u>	0.075	0.060	0.045	0.030	0.015	0
7	**0.135**	**0.120**	**0.105**	<u>**0.090**</u>	0.075	0.060	0.045	0.030
8	**0.155**	**0.140**	**0.125**	**0.110**	<u>**0.095**</u>	<u>**0.080**</u>	0.065	0.050

Table 9.9
Blood alcohol concentration for 120-pound female. Bold type indicates BAC in excess of 0.10 percent. Underlined and bold values exceed BAC of 0.08 percent.

	Hours since drinks were consumed							
Drinks	1	2	3	4	5	6	7	8
0	0	0	0	0	0	0	0	0
1	0.025	0.010	0	0	0	0	0	0
2	0.065	0.050	0.035	0.020	0.005	0	0	0
3	<u>0.095</u>	<u>0.080</u>	0.065	0.050	0.035	0.020	0.005	0
4	**0.135**	**0.120**	**0.105**	<u>**0.090**</u>	0.075	0.060	0.045	0.030
5	**0.175**	**0.160**	**0.145**	**0.130**	**0.115**	**0.100**	<u>**0.085**</u>	0.070
6	**0.215**	**0.200**	**0.185**	**0.170**	**0.155**	**0.140**	**0.125**	**0.110**
7	**0.255**	**0.240**	**0.225**	**0.210**	**0.195**	**0.180**	**0.165**	**0.150**
8	**0.285**	**0.270**	**0.255**	**0.240**	**0.225**	**0.210**	**0.195**	**0.180**

deadline, six states retain a 0.10 limit: New Jersey, Colorado, Delaware, Minnesota, Pennsylvania, and West Virginia (Martel 2003).

Even the 0.08 BAC limit may be too lenient, however, as alcohol impairs the driving skills of most people at far lower BAC levels. The American Medical Association (1997, 1998) finds that there is "substantial and consistent impairment" in driving ability and that the "risk of fatal crashes greatly increases" for most people when BAC levels reach 0.04 or 0.05 percent. As a result, the American Medical Association favors a "zero-tolerance" rule, but concedes that a 0.05 percent BAC limit is politically feasible. The American Academy of Family Physicians (1995) takes this further, recommending a BAC limit of 0.04 percent. This is consistent with the 0.04 percent BAC limit for commercial drivers, established by the Commercial Motor Vehicle Act of 1986.[17] The 0.04 percent limit seems sensible and even generous to the alcohol user, as it would allow a typical 180-pound male, for example, to legally drive a motor vehicle 2 hours after consuming three drinks.

Another strategy for deterring traffic fatalities is to limit youth access to alcohol. After Prohibition, most states restricted alcohol consumption to individuals 21 years of age and over. In the early 1970s, 29 states relaxed the minimum legal drinking age (MLDA) to under 21 (typically 18, 19, or 20).[18] Eighteen-year-olds won the right to vote in 1970, and many state politicians argued that an adult who is eligible to vote and to be drafted into the military should be extended the right to drink alcoholic beverages. Since then, many researchers have studied the effect of MLDA on alcohol-related accidents. Early studies from the 1970s reported substantial increases in motor vehicle crashes among teenagers when the MLDA was lowered. As the evidence mounted, public advocacy groups pressured states to raise the MLDA back to 21. Sixteen states raised their MLDA to 21 years of age during the years 1976–1983. Remaining states followed after the federal government passed the Uniform Drinking Act in 1984, which cut federal transportation funds to states that allowed drinking for anyone under 21. The National Highway Traffic Safety Association (2000: 4) estimates that returning to the MLDA of 21 has "reduced traffic fatalities involving drivers 18–20 years old by 13 percent and has saved an estimated 20,043 lives from 1975 to 2000." Overall, the alcohol-related fatality rate for youth dropped from 22 to 10 deaths per 100,000 young people from 1982 to 2000 (National Highway Traffic Safety Administration 2000; *Beer Industry Update: A Review of Recent Developments* 2002).

Strict penalties on drunk drivers may also deter alcohol-related motor vehicle crashes. The American Medical Association (1997) recommends suspending the driver's license of all who are convicted of driving under the influence (DUI) of alcohol; enacting and enforcing stronger penalties against repeat offenders; and linking DUI penalties with alcohol-abuse assessment and treatment services.

The American Medical Association is also urging the National Highway Safety Administration to investigate new technologies that will prevent the engine of an automobile from starting when the driver's BAC level exceeds legal limits. It is in the public interest to pursue these policy recommendations.

Excise Taxes

One policy recommendation that has received considerable support is raising the excise tax on beer. At least a portion of the tax increase is passed on to consumers in the form of higher prices, which in turn will discourage consumption (see chapter 2).[19] In a survey by Harwood et al. (1998) for the Robert Wood Johnson Foundation, 61 percent of those surveyed favor higher alcohol taxes to pay for alcohol treatment programs.[20]

For an excise, or Pigovian, tax to be efficient, it must adjust the price of a commodity so that consumers pay the full social cost of the product (Varian 1992). An excise tax may be especially effective when the tax revenue supports alcohol education, abuse assessment, and treatment programs. Estimates from the previous chapter indicate that the external cost of alcohol consumption lies between $0.81 and $1.03 per ounce of ethanol. Including a generous estimate of the external benefits to moderate consumption, the estimated tax rate commensurate with the net external cost of alcohol consumption ranges from $0.45 to $0.67 per ounce of ethanol (or from $1.52 to $2.28 per six-pack).[21]

These estimates far surpass current federal excise tax rates. The 2001 average tax rate per ounce of ethanol is about $0.10 for beer, $0.07 for wine, and $0.21 for spirits. One reason for low taxes today is that the tax is levied on output rather than dollar sales. As a result, inflation continually erodes the real value of the tax rate. Figure 9.1 tracks the federal tax rate in 1982 cents per ounce of ethanol for spirits, beer, and wine. For both spirits and beer, the current tax rate falls substantially below rates from the 1950s. Figure 9.2 plots the federal and average state excise tax rates per barrel of beer in real 1982 dollars. The average

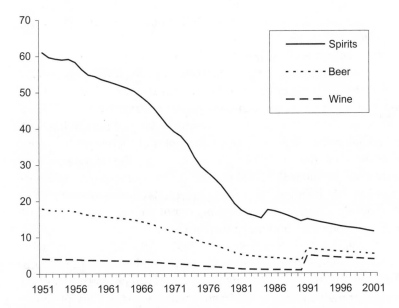

Figure 9.1
The real federal excise tax rate on spirits, beer, and wine (1982 dollars per ounce of
ethanol sold), 1951–2001. Sources: Federation of Tax Administrators; *Brewers Almanac*.

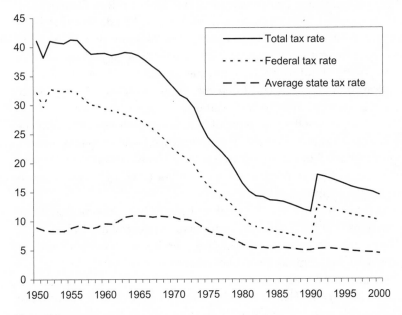

Figure 9.2
Total, federal, and state excise tax rates on beer (1982 dollars per barrel), 1950–2000.
Source: See appendix A.

state rate has also declined since the 1950s but not as steeply as the federal rate.

Another concern with current tax policy is the disparity among rates for beer, wine, and spirits. One could argue that an efficient tax should equalize rates per unit of ethanol. The Distilled Spirits Council of the United States (2002) claims that the current tax system discriminates against distilled spirits because a standard serving of beer, wine, and spirits contains the same amount of ethanol and therefore should be taxed at the same rate. To cover all external costs, the tax rate on beer must increase by more than 400 percent, wine by more than 600 percent, and spirits by more than 200 percent. Weinberg questions the merit of an equalization policy; spirits are not packaged in a standard serving, and one can become intoxicated more quickly with spirits (personal conversation, September 23, 2002). After all, a person who consumes 12 ounces of spirits would have to drink nine 12-ounce cans of beer to ingest the same amount of ethanol. Further, recent evidence suggests that highway safety diminishes with the availability of spirits but increases with the availability of beer and wine (Baughman et al. 2001). Thus, a higher tax rate on spirits may be warranted.

In addition to paying for the external cost of alcohol consumption, a higher excise tax can deter consumption via higher prices. Denney et al. (2002) estimate a demand and supply system to address this issue directly for the U.S. brewing industry. Results show that a 1 percent increase in the federal excise tax rate causes the equilibrium price of beer to rise by about 0.8 percent and the equilibrium level of beer consumption to fall by about 0.12 percent. Figure 9.3 charts the real price and excise (federal and average state) tax rate for beer from 1953 to 2001.[22] One can see that the price of beer jumped in 1991, the year the federal excise tax rate doubled. The downward trend in the tax and the apparent shortfall in the tax relative to the socially optimum tax appear to be policy concerns, particularly since lower taxes and prices encourage beer consumption.

Even if tax rates match the social cost of alcohol consumption, there is a fundamental problem with using taxes to deal with alcohol abuse problems in our society. Although an excise tax policy would be appropriate for commodities like cigarettes that generate negative externalities at all levels of consumption, it may be inappropriate for alcoholic beverages. Heavy drinking causes negative externalities, but moderate drinking generates positive externalities. If higher taxes and

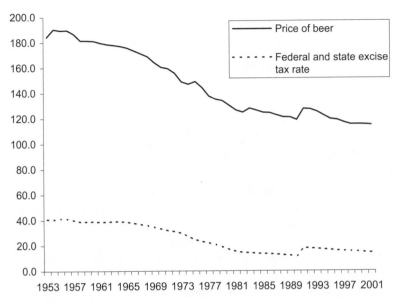

Figure 9.3
The price of beer and the total (federal and average state) excise tax rate on beer (1982 dollars), 1953–2001. Source: See appendix A. The price of beer is derived from the price index of beer (see appendix A) and Standard and Poor's (2001) estimate that the average excise tax rate on beer was 17 percent of the price in 1997.

prices reduce moderate drinking and have little or no effect on heavy drinking and alcohol abuse, a policy to raise taxes could actually lower social welfare. At issue is the extent to which a higher price affects alcohol abuse not use.

Several studies suggest a negative link between alcohol prices and abuse.[23] Alcohol taxes appear to depress rates of mortality arising from cirrhosis of the liver (Cook and Tauchen 1982) and highway fatalities (Chaloupka et al. 1993). Ohsfeldt and Morrisey (1997) find that higher beer taxes are related to lower rates of injury in the work place. Furthermore, alcohol consumption appears to be associated with sexually transmitted diseases and violent crimes. (See chapter 8.) In all, this research implies that higher taxes on alcohol would mitigate external effects.

Two main criticisms call these studies into question. First, the evidence reveals correlation but not necessarily causation. For example, a decline in alcohol consumption and abuse may induce state government officials to increase tax rates to recover lost tax revenues. Both

Cook and Tauchen (1981) and Ohsfeldt and Morrisey (1997) perform specification tests, however, indicating that causality runs from taxes to cirrhosis and from taxes to work place injuries. Still, a third cause may explain the link between taxes and abuse. For example, public sentiment or concern for health may cause both moderate drinking and higher alcohol taxes.

Sloan et al. (1994), Mast et al. (1999), Dee (1999), Stout et al. (2000), and Young and Likens (2000) provide convincing evidence of a third cause that influences both taxes and alcohol-related outcomes. To illustrate, Dee (1999) analyzes the effect of alcohol policies on teenage drinking and traffic fatalities. Unobserved state specific attributes, like culture and drinking sentiment, partially explain the negative correlations between beer taxes and youth drinking and traffic fatalities. With better controls, such as distinguishing between nighttime and daytime driving fatalities, Dee finds that beer taxes have a relatively small and insignificant effect on teenage alcohol consumption and traffic fatalities. These studies cast doubt on previous research which fails to consider all important determinants of alcohol-related outcomes.

The complexity of these relationships comes to light by comparing the rates of per-capita ethanol consumption, liver disease, and alcohol-related traffic fatalities by state. Figure 9.4 orders states from those with the highest to the lowest alcohol consumption rates for 2000.[24] Simple inspection of the data reveals no obvious correlation between variables but shows that individual state effects are important. For example, Nevada leads in alcohol consumption because of tourism and legalized gambling. States with a large proportion of people who oppose alcohol consumption for religious reasons, such as Kentucky, Utah, and Alabama, have low alcohol consumption and low rates of liver disease. And while Kentucky and Utah have low alcohol-related traffic fatality rates, Alabama's fatality rate matches the national average. Alabama levies the highest tax rate of all states on alcoholic beverages, while Kentucky's tax rate falls far below the national average. (See table 9.10.) Furthermore, states with substantial alcohol production, such as California (wine and beer), Colorado (beer), Kentucky (Spirits), Missouri (beer), and Wisconsin (beer), keep tax rates down. This is consistent with the evidence that state legislatures favor industries with a large number of employees and a lobbying presence (Benjamin and Dougan 1997; Feng 1998). In spite of very low tax rates, California and Colorado witness proportionally fewer than average

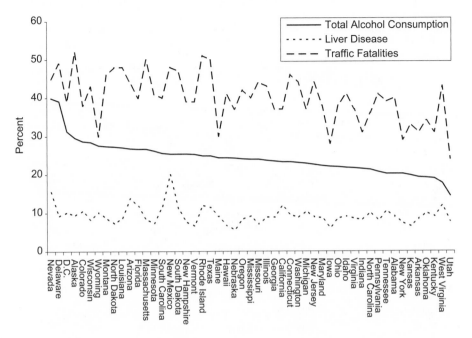

Figure 9.4

Total alcohol consumption (0.1 gallon per capita), age-adjusted liver disease rate (per 1,000 people), and percent of traffic fatalities involving alcohol for 2000. Sources: *Beer Industry Update: A Review of Recent Developments* (2002); Department of Health and Human Services, National Vital Statistics Reports 50, no. 15, September 16, 2002; Department of Transportation; National Center for Statistics Analysis.

traffic fatalities while Missouri and Wisconsin have below-average rates of liver disease. These simple comparisons lack proper control of unobservable variables necessary for drawing valid conclusions as was discussed earlier and illustrate that to fully understand the relationship between taxes and alcohol abuse, one must control for numerous effects.

The complexity of these relationships and the evidence from Dee and others, warrants further research on the extent to which higher taxes curb alcohol abuse. If higher taxes dissuade moderate drinkers but have little or no effect on alcohol abusers as the work of Manning et al. (1995) suggests, then higher excise taxes would lower social welfare. At this point, the evidence suggests that an excise tax is too blunt an instrument to alleviate the social costs associated with alcohol abuse.[25]

Table 9.10
State sales tax information and excise tax rates on beer, wine, and spirits, 2002. Source:
Federation of Tax Administrators. Letter "a" in column indicates that revenues are generated from various taxes and fees.

	Excise tax rate ($/gallon)			
	Beer	Wine	Spirits	State sales tax?
Alabama	0.53	1.70	a	Yes
Alaska	0.35	0.85	5.60	No
Arizona	0.16	0.84	3.00	Yes
Arkansas	0.23	0.75	2.50	Yes
California	0.20	0.20	3.30	Yes
Colorado	0.08	0.32	2.28	Yes
Connecticut	0.19	0.60	4.50	Yes
Delaware	0.16	0.97	3.75	No
D.C.	0.09	0.30	1.50	Yes
Florida	0.48	2.25	6.50	Yes
Georgia	0.48	1.51	3.79	Yes
Hawaii	0.92	1.36	5.92	Yes
Idaho	0.15	0.45	a	Yes
Illinois	0.185	0.73	4.50	Yes
Indiana	0.12	0.47	2.68	Yes
Iowa	0.19	1.75	a	Yes
Kansas	0.18	0.30	2.50	—
Kentucky	0.08	0.50	1.92	Yes
Louisiana	0.32	0.11	2.50	Yes
Maine	0.35	0.60	a	Yes
Maryland	0.09	0.40	1.50	Yes
Massachusetts	0.11	0.55	4.05	Yes
Michigan	0.20	0.51	a	Yes
Minnesota	0.15	0.30	5.03	—
Mississippi	0.43	0.35	a	Yes
Missouri	0.06	0.36	2.00	Yes
Montana	0.14	1.06	a	No
Nebraska	0.23	0.75	3.00	Yes
Nevada	0.09	0.40	2.05	Yes
New Hampshire	0.30	a	a	No
New Jersey	0.12	0.70	4.40	Yes
New Mexico	0.41	1.70	6.06	Yes
New York	0.135	0.19	6.44	Yes
North Carolina	0.53	0.79	a	Yes
North Dakota	0.16	0.50	2.50	—
Ohio	0.18	0.32	a	Yes

Table 9.10
(continued)

	Excise tax rate ($/gallon)			State sales tax?
	Beer	Wine	Spirits	
Oklahoma	0.40	0.72	5.56	Yes
Oregon	0.08	0.67	a	No
Pennsylvania	0.08	a	a	Yes
Rhode Island	0.1	0.60	3.75	Yes
South Carolina	0.77	0.90	2.72	Yes
South Dakota	0.27	0.93	3.93	Yes
Tennessee	0.13	1.10	4.00	Yes
Texas	0.19	0.20	2.40	Yes
Utah	0.35	a	a	Yes
Vermont	0.265	0.55	a	No
Virginia	0.26	1.51	a	Yes
Washington	0.261	0.87	a	Yes
West Virginia	0.18	1.00	a	Yes
Wisconsin	0.06	0.25	3.25	Yes
Wyoming	0.02	a	a	Yes
Mean	*0.239*	*0.739*	*3.618*	

9.3 Advertising, Advertising Restrictions, and Social Welfare

Beer, wine, and spirits producers spend almost $1.5 billion each year on advertising. Of the three, the beer industry spends by far the most on advertising in total and per unit of ethanol. (See table 9.11.) The advertising gap per ounce of ethanol between beer and the other alcoholic beverages is narrowing, as wine and spirits advertising have increased relative to beer advertising from 1995 to 2000.

An important change in advertising strategy occurred in November 1996 when the Distilled Spirits Council of the United States voted unanimously to drop its 48-year voluntary ban of advertising on television.[26] The vote was motivated by sagging sales, as spirits share of all ethanol consumed in the United States declined from 44.3 percent to 28.8 percent from 1970 to 1996 (*Beer Industry Update: A Review of Recent Developments* 2002). Spirits producers argued that they should be allowed to compete on a "level playing field" with beer and wine producers, since the standard servings of beer, wine, and spirits contain the same amount of ethanol.

Table 9.11

Advertising spending in the brewing, wine, and distilled spirits industries. Source: *Beer Industry Update: A Review of Recent Developments* (various issues) and *Adams Business Media, Beer, Wine, and Liquor Handbooks* (various issues). Data include spending on magazine, newspaper, outdoor, and broadcast advertising.

	Advertising expenditures ($1,000)				Advertising expenditures ($) per ounce of ethanol			
	Beer	Wine	Spirits	Total	Beer	Wine	Spirits	Total
1995	736,283	68,265	230,487	1,035,035	20.36	9.68	13.12	17.03
1996	713,148	83,104	226,842	1,023,094	19.48	10.87	12.67	16.47
1997	726,082	101,463	256,332	1,083,877	19.68	12.71	14.26	17.25
1998	764,228	131,577	291,230	1,187,035	20.46	16.34	16.17	18.72
1999	799,690	120,511	321,323	1,241,524	21.08	14.43	17.42	19.18
2000	910,442	133,183	377,013	1,420,628	23.76	15.24	19.71	21.46

With the ban rescinded, television advertising of spirits increased from $3.5 million in 1996 to $25.2 million in 2000. In spite of this surge in advertising spending overall and relative to beer and wine producers, spirits' share of alcoholic beverage sales remained flat between 1995 and 2001. This is consistent with previous work discussed in chapter 2 which shows that advertising has little effect on the market demand for alcoholic beverages and that spirits advertising may attract few if any beer and wine drinkers. Of course, the market share of spirits may have fallen without this advertising boost. Further research is needed to determine the effect of this new spirits advertising on the consumption of spirits, wine, and beer.

Several consumer advocacy groups and recent surveys convey concern that television advertising may promote alcohol use and abuse.[27] In one survey (Harwood et al. 1998), 58 percent of respondents believe that alcohol advertising increases how much people drink, 61 percent favor a ban on television advertising of beer and wine, and 67 percent favor a ban on television advertising of spirits. When spirits producers began to advertise on television in 1996, President Clinton, Mothers Against Drunk Driving, and the Center for Science in the Public Interest voiced immediate concern. Further, the American Medical Association asked network and cable television companies to ban beer and wine ads from prime-time television (*Modern Brewery Age, Weekly News Edition*, December 16, 2002). The Federal Trade Commission responded by reviewing the merits of alcohol advertising. Citing protection of advertising as free speech under the Constitution and insufficient evidence linking advertising to alcohol abuse, the Federal Trade Commission (1999) did not favor formal restrictions; instead it encouraged the beer, wine, and spirits industries to improve their self-regulation of advertising.[28]

The Federal Trade Commission report did recommend that advertisers of alcoholic beverages follow the industry's "current best practices." These include prohibiting advertisements with substantial underage appeal, placing advertisements where most of the audience is reasonably expected to be of legal drinking age, curbing advertising and sponsorships on college campuses, and restricting the promotional placement of alcoholic beverages to films rated R and NC-17. The Beer Institute (2002) lists 13 guidelines to which its members subscribe. In addition to those listed in the Federal Trade Commission report, the guidelines state that advertising should "portray beer in a responsible manner." Specifically, beer ads should not depict the act of drinking or intoxication, not link beer to activities that require alertness or coordination, and not disparage competing brands.[29] The guidelines also ban ads that contain lewd or amorous activity, depictions of Santa Claus, and cartoon characters "intended to appeal primarily to persons below the legal drinking age."

Had all brewers followed the principles of the voluntary guidelines, the industry would have avoided the objections leveled at beer advertising. (See chapter 8.) For example, they would have eliminated the popular Hamm's bear cartoon character of the 1960s and the Anheuser-Busch spokesdog (Spuds McKenzie), frogs, lizards, and the Bud Man characters in Budweiser advertisements during the 1980s and the 1990s. In fact Miller, which owns the Hamm's label, recently objected to a planned fiftieth-birthday celebration of the Hamm's Bear by the Hamm's Club of Minneapolis for fear that the celebration "might appear to condone or target underage drinkers" (*Modern Brewery Age, Weekly News Edition*, July 22, 2002: 3). Brewers would also have refrained from introducing Nude Beer in the early 1980s and Stroh's Swedish Bikini Team, Heileman's PowerMaster Malt Liquor, and the Heileman-Stroh Crazy Horse Malt Liquor of the 1990s. Today's "sexy new ads" from Miller, Coors, and Boston demonstrate that the major brewers do not always conform to the guidelines.

Even if the content of all beer advertisements meets socially acceptable standards, the brewing industry may still advertise excessively from society's perspective. Chapter 8 shows that the welfare effect of socially acceptable forms of advertising depends on how advertising affects consumer surplus, producer surplus, and the externalities associated with alcohol consumption. Tremblay and Tremblay (1995) estimate these effects for a marginal change in beer advertising and find that advertising leads to higher prices and is oversupplied. Tremblay and Tremblay's result should be interpreted with caution, however, as it ignores the potential health benefits associated with the moderate consumption of alcohol. It also ignores the finding by Manning et al. (1995) that price changes have little or no effect on alcohol abuse, the true policy target.

If Tremblay and Tremblay's result is correct, a complete ban on advertising might not improve welfare, since their work analyzes the welfare effect of a marginal change in advertising. The effect of an advertising ban on price and social welfare remains uncertain.[30] In addition, Sass and Saurman (1995) find that state restrictions on price advertising benefit national producers and increase concentration. If their result is generally true, a ban on beer advertising would be illegal under current law.

9.4   Policy Issues Involving Specialty and Import Brewers

The continued success of the specialty and import brewers eases some of the concerns with the trend toward concentration in the mass-producing segment of the industry. The beers that survived the consolidation of the mass producers in the 1960s through the 1980s were light in flavor and remarkably similar. The uniformity of regular beer in the United States along with an increased demand for variety and quality among consumers sparked an interest in import and specialty products.

Initially, the import and specialty sector was so small that it was ignored by policy economists. When commenting on the policy implications of the success of the microbreweries, for example, Scherer (1996: 423) states that there are "precisely none." Today, if one includes import as well the specialty brewers, the sector cannot be ignored. Imports and specialty brewers now account for more than 13 percent of beer sales in the United States. Success of the micros has also changed the behavior of the mass producers, inducing them to be more innovative and to offer their own versions of specialty beer, albeit with limited success. At the very least, the entry of more than 1,500 specialty brewers from 1980 to 2001 is a testament to consumer sovereignty and entrepreneurial zeal. Today, consumers have access to a wide array of brands of light lager, all-malt lager, ale, porter, and stout from a variety of domestic and import brewers. Since most specialty and imported brands differ significantly from regular domestic beer, however, the effect of entry into this sector on competition is likely to be limited to the higher-priced super-premium brands.

9.5 Policy Recommendations and Conclusions

The U.S. brewing industry is particularly interesting as a subject of policy analysis. There are three areas of concern: anti-trust matters, alcohol abuse, and socially undesirable beer ads.

An evaluation of the enforcement of the anti-trust laws is mixed. For the most part, the U.S. government has dealt appropriately with price fixing, predatory pricing, and exclusive dealing contracts detrimental to competition. Of greater concern has been the government's enforcement of the anti-merger laws. With increasing concentration and considerable merger activity, the U.S. Department of Justice prevented almost all mergers that involved one or more brewers from the top two tiers. In hindsight, it is clear that this policy was misguided. The legal mergers that involved third-tier brewers have not produced a single mass-producing brewer that is competitive with the industry leaders. In addition, constraining second-tier firms from growing by merger left most of them inefficiently small and led to their eventual demise. Had the Department of Justice allowed the proposed mergers between Pabst and Carling in 1978, Heileman and Schlitz in 1982, and Coors and Stroh in 1989, growth of Anheuser-Busch might have been checked and a greater number of viable competitors might be in existence today.

Pabst continues to decline and is expected to exit the market soon. Anheuser-Busch, Miller, and Coors will then claim about 95 percent of all domestic beer sales. In this setting, it would be socially undesirable to allow any of the top three firms to merge unless one was clearly failing. With so few major competitors, non-competitive prices and profits are expected. Even with positive economic profits, substantial scale economies and sunk costs block domestic entry and make the mass-producing sector a natural oligopoly. Higher profits may increase the supply of imported beer, however, especially from neighboring countries that produce lighter brands (e.g., Corona) that are close substitutes for regular domestic beer. Therefore, additional policy recommendations include eliminating trade barriers and encouraging a competitive specialty sector.

With respect to externalities, there is little doubt that the cost of alcohol abuse is substantial and that stricter policies are needed to reduce the social cost of alcohol consumption in the United States. A number of policies have been proposed and implemented with varying degrees of success. The primary policy tools include providing consumers with information about the risks of alcohol abuse, raising the excise tax, and imposing stiffer penalties on alcohol abusers.

A discussion of alcohol policy would be incomplete without a reference to prohibition. Some religious groups and public health organizations continue to support government policies that would limit access and even prohibit the consumption of alcoholic beverages in the United States.[31] The most passionate groups are religious organizations that cast alcohol consumption as sinful. Even if this is true, however, appropriate policy analysis in a society that values individual freedom must consider the social benefits and costs of prohibiting alcohol consumption. Most developed countries considered or implemented some form of prohibition during the early 1900s. Iceland holds the record, with 23 years of prohibition. The United States is second, having prohibited consumption of all alcoholic beverages for 14 years (*Brewers Digest*, November 1938). These experiments failed, and alcohol consumption is legal in all developed countries today. In view of the apparent health benefits of moderate alcohol consumption and the failure of prohibition to curtail alcohol consumption, policies to reduce excessive alcohol consumption are more prudent than prohibiting alcohol consumption altogether.

A first step toward limiting alcohol abuse is to ensure that all consumers are fully informed about the benefits and costs of alcohol consumption. Information about the definition of moderate drinking, the health risks associated with excessive drinking, and the consumption rates of beer, wine, and spirits expected to impair driving should be a part of the health curriculum in junior and senior high schools. In addition, those convicted of driving a motor vehicle while intoxicated should be counseled about the health consequences of heavy drinking and the increased risk of a fatal traffic accident when driving under the influence of alcohol. Encouraging research that would allow individuals to identify their predisposition toward alcoholism may also prove fruitful. Government warning labels should be changed in accordance with the recommendations of public-interest organizations, as was discussed earlier in the chapter. It would be beneficial to rotate these warnings with information about lesser-known health risks, about beer-consumption rates consistent with moderate and excessive drinking, and about new research findings on alcohol use as they emerge.

The connection between alcohol consumption and motor vehicle crashes is unequivocal, and more stringent policies are warranted. The first policy recommendation is to lower the BAC limit. The ideal would be to adopt a "zero-tolerance rule," making it illegal to drink and drive (i.e., set the BAC limit to just over 0 percent). After even one drink, some impairment occurs. Zero tolerance would save lives and send a strong signal that drinking and driving is socially unacceptable. Although the political feasibility of such a policy has been questioned, it has been adopted in several Eastern European countries and in parts of Japan. A zero-tolerance rule encourages a designated driver or planned use of a taxi when individuals drink away from home. Perhaps a more realistic goal would be to set the BAC limit at 0.04 percent, the limit imposed on commercial drivers and recommended by the American Academy of Family Physicians. This would allow an average person to drink in excess of a moderate amount of alcohol and still drive legally within 2 hours. The second policy recommendation is to impose strict penalties on those who drink to excess and drive a motor vehicle. The recommendations of the American Medical Association that are discussed in this chapter should be implemented.

An excise tax is commonly used to mitigate the social costs of negative externalities. The issue is more complex for alcoholic beverages, however, since moderate consumption generates positive externalities and excessive consumption generates negative externalities. In a case like this, the ideal excise tax rate would be non-linear, with a subsidy to encourage moderate consumption and a very high tax rate on excessive consumption. Because such a policy is impractical, the use of an excise tax to mitigate the negative externalities associated with alcohol abuse appears (pending additional research) to be misguided. A moderate tax may be warranted, however, if it finances alcohol-education and anti-alcohol-abuse programs. Some have called for equalization of the tax rates on beer, wine, and spirits. Recall that the average tax rate per ounce of alcohol in 2001 is about $0.10 for beer, $0.07 for wine, and $0.21 for spirits. The main concern with this recommendation is that a person can become intoxicated much more quickly on spirits than on beer; one can down six shots of spirits much faster than six cans of beer, for example, and ingest the same amount of alcohol. Thus, a higher tax rate on spirits may be warranted. There appears to be no social justification for the higher tax rate on beer than wine, however.[32]

Is beer advertising socially desirable? The industry's voluntary guidelines encourage socially responsible advertising, but some beer ads clearly violate the guidelines by promoting sexist stereotypes and underage drinking. It is in the industry's interest to enforce existing guidelines strictly. Without better self-regulation, greater government intervention can be expected. The evidence suggests that beer advertising is socially excessive, but it is not clear that an advertising ban would improve welfare. On the other hand, consumers' general lack of knowledge about the health risks associated with heavy drinking suggests that society may benefit from product labeling and publicly sponsored advertising campaigns that provide consumers with accurate information concerning the costs of alcohol abuse.

10 Concluding Remarks, Forecasts, and Directions for Future Research

We should all be concerned about the future because we will have to spend the rest of our lives there.

—Charles Kettering, *Seed for Thought* (1949)

History, economic theory, firm and industry data, and empirical analysis have guided this investigation of the U.S. brewing industry in the later half of the twentieth century. Three features of the industry stand out: the tremendous increase in industry concentration, the continued success of Anheuser-Busch, and the emergence of the "domestic specialty" and "import" segments of the market.

The evidence shows that changes in technology and marketing conditions allowed for only a few viable firms, provoking a war-of-attrition game in brewing. The advent of television gave national firms a competitive advantage and caused a preemption race in advertising as brewers fought for marketing superiority. Greater advertising competition also raised the sunk costs of doing business in brewing. As a result, most of the mass-producing beer companies exited the industry, and sales became concentrated in fewer and fewer hands. Brewers able to market their beer effectively and reach minimum efficient scale or to serve a regional-niche market were most likely to survive.

As the war of attrition continued, battles were waged along a number of strategic fronts. The national brewers introduced new products and increased advertising spending in an effort to take advantage of the new television medium, to maintain a premium image for their flagship brands, and to promote new products. They also built super-sized breweries in order to attain scale efficiency. A handful of regional brewers survived by retreating to small niche markets. Price competition remained high, as firms with shrinking sales and idle equipment resorted to price cuts. Many firms that exited were purchased by other brewers, a process that effectively transferred assets from failing to more successful firms. As a result of strict enforcement of the anti-trust laws, most mergers were a consequence of the attrition war and not a direct cause of high concentration or market power in brewing.

Anheuser-Busch played a prominent role in the evolution of the industry and continues to do so today. Since the 1950s, Anheuser-Busch has established a number of efficiently sized plants throughout the country, saving on transportation costs and exploiting scale economies. In addition, Anheuser-Busch was the first to offer brands in the popular-priced, premium, and super-premium categories. In contrast, the company was slow to develop a winning brand of light beer. Once introduced, however, Bud Light became popular, and it has been the best-selling light beer since 1994. Studies confirm that Anheuser-Busch's marketing is the most efficient in the industry. With strategically located plants of efficient size, an efficient product mix, and a successful marketing program, Anheuser-Busch has been consistently successful and has become the largest brewer in the United States.

One can gain a deeper understanding of business strategy by studying the actions of winning firms like Anheuser-Busch, but lessons can also be learned from failing firms. The Schlitz Brewing Company provides an excellent case study. During the 1950s, Schlitz and Anheuser-Busch were competitive equals that battled back and forth for the top spot in brewing. Anheuser-Busch edged ahead during the 1960s and the early 1970s, but Schlitz remained a strong number two. Schlitz went into a tailspin in the late 1970s, primarily because management failed to maintain quality and to protect the reputation of its flagship brand. An important lesson to be learned from the Schlitz mistake is that product reputation is essential to market success in consumer-goods markets.

Since the late 1970s, three main forces have fostered the domestic specialty and import segments of the market. First, economic prosperity stimulated demand for brands with social status and an image of quality, including premium and super-premium beer as well as the domestic specialty and imported brands. Second, as the mass producers continued to consolidate, the domestic brands that remained became lighter and more alike. At the same time, consumers began to demand greater variety, which created a niche for domestic specialty and imported brands. Third, small domestic specialty brewers benefited from changes in legislation. For example, the federal excise tax on beer produced by microbreweries and brew pubs was lowered in 1977; today the rate is 61 percent below the rate paid by the mass producers. Thus, while the mass producers continued to exit, domestic and import brewers entered the U.S. market and flourished for most of the 1980s and the 1990s.

Another important goal of this book is to assess the predictions of game theory in light of the observed strategic behavior of firms in brewing over time. The evidence verifies that game theory is useful in many ways. Historical and empirical evidence indicate that changes in technology and marketing opportunities forced brewers into a pre-emption race in advertising and into a war-of-attrition game that would force most firms out of business. In this setting, a firm's alter-natives are to grow and survive, to find a profitable niche market, to exit, and to continue for a time by harvesting the value of physical assets and product goodwill. During the battle to survive, a "Hail Mary" strategy may be optimal for a marginal firm, as only the upside risk counts for a firm on the brink of failure. The evidence shows that all of these strategies were used in brewing. Anheuser-Busch, Miller, and Coors have grown in size and are national in scope, supporting the hypotheses that size matters and that a national distribution pro-vides a competitive advantage in brewing. Genesee, Yuengling, and many microbrewers serve regional niche markets. Former leaders like Ballantine, Falstaff, and Schlitz exited without much fight. Heileman, Pabst, and Stroh pursued a harvesting strategy as they began their long and slow decline. Brewers under financial stress resorted to blind-taste-test commercials and to gimmick brands (e.g., generic beer, Nude Beer, Billy Beer) in a desperate effort to survive. The evidence also indicates that brewers use a mixed pricing strategy to market premium brands and a trigger strategy to maintain high prices, actions that are optimal in certain game-theoretic settings. The shakeout in the spe-cialty sector during the late 1990s indicates that early entrants are more likely to survive. That result suggests the importance of experience and a first-mover advantage.

Of course, not all the actions of brewing firms have aligned with the predictions of game theory. For example, simple game-theory models cannot explain the failure of Schlitz and the success of Anheuser-Busch, two companies that were equals in the 1950s. Neither can the principles of game theory shed light on idiosyncrasies of Coors. The behaviors of Schlitz and Coors are better understood by studying the histories of the companies and the personalities of their owners and managers. It is likely that Coors and Schlitz would have made wiser economic decisions in the 1970s if they had developed a strategic planning department to rival the one at Anheuser-Busch. Until the 1980s, all strategic decisions at Coors were made by the Coors family. With adequate strategic advice, Coors might have responded more quickly to the obvious success of Miller Lite in the mid 1970s, as the principles of game theory indicate. Likewise, with an adequate strategic planning staff at Schlitz, the sudden death of company president Robert Uihlein in 1976 may not have left such a void in leadership and management skills at Schlitz.

10.1   Forecasts

When making an economic forecast, perhaps the best one can hope for is to be "intelligently wrong or fortunately right."[1] With this forewarning in mind, the primary predictions for the industry follow. There is little doubt that Pabst will exit the industry. It is more difficult to predict when this will occur, as this forecast is conditional upon the future state of the economy. With greater economic prosperity, Pabst would likely exit quickly as demand for the popular-priced brands marketed by Pabst would decline. Alternatively, a prolonged economic downturn could keep the Pabst brands afloat for some time.

Once Pabst exits, Anheuser-Busch, Coors, and Miller will command about 95 percent of the domestic market. This may or may not mean the end of the attrition war and the attainment of a steady state. Anheuser-Busch, Coors, and Miller have attained minimum efficient scale, but Anheuser-Busch still retains a competitive advantage. Coors has successful brands, but its transportation costs are relatively high because it has only three plants. Miller has a better mix of facilities but a mediocre marketing record of late. The future of Coors and Miller will depend not only on their own behavior but also on the behavior of Anheuser-Busch and the Department of Justice. The status quo is likely to persist if Anheuser-Busch refrains from using an aggressive advertising and pricing policy and if Anheuser-Busch, Coors, and Miller avoid making strategic blunders. Tougher competition or a firm mistake could put Coors or Miller in a tailspin, leaving the devolution and merger strategies as their only options. With the current level of concentration, the Department of Justice will not approve a Coors-Miller merger unless one firm is failing. Speculation has already started regarding such a merger, as the market share of Miller has deteriorated since 1996 and the share of Coors has declined since 2000 (*Forbes*, December 24, 2001; *Modern Brewery Age*, March 31 and May 19, 2003). Either scenario suggests that the brewing industry will be less competitive and will realize higher profits in the years to come.

The future of the domestic specialty brewers is more difficult to forecast. Growth in the number of small brew pubs and micro-breweries probably has peaked, and the continued success of existing firms probably will depend on local demographic and economic conditions. Growth by merger seems unlikely, since a microbrewery's strength comes from an ability to cater to a local market. Certainly the leading domestic specialty brewers, Boston and Sierra Nevada, have a bright future if they maintain product quality and find creative ways to market domestic craft beer on a large scale. Marketing may become increasingly important if they are going to compete successfully at the national level with the imports and micro-clones from Anheuser-Busch, Miller, and Coors and continue to maintain their "micro" image.

Growth in the high-priced segment (i.e., super-premium, specialty, and import beer) will depend on growth of the macro-economy, and the domestic share of this segment of the market is uncertain. Super-premium brands are unlikely to grow unless new brands are developed that compete well with the lighter imports from Canada and Mexico. Most local markets are saturated with microbreweries, so the entry opportunities are limited. Substantial growth of the domestic specialty sector will depend on the success of Boston, Sierra Nevada, and other larger specialty brewers. With luck and a more focused effort on a few quality brands, the domestic specialty brewers could capture sales from the imports and reach a 5 percent share of total U.S. beer consumption. In part, this will depend on changes in the prestige value of microbrews relative to imported brands. With continued free trade and income growth, the high-priced segment of the market will remain dynamic and competitive in the years to come. Competition in this segment of the market may also keep a lid on price increases for regular domestic beer.

The issue that will probably receive the most attention in the future is society's concern with the high costs associated with alcohol consumption and abuse. Some religious groups will continue to promote laws that prohibit alcohol consumption entirely, and public health organizations will lobby for stiffer laws to curb drunk driving, underage drinking, and alcohol abuse. In view of the experience with

Prohibition and the recent scientific evidence supporting the health benefits associated with moderate alcohol consumption, a new prohibition movement seems unlikely. Increasing the excise tax on beer and other alcoholic beverages may not be in the public interest. This issue may be moot, however, as federal and state governments may increase the excise tax on alcohol simply as a way of raising tax revenue. In any case, there is little social justification for using a simple linear excise tax to mitigate the externalities associated with alcohol abuse.

Pressure to reduce the blood-alcohol-content limit for driving will continue. As the evidence indicates that driving is substantially impaired at a BAC level of 0.04 percent, MADD and other public health organizations will continue to pressure for a lower legal BAC limit. A "zero-tolerance rule" is in society's interest and has been successfully applied in foreign countries, but it is unlikely to be politically feasible in the United States. An appropriate first step is to lower the BAC limit to 0.04. If this occurs, continued pressure for a zero-tolerance rule will depend on the effectiveness of the 0.04 limit. The availability of alternative transportation modes and devices that make it impossible for an intoxicated individual to start a motor vehicle will also affect the call for zero tolerance.

There will undoubtedly be continued debate about the social desirability of alcohol advertising. The industry has established a reasonable set of voluntary guidelines on acceptable advertising practices, but brewers continue to push the boundaries of the guidelines. It is in the industry's interest to impose strict penalties on violators to avoid government involvement. The imposition of government regulations on beer advertising will depend on the advertisements produced by the leading brewers, the outcome of continued research on this issue, and public sentiment.

10.2   Future Research

The constant change in the industry's structure, the vast heterogeneity among brewers, and the important policy concerns associated with alcohol consumption make the U.S. brewing industry worthy of study from economic, strategic management, and policy perspectives. Many questions remain unresolved.

Several facts regarding the behavior of brewers raise questions that are important to strategy theory. For example, the evidence indicates that gimmicks and "Hail Mary" strategies are common among failing brewers. Gimmicks are also used on occasion by successful firms (i.e.,

Miller's catfight commercials), however, and further research is needed to determine if this is a signal of an imminent decline in fortune or is attributable to some other cause. In addition, in view of the divergent set of strategic paths and performance outcomes of surviving brewers at the end of the war-of-attrition game, it would be useful to identify which set of initial firm conditions generates a particular strategic path. This would make it possible to determine whether a surviving firm's strategy was merely satisficing or truly optimal.

At the industry level, at least three important areas warrant further empirical research. First, the causes of high concentration in brewing merit further empirical analysis. Advertising and scale economies have been shown to be important, but endogeneity may be a problem and other industry and firm effects may play a part. Second, with so few mass producers, there is continued concern about cooperative behavior among the leading brewers. Further research is needed to monitor the degree of market power in the industry. Third, the U.S. distilled spirits industry has recently voted to eliminate its voluntary ban on broadcast advertising, and future research should investigate the effect of this change on spirits, wine, and beer consumption.

The basic economic conditions of Anheuser-Busch have been investigated, but further research is needed to understand the demand and cost conditions of other brewers. Important unresolved questions include the following: How do the demand and cost conditions differ by firm? To what extent does Anheuser-Busch have a goodwill and/or cost advantage over Coors, Miller, failing mass producers, and the leading specialty brewers? To what extent is firm success linked to scale efficiency, marketing efficiency, and other market and firm effects?

Research at the brand level using scanner data (Ackerberg 2001; and Tenn 2003) may also prove useful. Ackerberg uses brand-level data to test the importance of the informative and persuasive effects of advertising for a new brand of yogurt and finds that advertising affects the demand of inexperienced consumers alone, suggesting that the advertising for a new product is primarily informative in nature. This book does not contain enough brand-level data for such a study on brewing, but the data here combined with scanner data could make such research possible.

Further research is needed if we are to understand the direct effects of taxes, advertising, and other policy variables on the alcohol demands of moderate drinkers, underage alcohol consumers, and alcohol abusers. A complete understanding of the social effects of alternative policy instruments is critical to effective public policy.

Appendix A
Data and Sources

The tables, figures, and regression results in this book are based on three main data sets, unless otherwise noted in the text. The first data set, called "industry data," consists of annual observations on the brewing industry from 1950 to 2001. Table A.1 lists the variable definitions and data sources for these industry-level data.

The second data set, "firm data," contains annual observations of 34 major brewers from 1950 to 2001. Table A.2 lists the brewers included in the sample, the years for which financial data are available (i.e., total revenue, profit, assets, and advertising), the year that they exited from the industry if they did so, and the tier status of each firm in each year (based on table 3.3). Table A.3 lists the variable definitions and data sources. Our previously published work that used firm-level data included observations from two additional privately owned brewers. Because the owners requested that their data remain confidential, they are not included here.

The third data set, "firm output data," provides annual output figures for the 100 largest brewers from 1947 to 2001, ranked by firm size from largest to 100th largest in the industry for each year. The authors gratefully acknowledge the generosity of Robert S. Weinberg in donating this unique and extensive information.

To obtain the data sets described in this appendix, send a request to CTremblay@oregonstate.edu.

Table A.1
Industry-level variables and data sources.

Variable	Description, measurement, and data source
Advertising	Total advertising expenditures, millions of dollars[a]
Capacity	Total U.S. brewing capacity, million barrels, *Brewers Digest*, "Brewer's Guide and Brewery Directory"
Cost-Labor	Payroll: salaries and wages paid out by brewers, million dollars, *Brewers Almanac*
Cost-Mat	Cost of materials used in production, million dollars, *Brewers Almanac*
CPI	Consumer price index, base year 1982, *Statistical Abstract of the United States*
CR4	Four-firm concentration ratio, percent, Office of R. S. Weinberg
Exports	Total U.S. exports of malt beverages, million barrels, Office of R. S. Weinberg
HHI	Herfindahl-Hirschman Index for the largest 100 firms in the industry, percent, Office of R. S. Weinberg
Imports	Total U.S. imports of malt beverages, million barrels, Office of R. S. Weinberg
Income	Total U.S. disposable personal income, billion dollars, *Statistical Abstract of the United States*
K-Index	Capital equipment, finished goods producer price index, base year 1982-84, *Statistical Abstract of the United States*
L	Number of employees in the brewing industry, thousands, *Brewers Almanac*
M-Index	Crude food materials and foodstuffs price index, base year 1982-84, *Statistical Abstract of the United States*
MES	Estimate of minimum efficient scale, or the smallest level of firm output needed to reach minimum long-run average cost, million barrels, see chapters 2 and 3
N-Macro	Number of macro or mass-producing beer companies, Office of R. S. Weinberg
N-Specialty	Number of specialty (brewpub, micro, and regional craft) beer companies, Office of R. S. Weinberg
P-Beer	Price index of beer (nominal), base year 1982-84, *CPI Detailed Report*
P-Soft-Drinks	Price index of cola (nominal), base year 1982, *CPI Detailed Report*
P-Spirits	Price index of distilled spirits (nominal), base year 1982-84, *CPI Detailed Report*
P-Wine	Price index of wine (nominal), base year 1982-84, *CPI Detailed Report*
Packaged	Percent of beer sold in packages (non-kegs), *Brewers Almanac*.
Population	Total U.S. population, millions, *Statistical Abstract of the United States*

Table A.1
(continued)

Variable	Description, measurement, and data source
Pop < 18	Total U.S. population less than 18 years old, *Statistical Abstract of the United States* and *Current Population Report*
Pop (18–44)	Total U.S. population from 18 to 44 years old, *Statistical Abstract of the United States* and *Current Population Reports*
PPI	Producer price index, base year 1982, *Statistical Abstract of the United States*
Profit/Sales	Net profit (after deducting federal income taxes) divided by gross sales for the U.S. brewing industry, percent[a]
Profit/Sales-M	Net profit (after deducting federal income taxes) divided by gross sales for all U.S. manufacturing, percent[a]
Qc	Beer industry consumption, thousand barrels, Office of R. S. Weinberg
Q-Macro	Shipments of macro or mass-producing beer companies, thousand barrels, Office of R. S. Weinberg
Qp	Beer industry production, thousand barrels, Office of R. S. Weinberg
Q-Specialty	Shipments of specialty producing beer companies, thousand barrels, Office of R. S. Weinberg
Taxes	Beer taxes for the industry, thousand dollars[a]
Tax-Federal	Federal excise tax rate per barrel of beer (dollars), *Brewers Almanac*
Tax-State	Average state excise tax per barrel of beer (dollars), *Brewers Almanac*
Total-Cost	Total cost or deductions, thousand dollars[a]
Total-Assets	Total industry assets, thousand dollars[a]
Total-Net-Pro	Total net profit or income in brewing, thousand dollars[a]
Wages-Brewing	Average hourly earnings in brewing (dollars per hour), U.S. Department of Labor, Bureau of Labor Statistics as reported in *Brewers Almanac*
Wages-Man	Average hourly earnings in all manufacturing industries in the U.S. (dollars per hour), U.S. Department of Labor, Bureau of Labor Statistics as reported in *Brewers Almanac*

a. U.S. Treasury Department, Internal Revenue Service, Source Book, as reported in *Brewers Almanac* (various issues).

Table A.2
Major U.S. brewing companies, years firms exited the industry, years for which financial data are available, and tier classifications.

Company name[a]	Exit date	Financial data[b]	Tier	
			First	Second
Anheuser-Busch Inc.	—	1950–2001	1950–	—
Associated Brewing Co.	1972	1950–1971	—	—
P. Ballantine & Sons	1972	—	—	1950–1964
Burgermeister Brewing	1961	1950–1959	—	—
Carling Brewing Co.	1979	1962–1979	—	1950–1964
Adolph Coors Co.	—	1972–2001	1987–	1975–1986
Drewerys Limited Inc.	1965	1950–1964	—	—
Duquesne Brewing Co.	1972	1950–1971	—	—
Falstaff Brewing Co.	1975	1950–1988	—	1950–1974
Genesee (High Falls) Brewing	—	1968–1987	—	1975–1986
Goebel Brewing Co.	1964	—	—	—
Grain Belt Breweries Inc.	1975	1950–1974	—	—
Gunther Brewing Co.	1960	—	—	—
Theodore Hamm Brewing Co.	1975	—	—	1950–1964
Harvard Brewing Co.	1956	—	—	—
Heileman Brewing Co.	1996	1950–1994	—	1965–1996
Jackson Brewing Co.	1974	—	—	—
Lone Star Brewing Co.	1976	1950–1975	—	—
Lucky (General) Brewing Co.	1973	1950–1970	—	—
Meister Brau Inc.	1972	1966–1970	—	—
Miller Brewing Co.	—	1977–2000	1965–	1950–1964
Narragansett Brewing Co.	1965	—	—	—
National Brewing Co.	1975	1955–1965	—	—
Olympia Brewing Co.	1982	1956–1978	—	—
Pabst Brewing Co.	—	1950–1983	1950–1974	1975–2000
Pearl Brewing Co.	1978	1950–1968	—	—
Piel Bros. Inc.	1962	—	—	—
Pittsburgh Brewing Co.	—	1950–1985	—	—
Rheingold Breweries Inc.	1977	1966–1972	—	—
Jacob Ruppert Brewing Co.	1965	1950–1962	—	—
F. & M. Schaefer Brewing Co.	1980	1968–1979	—	1965–1974
Joseph Schlitz Brewing Co.	1982	1950–1981	1950–1982	—
C. Schmidt & Sons Inc.	1987	—	—	—
Stroh Brewing Co.	1999	1977–1993	1982–1986	1965–1981, 1987–1999

a. Lucky became General in 1973. Genesee became High Falls in 2000. Stroh purchased Schlitz in 1982, bumping Stroh temporarily into the top tier. S&P purchased Falstaff in 1972, Lucky in 1973, and Pabst in 1986, but these companies operated separately for years after the S&P acquisition. Pabst's corporate office is in San Antonio, and Pabst markets the Falstaff and Lucky brands.
b. Years for which financial data are available for total revenue, profit, assets, and advertising.

Table A.3
Firm-level variables and data sources.

Variable	Description, measurement, and data source
Year	Year of observation
Name	Company name (identified by the first four letters of company name)
Total Revenue	Total revenue (thousands of dollars), company financial reports (1950-1976) and *Beer Industry Update: A Review of Recent Developments* (1977-2001).
Profit	Net profit (thousands of dollars), company financial reports and *Beer Industry Update: A Review of Recent Developments* (various issues)
Output	Output (thousands of barrels), Office of R. S. Weinberg
Adv	Advertising expenditures (thousands of dollars), TNS Media Intelligence/CMR as reported in *Beer Industry Update: A Review of Recent Developments* (1982-2001). For 1950-1981: Schonfeld & Associates Inc. as reported in *Advertising Age*, February 3, 1958, 82-83; October 9, 1961, 70-72; January 20, 1964, 102; October 5, 1964, 158-160; August 23, 1965, 79-80; August 22, 1966, 122-123; September 18, 1967, 63-64; September 9, 1968, 106-107; October 20, 1969, 272-273; October 26, 1970, 40-41; September 20, 1971, 31-32; October 30, 1972, 145-146; October 1, 1973, 34-35; September 23, 1974, 41-42; November 3, 1975, 29-30; September 26, 1977, 112; October 9, 1978, 122; September 24, 1979, 18; January 16, 1984, M9-M10
Assets	Total assets (thousands of dollars), company financial reports.
Capacity	Total brewing capacity (thousands of barrels)[a]
D-Buy	Horizontal merger dummy variable, equals 1 if firm buys plant/brands of another brewer and equals 0 otherwise. See chapter 7 for sources.
D-Sell	Horizontal merger dummy variable, equals 1 if firm sells plant/brands to another brewer. See chapter 7 for sources.
Cap-Seller	Capacity of the selling firm in a horizontal acquisition, million barrels.[a]
D-Brand	Brand dummy variable, equals 1 if firm purchases only the brands of another brewer. See chapter 7 for sources.
D-Litigation	Antitrust litigation dummy variable, equals 1 if a horizontal merger is challenged by the Department of Justice. See chapter 7 for sources.
D-Popular	Popular priced brand dummy variable, equals 1 if firm produces a popular priced brand.[a]
D-Premium	Premium priced brand dummy variable.[a]
D-Super	Super premium priced brand dummy variable.[a]
D-Light-Pop	Light popular priced brand dummy variable.[a]
D-Light-Prem	Light premium priced brand dummy variable.[a]
D-Light-Super	Light super premium priced brand dummy variable.

Table A.3
(continued)

Variable	Description, measurement, and data source
D-Malt-Liquor	Malt liquor brand dummy variable.[a]
D-Ale	Ale brand dummy variable.[a]
D-Dark	Dark beer brand dummy variable.[a]
D-LA	Low alcohol brand dummy variable.[a]
D-Cooler	Cooler brand dummy variable.[a]
D-Dry	Dry beer brand dummy variable.[a]
D-Ice	Ice beer brand dummy variable.[a]
D-NA	Non-alcohol beer (near beer) brand dummy variable.[a]
D-Specialty	Specialty brand dummy variable.[a]
Total-Labels	Total number of labels (brands) sold by the firm.[a]

a. Sources: Firm documents, *Brewers Digest, Brewer's Guide and Brewery Directory* (1950-1996, 1998-2001), and *Modern Brewery Age Blue Book* (1997). Information about coolers and non-alcoholic brands are provided for completeness but are not used in any analyses in the book.

Appendix B
Beer Containers

Table B.1 lists the primary container sizes found in the United States. The official government definition of a standard serving of beer is 12 ounces (at 5 percent alcohol by volume). For additional information on the definition of a standard serving size and the measurement of alcohol content, see appendix D. For a brief history of packaging in brewing, see www.allaboutbeer.com.

Table B.1
Standard sizes of beer containers and alternative units of measurement. For example, a U.S. case contains 24 12-ounce cans or bottles. In the U.S., beer sales are recorded in 31-gallon barrels. The standard metric measure for beer is the hectoliter. One U.S. barrel equals 1.1734 hectoliter (117.34 liters). In Europe, beer is frequently measured in imperial barrels. An imperial barrel contains 163.66 liters.

Units of measure	Standard sizes of beer containers in U.S.					
	Barrel	Keg	Case	Quart	16 ounces	12 ounces
Kegs (1,024 ounces)	3.875	1	0.2813	0.0313	0.0156	0.0117
Gallons (128 ounces)	31	8	2.25	0.25	0.125	0.0938
Cases (288 ounces)	13.778	3.5556	1	0.1111	0.0556	0.0417
Quarts (32 ounces)	124	16	9	1	0.5	0.375
Cans (16 ounces)	248	64	18	0.5	1	0.75
Cans (12 ounces)	330.667	85.333	24	2.667	1.333	1
Ounces	3,968	1,024	288	32	16	12

Appendix C
Mergers, Ordered by
Acquired Firm

Table C.1 (pp. 294–306) is the reverse of table 7.9, as it orders mergers and acquisitions by the *acquired* firm instead of the acquiring firm. An acquisition includes the purchase of brands and facilities unless otherwise noted; the phrase "purchased brands only" means that the facilities were not purchased or were immediately sold. See table 7.9 for sources.

Table C.1
Major mergers and acquisitions, by acquired firm, 1950–2002. An asterisk indicates that the acquisition was challenged or investigated by U.S. Department of Justice for violation of anti-trust laws. An acquisition includes the purchase of brands and facilities unless otherwise noted. "Purchased brands only" means that facilities were not purchased or were immediately sold. See table 7.9 for sources.

Acquired firm, year	Acquiring firm	Comments
Acme 1954	Rheingold	Purchased plants in Los Angeles and San Francisco.
Altes 1954	National	
Ambrosia 1959	Atlantic	
American (Miami) 1958	*Anheuser-Busch	Purchased Regal brand and facilities. Dept. of Justice issued consent decree to divest in 1960.
American (New Orleans) 1962	Atlantic	
American (Baltimore) 1973	Queen City	Purchased brands only.
Anheuser-Busch 1961	*National	Bought Miami (American) plant and brands from Anheuser-Busch because of Dept. of Justice consent decree.
Arizona 1964	Carling	Sold to National in 1966.
Associated 1972	*Heileman	Purchased Drewerys, Sterling, and J. Schmidt plants. Was forced to divest of some brands by 1974.
1972	Pickett	Purchased Edelweiss and Champagne Velvet brands.
1973	Schaefer	Purchased Piel and Trommer brands.
Atlantic 1965	Drewerys	Purchased brands only.
Atlas 1951	Drewerys	
Ballantine 1968	Investors Funding Corp.	Conglomerate merger.
1972	Falstaff	Purchased brands and closed plant.

Table C.1
(continued)

Acquired firm, year	Acquiring firm	Comments
Bartels 1967	Lion	Purchased brands only.
Bavarian 1959	International	
Berghoff 1954 1954	Falstaff Walter	Purchased Berghoff brand; Falstaff purchased Berghoff plant.
Blatz 1958	*Pabst	Purchased brand and closed plant. Court ordered Pabst to divest of Blatz in 1969.
Blitz-Weinhard 1979	Pabst	
Bohemian (Boise) 1956	Atlantic	
Bohemian (Spokane) 1956	Atlantic	
Boston Celtics 1968	Ballantine	Conglomerate merger.
Bridgeport 1995	Gambrinus	Conglomerate merger.
Bub 1969	Walter	Purchased brands only.
Buckeye 1966	Meister Brau	
Burger 1973	Hudepohl	Purchased brands only.
Burgermeister 1961	*Schlitz	Court ordered divestiture in 1966.
Burkhardt 1956	Burger	
Burlington 1954	Weber Waukesha	
Busch 1973	Leinenkugel	Purchased brands only.
Butte 1963	Dakota	Purchased brands only.
Canadian Ace 1968	Eastern	Purchased brands only.

Table C.1
(continued)

Acquired firm, year	Acquiring firm	Comments
Carling		
1966	Miller	Purchased Fort Worth plant.
1966	National	Bought Arizona Brewing Co. plant in Phoenix from Carling.
1978	*Pabst	Attempted merger was stopped by Dept. of Justice.
Carling (Baltimore)		
1979	Heileman	
Carling (U.K.)		
2002	Coors	Market-extension merger.
Celis		
1995	Miller	Purchased partial interest.
Champale		
1986	Heileman	Purchased brands only.
F. W. Cook		
1955	Associated	Closed plant.
Croft		
1952	Narragansett	Purchased brands only.
Cumberland		
1969	Queen City	Purchased brands. Closed plant in 1970.
Dakota		
1966	Cold Spring	
Dawson		
1967	Associated	Purchased brands. Plant sold to Rheingold.
1967	Rheingold	Purchased plant; brands purchased by Associated.
Drewerys		
1965	Associated	
DuBois		
1967	Pittsburgh	Purchased brands only.
Duluth		
1966	Heileman	Purchased brands only.
Duncan		
1980	Heileman	Purchased brands and facilities, sold in 1983 to become independent firm (Florida Brewing).
Duquesne		
1965	*Pittsburgh	Dept. of Justice issued consent decree to stop merger in 1966.
1972	C. Schmidt	Purchased brands only.

Table C.1
(continued)

Acquired firm, year	Acquiring firm	Comments
E & B 1962	Associated	
Erie 1978	C. Schmidt	Purchased brands only.
Esslinger 1964	Ruppert	Purchased brands only.
Evansville 1997	Pittsburgh	Closed plant. Purchased Drewerys, Cook's, Falls City, Drummond Brothers, and Lemp brands.
Falls City 1979	Heileman	Purchased brands only.
Falstaff 1975	S&P	Conglomerate merger.
Fehr 1966	Hudepohl-Schoenling	Purchased brands only.
Fisher 1957	*General	Dept. of Justice issued consent decree ordering divestiture in 1958.
Fitger 1973	Schell	Purchased brands only.
Fort Pitt 1956	Gunther	Purchased brands only.
Fox Head 1962	Heileman	Purchased brands only.
P. Fox 1955	Fox Head	
Frankenmuth 1955	International	
Franklin 1952	Pilsener	
Fred Koch 1986	Genesee	
Fuhrmann and Schmidt 1966	H. Ortlieb	
Galveston-Houston 1956	Falstaff	

Table C.1
(continued)

Acquired firm, year	Acquiring firm	Comments
General		
1966	Miller	Purchased Azusa plant.
1973	S&P	Conglomerate merger.
Genesee		
1999	Platinum Holdings	Attempted conglomerate merger. Genesee was purchased by a New York management group; the name was changed to High Falls.
Gettelman		
1961	Miller	
Gluek		
1964	Heileman	Purchased brands only.
Goebel		
1964	Stroh	Purchased brands only.
Goetz		
1961	Pearl	
Golden West		
1950	Goebel	
Grain Belt		
1975	Heileman	Purchased brands only.
Grapette		
1970	Rheingold	Conglomerate merger.
Gretz		
1960	Esslinger	Purchased brands only.
Griesedieck-Western		
1954	Carling	Purchased Stag brand and plant.
Griesedieck Brothers		
1957	Falstaff	
Gulf		
1963	Hamm	Purchased plant only.
Gunther		
1957	Jones	Purchased Fort Pitt brands only.
1960	Hamm	Purchased plant only.
Haberle Congress		
1962	Standard-Rochester	Purchased brands only.
Haffenreffer		
1964	Narragansett	Purchased brands only.
Hamm		
1963	Schaefer	Purchased Baltimore (Gunther) plant from Hamm.
1965	Heublein	Conglomerate merger.

Table C.1
(continued)

Acquired firm, year	Acquiring firm	Comments
1965	*Molson	Successfully challenged by Dept. of Justice.
1975	Olympia	Purchased from Heublein.
1975	Pabst	Purchased Burgermeister brand only.
Hampden-Harvard		
1961	Drewerys	
P. Hand		
1980	Huber	Purchased brands only.
Hanley		
1957	Narragansett	Purchased brands only.
Harvard		
1956	Hampden	Changed name to Hampden-Harvard; closed Lowell plant.
Hauenstein		
1970	Grain Belt	Purchased brands only.
Hawaii		
1964	Schlitz	Purchased Primo brand and facilities.
Heidelberg		
1959	Carling	
Heileman		
1973	*Cold Spring	Purchased Duluth brands (Karlsbrau) and Gluek brands (Gluek and North Star) from Heileman because of Dept. of Justice consent decree.
1987	Bond Corporation Holdings	Conglomerate merger, purchase price was $1,200 million.
1988	Evansville	Purchased Evansville plant and Cook's, Sterling, Falls City, and Drewerys brands.
1993	Hicks, Muse, and Co.	Conglomerate merger. Purchase price was $300 million.
1996	Stroh	
Huber		
1988	Stroh	Purchased Augsburger brand only.
Hudepohl		
1986	Hudepohl-Schoenling	Purchased brands and facilities; closed Schoenling plant.

Table C.1
(continued)

Acquired firm, year	Acquiring firm	Comments
Hudepohl-Schoenling 1997	Boston	Purchased plant only. Boston Beer Co. brews Hudepohl-Schoenling brands under contract.
Hyde Park 1950	Griesedieck Western	
Independent Milwaukee 1963	Heileman	Purchased brands only.
International 1956	Carling	Purchased brands only.
International 1971	Koch	Purchased Iroquois brands only.
Interstate 1950	General	
Iroquois 1955	International	
Jackson 1974	Pearl	Purchased brands only.
Judson Candy 1965	Pearl	Conglomerate merger.
Kaier 1968	H. Ortlieb	Purchased brands only.
Kiewel 1959	Grain Belt	Leased plant, but then closed it in 1961.
Kingsbury 1961	Heileman	
Krantz 1956	International	
Krueger 1961	Narragansett	Purchased brands only.
L.A. 1952	Pabst	
Labatt 1964	*Schlitz	Labatt owned General; Schlitz bought 39% interest in Labatt; court ordered divestiture in 1966.
Latrobe 1988	Labatt Importers	

Table C.1
(continued)

Acquired firm, year	Acquiring firm	Comments
Lebanon 1959	Yuengling	Purchased brands only.
J. Leinenkugel 1988	Miller	
Lone Star 1976	Olympia	
Maier 1972	General	
Mankato 1951	Cold Spring	
Marlin 1956	National	
Meister Brau 1972	Miller	Purchased brands only.
1972	Hamm	Purchased Burgermeister brand; closed plant.
Metz 1962	Walter	Purchased brands only.
Miller 1967	W. R. Grace	Conglomerate merger.
1969	Philip Morris	Conglomerate merger.
2002	South African Breweries	Purchased from Philip Morris by international brewer.
Minnesota 2002	Schell	Purchased Grain Belt brand only. Minnesota plant closed.
Missoula 1964	Rainier	Purchased brands only.
Mitchell 1956	Falstaff	
Molson 1995	Miller	International merger. Miller sold its equity interest in Molson in 1997.
Monarch 1958	Van Merritt	Purchased brands only.
Mt. Carbon 1976	Yuengling	Purchased brands only.
Muehlbach 1956	Schlitz	Purchased facilities only.

Table C.1

(continued)

Acquired firm, year	Acquiring firm	Comments
Narragansett 1965	*Falstaff	Purchased brands and facilities. Acquisition was unsuccessfully challenged by Dept. of Justice.
National 1975	Carling	
Neuweiler 1968	H. Ortlieb	Purchased brands only.
Oconto 1966	Van Merritt	
Oertel 1967	Heileman	Purchased brands only.
Old Crown 1973	P. Hand	Purchased brands only.
Olympia 1982	Pabst	Part of merger with Heileman in 1982.
H. Ortlieb 1981	C. Schmidt	Purchased brands only.
Pabst 1969	Heileman	Purchased Blatz brand only
1982	*Heileman	Purchased plants in Perry, GA (Pabst), San Antonio (Lone Star), and Portland (Blitz-Weinhard) and the following brands: Blitz-Weinhard, Henry Weinhard, Red, White & Blue, Burgermeister, Lone Star, and Buckhorn. To ensure Dept. of Justice approval, remaining plants and brands of Pabst and Olympia were spun off as an independent Pabst brewer.
1982	*Stroh	Purchased St. Paul (Hamm/ Olympia) plant but sold Tampa (Schlitz) plant to Pabst; Dept. of Justice required Stroh to sell Schlitz plant.
1986	S&P	Conglomerate merger.
1987	Stroh	Purchased Tampa (Schlitz) plant.
2001	Guinness UDV	Purchased Lehigh Valley plant only.
Pacific 1952	Falstaff	

Table C.1
(continued)

Acquired firm, year	Acquiring firm	Comments
Pearl 1978	S&P	Conglomerate merger. Pearl was listed as a subsidiary of General Brewing Company.
Pepsi Cola 1969	Rheingold	Conglomerate merger of Pepsi distributor.
Phoenix 1957	International	
Piel Bros. 1962	Drewerys	
Pilsener 1963	Duquesne	Purchased brands only.
Pittsburgh 1986	Bond Corp. Holdings	Conglomerate merger. Pittsburgh became an independent brewer again in 1991.
Potosi 1972	Huber	Purchased brands only.
Progress 1959	Lone Star	
Queen City 1974	Pittsburgh	Purchased brands only.
Rahr 1966	Oshkosh	Purchased brands only.
Rainier 1954	Hamm	Purchased Rainier's San Francisco plant.
1977	Heileman	
Reading 1976	C. Schmidt	Purchased brands only.
Reality 1950	Miller	Conglomerate merger.
Redhook 1994	Anheuser-Busch	Purchased 25% of company's equity.
Regal 1962	Maier	Purchased brands only.
Rheingold 1957 1964	Hamm Pub United Corp.	Purchased Los Angeles plant Conglomerate merger.

Table C.1
(continued)

Acquired firm, year	Acquiring firm	Comments
1972	PepsiCo	Conglomerate merger.
1974	Chock-Full-O-Nuts	From Pepsi Cola; conglomerate merger.
1977	C. Schmidt	Purchased two plants and two brands.
Rice Lake		
1973	Walter	Purchased brands only.
Ruppert		
1965	*Rheingold	Challenged by Dept. of Justice. Purchased brands only.
Schaefer		
1963	C. Schmidt	Purchased Standard brands and facilities.
1980	Stroh	
Scheidt		
1955	C. Schmidt	
Schlitz		
1969	Meister Brau	Purchased Burgermeister brand and San Francisco plant.
1979	Anheuser-Busch	Bought Syracuse plant.
1982	*Stroh	Dept. of Justice required Stroh to sell Schlitz plant in Tampa.
C. Schmidt		
1978	H. Ortlieb	Purchased McSorley Cream Ale brand.
1987	Heileman	Purchased brands only.
J. Schmidt		
1955	Associated	
Schoenhofen Edelweiss		
1951	Drewerys	
Shipyard Brewing		
1995	Miller	Purchased partial interest.
Sick's Spokane		
1955	Rainier	
Simon of Buffalo		
1971	Koch	Purchased brands only.
Sioux City		
1959	Kingsbury	
Spoetzl (Shiner, TX)		
1989	Gambrinus	Conglomerate merger.
Standard		
1961	Schaefer	

Table C.1
(continued)

Acquired firm, year	Acquiring firm	Comments
Stegmaier 1974	Lion	Purchased brands.
Sterling 1964	Associated	
Storz 1967	Grain Belt	Leased plant. Purchased brands and facilities in 1970.
Stroh 1982	*Pabst	Purchased Tampa (Schlitz) plant. Pabst sold its St. Paul (Pabst, Olympia) plant to Stroh. Dept. of Justice required Stroh to sell Schlitz plant.
1989	*Coors	Attempted merger opposed by Dept. of Justice. Purchased Memphis plant only.
1999	Miller	Miller purchased Olde English 800 and Hamm brands from Stroh. As part of the Pabst-Stroh merger, Pabst sold its Tumwater (Olympia) plant and the Mickey's Malt Liquor and Henry Weinhard brands to Miller.
1999	*Pabst	Pabst purchased Stroh's Lehigh Valley plant and the Ballantine, Falstaff, Lone Star, Old Style, Olympia, Rainier, Schmidt, and Special Export brands. Pabst also took over Stroh's contract brewing for the Boston Beer Company. Miller purchased the Hamm and Olde English 800 brands from Stroh. As part of the agreement, Miller purchased the Tumwater (Olympia) plant and the Mickey's Malt Liquor and Henry Weinhard brands from Pabst. Yuengling purchased Stroh's Tampa plant. Platinum Holdings purchased the La Crosse (Heileman) plant, which later became the City Brewing Company. The following Stroh plants were closed: Longview (Lone Star); Portland (Blitz-Weinhard); Seattle (Rainier); Winston-Salem (Schlitz).

Table C.1
(continued)

Acquired firm, year	Acquiring firm	Comments
1999	Platinum Holdings	Purchased La Crosse (Heileman) plant only. Conglomerate merger. Became City Brewery Company.
1999	Yuengling	Purchased Tampa plant only.
Tampa Florida 1961	International	
Terre Haute 1958	Atlantic	
Trommer 1950	Rheingold	
Tsingtao 1993	Anheuser-Busch	Purchased 4.5% interest in company.
Utica 1959	West End	Purchased brands only.
Wagner 1974	Pittsburgh	Purchased brands only.
Weber Waukesha 1958	Fox Head	
Weidemann 1967	Heileman	Purchased brands only.
West Bend Lithia 1972	Walter	Purchased brands only.
Widmer Bros. 1997	Anheuser-Busch	Purchased 30.9% interest.
William Simon 1973	Koch	Purchased brands only.

Appendix D
Alcohol Content, Standard Serving Size, and Blood Alcohol Concentration

The alcohol content of beer is measured by weight or by volume. Beer with an alcohol content of 5 percent by weight contains 5 grams (or other weight unit) of alcohol per 100 grams of beer. Alcohol content of 5 percent by volume means that a beer contains 5 liquid ounces (or other volume unit) of alcohol per 100 liquid ounces of beer. Because alcohol weighs 79.6 percent as much as water, a brand of beer that is 5 percent alcohol by volume is 3.98 percent alcohol by weight. Throughout the book, alcohol content is measured by volume.

The official government definition of a standard drink varies from country to country. For example, a standard serving of beer is about 17 ounces in Japan and about 7 ounces in the United Kingdom (Brewers Digest 1999). In the United States, a drink or standard serving contains 0.6 ounces of ethanol or absolute alcohol (U.S. Department of Agriculture and the U.S. Department of Health and Human Services 1995). This is equivalent to one 12-ounce container of regular beer (at 5 percent alcohol by volume), one 6-ounce glass of wine (at 10 percent alcohol by volume), one 5-ounce glass of wine (at 12 percent alcohol by volume), and one 1.5-ounce shot of distilled spirits (80 proof, 40 percent alcohol by volume).

An individual's level of intoxication is measured by blood alcohol concentration (BAC). Blood alcohol levels are calculated as the ratio of alcohol by weight (in milligrams) to volume of blood (in deciliters). BAC is expressed as a percent, where 10 percent alcohol by volume is equivalent to 100 milligrams (or 10 grams) of alcohol per deciliter of blood.

Tables D.1–D.3 show the link between alcohol consumption and BAC level. The numbers are averages for typical individuals with normal body weight-height ratios. Table D.1 provides BAC levels by weight class for men. For example, an average 200-pound male who

Table D.1
BAC levels of men by weight class and number of alcoholic drinks consumed. For example, if a typical 200-pound man consumes four drinks, his BAC level is expected to be 0.07 percent. At this BAC level, he could legally drive an automobile in any state. To adjust BAC level for time since consumption, see table D.3.

	Weight (pounds)							
Drinks	100	120	140	160	180	200	220	240
0	0	0	0	0	0	0	0	0
1	0.04	0.03	0.03	0.02	0.02	0.02	0.02	0.02
2	0.07	0.06	0.05	0.05	0.04	0.04	0.03	0.03
3	0.11	0.09	0.08	0.07	0.06	0.06	0.05	0.05
4	0.15	0.12	0.11	0.09	0.08	0.07	0.08	0.06
5	0.19	0.16	0.13	0.12	0.10	0.09	0.08	0.08
6	0.22	0.19	0.16	0.14	0.12	0.11	0.10	0.09
7	0.26	0.22	0.19	0.16	0.15	0.13	0.12	0.11
8	0.30	0.25	0.21	0.19	0.17	0.15	0.14	0.12

Table D.2
BAC levels of women by weight class and number of alcoholic drinks consumed. For example, if a typical 140-pound woman consumes two drinks, her BAC level is expected to be 0.06 percent. At this BAC level, she could legally drive an automobile in any state. To adjust BAC level for time since consumption, see table D.3.

	Weight (pounds)							
Drinks	100	120	140	160	180	200	220	240
0	0	0	0	0	0	0	0	0
1	0.05	0.04	0.03	0.03	0.03	0.02	0.02	0.02
2	0.09	0.08	0.06	0.06	0.05	0.05	0.04	0.04
3	0.14	0.11	0.10	0.09	0.08	0.07	0.06	0.06
4	0.18	0.15	0.13	0.11	0.10	0.09	0.08	0.08
5	0.23	0.19	0.16	0.14	0.13	0.11	0.10	0.09
6	0.27	0.23	0.19	0.17	0.15	0.14	0.12	0.11
7	0.32	0.27	0.23	0.20	0.18	0.16	0.14	0.13
8	0.36	0.30	0.26	0.13	0.20	0.18	0.17	0.15

Table D.3
Time adjustment factors, for men and women, that may be used to correct BAC levels in tables D.1 and D.2 for time since consumption. Subtract the time adjustment factor from the BAC level in table D.1 or D.2 to estimate the time-adjusted BAC level. For example, if a typical 120-pound woman consumes four drinks at time 0, then after 2 hours her BAC level is expected to be $0.15 - 0.03 = 0.12$ percent. At this BAC level, it would be unlawful for her to drive an automobile in every state.

Hours since drinks were consumed

1	2	3	4	5	6	7	8
0.015	0.030	0.045	0.060	0.075	0.090	0.105	0.120

consumes six drinks will have a BAC level of 0.11 percent. A person's BAC level drops over time, however, at the rate of 0.015 per hour. (See table D.3.) Three hours after consuming alcohol, this 200-pound male will have a BAC level of 0.065 ($= 0.11 - 0.045$). Table D.2 provides BAC levels for women. For example, if an average 140-pound female consumes four drinks, her BAC level will be 0.07 after 4 hours ($= 0.13 - 0.06$).

As of October 1, 2003, New Jersey, Colorado, Delaware, Minnesota, Pennsylvania, and West Virginia have a legal BAC limit of 0.10; all other states have a BAC limit of 0.08 (Martel 2003). BAC information is available from many public health organizations, including web pages of the U.S. Department of Health and Human Services (www.health.org), the Minnesota Department of Public Safety (www.dps.state.mn.us), and the Indiana Prevention Resource Center (www.drugs.indiana.edu).

Notes

Chapter 1

1. The discussion of the early history of the U.S. brewing industry and Prohibition era borrows from Baron 1962, Downard 1980, *Modern Brewery Age*, September-October 1983, Robertson 1984, Jackson 1988, McGahan 1991, Stack 2000, and Glover 2001 and from the American Brewery History web site (www.beerhistory.com). On the prohibition histories of other countries, see *Brewers Digest*, November 1938.

2. On brewing history, see *Modern Brewery Age*, September-October 1983 and March 26, 2001; Robertson 1984; Glover 2001; www.beerhistory.com.

3. Table B.1 in appendix B lists the primary container sizes used in the U.S.

4. Producing a gallon of beer requires at least 5 gallons of water for cleaning and cooling (Glover 2001: 31). For this reason, early brewing facilities were located near rivers, springs, and wells. Although water quality is still commonly referred to in advertising, it has not been an issue in brewing since about 1950; water can be chemically treated and standardized.

5. For a more complete discussion of beer styles around the world, see *Modern Brewery Age*, December 30, 1991: 3, *Consumer Reports*, June 1996, Glover 2001, *Brewers Digest*, September-October 2002, the web site of the Beer Institute (www.beerinstitute.org), and individual brewers' web sites.

6. The mass producers have also experimented with wine coolers and malt alternatives, such as Zima, Tequiza, and Skyy Blue. These flavored alcoholic beverages receive most of their alcohol content from fermentation rather than distilling. We ignore this category because malt alternatives are not a close substitute for beer and because the category is small and dwindling (*Modern Brewery Age, Weekly News Addition*, November 19, 2001, December 4, 2002, and September 1, 2003).

7. For more on the factors that affect beer quality, see *Fortune*, November 1972, Robertson 1984, *Consumer Reports* 1996, *Modern Brewery Age*, May 18, 1998 and May 10, 1999, and Goldammer 1999.

8. Many women and residents of warmer climates appear to prefer lighter beer. In 2001, for example, 43% of the drinkers of Corona (a light imported beer) were women, and only 25.6% of the drinkers of Guinness Stout (a dark imported beer) were women (*Beer Industry Update: A Review of Recent Developments*, 2002).

9. For beer rankings, see *Consumer Reports* 1983, 1996, 2001, Robertson 1984, Klein 1995, *Brewers Digest*, July-August 2002, *Modern Brewery Age Weekly News Edition*, July 8, 2002, and numerous web sites, including "The Beer World Cup" (www.allaboutbeer.com), "The Best American Beers" (www.ratebeer.com), "Great American Beer Festival" (www.gabf.org), and "World Beer Cup 2002 Awards" (www.realbeer.com).

10. Accurate data on legal beer production became available after the Internal Revenue Act of 1862, a law that imposed a federal excise tax of $1 per barrel.

11. In the industry as a whole, 6.9% of the beer produced in 1996 was lost through spillage or was destroyed because it was of inferior quality (*Brewers Almanac* 1998: 9).

Chapter 2

1. Productive efficiency occurs if the industry level of output is produced at minimum aggregate industry cost. An industry is allocatively efficient if it produces the socially optimal level of output. This occurs when price equals marginal social cost. A firm is said to be technically efficient when it produces output with the minimum of inputs and is economically efficient if it produces output at minimum cost. For descriptions of these and other forms of efficiency, see Baumol et al. 1982; Sutton 1991; Färe and Grosskopf 1994.

2. For another discussion of how culture and consumption capital affect the demand for alcoholic beverages, see Heien and Pompelli 1989.

3. Other sources provide similar estimates by age group. A survey reported in *Business Week* (March 9, 1957) indicates that 61% of those in the 21–40 age group drink beer, 53% of those in the 40–60 age group, and 33% of those over 60. In a survey by *Advertising Age* (January 16, 1984), 61% of those in the 18–24 age group are beer drinkers, 58% of those in the 25–34 age group, 44% of those in the 35–49 age group, 26% of those in the 50–64 age group, and 24% of those over 64.

4. A recent study by the Scarborough Research Company (2002) indicates that enthusiasts of different sport activities have different preferences for alcoholic beverages. Snow skiers are 89% more likely to drink red wine, "xtreme sports" enthusiasts are 107% more likely to drink imported beer, golfers prefer light beer, and auto racing fans prefer popular-priced beer.

5. Using household rather than market data, Gao et al. (1995) estimate that the price elasticity of demand is −0.230 for beer, −0.404 for wine, and −0.249 for spirits. The income elasticity of demand for beer is −0.088 but is not significantly different from zero. Beer's cross-price elasticity of demand with wine and spirits is 0.156 and 0.074 respectively. Manning et al. (1995) find that the demand for alcoholic beverages becomes more price inelastic among households with heavy drinkers (i.e., the top 20% in terms of ethanol consumption).

6. Grabowski (1977–78) also finds that the effect of beer advertising on firm demand dissipates within one year, a result that is consistent with Boyd and Seldon's (1990) findings for cigarettes.

7. Abbot et al. (1997) find that advertising has no effect on beer demand in the United Kingdom. Calfee and Scheraga (1994) find that advertising has no significant effect on alcohol consumption in their study of seven countries. After reviewing the evidence for several foreign countries, Ambler (1996) concludes that advertising restrictions do not

cause alcohol consumption to decline. Saffer (1991) discovers that advertising bans in foreign countries reduced alcohol consumption, motor vehicle fatalities, and cirrhosis deaths, but Young (1993) questions the methodology used in the Saffer study.

8. For further discussion, see chapter 6. A similar trend appears to be underway in Japan, as beer consumers are switching to lighter beers (*Modern Brewery Age, Weekly News Edition*, June 24, 2002).

9. A Veblen effect exists when a person is motivated to buy a superior product because the purchase signals to others that the buyer is wealthy (Veblen 1899). Veblen effects are more likely for commodities that are expensive and can be observed by others. For example, these effects would be more important for a Rolls Royce than a Honda automobile and more important for the landscaping of one's front yard than one's back yard.

10. The percentage of beer consumed in bottles and cans grew continuously since Prohibition. It was 30% in 1935, 64.3% in 1945, 80.2% in 1960, 87.9% in 1980, and 90.7% in 2000 (*Brewers Almanac*, various issues).

11. Data on direct capital costs or the rental cost of capital services in brewing are unavailable. Total cost minus labor and material costs provide an inaccurate estimate because total costs include long-run investment expenditures which are not current capital expenses (Carlton and Perloff 2000; Martin 2002).

12. Although Elyasiani and Mehdian (1993) reject the hypothesis of technological change in brewing, Kerkvliet et al. (1998) show that their test is invalid.

13. There is no evidence of significant or important economies of scope in the U.S. brewing industry (Tremblay and Tremblay 1996).

14. During the early 1970s, Cockerill (1977) found that MES was about 2.55 million barrels in the United Kingdom, which is consistent with U.S. estimates.

15. On the strengths and weaknesses of the survivor technique to measure MES, see Stigler 1958; Shepherd 1967; Hallagan and Joerding 1983.

16. In the mid 1980s, Robert Rechholtz, president of marketing at Coors, argued that a brewer would have to sell from 25 million to 35 million barrels of beer a year to be competitive with Anheuser-Busch and Miller. These figures may have been inflated, as Rechholtz was using them to make a case for a larger advertising budget at Coors (Baum 2001).

17. Annual unit costs are obtained for the three leading brewers (Anheuser-Busch, 1996 and 2000; Coors, 1996 and 2000; Miller, 2000); for two second-tier brewers (Heileman, 1995; Stroh, 1993); for a large contract brewer (Boston, 2000); for a large specialty brewer (Redhook, 1996 and 2000). Also included is the mean unit cost of three microbreweries (Frederick, Portland, and Pyramid, 1996 and 2000). The small micros have a unit cost that ranges from $140 to $148, Redhook's unit cost ranges from $110 to $115, Boston's is $68, Heileman's is $67, Stroh's is $63, Coors's ranges from $66 to $68, Miller's is $54, and Anheuser-Busch's ranges from $57 to $58. Note that part of the higher cost of the microbrewers is due to their use of more expensive inputs. (See chapter 5.) The data are obtained from *Beer Industry Update: A Review of Recent Developments* (various issues).

18. See, for example, *Modern Brewery Age*, April 1955. Water treatment was highly efficient by late 1970s, as Greer (2002: 40) quotes William Coors as saying that "you could make Coors from swamp water and it would be exactly the same."

19. According to *Brewers Digest, Buyer's Guide and Brewery Directory* (various issues), Anheuser-Busch, Associated, Carling, Drewerys, Falstaff, Hamm, Lucky, National, Pabst, Rheingold, Schaefer, Schlitz, and C. Schmidt operated more than one brewery by 1956. Second plants were purchased by Heileman in 1961, Miller in 1961, Stroh in 1981, and Genesee in 1985. Of the major brewers, Coors is the notable exception, as it did not use a second plant until 1987. (See chapter 4.) The slow response of Coors was probably due, in part, to the fact that the Coors flagship brand used the following slogan: "Brewed with Pure Rocky Mountain Spring Water."

20. Industry experts classified Anheuser-Busch, Pabst, and Schlitz as national producers in 1949 (*Business Week*, August 27, 1949) and added Miller to this group by 1952 (*Business Week*, April 19, 1952; *Printers' Ink*, February 6, 1959).

21. Recall that full efficiency is reached with a score of 1.0. These estimates are similar to the overall efficiency scores of 0.93–0.95 for the Finnish brewing industry found by Kumbhakar and Summa (1989).

22. Denney et al. (2002) find that the main results are unaffected when the model includes advertising.

23. For a description of the myopic addiction or partial adjustment model, see Greene 2003: 568–569. For an excellent defense of the myopic model, see Ackerlof 1991.

24. For details, see Denney et al. 2002.

25. An inverse demand function is estimated because output data are more reliable than price data. Addiction is not an issue at the firm level and is ignored.

26. First-order autocorrelation is detected, and autocorrelation corrections are made, with the autoregressive parameters estimated to be 0.297 for demand and 0.503 for supply.

27. The maintained hypothesis that advertising is predetermined may also be a concern. To address the possible endogeneity issue, the model is estimated using the following instrumental variables on advertising: capacity utilization rate, percentage of beer sold in packaged form at the industry level, and all exogenous variables in the model. Unusually large t-ratios in the supply relation and few degrees of freedom justify skepticism toward the results, however.

28. Labor is measured as the cost of labor divided by the consumer price index. Materials are measured as the cost of materials divided by the crude food materials producer price index. Capital is measured as capital costs divided by the capital equipment producer price index.

29. On this technique, see Pindyck and Rubinfeld 1991.

30. On techniques designed to estimate a frontier production function, see Kerkvliet et al. 1998.

Chapter 3

1. On different measures of industry concentration, see Schmalensee 1977; Kwoka 1981.

2. This is sometimes called the "numbers equivalent." In the special case where firms are of equal size and there are four or more firms in the industry, then $HHI = 1/n = CR4/4$.

A one-to-one correspondence between HHI and CR4 does not exists when there are fewer than four firms in the industry or when firms are of unequal size (Sleuwaegen and Dehandschutter 1986).

3. A more precise measure of concentration would require information on all of the relevant moments of the distribution (e.g., the mean, variance, skewness, kurtosis) (Greene 2003: 878–879).

4. A similar pattern occurred in other countries. In England, the number of breweries fell from 567 to 94 from 1950 to 1993 (Millins 1998), and in New Zealand the number fell from 26 to 4 between 1951 and 1972 (Jones 1998). On other countries, see Mueller and Schwalbach 1980; Brouwer 1988; Wilson and Gourvish 1998.

5. The Merger Guidelines classify an industry as moderately concentrated when HHI ranges from 10 to 18 and to be highly concentrated when HHI exceeds 18. For further discussion of the Merger Guidelines as they apply to the brewing industry, see chapter 9.

6. For a review of the main causes of rising industry concentration, see Scherer and Ross 1990; Geroski and Mazzucato 2001; Martin 2002.

7. On preemption and wars of attrition, see Ghemawat and Nalebuff 1990; Fudenberg and Tirole 1992; Bulow and Klemperer 1999; McAfee 2002.

8. The availability of local spot television advertising has not eliminated the marketing advantage of the national producer. In 1982, for example, the cost of reaching 1,000 male viewers aged 18–49 during prime time was $14.14 for network television advertising and $23.49 for spot television advertising (Greer 1998: 37).

9. Michael Roarty, former vice president of marketing at Anheuser-Busch, makes a very similar statement (Greer 2002: 35).

10. This is also consistent with the models of Tremblay and Martins-Filho (2001) and Tremblay and Polasky (2002), which show how leading firms can use advertising to create an image of quality that leads to growth and an increase in industry concentration.

11. Brewing vats and other equipment can last up to 50 years (*Forbes*, October 1, 1977; McGahan 1991).

12. Sutton (1991) identifies three periods between 1953 and 1985: from 1953 to the mid 1960s, from the mid 1960s to the mid 1970s, and from the mid 1970s to 1985. Alternatively, Weinberg (1978) and *Beverage World* (1991) identify six competitive periods or distinct "beer wars" since prohibition: 1933–1947, 1947–1973, 1973–1977, 1977–1980, 1980–1991, 1991 on.

13. Miller is classified as a second-tier instead of a third-tier firm, as in Sutton 1991, because Miller's market share is comparable to other second-tier firms. Industry experts classified Miller as a small national brewer by the mid 1950s (*Business Week*, April 19, 1952; *Printers' Ink*, February 6, 1959).

14. Advertising data are not available for third-tier firms, and one cannot obtain advertising spending from this group by subtracting the advertising spending of the top two groups from industry advertising. Industry data include advertising expenditures on all media, while firm data include spending on television, radio, and print, and outdoor advertising. The advertising intensities for a sample of third-tier firms (Associated,

Drewerys, and Lucky) indicate that this group of third-tier firms advertised less intensively than firms in the top tiers.

15. Advertising intensities of a sample of third-tier firms (Olympia, Rheingold, and
Schmidt) also fell and were below those of the top tiers.

16. It is also possible that advertising has a delayed effect on industry concentration, an
issue that will be discussed further at the end of the chapter. Previous research indicates,
however, that the effect of advertising on firm demand dissipates within one year in the
U.S. brewing industry (Ackoff and Emshoff 1975a; Grabowski 1977–78).

17. This war is also discussed in *Business Week*, November 8, 1976 and March 4, 1996;
Newsweek, September 4, 1978 and August 16, 1982; *Sports Illustrated*, August 8, 1988,
Burgess 1993; Greer 1996.

18. Stroh purchased Schlitz in 1982, and the joint company remained a national producer
through the mid 1980s. The period 1975–1981 includes Schlitz data, and the period 1982–
1986 includes combined Stroh-Schlitz data. See chapter 4 for further discussion of this
merger.

19. For example, Miller increased its brewing capacity by 259%, Schlitz increased capacity by 31%, Anheuser-Busch by 26%, and Pabst by 5% from 1975 to 1979. Schlitz experienced a number of problems in the late 1970s, documented in chapter 4, before being
purchased by Stroh in 1982.

20. Falstaff and Schaefer are relegated to third-tier status because they experienced a
dramatic drop in market share during the period. Falstaff's market share fell from 3.93%
in 1974 to 0.39% by 1986, and Schaefer was purchased by Stroh in 1980.

21. Advertising intensities from a sample of third-tier firms (Olympia, Pittsburgh, and
Schmidt) were generally below those of first-tier brewers.

22. This classification is consistent with Weinberg 1999. Coors served customers in every
state but Indiana by 1988 and distributed to every state by 1991. See chapter 4 for further
detail.

23. State-level market share data are obtained from *Beer Industry Update: A Review of
Recent Developments* (various issues).

24. Given the small sample and problems with multicollinearity, the effect of other
demand and individual firm effects are ignored. For a more complete discussion, see
Martin 1979 and Geroski and Mazzucato 2001.

25. Estimates of MES are taken from table 3.1 and are assumed to be a linear combina-
tion of these estimates for missing years.

26. This parameter should be interpreted with caution, since SE and individual firm
effects may also influence concentration with a lag.

Chapter 4

1. Several third-tier brewers had important but short-lived influence on the industry. For
example, the Associated Brewing Company of Detroit became the tenth-largest brewer in
1970 but soon experienced financial difficulties and was purchased by Heileman and
Schaefer in 1972. The Olympia Brewing Company of Olympia, Washington became the

sixth-largest brewer in 1976 after it purchased Hamm in 1975 and Lone Star in 1976. Olympia's profits and market share soon declined before being purchased by Pabst in 1982. C. Schmidt & Sons Brewing Company of Philadelphia became the tenth-largest brewer in 1980 but quickly lost market share before selling to Heileman in 1987.

2. Rheingold and Boston briefly made it into the top five but are not included among the industry leaders. Rheingold is excluded because its output level and market share fell dramatically from 1954 through 1964, relegating it to the third tier by the late 1950s. Boston, a contract-specialty brewer, will be discussed in chapter 5.

3. Although August II was forced to resign by the board of directors and his son, August III, August II remained on as company chairman (Hernon and Ganey 1991, chapter 59).

4. The company's percentage of total revenue from beer sales grew from about 75% in 1947 (*Business Week*, September 6, 1947) to about 92% by 1980 (*Financial World*, June 1, 1980).

5. *U.S. v. Anheuser-Busch*, 1960. Enforcement of the anti-merger laws in brewing will be discussed in more detail in chapter 9.

6. The Baldwinsville plant had a capacity of 4.4 million barrels in 1979, more than 13% of Schlitz's total capacity. The acquisition increased Anheuser-Busch's total capacity by almost 10%.

7. For a description of Redhook and a detailed account of this agreement, see Barndt 2002.

8. Of the seven Stroh breweries, four were closed: Longview (Lone Star), Portland (Blitz-Weinhard), Seattle (Rainier), and Winston-Salem (Schlitz). The Lehigh Valley (F. & M. Schaefer) plant was purchased by Pabst. The Tampa (Schlitz) brewery was sold to D. G. Yuengling & Sons, and the La Crosse (Heileman) brewery went to the newly formed City Brewing Company. In addition, Pabst took over Stroh's contract brewing agreement with the Boston Beer Company and obtained the Ballantine, Falstaff, Lone Star, Old Style, Olympia, Rainier, Schmidt, and Special Export brands from Stroh.

9. For more detailed information about this merger, see *Modern Brewery Age, Weekly News Edition*, June 10, 2002: 1 and June 10, 2002: 3.

10. For more detailed accounts of Coors, see Barnett and Wilsted 1988c and Baum 2001.

11. For an account of the life of Joe Coors, who died in the spring of 2003, see *Modern Brewery Age*, Weekly Edition, March 24, 2003.

12. Whatever its source, success at Coors during this period pushed up the company's value well above the replacement cost of its plant and equipment. When the company first sold stock to the public in 1974, its market price indicated that the company was worth more than $100 per barrel at a time when new production capacity cost about $40 per barrel (Baum 2001: 124; chapter 3 of present volume).

13. Problems at Coors during this time are documented in *Business Week*, May 8, 1978; *Forbes*, October 16, 1978; *Business Week*, July 20, 1981; *Forbes*, July 19, 1982; Burgess 1993; Van Munching 1997; Baum 2001.

14. Coors bought land for the Virginia facility by 1983 and began blending, finishing, and packaging beer in the Virginia plant in April of 1987 (*Forbes*; October 24, 1983; correspondence with the Coors Consumer Information staff).

15. For an excellent account of these events, see Barnett and Wilsted 1988d.

16. Born in Poland in 1909, Paul Kalmanovitz emigrated to the U.S. in 1926. With little wealth and no formal education, he was able to acquire a number of once-popular regional brands, including Falstaff, Narragansett, Ballantine, Ballantine Ale, Lucky, Pearl, Jax, Country Club Malt Liquor, and Pabst. This merger devolution strategy will be discussed in more detail in chapter 7.

17. One reason for the Burgermeister merger was to acquire a successful popular-priced brand that would compete with Anheuser-Busch's Busch brand. Schlitz introduced Old Milwaukee after being forced by the courts to divest of Burgermeister (*Advertising Age*, June 30, 1975).

18. Unless otherwise referenced, this discussion borrows from *Advertising Age*, April 13, 1981 and April 20, 1981.

19. Within Schlitz, this was initially called STP for the "save the president" campaign (*Advertising Age*, April 20, 1981: 52).

20. Personal conversation, September 16, 2002.

21. Gelb and Gelb (1986) argue that a simple change or even an improvement in the formula of a traditional product like Coca-Cola or Schlitz beer can be a fiasco because consumers have emotional ties to the established brand.

22. The Arizona Brewing Company was sold to National in 1966.

23. Although S&P has owned several brewers, the company continued to report production data separately. Thus, tables 4.2–4.6 show Falstaff's market share though 2000.

24. For a personal account of the hardships Kalmanovitz imposed on the employees at Falstaff, see www.jadetech.com.

25. On this merger, see *Wall Street Journal*, September 24, 1987. Robert Weinberg, who argues that Bond substantially overvalued Heileman, estimates that the company's true market value was about $300–400 million (*Modern Brewery Age*, March 26, 2001).

26. A third group of present-day brewing firms, the craft or specialty brewers, will be discussed in chapter 5.

27. They are dwarfed by the nationals, however. In 2002, Yuengling had 0.68% of the domestic market, Latrobe had 0.58%, Genesee had 0.49%, Pittsburgh had 0.22%, and Stevens Point had 0.03%.

Chapter 5

1. The term "small beer" was used in England to describe beer that was light and weak, much like today's domestic light beer.

2. For further discussion of the calorie and alcohol content of different brands of beer, see chapter 9.

3. In a small sample survey published in the August 2001 issue, *Consumer Reports* found that the average six-pack of 12-ounce containers of premium domestic beer sold for $4.57, the average domestic craft (specialty) lager sold for $5.44, and the average import sold for $6.26.

4. As discussed in chapter 1, beer is a perishable product that deteriorates once it is packaged. It takes about 45 days for beer from Belgium to reach the U.S. (*Modern Brewery Age*, May 16, 1994).

5. For more on the Reinheitsgebot, see Mayer 1987; Jackson 1988; Glover 2001.

6. As was discussed in chapter 1, more important quality concerns include ensuring that beer is adequately aged and properly handled during brewing and shipping, qualities that have nothing to do with being a light or a craft beer.

7. On consumers' concerns with product identity, see Carroll and Swaminathan 2000. For a further discussion of foreign direct investment and contract brewing activity in the international brewing market, see Karrenbrock 1990.

8. The discussion of the early microbrewery movement borrows from the *New York Times*, April 29, 1979; *Wall Street Journal*, March 15, 1983; *Barron's*, May 9, 1983; Robertson 1984; *Modern Brewery Age*, May 22, 1995; Johnson 1993; Rhodes 1995.

9. Contract brewing is not simply a craft brewing phenomena. For example, the Narragansett Brewing Company (Cranston, Rhode Island) had a 5-year contract to brew beer for the Krueger Brewing Company in 1961 (www.americanbreweriana.org). Today, all Pabst beer is brewed by Miller. According to *Modern Brewing Age* (March 17, 1997: 9), there were about 130 contract brewers in the U.S. in 1996.

10. A spokesperson for the Association of Brewers, the trade association of the U.S. craft brewing industry, notes that some variation is allowed to encourage more innovation than allowed by the strict German Reinheitsgebot (*Modern Brewery Age, Weekly News Edition*, December 30, 1996: 3).

11. For the remainder of the book, Anchor is classified as a domestic specialty brewer.

12. The calculation is made for a sample of two macrobrewers (Anheuser-Busch and Coors) and three specialty brewers (Frederick, Portland, and Pyramid) (*Import Specialty Insights: A Review of Recent Developments*, 2002).

13. The law made it legal for a single adult household to brew up to 100 barrels of beer annually for personal use and not for sale. A household with two or more adults could brew up to 200 barrels. For discussions of the law, see Mares 1984; Johnson 1993; www.cascadebrewersguild.org.

14. On laws pertaining to brew pubs, see *Los Angeles Times*, July 18, 1984; *Newsweek*, February 9, 1987; *Brewers Digest*, March 1987; *Modern Brewery Age*, May 13, 1991, May 15, 1992, and March 25, 1996; *Restaurant Business*, March 1, 2000; www.brewpubzone.com.

15. Our information about the tax laws in Hawaii and the experience of the Kona Brewing Company was obtained from *Hawaii Business Magazine* (2000) and from personal conversation with Danny Sam, manager of the Kona Brewing Company, July 1, 2002. Regarding the purchase of used equipment, Kona purchased 5-year-old fermenters with 60 barrels of capacity for $1,000 which would sell for $4,000 when new.

16. According to *Brewers Digest* (March 1987) and *Modern Brewery Age* (July 10, 1989), there were five contract craft brewers in the late 1980s. *Modern Brewery Age* identified 25 contract-craft brewers in 1990 (May 13, 1991: 9) and ten in 1994 (May 22, 1995: 10). The Boston and Pete's brewing companies are the major contract-craft brewers today. Like Boston, Pete's experienced very rapid growth from its inception in 1985 through the mid 1990s.

17. See the May 20, 1996 issue of *Modern Brewing Age* and the company's web page (www.samadams.com).

18. The sample of small microbrewers includes Frederick, Portland, and Pyramid. In contrast, the average cost for Coors was $68 and for Anheuser-Busch was $57. Cost data are obtained from *Beer Industry Update: A Review of Recent Developments* (2002) and *Import Specialty Insights* (2002).

19. In early 1996, Anheuser-Busch and the Oregon Brewers Guild for craft brewers brought an unsuccessful petition before the U.S. Bureau of Alcohol, Tobacco, and Fire-arms that would have required all brewers to disclose where their beers are brewed (*Wall Street Journal*, April 15, 1996; *Modern Brewery Age*, May 20, 1996). This would pose a spe-cial problem for Boston and Pete's, as they brew little if any of their own beer. In response to the petition, Jim Koch, president of Boston, expressed concern that this would effectively abolish trade names and argued that it is the brewer and not the brewing facilities that are responsible for a particular brand of beer. In Koch's words (*Wall Street Journal*, April 15, 1996), "if Julia Child comes to your kitchen, brings her own ingredients and makes dinner, but you own the kitchen, is it you or Julia Child who made the dinner?" Missouri, home of Anheuser-Busch, is the only state to require such disclosure on beer packaging (*Modern Brewery Age Weekly News Addition*, December 1, 1997).

20. For accounts of this episode, see *Newsweek*, June 9, 1986; Van Munching 1997, chapter 11.

21. Robert Weinberg warned of a shakeout in 1995 (*New Brewer*, January-February 1996; *Modern Brewery Age*, May 20, 1996). Others made similar predictions in late 1996 (*Modern Brewery Age*, May 12, 1997).

22. On the problems faced by microbrewers in the late 1990s, see *Brandweek*, March 31, 1997; *Modern Brewery Age*, May 12, 1997, May 18, 1998, May 10, 1999, May 8, 2000, May 21, 2001, and January 27, 2003; *Beverage Industry*, January 1998. According to *Restaurant Business* (March 1, 2000), brew pubs fared better than microbreweries during the late 1990s.

Chapter 6

1. Dunn, Roberts, and Samuelson (1988) find that 36.1% of all entry into the U.S. manu-facturing sector comes from firms that already have a presence in the market.

2. By 1951, Anheuser-Busch, Pabst, and Schlitz were multiple-plant producers. Miller joined them in 1961.

3. The ability to command higher prices suggests that the national brands are of superior quality, at least in the eyes of the consumer. The extent to which this difference is subjec-tive will be discussed in the next chapter.

4. This discussion focuses on the first firm to actually bring the product to market rather than the inventor. For example, Baum (2001) claims the Bill Coors invented malt liquor, a product that Coors never marketed, in 1940. Unless otherwise noted, the source of all brand information is *Brewers Digest, Buyer's Guide and Brewery Directory* (various issues).

5. This account is derived from *Advertising Age*, March 30, 1970, January 9, 1978, and March 29, 1982; *Business Week*, August 22, 1970 and October 13, 1975; *Forbes*, January 15, 1976; Baum 2001.

6. The 1946 sample includes 385 American lagers (Master Brewers Association of America 1946). The 1996 sample includes 16 brands of regular beer (*Consumer Reports* 1996).

7. In the mid 1990s, the major brewers began producing phantom specialty products in response to the success of the micro and regional specialty brewers. (See chapter 5.) Coors was the first to introduce a malt-alternative with its Zima brand in 1993; Anheuser-Busch followed with Tequiza in 1998; Miller followed with Skyy Blue in 2001. This category is ignored because it is small and because malt-alternatives are not close substitutes for beer. (See chapter 1.)

8. For a review of the literature, see Tremblay and Tremblay 1996.

9. Alternatively, firm success and pioneering activity may be correlated because unsuccessful firms are more myopic (Dutta and Sundaram 2001) or risk loving (Friedman and Savage 1948).

10. Burgess (1993: 112) uses this very term to describe some of the high-risk strategies undertaken by Coors during the mid 1980s when Coors was under financial stress. This strategy is also discussed by McAfee (2002: 135–136).

11. This condition appears to hold in brewing as a new recipe is easily replicated and a brewery can switch production from one type of beer to another within an hour (*Fortune*, September 19, 1994: 79–86). For example, Schlitz Light was introduced 9 months after Miller Lite, and Michelob Dry was introduced within 6 months of the entry date of the first Japanese dry beer into the U.S.

12. This discussion excludes ale, which was introduced before Prohibition, and low-alcohol beer, which had limited entry.

13. One might expect more activity from third-tier firms simply because there are more of them. This is not the case for first-tier and second-tier firms, however, as the number in each group is about the same. (See table 3.3.)

14. Industry characteristics are ignored because they were never significant in the 1996 work. Multicollinearity may be the problem, however, as many important variables in brewing move together over time. For example, the Herfindahl-Hirschman index and per-capita income have increased with time and have a correlation coefficient of 0.95. Thus, the data make it difficult to distinguish the effect of income from the effect of concentration on the introduction of new products.

Chapter 7

1. For a summary of the pricing outcomes that result from different oligopoly models, see Vives 1999.

2. For reviews of the economics of advertising, see Schmalensee 1986; Carlton and Perloff 2000; Martin 2002.

3. Estimating the tax burden on consumers is complicated because taxes are levied in the form of corporate, sales, and excise taxes at the state and federal levels. Weinberg and *Consumer Reports* provide lower estimates than *Standard and Poor's DRI* (2001), which estimates the proportion of sales devoted to taxes at about 44% in 1997. Beer taxes will be discussed in more detail in chapter 9.

4. See *Printers' Ink*, January 12, 1962; Allison and Uhl 1964; Rewoldt et al. 1973. For an excellent review of these and other blind taste test studies, see Greer 1980: 87–91.

5. These tests for quality appear to be flawed, however, as reviewer comments indicate some confusion about the difference between vertical and horizontal differentiation. In one *Consumer Reports* test (2001), evaluators rated premium Budweiser superior to popular-priced Busch but stated that Busch has a slight taste of honey. As some consumers may prefer this taste, the evaluations may represent the horizontal preferences of the reviewers more than real quality differences between brands.

6. *Brewers Almanac* (1998: 9) reports that 6.9% of the beer produced in 1996 was lost through spillage or destroyed because it was of inferior quality.

7. Depending on handling, regular domestic lager is best when consumed within 3 months of manufacture. (See chapter 1.)

8. Pabst's market share grew considerably faster than the other national brewers from 1960–1962. In 1976, Pabst made an unsuccessful attempt to return Blue Ribbon to the premium category (*Advertising Age*, January 30, 1961 and September 11, 1961; *Barrons*, September 4, 1961 and March 8, 1976; *Printers' Ink*, January 31, 1964).

9. From 1989 to 1992, sales of Miller High Life fell by 41%. On Miller's discounting strategy, see *Modern Brewery Age*, March 21, 1994 and *Business Week*, May 2, 1994. Some speculate that problems with High Life began in the early 1980s when its "Miller Time" theme became old and stale (*Fortune*, March 18, 1985: 26).

10. To compete more effectively, the national brewers also introduced their own versions of popular-priced beer: Anheuser-Busch with Busch (in 1957), Coors with Keystone (in 1990), Miller with Milwaukee's Best (in 1961), Pabst with Blatz (in 1959), and Schlitz with Burgermeister (in 1961).

11. According to McGahan (1991), the price differential between premium and popular-priced brands was about 50% in the late 1930s because the shipping brewers were afraid that an aggressive pricing policy to increase sales would fuel the neo-prohibitionist movement and lead to greater government regulation. Cockerill (1977) finds a differential of 8%–60% between premium and popular-priced brands in the U.K.

12. Although this section focuses on a mixed strategy in prices (Varian 1980; Gibbons 1992), there is limited evidence that brewers also use a mixed strategy in advertising (Ackoff and Emshoff 1975a, 1975b). It is likely, as Ulrich Doraszelski has suggested in personal correspondence, that a brewer coordinates its mixed strategy in prices and advertising.

13. This is also true for Cournot type games where firms compete in output instead of price. A trigger strategy can also support collusion in a finite horizon game (Vives 1999: 302–305).

14. See also *Business Week*, December 18, 1989; Greer 1989; *Modern Brewery Age Weekly News Edition*, January 20, 2003.

15. Brooks (1970) argues that Anheuser-Busch chose to discipline its Midwest rivals in the St. Louis region because this was one of the few areas of the country where Anheuser-Busch marketed beer directly to retailers, and, therefore, had greater control over the retail price of Budweiser. For further discussion, see *Modern Brewery Age*, August 1954b and August 1958.

16. *Federal Trade Commission,* 277, 281 (1957), 54. For further account of this case, see Brooks 1970; Koller 1971; Greer 1980: 343–344; *Federal Trade Commission v. Anheuser-Busch, Inc.,* 363 U.S. 536 (1960), and *Anheuser-Busch, Inc. v. Federal Trade Commission,* 289 F. 2d 835 (1961).

17. A price war or tough price competition can be privately optimal if it eliminates weaker competitors and produces greater cooperation in the future. For further discussion of these events, see the *Wall Street Journal,* October 26, 1989; *Business Week,* December 18, 1989; Scherer 1996; Greer 1998.

18. Miller initiated price cuts in 1997–1998, but Anheuser-Busch, Coors, and Stroh did not follow (*Modern Brewery Age,* March 22, 1999: 10; *Wall Street Journal,* July 2, 1998). According to Robert Weinberg, the other three brewers may not have followed Miller because they feared that all the discounting was tarnishing the image of their flagship brands (*Wall Street Journal,* July 2, 1998).

19. These are rough estimates since most brewers generate some of their revenue from non-beer sales. For example, Anheuser-Busch generated about 92% of its 1979 sales from beer (*Business Week,* April 21, 1980), Coors generated about 90% of sales from beer in 1977 (*Forbes,* October 16, 1978), and Heileman generated about 93% of its sales from beer in 1976 (*Beverage World,* January 1977). For much of the period, Miller was owned by a conglomerate firm, Philip Morris, making it difficult to identify Miller's beer revenues. In addition, the revenue for Pabst in 1958 is inaccurate because of a complex merger with Blatz. The price discounting episode at Anheuser-Busch in the mid 1950s is unobservable because it involved the St. Louis area only.

20. McGahan (1995) finds evidence that brewers also used a trigger strategy to support more cooperative pricing during the Great Depression.

21. For further discussions of persuasive advertising, see Lee 1997; Tremblay and Martins-Filho 2001; Eaton and White 2002; Tremblay and Polasky 2002. On cognitive dissonance theory and advertising, see Akerlof and Dickens 1982. Cognitive dissonance also explains why anti-smoking ads that show real smokers with appalling health problems due to long-term smoking can be so effective at reducing demand (Hu and Keeler 1995; Tremblay and Tremblay 1995a).

22. This may explain the decline of High Life, as its image was squeezed between Budweiser and Coors.

23. However, Sass and Saurman (1995) find that restrictions on price advertising in brewing led to higher concentration in various states in the U.S. In addition, Benham (1972) and Milyo and Waldfogel (1999) find that a complete ban on advertising leads to higher prices for eyeglasses and alcoholic beverages, respectively. This suggests that price advertising leads to lower prices and that a complete ban may eliminate the informational content of advertising and result in higher prices.

24. For a more complete discussion of the possible effect of advertising on market prices, see Becker and Murphy 1993; Carlton and Perloff 2000; Tremblay and Okuyama 2001; Tremblay 2003.

25. These results are not surprising if most beer drinkers cannot distinguish one brand of mass-produced beer from another. If true, then the probability of at least 46 out of 100 Budweiser drinkers favoring Schlitz is 80.3%. For further discussion of these comparison advertisements, see Byars 1984; Aaker 1991; *Advertising Age,* December 8, 1980; *Fortune,* January 26, 1981.

26. In 1992, Anheuser-Busch created advertisements that informed consumers on the East Coast that Coors beer contained Virginia water. Coors made an unsuccessful attempt to block these negative advertisements, but the Bureau of Alcohol, Tobacco, and Firearms responded by ordering Coors to remove its Rocky Mountain reference from labels and advertising. For an account of these events and the Coors Rocky Mountain theme, see *Fortune*, November 1972; *New York Times*, August 14, 1992 and August 20, 1992; Burgess 1993: 144; Baum 2001.

27. The advertising expenditures of the leading brewers follow the general pattern of the industry (discussed in chapter 3).

28. The "Schlitz-Stroh" data in figure 7.4 are for Schlitz until its purchase by Stroh in 1982.

29. Miller High Life was no longer a premium brand during this period.

30. Unfortunately, data on advertising per barrel are not available for Miller Lite, the first successful light beer that was introduced nationally in 1975. Miller Lite's advertising intensity was relatively low, at $2.39, by 1977 because its sales were quite high by then. Data for Gablinger come from *Advertising Age*, April 1, 1968.

31. Anti-trust issues will be discussed in chapter 9.

32. The glaring exception is Anheuser-Busch's 1979 purchase of the Schlitz plant in Syracuse, New York. Anheuser-Busch received Department of Justice approval to purchase the plant because Schlitz was failing and Anheuser-Busch was the only brewer large enough to use the Syracuse plant's 4.4 million barrels of capacity (Elzinga 1986).

33. For further discussion of the theoretical motives for mergers and motives for merger in brewing, see *Beverage World*, October 1982; Carlton and Perloff 2000; Pautler 2001; Martin 2002.

34. Average capacity utilization rates for Heileman were 95.2% for 1965–1983 and 64.7% for 1984–1993.

35. This is in conflict with the result of Andrade et al. (2001), who find that mergers generally do not produce an efficiency gain. More recently, Pesendorfer (2003) finds that horizontal mergers lead to efficiency gains in the paper industry. Brewing may be more like the paper industry, since the rise in MES relative to the size of the market forced the least efficient brewers out of business and allowed surviving firms to benefit from the devolution strategy.

36. For an excellent review of the theoretical and empirical research on exclusive dealing contracts, see Sass 2001.

37. On federal and state law regarding exclusive dealing contracts in brewing, see Sass and Saurman 1993.

38. On the relationship between exclusive dealing clauses and beer prices in the U.K., see Slade 1998.

39. For a personal account of the hardships that Mr. Kalmanovitz imposed on employees, see www.jadetech.com.

40. Although true generic brands accounted for up to 10% of all retail grocery sales in the 1980s, they account for less than 0.5% today (Pride and Farrell 2003).

41. General's total production rose during the years 1980–1982 but showed a steady decline thereafter. On generic beer, see *Journal-American* (Kirkland, Washington), May 7, 1980; *Seattle Post Intelligencer*, April 28, 1980; *Los Angeles Times*, December 25, 1979.

42. For an account of Olde Frothingslosh and photographs of several cans, see *Advertising Age*, December 12, 1966; Robertson 1984; www.rustycans.com; www.santjoe.edu.

43. On Billy Beer, see *Advertising Age*, September 26, 1977; Robertson 1984; www.jadetech.com.

Chapter 8

1. Tirole (1988) and Shy (1995) focus on efficiency and technological progress. Scherer and Ross (1990) and Carlton and Perloff (2000) add equity. Shepherd (1990) includes social responsibility.

2. A review of the posters to promote the German import St. Pauli Girl suggests little downplay of sexual imagery over time. Posters from the years 1977–2003 can be seen at www.stpauligirl.com.

3. A similar concern was raised with Anheuser-Busch's marketing of its "Hurricane" brand malt liquor, first introduced in 1996 (National Council on Alcoholism and Drug Dependence at www.ncadd.org).

4. For an account of these events, see www.naacpi.org, www.crazyhorsedefense.org, www.ableza.org, and the ABC News *Nightline* television program on PowerMaster (June 26, 1991).

5. Under the Civil Rights Act of 1964, race, religion, national origin, and gender discrimination are illegal. The Age Discrimination in Employment Act of 1967 made age discrimination illegal.

6. Pittsburgh's production fell about 28% in 1972 and remained constant until 1980. For an account of these events, see *Advertising Age*, July 17, 1972 and *Business Week*, September 29, 1980.

7. Coors claims that these allegations are exaggerated, however (*Facts About Coors*, 1982).

8. For a review of the empirical evidence of the relationship between discrimination and market power in other markets, see Shepherd 1997, chapter 5.

9. Exceptions are the development of the aluminum can by Coors (see chapter 4) and William Sealy Gosset's contribution to the field of statistics (Pearson 1990). While working as a chemist at the Guinness brewery in Ireland, Gosset developed the Student t-distribution and small sample hypothesis testing techniques in order to ensure consistent quality from each batch of Guinness beer. Guinness allowed Gosset to publish his results, but only under the condition that the data remain confidential and that he publish under a different name. Such secrecy agreements were common practice at the time. As a result, Gosset published under the pseudonym "Student."

10. Externalities associated with excessive alcohol consumption will be discussed in the next section.

11. When marginal and average costs differ, however, price may exceed marginal cost even though long-run profits are 0.

12. On the strengths and weaknesses of these and other measures of profitability and market power, see Martin 2002.

13. In a simple Cournot model, for example, equilibrium price and industry profits fall with the number of competitors (Vives 1999).

14. For summaries, see Bresnahan 1989; Martin 2002, chapter 3.

15. The conjectural variation (v) equals $\partial Q_{-i}/\partial q_i$, and Θ equals $1 + v$. In a cartel, $v = n - 1$. In a Cournot or monopoly setting, $v = 0$. In a Bertrand or competitive market, $v = -1$.

16. Gallet and Euzent (2002) also find little evidence of market power in brewing using annual industry data. McGahan (1995) finds evidence of cooperative behavior in brewing in the years 1933–1942. The National Recovery Act, requests from legislators that brewers not compete too vigorously on price during the Great Depression, and subsequent support from local trade associations encouraged cooperation in brewing during the late 1930s. In the unregulated period of the 1880s, Manuszak (2002) finds that brewing firms did not engage in collusive behavior.

17. The main exceptions result from merger activity. Carling purchased National in period 4, which substantially raised Carling's market share and capacity utilization rate in that year. In addition, Drewery bought Hampton-Harvard and Piels in periods 4 and 3, respectively. Falstaff purchased Ballantine in period 3. Narragansett purchased Krueger in period 4. Ruppert purchased the Esslinger brands in period 1. Stroh purchased Heileman in period 3.

18. Firms may have a capacity utilization rate in excess of 100% for two reasons. First, capacity information is published in February of each year and will understate a firm's average capacity during the year if it is expanded after February. Second, one firm may contract with another firm to brew some of its beer. Thus, beer sales could exceed a firm's capacity. In 2002, for example, Pabst had no production capacity but sold about 7.5 million barrels of beer, beer that was produced under contract by Miller.

19. This information derives from personal conversation with Robert Weinberg on September 16, 2002. The range of estimates is due to the age of plant and equipment, the size of overhead costs, and demand conditions. This range is also consistent with those of Elzinga (1973) and Navir (1999) for regular and craft brewing, respectively.

20. For an alternative representation of strategic groups in brewing, see Hatten and Schendel 1977.

21. Rather than superiority, the variance in performance among brewers might be attributed to luck or to a disequilibrium phenomena that will dissipate over time (Mancke 1974).

22. The National Institute of Alcohol Abuse and Alcoholism, at www.niaaa.nih.gov, provides an excellent summary of the health risks associated with alcohol abuse.

23. Source of motor vehicle accident data: National Highway Traffic Safety Administration 2000.

24. Although litter is also a problem, it is ignored here because deposit laws help mitigate the negative externalities associated with litter. For example, Oregon requires a 5 cent deposit per container and recycles about 85% of its beverage containers (Gitlitz 2001). Externalities are minimal in production. The major pollutants are cleaning agents

and alcohol from spent grains and beer spills that enter the environment through faulty sewer lines (Smith and Sims 1985). Although Coors inadvertently polluted its ground water in this way in the early 1980s (Baum 2001), most brewers are environmentally friendly. For example, Coors was the first U.S. company to open up an aluminum recycling center back in 1959. Coors also received a "Climate Wise" award from the U.S. Environmental Protection Agency (EPA) in 1999 for its efforts to save energy and reduce pollution. Similarly, Anheuser-Busch received the EPA's "Waste Wise" award in 2002 for improvements in recycling. New Belgium (Fort Collins, Colorado) plans to be the first wind-powered brewery in the U.S.

25. These numbers are derived from Miller and Blincoe's (1994) and Kenkel's (1996) estimates of the optimal excise tax rate per six-pack, which would be the external cost to society of consuming an additional six-pack of beer divided by the net price of beer. The net price is the market price minus the current excise tax rate. In the late 1990s, the average market price was about $4.25 and the average excise tax rate was $0.83, producing a net price of $3.42. Estimates of the optimal tax rate were 51% (of $3.42) from Pogue and Sgontz, 137% from Miller and Blincoe, and 106% from Kenkel. The external-cost numbers in table 8.4 imply an optimal excise tax rate of between 80% and 102%. Tax issues are also discussed in chapter 9.

26. Moderate drinking is defined as no more than two drinks per day for men 21–65 years of age and no more than one drink per day for men over 65 and for women over 20 who are not pregnant. One drink is equivalent to 0.6 ounce of ethanol (pure alcohol) or a single 12-ounce serving of beer (at 5% alcohol by volume), a 6-ounce serving of wine (at 10% alcohol), and a 1.5-ounce serving of spirits (at 40% alcohol or 80 proof). See chapter 9 and appendix D for further discussion.

27. See, for example, *Wall Street Journal*, August 13, 2002; "Alcohol and Coronary Heart Disease" (www.niaaa.nih.gov); "Beer, In Moderation, Cuts Risk of Cataracts and Heart Disease," *Science Daily* (www.sciencedaily.com). John Folts of the University of Wisconsin at Madison finds that the flavonoids in beer, especially dark beer, may prevent heart disease (*Gazette-Times*, November 1, 2003). For an early discussion of the health benefits of beer consumption, see *Modern Brewery Age*, April 1958.

28. These and other statistics on heart disease can be found at www.umm.edu.

29. These issues are addressed by Fisher and McGowan (1979), Shapiro (1980), Kaserman and Mayo (1991), Becker and Murphy (1993), Melese et al. (1996), and Tremblay (2001, 2003).

30. Becker and Murphy allow for positive externalities when advertising pays for radio and television programming. This effect is subsumed in the general external effects described in our model.

31. In a monopoly setting, for example, $\Theta = 1$ and $\lambda = -\partial P / \lambda Q > 0$. In a competitive or simple Bertrand setting, $\Theta = \lambda = 0$.

32. Aggregation requires that marginal cost is the same for all firms and that the market-power parameter is either a constant or defined as a measure of average industry conduct. On the strengths and weaknesses of this approach, see Bresnahan 1989; Genesove and Mullen 1998; Corts 1999; Clay and Troesken 2003.

33. The supply relation was corrected for first-order autocorrelation, but no autocorrelation was detected in the demand equation.

34. On the effect of beer taxes, see Denney et al. 2002.

35. This is a reasonable assumption for Anheuser-Busch, since it is large enough to take advantage of scale economies. (See figure 2.10.)

36. This conclusion is qualitatively similar to the conclusion drawn by Manuszak (2002). Manuszak finds that competition diminished in brewing during the 1880s as the number of competitors declined.

Chapter 9

1. Of course, excessive caution will lead to no action at all, which is inappropriate if the status quo is socially unacceptable. For further discussion of concerns with applied policy analysis, see Demsetz 1969.

2. For a review of the U.S. anti-trust laws and the anti-merger cases discussed in this section, see Greer 1980, 1998; Scherer 1980, 1996; Elzinga 1982; Seplaki 1982; Waldman 1986; Martin 1988; Kwoka and White 1999.

3. Scherer (1980: 554) argues that these court decisions may illustrate "a different sort of consistency," one that provides a "faithful stewardship to the will of Congress."

4. The 1982 Guidelines (at 28,497) indicate that the "critical HHI thresholds of 1,000 and 1,800 correspond roughly to a CR4 of 50% and 70%, respectively."

5. The change in HHI due to a merger equals twice the product of the market shares of the two merging firms. For example, a merger between firms with market shares of 10% and 5% would raise HHI by 100 points.

6. Robert Weinberg believes that the merger between Coors and Stroh would have been approved if the companies had continued negotiation with the Department of Justice (personal conversation, September 23, 2002).

7. For strong criticism of the government's unwillingness to allow Pabst to purchase Carling, see *Advertising Age*, July 3, 1978.

8. For more complete descriptions of price discrimination and the law, see Scherer and Ross 1990; Varian 1992.

9. In 1973, the FTC ordered Coors to stop using cancellation clauses in its contracts with distributors in an effort to fix the price of Coors beer at the retail level, but there was no allegation of price fixing with another brewer (*Wall Street Journal*, June 6, 1974). On the input side of the market, Hallagan (1985) finds that U.S. hops growers remain competitive in spite of legal opportunities to collude.

10. For example, McAfee (2002: 129) argues that cartels are unlikely in industries with more than eight rivals and that price-fixing agreements are unlikely in industries with more than five.

11. In the U.S., a drink or standard serving contains 0.6 ounce of ethanol or absolute alcohol. This is equivalent to one 12-ounce container of regular beer (at 5% alcohol by volume), one 6-ounce glass of wine (at 10% alcohol by volume), and one 1.5-ounce shot of distilled spirits (80 proof, 40% alcohol). See appendix D for further discussion.

12. A new method that appears to be effective at curbing cigarette smoking and alcohol abuse on college campuses is "social norming." Many students overestimate the percent-

age of peers who smoke and drink to excess and try to fit in by pursuing the mis-perceived behaviors of their peers. A social norming program correctly informs students of campus norms, information that leads to more responsible behavior. On the pros and cons of this method, see *USA Today*, May 27, 2002; Perkins 2003; Wechsler and Wuethrich 2002.

13. The Act did not apply to ten states with laws requiring that alcohol content appear on the label: Arkansas, California, Colorado, Kansas, Massachusetts, Minnesota, Missouri, Montana, Oklahoma, and Oregon.

14. This data set is used because it comes from a reliable source, the Connecticut Agri-cultural Experiment Station, and because it includes information from all of the major brands of domestic beer that are discussed in this book. Brand characteristics change. The interested reader can find more recent estimates of the alcohol and calorie content of the major brands in *Consumer Reports* (June 1996 and August 2001), on individual firms' web pages, and on the web page of Dr. Aaron M. White of the Duke University Medical School (www.duke.edu).

15. Blood alcohol levels are calculated as a ratio of alcohol by weight (in milligrams) to volume of blood (in deciliters). BAC is expressed as a percentage, where 10% alcohol by volume is equivalent to 100 milligrams (10 grams) of alcohol per deciliter of blood. See appendix D for further discussion.

16. For a review of the evidence, see National Institute on Alcohol Abuse and Alcoholism 2001.

17. For more on the Act, see "Commercial Motor Vehicle Traffic Enforcement" at www.nhtsa.dot.gov.

18. This discussion is based on reports by the American Medical Association (2002) and the National Institute on Alcohol Abuse and Alcoholism (2001).

19. Demand is inelastic but not perfectly so, especially in the long run. Although Denney et al. (2002) find that about 80% of the federal excise tax on beer is passed on to consum-ers, a 100% rate is assumed to simplify the discussion. If part of the tax is paid for by producers as Denney et al. find, however, this may explain why producers strongly oppose higher beer taxes. See, for example, Anheuser-Busch's arguments for lowering beer taxes at www.rollbackthebeertax.org.

20. More than 7,000 adults were randomly selected from the 48 contiguous states, the District of Columbia, and Puerto Rico. The sample matches the actual gender, age, race, education, and income composition of the U.S. closely.

21. For a six-pack with a market price of $4.25, this would translate to a tax rate of 47%–70% over the net price (market price less the excise tax). Even with these positive external benefits, the estimates of 47%–70% are similar to previous estimates of the optimal tax on ethanol, which range from 40% to 137% (Phelps 1988; Pogue and Sgontz 1989; Miller and Blincoe 1994; Kenkel 1996).

22. The price of beer is derived from the price index of beer (see chapter 2) and Standard and Poor's DRI (2001) estimate of the average excise tax rate on beer at 17% of the price in 1997.

23. For reviews of the early literature, see Leung and Phelps 1993; Cook and Moore 1994.

24. Data sources: for age-adjusted liver disease rate, *National Vital Statistics Report* 50, no 15, September 16, 2002; for traffic fatalities, National Highway Traffic Safety Administration 2000; for per-capita beer consumption, *Beer Industry Update: A Review of Recent Developments*, 2001; for taxes per barrel, *Brewers Almanac*, 2002.

25. For additional arguments against higher beer taxes, see Beer Institute 2002; Standard and Poor's DRI 2001. Cook and Moore (1994) and Kenkel (1996) favor higher excise taxes on alcoholic beverages.

26. For further discussion, see *Wall Street Journal*, June 12, 1996; Bang 1998; Hacker 1998; Tremblay and Okuyama 2001; *Advertising Age*, April 15, 2002. See also Center for Science in the Public Interest, "Chronology of Broadcast Liquor Advertising" (www.cspinet.org).

27. This concern dates back at least as far as the mid 1950s (*Modern Brewery Age*, August 1954a, November 1954, July 1956).

28. In *Central Hudson Gas v. Public Service Commission* (447 U.S. 557, 1980), the U.S. Supreme Court ruled that bans or restrictions on commercial speech are legal only when they promote the interests of society and are the least restrictive alternative.

29. This guideline would benefit all firms, as negative advertising by one firm may induce others to resort to negative advertising and persuade consumers that none of the products are any good (McAfee 2002: 114). In addition, firms most likely to violate the guideline would be failing firms with little interest in the long term welfare of the industry.

30. On the theoretical issues and empirical evidence regarding the effect of advertising restrictions on price and social welfare, see Benham 1972; Dixit and Norman 1978; Milyo and Waldfogel 1999; Tremblay and Okuyama 2001; Tremblay 2003.

31. For more on the position of the Women's Christian Temperance Union, see the October 1954 issue of *Modern Brewery Age* and www.wctu.org. For the views of Mothers Against Drunk Driving, see www.madd.org.

32. There is probably a stronger argument for imposing a higher tax on malt liquor and fortified wine (i.e., wines with an alcohol content that ranges from 17% to 21%), as their tax rates and prices per unit of alcohol are relatively low. Higher taxes on these alcoholic beverages would be regressive, however, as low-income consumers are more likely to buy malt liquor and fortified wine.

Chapter 10

1. Anonymous, quoted on p. 79 of James 1981.

References

Print Materials

Aaker, David A. 1991. *Managing Brand Equity: Capitalizing on the Value of a Name Brand.* Free Press.

Abbott, A. J., K. A. Lawler, and M. C. H. Ling. 1997. "Advertising Investment in the UK Brewing Industry: An Empirical Analysis." *Economic Issues* 2, no. 1: 55–66.

Abreu, Dilip. 1986. "Extremal Equilibria for Oligopolistic Supergames." *Journal of Economic Theory* 39, no. 1: 191–225.

Ackerberg, Daniel A. 2001. "Empirically Distinguishing Informative and Prestige Effects of Advertising." *Rand Journal of Economics* 32, no. 2: 316–333.

Ackoff, Russell L., and James R. Emshoff. 1975a. "Advertising Research at Anheuser-Busch Inc. (1963–68)." *Sloan Management Review* 16, no. 2: 1–15.

Ackoff, Russell L., and James R. Emshoff. 1975b. "Advertising Research at Anheuser-Busch Inc. (1968–74)." *Sloan Management Review* 16, no. 3: 1–15.

Adams Beer Handbook. 2002. Adams Business Media.

Adams Liquor Handbook. 2002. Adams Business Media.

Adams Wine Handbook. 2002. Adams Business Media.

Adams, Walter, and James W. Brock. 1988. "Reaganomics and the Transmogrification of Merger Policy." *Antitrust Bulletin* 33, no. 2: 309–359.

Advertising Age. 1958. "Per-Case and Per-Barrel Costs of Beer and Ale Advertising." February 3: 82–83.

Advertising Age. 1958. "Pabst Shifts to 'Since 1844' Stress." June 23.

Advertising Age. 1959. "Hamm Invades East in Buy of Gunter Brewing." December 21: 6.

Advertising Age. 1961. "Hamm Brewing Builds to National Brand." January 16: 3.

Advertising Age. 1961. "Pabst Price Cuts Mean End of Premium Status." January 30: 3.

Advertising Age. 1961. "Krueger Deal with Narragansett Set." April 17: 12.

Advertising Age. 1961. Piel Bros. Unit Introduces New Low Calorie Beer." September 11: 42.

Advertising Age. 1961. "Per-Case and Per-Barrel Costs of Beer and Ale Advertising." October 9: 70–72.

Advertising Age. 1962. "Heileman Acquires Fox Head." July 9: 12.

Advertising Age. 1963. "Hamm Acquires Gulf Brewing." April 1: 111.

Advertising Age. 1964. "Antitrust Suit against Schlitz Is Filed by U.S." February 24: 199.

Advertising Age. 1964. "Per-Case and Per-Barrel Costs of Beer and Ale Advertising." October 5: 158–160.

Advertising Age. 1965. "Oly Beer Drive Ties Brew to Pizza Sales." March 22: 58.

Advertising Age. 1965. "Drewery Acquires Atlantic Brewing's Brand of Beer, Ale." June 7: 85.

Advertising Age. 1965. "Falstaff Purchases Narragansett: U.S. to Push Anti-Trust Suit." July 26: 82.

Advertising Age. 1965. "Advertising Costs for Beer, Ale, and Malt Liquor." August 23: 79–80.

Advertising Age. 1965. "Heublein Acquires Theo. Hamm Brewing for $92,750,000." October 18: 130.

Advertising Age. 1965. "Associated Joins Drewery's to Form #8 U.S. Brewer." December 13: 1.

Advertising Age. 1966. "Advertising Costs for Beer, Ale, and Malt Liquor." August 22: 122–123.

Advertising Age. 1966. "Good News for Nocturnal Beer Bibbers Olde Frothingslosh Is Back Clad in Day-Glo." December 12: 18.

Advertising Age. 1967. "Rheingold Unit Markets Gablinger's Beer, Containing No Carbohydrates." January 9: 3.

Advertising Age. 1967. "Forest Expands Markets for Its Gablinger's Beer." June 12: 94.

Advertising Age. 1967. "Advertising Costs for Beer, Ale, and Malt Liquor." September 18: 63–64.

Advertising Age. 1967. "'Hamm It Up' Goes on the Road after Testing in Land of Sky Blue Waters." September 25: 24.

Advertising Age. 1968. "Intro of Gablinger's Leads to Top Level Shift at Rheingold." April 1: 6.

Advertising Age. 1968. "Pearl Brewing Expands Markets." April 15: 2.

Advertising Age. 1968. "In 67 Brewers Cut per Barrel Ad Costs." September 9: 106–107.

Advertising Age. 1969. "Philip Morris Acquires Miller." June 16: 94.

Advertising Age. 1969. "Brewers' Ad Spending Dipped in 68 but Sales Climbed, Despite Strikes." October 20: 273.

Advertising Age. 1970. "Meister Brau Wins Amylase Patent Suit." March 30: 62.

Advertising Age. 1970. "CU Fails to Get Injunction vs. Hamm, but Makes Points Anyhow." June 1: 2.

Advertising Age. 1970. "Advertising Costs for Beer, Ale, and Malt Liquor." October 26: 40–41.

Advertising Age. 1971. "Miller Edges Away from Champagne Motif in Initial Campaign by McCann." February 1: 58.

Advertising Age. 1971. "Ballantine Is Seen Getting Token Support." February 22: 129.

Advertising Age. 1971. "Advertising Costs for Beer, Ale, and Malt Liquor." September 20: 31–32.

Advertising Age. 1971. "Hamm Buys Burgie Beer." December 20: 8.

Advertising Age. 1972. "Hamm's Bear Back after Hibernation." February 28: 2.

Advertising Age. 1972. "Ballantine's New Owner Looks Ahead." March 20: 25.

Advertising Age. 1972. "3 Meister Brau Brand Names Bought by Miller." July 3: 8.

Advertising Age. 1972. "Carling Choice of Lois Shop Highlights Beer Development." July 17: 3.

Advertising Age. 1972. "Iron City Beer's Sales Drives Aim at Backlash." July 17: 18.

Advertising Age. 1972. "Its Customers Couldn't Bear It—So Hamm Has Brought Him Back." July 31: 4.

Advertising Age. 1972. "Advertising Costs for Beer, Ale, and Malt Liquor." October 30: 145–146.

Advertising Age. 1973. "Drive Set for Bud 73 Push." May 7: 42.

Advertising Age. 1973. "A-B Will Stop Marketing Bud Malt Liquor." August 6: 54.

Advertising Age. 1973. "Advertising Costs for Beer, Ale, and Malt Liquor." October 1: 34–35.

Advertising Age. 1974. "Grain Belt Shifts Ad Dollars to Stave Off Oly Invasion." March 18: 56.

Advertising Age. 1974. "Top Brewer Ad Spending Slipped 8.7% Last Year." September 23: 41–42.

Advertising Age. 1975. "Sale of Hamm Signaling Burgie's Chicago Exit?" March 3: 59.

Advertising Age. 1975. "Coors Initial Stock Offering Well Received." June 23: 8.

Advertising Age. 1975. "Changes Seen in Latest Schlitz Ads, More on Tap." June 30: 51.

Advertising Age. 1975. "Schlitz Readying Regional Launch of Light Beer." October 20: 1.

Advertising Age. 1975. "Advertising Costs for Beer, Ale, and Malt Liquor." November 3: 29–30.

Advertising Age. 1975. "Miller Wants Competitors to Shed Light." November 10: 93.

Advertising Age. 1977. "Two Agencies Help Introduce A-B Light Beer." January 10: 1.

Advertising Age. 1977. "Stroh's Says It's Ready to Take on the Big Boys." March 21: 91.

Advertising Age. 1977. "We Don't Change Beer—Why Change Ads?" May 16: 102.

Advertising Age. 1977. "Oly Mining Gold—'Big 5 Beware,'" July 4: 25.

Advertising Age. 1977. "No More Pabst for Bill Carter—Falls City Creates His 'Personal' Brew." September 26: 6.

Advertising Age. 1977. "Ad Costs for Beer, Ale, and Malt Liquor." September 26: 122.

Advertising Age. 1978. "John Murphy of Miller Is Adman of the Year." January 9: 1.

Advertising Age. 1978. "A-B Budget Is Heavier Than Ever." February 13: 4.

Advertising Age. 1978. "A-B Cracks New Area with Michelob Light." February 20: 64.

Advertising Age. 1978. "Schlitz Payoff Indictment Names Burnett, Other Shops as Conduits." March 20: 1.

Advertising Age. 1978. "U.S. Ready to Settle with Nine in Beer, Liquor Payoff Probe." March 27: 1.

Advertising Age. 1978. "A-B to Pay $750,000 to Settle Charges." April 3: 14.

Advertising Age. 1978. "FTC May Ask for Fines in Löwenbräu Ad Case." June 26: 1.

Advertising Age. 1978. "Analysts Assail Government Move to Halt Pabst, Carling Deal." July 3: 46.

Advertising Age. 1978. "Ad Costs for Beer, Ale, and Malt Liquor." October 9: 122.

Advertising Age. 1978. "Schlitz Case Settled Out of Court." November 6: 8.

Advertising Age. 1978. "Carling Set to Pour Out New Dark Beer." September 18: 11.

Advertising Age. 1978. "After 105 Years, Coors Diversifies." December 18: 12.

Advertising Age. 1979. "Pabst Plans to Acquire Blitz-Weinhard Brewing." February 5: 70.

Advertising Age. 1979. "Top Breweries Hike Ad Spending 33%." September 24: 18.

Advertising Age. 1980. "Schlitz to Taste-Test." December 8: 1.

Advertising Age. 1980. "Pabst Sets New Light, Blue Ribbon TV Effort." April 14: 4.

Advertising Age. 1980. "Taste That's Key to Schlitz Drive." April 28: 2.

Advertising Age. 1980. "Schlitz to Taste-Test." December 8: 1.

Advertising Age. 1981. "Schlitz, What Went Wrong." April 13: p. 61–64.

Advertising Age. 1981. "Schlitz, Lost at Sea, Part 2." April 20: p. 49–52.

Advertising Age. 1981. "Small but Feisty Brewers Survive." July 27: S49–50.

Advertising Age. 1982. "The 'Big 2' Strengthen Their Grip." March 29: m31.

Advertising Age. 1982. "Stroh Mulls Post-Merger Plan." April 26: 4.

Advertising Age. 1982. "Miller Lite Spots Draw Heavy Acclaim." April 26: m1.

Advertising Age. 1982. "Pabst Ads Draw Fire by Jacobs." March 29: 26.

Advertising Age. 1984. "Beer Marketing." January 16: 10.

Advertising Age. 1985. "Whole World Is Watching U.S. Alcohol Ad Debate." February 11: 70.

Advertising Age. 1985. "Coors Pores Over Plans to Expand." April 15: 4.

Advertising Age. 1986. "Adolph Coors Co." November 3: 103.

Advertising Age. 1988. "Pabst on Attack." June 27: 92.

Advertising Age. 1989. "Heileman in High Gear." February 13: 1 and 66.

Advertising Age. 1989. "New Dry Beer Gets Bud Name." March 27: 3.

Advertising Age. 1990. "A-B Tries to Bolster Bud, Bud Light." February 12: 51.

Advertising Age. 1991. "Coors to Modify 'Spring Water' Claim." March 18: 4.

Advertising Age. 1993. "Ice Beer Cracks into Market." November 29: 1 and 36.

Advertising Age. 2002. "Beer Group Warns of Possible Ad Restrictions." April 15. www.adage.com.

Advertising Age. 2002. "Should BBB Approve Beer Ads?" April 16: 1.

Advertising Age. 2002. "Radio Show Canceled after Sex Contest Goes Awry." August 23. www.adage.com.

Advertising Age. 2002. "Can Sex Show Scandal Boost Brewer's Profile?" September 3. www.adage.com.

Advertising Age. 2002. "Anheuser-Busch Boosts Prices, Increases Ad Budget." October 24. www.adage.com.

Advertising Age. 2002. "Michelob to Get Increased Ad Spending." November 13. www.adage.com.

Advertising Age. 2003. "Why the Miller Beer Sex Ad Doesn't Work." January 27. www.adage.com.

Advertising Age. 2003. "Can Miller Beer Survive the Mess It's In?" July 7. www.adage.com.

Adweek. 1985. "Low-Alcohol Beer Struggles for Glass Distinction." August 19: 12.

Adweek's Marketing Week. 1987. "With Spuds for Bud, It's a Dog's Light with Real Bite." June 29: 21.

Akerlof, George A. 1991. "Procrastination and Obedience." *American Economic Review* 81, no. 2: 1–19.

Akerlof, George A., and William T. Dickens. 1982. "The Economic Consequence of Cognitive Dissonance." *American Economic Review* 72, no. 3: 307–319.

Akerlof, George A., and Rachel E. Kranton. 2000. "Economics of Identity." *Quarterly Journal of Economics* 115, no. 3: 715–753.

Allison, Ralph I., and Kenneth P. Uhl. 1964. "Influence of Beer Brand Identification on Taste Perception." *Journal of Marketing Research* 1, no. 3: 36–39.

Ambler, Tim. 1996. "Can Alcohol Misuse Be Reduced by Banning Advertising?" *International Journal of Advertising* 15, no. 2: 167–174.

American Academy of Family Physicians. 1995. "Alcohol." www.aafp.org.

American Brewer. 2003. "Craft Beer and Imports." 19, no. 1: 22–27.

American Medical Association. 1996. "Alcohol and Driving: Key Facts." www.ama-assn.org.

American Medical Association. 1997. "Drivers Impaired by Alcohol." www.ama-assn.org.

American Medical Association. 1998. "Congressional Approval Sought for Lower Nationwide Blood-Alcohol Level." ww.ama-assn.org.

American Medical Association. 2002. "Alcohol and Other Drug Education." www.ama-assn.org.

American Medical Association. 2002. "The Minimum Legal Drinking Age: Facts and Fallacies." www.ama-assn.org.

American Medical Association. 2002. "Youth, Young Adults, and Alcohol: Key Facts and Prevention Strategies." www.ama-assn.org.

American School Health Association. 1994. "Guidelines for Comprehensive School Health Programs." www.ashaweb.org.

Andrade, Gregor, Mark Mitchell, and Erik Stafford. 2001. "New Evidence and Perspectives on Mergers." *Journal of Economic Perspectives* 15, no. 2: 103–120.

Anheuser-Busch Inc. v Federal Trade Commission. 1961. *Federal Reporter* 289, F.2d 835.

Appelbaum, Elie. 1979. "Testing for Price Taking Behavior." *Journal of Econometrics* 9, no. 3: 283–294.

Appelbaum, Elie. 1982. "The Estimation of the Degree of Market Power." *Journal of Econometrics* 19, no. 2–3: 287–299.

Apps, Jerry. 1992. *Breweries of Wisconsin.* University of Wisconsin Press.

Aron, Debra J., and Edward P. Lazear. 1990. "The Introduction of New Products." *American Economic Review* 80, no. 2: 421–426.

Aronson, Elliot. 1999. *The Social Animal.* Worth.

Bain, Joe S. 1959. *Industrial Organization.* Wiley.

Baker, Jonathan B., and Timothy F. Bresnahan. 1985. "The Gains from Merger or Collusion in Product-Differentiated Markets." *Journal of Industrial Economics* 33, no. 2: 427–444.

Baker, Jonathan B., and Timothy F. Bresnahan. 1988. "Estimating the Residual Demand Curve Facing a Single Firm." *International Journal of Industrial Organization* 6, no. 3: 283–300.

Bang, Hae-Kyong. 1998. "Analyzing the Impact of the Liquor Industry's Lifting of the Ban on Broadcast Advertising." *Journal of Public Policy and Marketing* 17, no. 1: 132–138.

Barndt, Stephen E. 2002. "Redhook Ale Brewery." In T. Wheelen and J. Hunger, eds., *Strategic Management and Business Policy.* Prentice-Hall.

Barnett, John H., and William D. Wilsted. 1988a. "The Alcoholic Beverage Industry." In *Strategic Management: Concepts and Cases*. PWS-Kent.

Barnett, John H., and William D. Wilsted. 1988b. "Joseph Schlitz Brewing Company." In *Strategic Management: Concepts and Cases*. PWS-Kent.

Barnett, John H., and William D. Wilsted. 1988c. "The Adolph Coors Company." In *Strategic Management: Concepts and Cases*. PWS-Kent.

Barnett, John H., and William D. Wilsted. 1988d. "Pabst Brewing Company." In *Strategic Management: Concepts and Cases*. PWS-Kent.

Baron, Stanley W. 1962. *Brewed in America: A History of Beer and Ale in the United States*. Little, Brown.

Barron's. 1959. "Big Gains on Tap for Pabst Brewing as a Result of Consolidation with Blatz." March 16: 33.

Barron's. 1961. "Heileman Brews Bigger Sales, Net as Production Efficiency Improves." April 24: 31.

Barron's. 1961. "Growth of the Southwest a Stimulant to Operation of Pearl Brewing Co." June 12: 30.

Barron's. 1961. "Major Changes by Pabst Yield Blue Ribbon Results." September 4: 26.

Barron's. 1963. "Concentrates to Pull-Tabs." September 16: 11.

Barron's. 1967. "Roll Out the Barrels." May 8: 3.

Barron's. 1969. "Rheingold Brews Heady Comeback in Earnings." March 31: 36.

Barron's. 1970. "Cold Drafts?" July 13: 10.

Barron's. 1976. "Pabst Brewing Likely to Enjoy Big Blue Ribbon Year." March 8: 66.

Barron's. 1980. "Coors Seems to Have Halted Its Market Erosion." May 12: 63.

Barron's. 1982. "Crippling Competition: That Is What Antitrust Is Doing to the Beer Industry." April 26: 11.

Barron's. 1983. "Small Beer: But Microbrewers Are a Yeasty Lot." May 9: 16.

Bauer, Raymond A., and Stephen A. Greyser. 1968. *Advertising in America: The Consumer View*. Harvard University Press.

Baughman, Reagan, Michael Colin, Stacy Dickert-Colin, and John Pepper. 2001. "Slippery When Wet: The Effects of Local Alcohol Access Laws on Highway Safety." *Journal of Health Economics* 20, no. 6: 1089–1096.

Baum, Dan. 2001. *Citizen Coors: A Grand Family Saga of Business, Politics, and Beer*. HarperCollins.

Baumol, William J., John C. Panzar, and Robert D. Willig. 1982. *Contestable Markets and the Theory of Industry Structure*. Harcourt Brace Jovanovich.

Becker, Gary S., and Kevin M. Murphy. 1988. "A Theory of Rational Addiction." *Journal of Political Economy* 96, no. 4: 675–700.

Becker, Gary S., and Kevin M. Murphy. 1993. "A Simple Theory of Advertising as a Good or Bad." *Quarterly Journal of Economics* 108, no. 4: 941–964.

Beer Industry Update: A Review of Recent Developments. 2002. Beer Marketer's INSIGHTS, Inc.

Beer Institute. 2002. "Beer Tax Facts: The Economic and Societal Impacts of State and Federal Taxes on Beer."

Beer Institute. 2002. "Advertising and Marketing Code."

Beer Institute. 2002–03. "Annual Report."

Beer in the U.S. 2002. Beverage Marketing Corp.

Benham, Lee. 1972. "The Effect of Advertising on the Price of Eyeglasses." *Journal of Law and Economics* 15, no. 2: 337–352.

Benjamin, Daniel K., and William R. Dougan. 1997. "Efficient Excise Taxation: The Evidence from Cigarettes." *Journal of Law and Economics* 40, no. 1: 113–136.

Beuttenmuller, Rudolf W. 1979. "The Goal of the New Premerger Notification Requirements: Preliminary Relief against Anticompetitive Mergers." *Duke Law Review* 249, no. 1: 249–285.

Beverage Industry. 1977. "Russ Cleary Confounds the Experts." January: 29–48.

Beverage Industry. 1980. "The Fading Blue Ribbon Beer." December: 24–27.

Beverage Industry. 1982. "The Brewer's Survival Equation." October: 30–34.

Beverage Industry. 1988. "Marketing Moves." January 18.

Beverage Industry. 1991. "Beer Seer." December: 20–21, 24–26.

Beverage Industry. 1996. "Mind Games: Anheuser-Busch Wants Its Wholesalers Whole Attention." September: 70–74.

Beverage Industry. 1998. "Domestic Specialty Suffers Growing Pains in '97." January: 9.

Beverage Industry. 1998. "Beverage Industry's Top 100 Beverage Companies of 1998." 89, no. 6: 31.

Blau, Francine D., Marianne A. Farber, and Anne E. Winkler. 2001. *The Economics of Women, Men, and Work*. Prentice-Hall.

Bok, Derek C. 1960. "Section 7 of the Clayton Act and the Merging of Law and Economics." *Harvard Law Review* 74, no. 2: 226–355.

Boyd, Roy, and Barry J. Seldon. 1990. "The Fleeting Effect of Advertising: Empirical Evidence from a Case Study." *Economics Letters* 34, no. 4: 375–379.

Brander, James A., and Jonathan Eaton. 1984. "Product Line Rivalry." *American Economic Review* 74, no. 3: 37–45.

Brandweek. 1995. "Microbreweries More Amenable to Majors." October 16: 3.

Brandweek. 1997. "Tapped-In 'Outsider.'" February 10: 52.

Brandweek. 1997. "Beer Marketing for Dummies." March 31: 38.

Brandweek. 2000. "Having a Blast during the Great Beer Bust." January 17: 28.

Brean, Hebert. 1958. "Hidden Sell Technique Is Almost Here: New Subliminal Gimmicks Now Offer Blood, Skulls, and Popcorn to Movie Fans." *Life* 44, March 31: 102–114.

Bresnahan, Timothy F. 1989. "Empirical Studies of Industry with Market Power." In R. Schmalensee and R. Willig, eds., *Handbook of Industrial Organization*. North-Holland.

Brewers Almanac. 2002. United States Brewers Association.

Brewers Digest, Buyer's Guide and Brewery Directory. 2003.

Brewers Digest. 1938. "Prohibition Has Failed Everywhere." November: 22.

Brewers Digest. 1945. "The Doctrine of Regional Beers." June: 32–35.

Brewers Digest. 1985. "Tide May Have Turned on Beer-Wine Issue." February 1985: 18–23.

Brewers Digest. 1986. "The Micro Brewers." February 1986: 21–22.

Brewers Digest. 1987. The U.S. Beer Market: Part II– The Microbrewery Movement." March: 28–33.

Brewers Digest. 1997. "Anheuser-Busch Expands Partnership with Kirin Brewery." January: 33.

Brewers Digest. 1999. "What Is a 'Standard Drink'?" January: 20–22.

Brewers Digest. 2002. "2002 World Beer Cup Winners." July/August: 63–66.

Brewers Digest. 2002. "Classical Beer Styles." September-October: 35–36.

Brooks, Robert C., Jr. 1970. "How Can Government Best Promote an Efficient Market." U.S. Congress, House of Representatives *Hearings on Small Business and the Robinson-Patman Act*, Vol. 2, 91st Congress, Second Session, March 3, 4, and 11: 721–738.

Brouwer, Maria. 1988. "Evolutionary Aspects of the European Brewing Industry." In H. de Jong, ed., *The Structure of European Industry*. Kluwer.

Bull, Donald, Manfred Fredrich, and Robert Gottschalk. 1984. *American Breweries*. Bullworks.

Bulow, Jeremy I., John D. Geanokopolos, and Paul D. Klemperer. 1985. "Multimarket Oligopoly: Strategic Substitutes and Complements." *Journal of Political Economy* 93, no. 3: 488–511.

Bulow, Jeremy L., and Paul D. Klemperer. 1999. "The Generalized War of Attrition." *American Economic Review* 89, no. 1: 175–189.

Bureau of Alcohol, Tobacco, and Firearms. 2001. "Alcohol Beverage Health Warning Statement." Washington, D.C.: U.S. Department of the Treasury, Notice No. 917, May 22. www.atf.treas.gov.

Burgess, Robert J. 1993. *Silver Bullets: A Soldier's Story of How Coors Bombed in the Beer Wars*. St. Martin's Press.

Business Today. 1986. "Behind the Beer Label." Spring: 20.

Business Today. 1986. "What the 21-Laws Mean to Brewers." Spring: 23–24.

Business Week. 1945. "Embattled Beer." November 24: 42.

Business Week. 1947. "Brewing Stays in the Family." September 6: 15.

Business Week. 1948. "Shifts in Beer Picture." July 17: 70.

Business Week. 1949. "Beer Business Is Flush." August 27: 61.

Business Week. 1951. "U.S. Taste Buds Want It Bland." July 14.

Business Week. 1951. "High Life for Miller's Beer." September 8: 68.

Business Week. 1951. "Beer Flows, Labor Dispute Ends." November 3: 32.

Business Week. 1952. "Beer Drinkers Like Them Light and Dry." April 19: 147.

Business Week. 1954. "Big Brewers Move West." January 16: 128.

Business Week. 1954. "Not Just a Flicker." February 6: 12.

Business Week. 1954. "National Brewing Co." October 2: 60.

Business Week. 1955. "New Beer Champ Coming Up as A-B Sales Bad." November 19: 114.

Business Week. 1955. "Racial Storm." December 17: 52.

Business Week. 1957. "New Ideas Shake Up Old Brewing Industry." March 9: 89–90.

Business Week. 1959. "U.S. Brewers Thirst for a Boom." June 20: 45.

Business Week. 1963. "Are the Drinkers Doing Their Part?" April 13: 106.

Business Week. 1964. "Brewing a River of Beer." March 14: 27.

Business Week. 1966. "How Falstaff Brews New Markets." July 30: 47.

Business Week. 1969. "Keeping Your Head in the Beer Business." September 13: 138–140.

Business Week. 1970. "The Brewery That Breaks All the Rules." August 22: 60.

Business Week. 1970. "Rheingold's Rise with the Mets." August 22: 60.

Business Week. 1973. "A Struggle to Stay First in Brewing." March 24: 42–49.

Business Week. 1975. "The Schlitz Strategy to Bring a Beer Back." January 20: 59.

Business Week. 1975. "How Miller Won a Market Slot for Lite Beer." October 13: 116–118.

Business Week. 1976. "Another Setback for Troubled Schlitz." September 6: 20.

Business Week. 1976. "Turmoil Among the Brewers: Miller's Fast Growth Upsets the Beer Industry." November 8: 58–67.

Business Week. 1977. "Schlitz Raids the Competition." November 21: 54.

Business Week. 1978. "Schmidt Acquires a Taste for Schaefer." April 24: 31.

Business Week. 1978. "A Test for the Coors Dynasty." May 8: 69–71.

Business Week. 1979. "Another Regional Brewer Tries Going National." December 3: 88–90.

Business Week. 1980. "Anheuser's Plan to Flatten Miller's Head." April 21: 171–174.

Business Week. 1980. "Schlitz's Brew of Old and New." May 12: 31.

Business Week. 1980. "Adolf Coors: Brewing Up Plans for an Invasion of East Coast." September 29: 123–124.

Business Week. 1980. "Pitt Brewery: Big-Time Tactics with a Hometown Touch." September 29: 124.

Business Week. 1981. "Coors Eats the Dust as the Giants Battle." July 20: 14.

Business Week. 1981. "A National Beer That May Turn Regional." October 5: 30–31.

Business Week. 1982. "What Blew the Head off Miller's Profits." February 15: 39–40.

Business Week. 1982. "What's on Tap at Pabst." June 14: 40.

Business Week. 1982. "Anheuser-Busch—The King of Beers Still Rules." July 12: 50–53.

Business Week. 1982. "Heileman Jockeys for More Markets." November 22: 35.

Business Week. 1985. "Can Pete and Jeff Coors Brew Up a Comeback." December 16: 86–88

Business Week. 1986. "Small-Time Brewers Are Putting the Kick Back into Beer." January 20: 90–91.

Business Week. 1987. "Alan Bond Hoists Heileman." October 5: 44.

Business Week. 1988. "How Do You Follow an Act Like Bud?" May 2: 118–119.

Business Week. 1989. "Heileman in High Gear." February 13: 1.

Business Week. 1989. "Coors May Take a Gulp of a Rival Brew." August 21: 70.

Business Week. 1989. "A Thirsty Coors Chugs Down Stroh's." October 9: 52.

Business Week. 1989. "One Last Call for Fading Beer Brands." October 16: 68.

Business Week. 1989. "A Warning Shot from the King of Beers." December 18: 124.

Business Week. 1992 "A Tall Order for the Prince of Beers." March 23: 66–68.

Business Week. 1992 "Now, It's Jack MacDonough Time." December 7: 94–95.

Business Week. 1994. "Attack of the Fighting Brands." May 2: 125.

Business Week. 1995. "From the Microbrewers Who Brought You Bud, Coors." April 24: 66–70.

Business Week. 1996. "Is It Finally Miller Time?" February 12: 37.

Business Week. 1996. "How Eagle Became Extinct." March 4: 68–69.

Business Week. 1997. "Why Zima Faded So Fast." March 10: 110–114.

Business Week. 1998. "Inside Wall Street." March 3: 1.

Business Week. 1998. "Those New Brews Have the Blues." March 9: 40.

Business Week. 1998. "Microbrews—Without the Froth." March 16: 96

Business Week. 2001. "Miller's Genuine Drought." May 14: 72–73.

Business Week. 2002. "Is This Bud for You, August IV?" November 11: 72.

Byars, Lloyd. 1984. *Strategic Management: Planning and Implementation Concepts and Cases.* Harper & Row.

Calfee, John E., and Carl Scheraga. 1994. "The Influence of Advertising on Alcohol Consumption: A Literature Review and an Econometric Analysis of Four European Nations." *International Journal of Advertising* 13, no. 3: 287–310.

Cameron, A. Colin, and Pravin K. Trivedi. 1990. "Regression-Based Tests for Over-dispersion in the Poisson Model." *Journal of Econometrics* 46, no. 3: 347–364.

Carlton, Dennis W., and Jeffery M. Perloff. 2000. *Modern Industrial Organization*. Addison-Wesley.

Carroll, Glenn R., and Anand Swaminathan. 1992. "The Organizational Ecology of Strategic Groups in the American Brewing Industry from 1975 to 1990." *Industrial and Corporate Change* 1, no. 1: 65–97.

Carroll, Glenn R., and Anand Swaminathan. 2000. "Why the Microbrewery Movement? Organizational Dynamics of Resource Partitioning in the U.S." *American Journal of Sociology* 106, no. 3: 715–762.

Caves, Richard E., and Michael E. Porter. 1977. "From Entry Barriers to Mobility Barriers: Conjectural Decisions and Contrived Deterrence to New Competition." *Quarterly Journal of Economics* 92, no. 2: 241–261.

Center for Science in the Public Interest. 2001. Action Alert: Alcoholic-Beverage Health Warnings. www.cspinet.org.

Center for Science in the Public Interest. 2001. "Alcohol Warning Labels Go Unnoticed, Poll Finds." www.cspinet.org.

Certo, Samuel, and J. Paul Peter. 1993. "Anheuser-Busch Companies, Inc." In *Cases in Strategic Management*. Irwin.

Chalk, Andrew J. 1988. "Competition in the Brewing Industry: Does Further Concentration Imply Collusion?" *Managerial and Decision Economics* 9, no. 1: 49–58.

Chaloupka, Frank J. 1991. "Rational Addictive Behavior and Cigarette Smoking." *Journal of Political Economy* 99, no. 4: 722–742.

Chaloupka, Frank J., Henry Saffer, and Michael Grossman. 1993. "Alcohol Control Policies and Motor Vehicle Fatalities." *Journal of Legal Studies* 12, January: 161–186.

Chamberlin, Edwin H. 1933. *The Theory of Monopolistic Competition*, eighth edition. Harvard University Press.

Chang, Yang-Ming, and Victor J. Tremblay. 1994. "Duopsony Models with Consistent Conjectural Variations." *Applied Economics Letters* 1, no. 1: 4–8.

Chesson, Harrell, Paul Harrison, and William J. Kassler. 2000. "Sex under the Influence: The Effect of Alcohol Policy on Sexually Transmitted Disease Rates in the U.S." *Journal of Law and Economics* 43, no. 1: 215–238.

Chicago Tribune Magazine. 1977. "Nevermore the Local Lagers." April 24: 50–51.

Christensen, Laurtis R., Dale W. Jorgenson, and Lawrence J. Lau. 1971. "Conjugate Duality and the Transcendental Logarithmic Production Function." *Econometrica* 39, no. 4: 255–56.

Clark, Lauren. 2002. "Beer & Babes Go Back a Long Way." *All About Beer Magazine*, September: 28–77.

Clay, Karen, and Werner Troesken. 2003. "Further Tests of Static Oligopoly Models: Whiskey, 1882–1898." *Journal of Industrial Economics* 51, no. 2: 151–166.

Clements, Kenneth W., and Lester W. Johnson. 1983. "The Demand for Beer, Wine, and Spirits: A Systemwide Analysis." *Journal of Business* 56, no. 3: 273–304.

Cochran, Thomas Childs. 1948. *The Pabst Brewing Company: The History of an American Business*. New York University Press.

Cockerill, Anthony. 1977. "Economies of Scale, Industrial Structure and Efficiency: The Brewing Industry in Nine Nations." In A. Jacquemin and H. de Jong, eds., *Welfare Aspects of Industrial Markets*. H. E. Stenfert Kroese, Martinus Nijhoff Social Sciences Division.

Comanor, W. S., and Wilson, T. A. 1974. *Advertising and Market Power*. Harvard University Press.

Consumer Reports. 1983. "Beer." July: 342–351.

Consumer Reports. 1996. "Can You Judge a Beer by Its Label?" June: 10–17.

Consumer Reports. 2001. "Which Brew for You?" August: 10–16.

Cook, Philip J., and Michael J. Moore. 1994. "This Tax's for You: The Case for Higher Beer Taxes." *National Tax Journal* 47, no. 3: 559–573.

Cook, Philip J., and George Tauchen. 1982. "The Effect of Liquor Taxes on Heavy Drinking." *Bell Journal of Economics* 13, no. 2: 379–390.

Corts, K. S. 1999. "Conduct Parameters and the Measure of Market Power." *Journal of Econometrics* 88, no. 2: 227–250.

Coulson, N. Edward, John R. Moran, and Jon P. Nelson. 2001. "The Long-Run Demand for Alcoholic Beverages and the Advertising Debate: A Cointegration Analysis." In M. Baye and J. Nelson, eds., *Advances in Applied Microeconomics: Advertising and Differentiated Products*, volume 10. JAI.

Culbertson, W. Patton, and David Bradford. 1991. "The Price of Beer: Some Evidence from Interstate Comparisons." *International Journal of Industrial Organization* 9, no. 2: 275–289.

Dee, Thomas S. 1999. "State Alcohol Policies, Teen Drinking, and Traffic Fatalities." *Journal of Public Economics* 72, no. 2: 289–315.

Demsetz, Harold. 1969. "Information and Efficiency." *Journal of Law and Economics* 12, no. 1: 1–22.

Demsetz, Harold. 1973. "Industry Structure, Market Rivalry, and Public Policy." *Journal of Law and Economics* 16, no. 1: 1–10.

Denney, Douglas, Byunglak Lee, Dong Woon Noh, and Victor J. Tremblay. 2002. Excise Taxes and Imperfect Competition in the U.S. Brewing Industry. Working paper, Department of Economics, Oregon State University.

Dewey, Donald. 1961. "Mergers and Cartels: Some Reservations about Policy." *American Economic Review* 51, no. 2: 255–262.

Diewert, Erwin. 1974. "Applications of Duality Theory." In M. Intriligator and D. Kendrick, eds., *Frontiers of Quantitative Economics*. North-Holland.

Distilled Spirits Council of the United States. 1997. "Beverage Alcohol Equivalence."

Distilled Spirits Council of the United States. 2002. "Distilled Spirits Excise Taxes."

Dixit, Avinash, and Victor Norman. 1978. "Advertising and Welfare." *Bell Journal of Economics* 9, no. 1 Spring: 1–17.

Doraszelski, Ulrich, and Sarit Markovich. 2003. Goodwill and Awareness Advertising: Implications for Industry Dynamics. Working paper, Hoover Institution, Stanford University.

Downard, William L. 1980. *Dictionary of the History of the American Brewing and Distilling Industries.* Greenwood.

Dunn, William N. 1993. *Public Policy Analysis: An Introduction.* Prentice-Hall.

Dunne, Timothy, Mark J. Roberts, and Larry Samuelson. 1988. "Patterns of Entry and Exit in the U.S. Manufacturing Industries." *Rand Journal of Economics* 19, no. 4: 495–515.

Dunne, Timothy, Mark J. Roberts, and Larry Samuelson. 1989. "Firm Entry and Postentry Performance in the U.S. Chemical Industries." *Journal of Law and Economics* 32, no. 2: s233–s271.

Dutta, Prajit K., and Rangarajan K. Sundaram. 2001. "Survival and the Art of Profit Maximization." *Review of Economic Design* 6, no. 3: 429–446.

Eaton, B. Curtis, and William D. White. 2002. "Image Advertising." In B. Curtis Eaton, ed., *Applied Microeconomic Theory: Selected Essays of B. Curtis Eaton.* Elgar.

Economist. 1992. "Strategic Shopping." September 26: 82–87.

Economist: Pocket World Figures. 2001. Profile Books.

Elyasiani, E., and S. Mehdian. 1993. "Measuring Technical and Scale Inefficiencies in the Beer Industry: Nonparametric and Parametric Evidence." *Quarterly Review of Economics and Finance* 33, no. 4: 383–408.

Elzinga, Kenneth G. 1968. "Mergers: Their Causes and Cures." *Antitrust Law and Economics Review* 2, fall: 53–104.

Elzinga, Kenneth G. 1969. "The Antimerger Law: Pyrrhic Victories?" *Journal of Law and Economics* 12, April: 43–78.

Elzinga, Kenneth G. 1971. "The Beer Industry." In W. Adams, ed., *The Structure of American Industry.* Macmillan.

Elzinga, Kenneth G. 1973. "The Restructuring of the U.S. Brewing Industry." *Industrial Organization Review* 1, no. 2: 101–114.

Elzinga, Kenneth G. 1982. "The Beer Industry." In W. Adams, ed., *The Structure of American Industry.* Macmillan.

Elzinga, Kenneth G. 1986. "The Beer Industry." In W. Adams, ed., *The Structure of American Industry.* Macmillan.

Elzinga, Kenneth G. 1990. "The Beer Industry." In W. Adams, ed., *The Structure of American Industry.* Macmillan.

Elzinga, Kenneth G. 2001. "Beer." In W. Adams and J. Brock, eds., *The Structure of American Industry.* Prentice-Hall.

Elzinga, Kenneth G. Forthcoming. "The Beer Industry." In W. Adams and J. Brock, eds., *The Structure of American Industry.* Prentice-Hall.

Facts About Coors. 1982. Adolph Coors Company.

Färe, Rolf. 1975. "A Note on Ray-Homogeneous and Ray-Homothetic Production Functions." *Swedish Journal of Economics* 77, no. 3: 366–372.

Färe, Rolf, Shawna Grosskopf, and Knox Lovell. 1985. *Measurement of Efficiency of Production*. Kluwer.

Färe, Rolf, Shawna Grosskopf, and Knox Lovell. 1994. *Production Frontiers*. Cambridge University Press.

Färe, Rolf, Shawna Grosskopf, Barry Seldon, and Victor J. Tremblay. 2004. "Advertising Efficiency and the Choice of Media Mix: A Case of Beer." *International Journal of Industrial Organization* 22, no. 2: 503–522.

Farr, Stephen, Carol Horton Tremblay, and Victor J. Tremblay. 2001. "The Welfare Effect of Advertising Restrictions in the U.S. Cigarette Industry." *Review of Industrial Organization* 18, no. 2: 147–160.

Federal Trade Commission. 1999. Self-Regulation in the Alcohol Industry: A Review of Industry Efforts to Avoid Promoting Alcohol to Underage Consumers.

Federal Trade Commission v. Anheuser-Busch Inc. 1960. 363 U.S. 536.

Feng, Hongrong. 1998. State Excise Taxes and Public Choice: Evidence from the U.S. Brewing Industry. M.S. thesis, Oregon State University.

Financial World. 1967. "Big Brewers Lift Results." March 29: 13.

Financial World. 1968. "Big Brewers Cashing In." February 28: 6.

Financial World. 1969. "Brewers in Ferment." June 18: 13.

Financial World. 1971. "Beer and Soda Boosting Rheingold's Sales and Profits." April 7: 18.

Financial World. 1974. "The Better Brew in Chock-Full-O-Nuts Corp." August 14: 23.

Financial World. 1975. "Anheuser Finds Quality Pays Off, but Schlitz Encounters Problems." June 4: 16.

Financial World. 1980. "When the Best Is Busch League." June 1: 32.

Fisher, Alan A., and Robert H. Lande. 1983. "Efficiency Considerations in Merger Enforcement." *California Law Review* 71, no. 6: 1582–1696.

Fisher, Franklin M., and John J. McGowan. 1979. "Advertising and Welfare: Comment." *Bell Journal of Economics* 10, no. 2: 726–727.

Forbes. 1959. "Frustrated Bargain Hunter." April 15: 27.

Forbes. 1962. "Small but Cocky." September 15: 16.

Forbes. 1964. "Brewing Industry Survey." November 15: 30.

Forbes. 1967. "No Small Beers Allowed." November 1: 67.

Forbes. 1968. "Budweiser Pulls Ahead." March 1: 28–33.

Forbes. 1968. "Netting a Winner." September 15.

Forbes. 1969. "Ignoring the Rules." February 1: 34.

Forbes. 1969. "Battle for Survival." September 15: 95.

Forbes. 1970. "Schlitz Brewing Always an Avis, Never a Hertz." April 15: 25.

Forbes. 1972. "Who Rules the Foam?" December 15: 36–40.

Forbes. 1974. "Gussie Busch's Bitter Brew." June 1: 22–24.

Forbes. 1976. "The Light Beer Game." January 15: 30–31.

Forbes. 1976. "Make Way for Miller." May 15: 45.

Forbes. 1976. "Off Coors." June 1: 61.

Forbes. 1977. "Sing No Sad Song for Heileman." October 1: 51.

Forbes. 1977. "Homemade Imports." October 15: 33–34.

Forbes. 1978. "Getting Schlitz Back on Track." April 24: 46–51.

Forbes. 1978. "Coors Beer, What Hit Us?" October 16: 71.

Forbes. 1978. "We Missed The Boat. . . . We Were Unsmarted." August 7: 36–38.

Forbes. 1980. "Is the Gusto Forever Gone?" December 8: 34.

Forbes. 1981. "Coming Up Fast on the Outside." June 8: 88–91.

Forbes. 1982. "What Price Independence." July 19.

Forbes. 1983. "A Difference of Perspective." October 24: 88.

Forbes. 1984. "Is the Game Over?" January 1: 95.

Forbes. 1986. "Draft, or Daft." June 30: 112–113.

Forbes. 1991. "Shirtsleeves to Shirtsleeves." March 4: 56.

Forbes. 1995. "Get 'Em before They Get You." July 31: 88.

Forbes. 2001. "Cut to the Chase: Merge Miller and Coors?" December 24: 109–110.

Fortune. 1950. "The Brotherly Brewers." April: 98.

Fortune. 1964. "How They Put Gusto into Schlitz." October: 106.

Fortune. 1965. "What Business Wants from Lyndon Johnson." February: 228.

Fortune. 1972. "While the Big Brewers Quaff, the Little Ones Thirst." November: 103.

Fortune. 1975. "Why There's No Yeast in Brewers' Stocks." November: 91–93.

Fortune. 1978. "Getting Schlitz Back on Track." April 24: 47–49.

Fortune. 1979. "Heileman Toasts the Future with 34 Beers." June 18: 124.

Fortune. 1979. "Schaefer Brews a Barrel of Red Ink." June 18: 198.

Fortune. 1981. "Schlitz's Crafty Taste Tests." January 26: 32–34.

Fortune. 1981. "Bold Departures in Antitrust." October 5: 180–188.

Fortune. 1982. "Betting the Barn at Stroh." May 31: 118–121.

Fortune. 1985. "Living with the Limits of Marlboro Magic." March 18: 24–28.

Fortune. 1989. "Is Bigger Better for Philip Morris?" May 8: 66–71.

Fortune. 1990. "Busch Fights to Have It All." January 15: 81–88.

Fortune. 1993. "Bickering Beer Barons." January 11: 101.

Fortune. 1994. "Brands Disown Their Parents." September 5: 15–16.

Fortune. 1994. "A Whole New Ball Game in Beer." September 19: 79.

Fortune. 1994. "Putting a Face on Big Brands." September 19: 80.

Fortune. 1997. "Bud-Weis-Heir." January 13: 90–93.

Fortune. 1997. "Frogs, Beers, and Organisms." June 9: 153–156.

Fortune. 2002. "Battling the Bulge with Beer and Sugar." October 28: 22.

Foxall, Gordon R., and Ronald E. Goldsmith. 1994. *Consumer Psychology for Marketing.* Routledge.

Friedman, James. 1971. "A Non-Cooperative Equilibrium for Supergames." *Review of Economic Studies* 38, no. 1: 1–12.

Friedman, Milton, and Leonard J. Savage. 1948. "The Utility Analysis of Choices Involving Risk." *Journal of Political Economy* 56, no. 5: 279–304.

Fudenberg, Drew, and Jean Tirole. 1992. *Game Theory.* MIT Press.

Galbraith, J. K. 1958. *The Affluent Society.* Houghton Mifflin.

Galbraith, J. K. 1985. *The New Industrial State.* Houghton Mifflin.

Gallet, Craig A., and John A. List. 1998. "Elasticity of Beer Demand Revisited." *Economics Letters* 61, no. 1: 67–71.

Gallet, Craig A., and Patricia J. Euzent. 2002. "The Business Cycle and Competition in the U.S. Brewing Industry." *Journal of Applied Business Research* 18, no. 2: 89–96.

Gao, X. M., Eric J. Wiles, and Gail L. Cramer. 1995. "A Microeconomic Model Analysis of U.S. Consumer Demand for Alcoholic Beverages." *Applied Economics* 27, no. 7: 56–69.

Gazette-Times (Corvallis, Oregon). 2003. "Beers to Your Health: The Darker, the Better." November 12.

Gelb, Betsy D., and Gabriel M. Gelb. 1986. "New Coke's Fizzle—Lessons for the Rest of Us." *Sloan Management Review* 28, no. 1: 71–76.

Genesove, D., and W. P. Mullen. 1998. "Testing Static Oligopoly Models: Conduct and Cost in the Sugar Industry, 1890–1914." *Rand Journal of Economics* 29, no. 2 Summer: 355–377.

Geroski, P. A., and M. Mazzucato. 2001. "Modeling the Dynamics of Industry Populations." *International Journal of Industrial Organization.* 19, no. 7: 1003–1022.

Ghemawat, Pankaj. 1997. *Games Businesses Play: Cases and Models.* MIT Press.

Ghemawat, Pankaj. 2001. *Strategy and the Business Landscapes.* Prentice-Hall.

Ghemawat, Pankaj, and Barry Nalebuff. 1990. "The Devolution of Declining Industries." *Quarterly Journal of Economics* 105, no. 1: 167–186.

Gibbons, Robert. 1992. *Game Theory for Applied Economists.* Princeton University Press.

Gilbert, Richard J., and Carmen Matutes. 1993. "Product Line Rivalry with Brand Differentiation." *Journal of Industrial Economics* 41, no. 3: 223–240.

Gisser, Mica. 1999. "Dynamic Gains and Static Losses in Oligopoly: Evidence from the Beer Industry." *Economic Inquiry* 37, no. 3: 554–575.

Gitlitz, Jenny. "Oregon's Bottle Bill at 30: How Is It Doing?" Container Recycling Institute. www.container-recycling.org.

Glover, Brian. 2001. *The World Encyclopedia of Beer*. Lorenz.

Goldammer, Ted. 1999. *The Brewers' Handbook: The Complete Book to Brewing Beer*. KVP.

Goldfarb, Avi. 2000. Anatomy of Firm Failure: The Case of Schlitz. Working paper, University of Toronto.

Grabowski, Henry G. 1977–78. "The Effects of Advertising on the Interindustry Distribution of Demand." *Explorations in Economic Research* 4, no. 5: 674–701.

Grant, Bert. 1998. *The Ale Master*. Sasquatch.

Greene, William H. 2003. *Econometric Analysis*. Prentice-Hall.

Greer, Douglas F. 1971. "Product Differentiation and Concentration in the Brewing Industry." *Journal of Industrial Economics* 19, no. 3: 201–219.

Greer, Douglas F. 1980. *Industrial Organization and Public Policy*. Macmillan.

Greer, Douglas F. 1981. "The Causes of Concentration in the U.S. Brewing Industry." *Quarterly Review of Economics and Business* 21, no. 4: 87–106.

Greer, Douglas F. 1984. *Industrial Organization and Public Policy*. Macmillan.

Greer, Douglas F. 1998. "Beer: Causes of Structural Change." In L. Duetsch, ed., *Industry Studies*. Sharpe.

Greer, Douglas F. 2002. "Beer: Causes of Structural Change." In L. Duetsch, ed., *Industry Studies*. Sharpe.

Hacker, George A. 1998. "Liquor Advertisements on Television: Just Say No." *Journal of Public Policy and Marketing* 71, no. 1: 139–142.

Hallagan, William, and Wayne Joerding. 1983. "Polymorphic Equilibrium in Advertising." *Bell Journal of Economics* 14, no. 1: 191–201.

Hallagan, William. 1985. "Contracting Problems and the Adoption of Regulatory Cartels." *Economic Inquiry* 23, no. 1: 37–56.

Hamilton, James L. 1972. "The Demand for Cigarettes: Advertising, the Health Scare, and the Cigarette Advertising Ban." *Review of Economics and Statistics* 54, no. 4: 401–411.

Hanoch, Giora. 1975. "The Elasticity of Scale and the Shape of Average Costs." *American Economic Review* 65, no. 3: 492–97.

Harwood, Eileen M., Alexander C. Wagenaar, and Kay M. Zander. 1998. Youth Access to Alcohol Survey: Summary Report for Robert Wood Johnson Foundation. www.rwjf.org/publications.

Harwood, H. 2000. Updating Estimates of the Economic Costs of Alcohol Abuse in the United States: Estimates, Update Methods and Data. Report prepared by Lewin Group of National Institute on Alcohol Abuse and Alcoholism.

Harwood, H., D. Fountain, and G. Livermore. 1998. Costs of Alcohol and Drug Abuse in the United States, 1992. Publication 98-4327, National Institutes of Health.

Hatten, Kenneth J., and Dan E. Schendel. 1977. "Heterogeneity Within an Industry: Firm Conduct in the U.S. Brewing Industry, 1952–71." *Journal of Industrial Economics* 26, no. 2: 97–113.

Hausman, J. A. 1978. "Specification Tests in Econometrics." *Econometrica* 46, no. 6: 1251–1271.

Hawaii Business Magazine. 2000. "Primed to Be the Next Primo." July.

Heien, Dale, and Greg Poppelli. 1989. "The Demand for Alcoholic Beverages: Economic and Demographic Effects." *Southern Economic Journal* 53, no. 3: 759–770.

Heien, Dale, and David J. Pittman. 1993. "The External Cost of Alcohol Abuse." *Journal of Studies on Alcohol* 54, no. 3: 567–579.

Hernon, Peter, and Terry Ganey. 1991. *Under the Influence: The Unauthorized Story of the Anheuser-Busch Dynasty.* Simon and Schuster.

Hilke, John C., and Philip B. Nelson. 1984. "An Empirical Note from Case Documents on the Economies of Network Television Advertising." *Review of Industrial Organization* 4, no. 1: 131–145.

Hill, R. Carter, William E. Griffiths, and George G. Judge. 2001. *Undergraduate Econometrics.* Wiley.

Hogarty, Thomas F., and Kenneth G. Elzinga. 1972. "The Demand for Beer." *Review of Economics and Statistics* 54, no. 2: 195–198.

Horowitz, Ira and Ann R. Horowitz. 1965. "Firms in a Declining Market: The Brewing Case." *Journal of Industrial Economics* 13, no. 2: 129–153.

Horowitz, Ira and Ann R. Horowitz. 1967. "Markov Processes and the Declining Brewing Population." *American Statistical Association, Proceedings of the Business and Economic Statistics Section.*

Horowitz, Ira and Ann R. Horowitz. 1969. "Concentration, Competition, and Mergers in Brewing." In J. Weston and S. Peltzman, eds., *Public Policy Toward Mergers.* Goodyear.

Horvath, Michael, Fabiano Schivardi, and Michael Woywode. 2001. "On Industry Life-Cycles: Delay, Entry, and Shakeout in Beer Brewing." *International Journal of Industrial Organization* 19, no. 7: 1023–1052.

Hu, The-Wei, Hai-Yen Sung, and Theodore E. Keeler. 1985. "Reducing Cigarette Consumption in California: Tobacco Taxes vs an Anti-Smoking Media Campaign." *American Journal of Public Health* 85, no. 9: 1218–1222.

Import Specialty INSIGHTS: A Comprehensive Review of the Import and Specialty Beer Market. 2001. Beer Marketer's INSIGHTS, Inc.

Jackson, Michael. 1988. *The New World Guide to Beer.* Courage.

James, Simon. 1981. *A Dictionary of Economic Quotations.* Barnes and Noble.

Johnson, Richard L., and David D. Smith. 1987. "Antitrust Division Merger Procedures and Policy, 1968–1984." *Antitrust Bulletin* 32, no. 4: 967–988.

Johnson, Steve. 1993. *On Tap: Guide to North American Brew Pubs.* WBR.

Jones, S. R. H. 1998. "The New Zealand Brewing Industry, 1840–1995." In R. Wilson and T. Gourvish, eds., *The Dynamics of the International Brewing Industry since 1800*. Routledge.

Journal-American (Kirkland, Washington). 1980. "Beer—It's Selling So Fast, Some Truckloads Are Still Warm When They Reach Kirkland." May 7.

Karrenbroch, Jeffrey D. 1990. "The Internationalization of the Beer Brewing Industry." *Federal Reserve Bank of St. Louis Review* 72, no. 6, November/December: 3–19.

Kaserman, David L., and John W. Mayo. 1991. "Regulation, Advertising, and Economic Welfare." *Journal of Business* 64, no. 2: 255–267.

Keithahn, Charles F. 1978. The Brewing Industry. Staff report, Bureau of Economics, Federal Trade Commission.

Kelton, Christina M. L., and W. David Kelton. 1982. "Advertising and Intraindustry Brand Shift in the U.S. Brewing Industry." *Journal of Industrial Economics* 30, no. 3: 293–303.

Kenkel, Donald S. 1993. "Drinking, Driving, and Deterrence: The Effectiveness and Social Cost of Alternative Policies." *Journal of Law and Economics* 36, no. 2: 877–913

Kenkel, Donald S. 1996. "New Estimates of the Optimal Tax on Alcohol." *Economic Inquiry* 34, no. 2: 296–319.

Kerkvliet, Joe R., William Nebesky, Carol Horton Tremblay, and Victor J. Tremblay. 1998. "Efficiency and Technological Change in the U.S. Brewing Industry." *Journal of Productivity Analysis* 10, no. 3: 271–288.

Klein, Benjamin, and Keith Leffler. 1981. "The Role of Market Forces in Assuring Contractual Performance." *Journal of Political Economy* 89, no. 4: 615–641.

Klein, Bob. 1995. *Beer Lover's Rating Guide*. Workman.

Koller, Roland H., II. 1971. "The Myth of Predatory Pricing: An Empirical Study." *Antitrust Law and Economics Review* 4, no. 4: 105–123.

Kotler, Philip, and Gary Armstrong. 1998. *Marketing, An Introduction*. Prentice-Hall.

Krattenmaker, Thomas G., and Robert Pitofsky. 1988. "Antitrust Merger Policy and the Reagan Administration." *Antitrust Bulletin* 33, no. 2: 211–232.

Kumbhakar, Subal C., and Timo Summa. 1989. "Technical Efficiency of Finnish Brewing Plants: A Production Frontier Approach." *Scandinavian Journal of Economics* 91, no. 1: 147–160.

Kwoka, John E., Jr. 1981. "Does the Choice of Concentration Measure Really Matter?" *Journal of Industrial Economics* 29, no. 3: 445–453.

Kwoka, John E., and Lawrence J. White. 1999. *The Antitrust Revolution: Economics, Competition, and Policy*. Oxford University Press.

Lariviere, Eric, Bruno Larue, and Jim Chalfant. 2000. "Modeling the Demand for Alcoholic Beverages and Advertising Specifications." *Agricultural Economics* 22, no. 2: 147–162.

Lee, Byunglak, and Victor J. Tremblay. 1992. "Advertising and the U.S. Market Demand for Beer." *Applied Economics* 24, no. 1: 69–76.

Lee, Li Lee. 1997. "Persuasive Advertising and Socialization." *International Journal of the Economics of Business* 4, no. 2: 203–214.

Leffler, Keith. 1982. "Ambiguous Changes in Product Quality." *American Economic Review* 72, no. 5: 956–967.

Leibenstein, Harvey. 1966. "Allocative Inefficiency vs. X-Inefficiency." *American Economic Review* 5, no. 3: 392–415.

Lieberman, Marvin B. 1990. "Exit from Declining Industries: 'Shakeout' or 'Stakeout'?" *Rand Journal of Economics* 21, no. 4: 538–554.

Leong, Elaine K. F., Xueli Huang, and Paul-John Stanners. 1998. "Comparing the Effectiveness of the Web Site with Traditional Media." *Journal of Advertising Research* 38, no. 5: 44–51.

Lerner, Abba P. 1934. "The Concept of Monopoly and the Measurement of Monopoly Power." *Review of Economic Studies* 1, no. 1–3: 157–175.

Levit, Katherine R., et al. 1994. "National Health Expenditures, 1993." *Health Care Financing Review* 16, no. 1: 247–294.

Los Angeles Times. 1979. "A 'Beer' Brand Beer Is Just a Beer by No Other Name." December 25.

Los Angeles Times. 1984. "Pub Owner Brews the Beer He Sells." July 18.

Lynk, William J. 1984. "Interpreting Rising Concentration: The Case of Beer." *Journal of Business* 57, no. 1: 43–55.

Mancke, Richard B. 1974. "Causes of Interfirm Profitability Differences." *Quarterly Journal of Economics* 88, no. 2: 181–193.

Manne, Henry G. 1965. "Mergers and the Market for Corporate Control." *Journal of Political Economy* 73, no. 2: 110–120.

Manning, Willard G., Emmet Keeler, Joseph P. Newhouse, E. M. Sloss, and J. Wasserman. 1991. *The Cost of Poor Health Habits.* Harvard University Press.

Manning, Willard, Linda Blumberg, and Lawrene Moulton. 1995. "The Demand for Alcohol: The Differential Response to Price." *Journal of Health Economics* 14, no. 2: 123–148.

Manuszak, Mark D. 2002. "Endogenous Market Structure and Competition in the Nineteenth Century American Brewing Industry." *International Journal of Industrial Organization* 20, no. 5: 673–692.

Mares, William. 1984. *Making Beer.* Knopf.

Marketing/Communications. 1969. "Beer: The Big Three Get Even Bigger." January: 26.

Marketing/Communications. 1971. "Beer in 1970: Nationals Post Headiest Gains." January: 18–23.

Markowitz, Sara, and Michael Grossman. 1998. "Alcohol Regulation and Domestic Violence towards Children." *Contemporary Economic Policy* 16, no. 3: 309–320.

Marris, R. 1968. "Galbraith, Solow and the Truth about Corporations." *The Public Interest* 11: 37–46.

Martel, Brett. 2003. "Louisiana Lowers Blood-Alcohol Limit." Associated Press, September 30.

Martin, Stephen. 1979. "Advertising, Concentration, and Profitability: The Simultaneity Problem." *Bell Journal of Economics* 10, no. 2: 639–647.

Martin, Stephen. 1988. *Industrial Economics: Economic Analysis and Public Policy.* Macmillan.

Martin, Stephen. 2002. *Advanced Industrial Economics.* Blackwell.

Martin, Susan E. 1995. The Effect of the Mass Media on the Use and Abuse of Alcohol. U.S. Department of Health and Human Services, National Institute of Health.

Marvel, Howard. 1982. "Exclusive Dealing." *Journal of Law and Economics* 25, no. 1: 1–25.

Mas-Colell, Andreu, Michael D. Whinston, and Jerry R. Green. 1995. *Microeconomic Theor.* Oxford University Press.

Mast, Brent D., Bruce L. Benson, and David W. Rasmussen. 1999. "Beer Taxation and Alcohol-related Traffic Fatalities." *Southern Economic Journal* 66, no. 2: 214–249.

Master Brewers Association of America. 2001. *The Practical Brewer: A Manual for the Brewing Industry.*

Matraves, Catherine. 1999. "Market Structure, R&D and Advertising in the Pharmaceutical Industry." *Journal of Industrial Economics* 48, no. 2: 169–194.

Mayer, K. John. 1987. "The Verdict—Beer Purity on Trial." *Brewers Almanac*, June: 32–35.

McAfee, R. Preston. 2002. *Competitive Solutions: A Strategist's Toolkit.* Princeton University Press.

McConnell, J. Douglas. 1968. "The Price-Quality Relationship in an Experimental Setting." *Journal of Marketing Research* 5, no. 3: 300–303.

McGahan, Anita M. 1991. "The Emergence of the National Brewing Oligopoly: Competition in the American Market, 1933–1958." *Business History Review* 65, no. 2: 229–284.

McGahan, Anita M. 1995. "Cooperation in Prices and Capacities: Trade Associations in Brewing after Repeal." *Journal of Law and Economics* 38, no. 2: 521–559.

Melese, Francois, David L. Kaserman, and John W. Mayo. 1996. "A Dynamic Model of Advertising by the Regulated Firm." *Journal of Economics* 64, no. 1: 85–106.

Merrett, David T. 1998. "Stability and Change in the Australian Brewing Industry, 1920–94." In R. Wilson and T. Gourvish, eds., *The Dynamics of the International Brewing Industry since 1800.* Routledge.

Milgrom, Paul, and John Roberts. 1986. "Price and Advertising Signals of Product Quality." *Journal of Political Economy* 94, no. 4: 796–821.

Miller, Ted R., and Lawrence J. Blincoe. 1994. "Incidence and Cost of Alcohol-Involved Crashes in the United States." *Accident Analysis and Prevention* 26, no. 5: 583–592.

Millns, Tony. 1998. "The British Brewing Industry." In R. Wilson and T. Gourvish, eds., *The Dynamics of the International Brewing Industry Since 1800.* Routledge.

Milyo, J., and J. Waldfogel. 1999. "The Effect of Price Advertising on Prices: Evidence in the Wake of 44 Liquormart." *American Economic Review* 89, no. 5: 1081–1096.

Miron, Jeffrey A., and Jeffrey Zwiebel. 1991. "Alcohol Consumption during Prohibition." *American Economic Review* 81, no. 2: 242–247.

Modern Brewery Age. 1950. "Canadian 1950 Brewery Sales, Profits Drop Slightly from Preceding Year." April: 31–80.

Modern Brewery Age. 1953. "Breweries Spend $17 Million in Newspapers in '52." July: 47–48.

Modern Brewery Age. 1954. "Let's Take a Look at a TV Survey." April: 44.

Modern Brewery Age. 1954. "Calories Go Commercial." June: 43–52.

Modern Brewery Age. 1954. "Breweries Spend $18 Million in '53 for Newspaper Ads, Cut Some Mediums." July: 51–53.

Modern Brewery Age. 1954. "Curbs on Radio, TV Beer Commercials to Be Advocated by Congress Group." August 30: 101.

Modern Brewery Age. 1954. "Bud Violates Robinson-Patman, Small Brewers Group Charges." August: 36.

Modern Brewery Age. 1954. "Woman's Christian Temperance Union Leaders Link Alcoholic Beverages to Crime, Juvenile Delinquency, Traffic Deaths." October: 31–130.

Modern Brewery Age. 1954. "Washington Voters Reject Restrictions on TV Beer Ads: Other Election Developments." November: 46.

Modern Brewery Age. 1955. "Brewing Industry Typical Example of Monopoly Trend, Senate Group Reports." April: 35–36, 104–105.

Modern Brewery Age. 1956. "Brewing Industry Ranks First in Outdoor Advertising." March: 43–44.

Modern Brewery Age. 1956. "Congress Group to Decree Brewing Industry Curtail Ad Practices Voluntarily 'Or Else.'" July: 24, 92–93.

Modern Brewery Age. 1958. "Research Proves Beer Is a Healthful Drink." April: 82–152.

Modern Brewery Age. 1958. "Anheuser-Busch Appeals FTC's Cease & Desist Order in St. Louis Price Discrimination Case." August: 1.

Modern Brewery Age. 1961. "Evaluating Beer and Price." October: 22–51.

Modern Brewery Age. 1965. "Annual Report: Foreign Beers Continue Record Sales Growth." September: 14–15.

Modern Brewery Age. 1976. "Growth of Imported Beer Brands Continues." August 16, MS 20–21.

Modern Brewery Age. 1979. "Modest Sales Rise Escalates Competition." April 9: MS 13–18.

Modern Brewery Age. 1981. "Foreign Brewers Seek to Expand in the U.S." July 20: MS 36–38.

Modern Brewery Age. 1983. "Import Update." July 11. MS 10–28.

Modern Brewery Age. 1983. "Beer Is Back: Repeal Ends the Ignoble Experiment." September-October: MS 16–34.

Modern Brewery Age. 1985. "Specialty Beers: Regionals' Answer to Imports and to the Nationals." July 15: 61–76.

Modern Brewery Age. 1986. "Annual Statistical Study: Domestic Sales Down, Imports Up." March 17: 6.

Modern Brewery Age. 1987. "Beer Industry Sales Rebound in 1986." March 16: 6–42.

Modern Brewery Age. 1987. "Annual Statistical Study: Beer Industry Sales Rebounds in 1986." March 16: 6.

Modern Brewery Age. 1988. "Annual Statistical Study: Little Growth for Brewing Industry in 1987." March 14: 4.

Modern Brewery Age. 1989. "Upscale Beer Segment: Bucking the Trend." July 10: 42–63.

Modern Brewery Age. 1989. "1988 Statistical Study." March 13: 1–22.

Modern Brewery Age. 1989. "Industry Sluggishness Hits Import Category." July 10: 4–28.

Modern Brewery Age. 1989. "1989 Year in Review: A Summary of Industry Issues and Performance." March 12: 1–40.

Modern Brewery Age. 1990. "Microbrewing 1989." May 14: 4–40.

Modern Brewery Age. 1991. "1990: The Year in Review." March 11: 6–38.

Modern Brewery Age. 1991. "Microbrewery Survey." May 13: 6–40.

Modern Brewery Age. 1991. "Import Overview." July 15: 7–47.

Modern Brewery Age. 1991. "Beer Analysis." December 30: 3.

Modern Brewery Age. 1992. "The Year in Review." March 16: 6–26.

Modern Brewery Age. 1992. "1992 Micro Report." May 11: 20–37.

Modern Brewery Age. 1992. "Import Overview." July 13: 6–18.

Modern Brewery Age. 1993. "The Year in Review: 1992." March 22: 6–38.

Modern Brewery Age. 1993. "Annual Microbrewery Report." May 10: 12–40.

Modern Brewery Age. 1993. "Import Overview." July 12: 6–52.

Modern Brewery Age. 1994. "Craft Brewing in America." May 16: 10–40.

Modern Brewery Age. 1994. "The Year in Review: 1993." March 21: p. 8–39.

Modern Brewery Age. 1994. "Import Overview." July 11: 11–52.

Modern Brewery Age. 1995. "The Rise of America's Third-Tier Brewers." January 30: 32–35.

Modern Brewery Age. 1995. "1994 Year in Review." March 13: p. 8–43.

Modern Brewery Age. 1995. "The Craft Brewing Explosion." May 22: 6–10.

Modern Brewery Age. 1995. "Fritz Maytag: American Brewer." May 22: 12–39.

Modern Brewery Age. 1995. "The Wisdom of Weinberg." May 22: 20–23.

Modern Brewery Age. 1995. "Imported Beer Focus." July 10: 8–13.

Modern Brewery Age. 1995. "Beer from Around the World." July 10: 14–23.

Modern Brewery Age. 1996. "Craft & Specialty Beer Report." May 20: 7–38.

Modern Brewery Age. 1996. "1995: The Year in Review." March 25: p. 8–44.

Modern Brewery Age. 1996. "Jim Koch: America's Uber-Brewer." May 20: 16–40.

Modern Brewery Age. 1996. "Fighting the Seventh Beer War." May 20: 26–29.

Modern Brewery Age. 1996. "Import Overview." July 15: 8–13.

Modern Brewery Age. 1997. "Interview with Bill Henry of Stroh." January 27.

Modern Brewery Age. 1997. "1996 Statistical Study: The Year in Review." March 17: p. 8–26.

Modern Brewery Age. 1997. "The Great and Powerful Bob." March 17: 28–35.

Modern Brewery Age. 1997. "Micro & Specialty Beer Report." May 12: 10–18.

Modern Brewery Age. 1997. "Import Beer Focus." July 14: 11–16.

Modern Brewery Age. 1998. "1997 Statistical Review: Year in Review." March 23: p. 10–42.

Modern Brewery Age. 1998. "Specialty & Microbrewery Report." May 18: 12–42.

Modern Brewery Age. 1998. "Imports Rock." July 20: 8–50.

Modern Brewery Age. 1999. "1998 Statistical Study: Brave New World of Beer." March 22: p. 10–40.

Modern Brewery Age. 1999. "Specialty & Microbrewery Report." May 10: 10–41.

Modern Brewery Age. 1999. "Interview with Ken Grossman." May 10: 19–42.

Modern Brewery Age. 1999. "The Import Boom Continues." July 19: 10–35.

Modern Brewery Age. 1999. "A Talk with the Chairman." September 13: 8–16.

Modern Brewery Age. 2000. "1999 Statistical Report: The New Age." March 27: p. 6–25.

Modern Brewery Age. 2000. "Craft Brewers Bounce Back." May 8: 8–13.

Modern Brewery Age. 2000. "Imports on a Roll." July 10: 8–14.

Modern Brewery Age. 2000. "Talking with Dr. Bob." November 27: 10–15.

Modern Brewery Age. 2001. "2000 Statistical Report: The New Millennium." March 26: p. 6–23.

Modern Brewery Age. 2001. "Pre-1900 Regional Breweries." March 26: 4–32.

Modern Brewery Age. 2001. "Craft Brewers Demise Much Exaggerated." May 21: 6–11.

Modern Brewery Age. 2001. "Imports on a Roll." July 23: 7–35.

Modern Brewery Age. 2001. "Truth in Numbers: Analyst Robert S. Weinberg finds Anomalies in the Data." November 12: 29–31.

Modern Brewery Age. 2002. "Molson Says Spilled Beer Costs Millions Each Year." March 11: p. 1.

Modern Brewery Age. 2002. "The Next Beer War?" March 25: 8–19.

Modern Brewery Age. 2002. "The Next Beer War? The First Shots Have Been Fired, and the Ammumition Is a Cirtus–Flavored RTE." March 25: 8–15.

Modern Brewery Age. 2002. "The Big Picture: Analyst Robert S. Weinberg Takes Another Look at Changes in the Structure of the Market." March 25: 16–19.

Modern Brewery Age. 2002. "Craft Brew Update." May 13: 7–12.

Modern Brewery Age. 2002. "Import Trends." July 22: 4–18.

Modern Brewery Age. 2003. "Focusing on Craft."January 27: 24–26.

Modern Brewery Age. 2003. "Statistical Study." March 31: 6–17.

Modern Brewery Age. 2003. "Waking the Slumbering Giant: A New Team Seeks to Bring Genesee/High Falls Back to Life." May 19: 6–10.

Modern Brewery Age. 2003. "Craft & Regional Segment: Bigger Crafters on Track, Brew pubs Face Tough Climate." May 19: 11–16.

Modern Brewery Age. 2003. "Imports Hit a Rough Patch." July 21: 15–18.

Modern Brewery Age, Weekly News Edition. 1996. "Anheuser Soft-Pedals '100% Share of Mind.'" June 10: 1.

Modern Brewery Age, Weekly News Edition. 1996. "Institute for Brewing Studies Defines 'Craft Brewer.'" December 30.

Modern Brewery Age, Weekly News Edition. 1997. "Missouri Labeling Law Irks Some in Trade." December 1: 1.

Modern Brewery Age, Weekly News Edition. 2001. "Bacardi Silver Ready to Roll, A-B Says." November 19: 1 and 3.

Modern Brewery Age, Weekly News Edition. 2002. "Coors Buys Carling for $1.7 Billion." January 7: 1 and 3.

Modern Brewery Age, Weekly News Edition. 2002. "Coors Complete's Carling Purchase for $1.7 Billion. February 11: 1 and 3.

Modern Brewery Age, Weekly News Edition. 2002. "Analysts Say Stokes Will Maintain Course at Anheuser-Busch." May 6: 1–3.

Modern Brewery Age, Weekly News Edition. 2002. "The Miller/SAB Deal Promises Benefits (and Potential Costs) for Wholesalers." June 10: 1.

Modern Brewery Age, Weekly News Edition. 2002. "Miller to Get New Lease on Life as SABMiller." June 10: 1 and 3.

Modern Brewery Age, Weekly News Edition. 2002. "South African Breweries Is Strong Player in Developing World." June 10: 3.

Modern Brewery Age, Weekly News Edition. 2002. "Japanese Brewers Face Difficulties, Analysts Say." June 24: 1.

Modern Brewery Age, Weekly News Edition. 2002. "World Beer Cup Medal Winners." July 8: 2–3.

Modern Brewery Age, Weekly News Edition. 2002. "Hamm's Celebration Put on Hold by Miller." July 22: 3.

Modern Brewery Age, Weekly News Edition. 2002. "Schell Brewing Co. Purchases Grain Belt." August 26: 2.

Modern Brewery Age, Weekly News Edition. 2002. "Boston Beer Pulls TV Ads after Complaints." September 9: 1–2.

Modern Brewery Age, Weekly News Edition. 2002. "Busch IV Confident on U.S. Beer Business." September 16: 1–3.

Modern Brewery Age, Weekly News Edition. 2002. "Anheuser-Busch Profits Rise 11.5% in 3Q." November 4: 1–3.

Modern Brewery Age, Weekly News Edition. 2002. "Coors Reports Rise in Third Quarter Earnings." November 4: 1–3.

Modern Brewery Age, Weekly News Edition. 2002. "Anheuser-Busch Maintains Earnings Forecast." November 18: 1–3.

Modern Brewery Age, Weekly News Edition. 2002. "Fizzling Malternatives Are Much in the News." December 4: 1.

Modern Brewery Age, Weekly News Edition. 2002. "AMA Seeks Ban on Prime-Time Beer Ads." December 16: 1–3.

Modern Brewery Age, Weekly News Edition. 2003. "Anheuser-Busch Posts Record Volume in 02." January 20: 1 and 4.

Modern Brewery Age, Weekly News Edition. 2003. "Ad Age's Crain Calls Miller Ads Irrelevant." February 3: 2–3.

Modern Brewery Age, Weekly News Edition. 2003. "Anheuser Increases State in Tsingtao." April 14: 1–3.

Modern Brewery Age, Weekly News Edition. 2003. "Joseph Coors Dies at Age 85." March 24: 1.

Modern Brewery Age, Weekly News Edition. 2003. "Waking the Slumbering Giant." May 19: 6–32.

Modern Brewery Age, Weekly News Edition. 2003. "Miller Puts Catfight Girls on Its Bottles." August 25: 1.

Modern Brewery Age, Weekly News Edition. 2003. "Anheuser-Busch Rolls Out Newest Bacardi." September 1: 1–3.

Modern Brewery Age, Weekly News Edition. 2003. "Ultra Rising Fortunes of Michelob Brand Family." September 1: 1–3.

Modern Brewery Age, Weekly News Edition. 2004. "A-B Introduces Elk Mountain Red." November 7: 1–2.

Mueller, Juergen, and Joachim Schwalbach. 1980. "Structural Changes in West Germany's Brewing Industry." *Journal of Industrial Economics* 28, no. 4: 353–368.

Mueller, Willard F. 1978. Testimony, Merger, and Industrial Concentration Hearing. U.S. Senate Committee on the Judiciary, Subcommittee on Antitrust and Monopoly. 95th Congress. 2nd Session, May 12: 84–124.

Myers, James H., and William H. Reynolds. 1967. *Consumer Behavior and Marketing Management*. Houghton Mifflin.

National Association of Attorneys General Antitrust Enforcement. 1987. *Horizontal Merger Guidelines of the National Association of Attorneys General*, Washington, D.C.: The Association, March 10.

National Council on Alcoholism and Drug Dependence. 2000. Dietary Guidelines for Americans.

National Highway Traffic Safety Administration. 2000. "Traffic Safety Facts 2000." U.S. Department of Transportation. www.nhtsa.dot.gov.

National Institute on Alcohol Abuse and Alcoholism. 2000. Tenth Special Report to the U.S. Congress on Alcohol and Health. NIH Publication 00–1583. U.S. Department of Health and Human Services.

National Institute on Alcohol Abuse and Alcoholism. 2001. "Alcohol and Transportation Safety." U.S. Department of Health and Human Services.

Navir, Nancy Ann. 1999. An Analysis of Firm Performance in the U.S. Craft Brewing Industry. Ph.D. dissertation, University of Minnesota.

Nelson, Jon P. 1999. "Broadcast Advertising and U.S. Demand for Alcoholic Beverages." *Southern Economic Journal* 65, no. 2: 774–790.

Nelson, Jon P. 2003. "Advertising Bans, Monopoly, and Alcohol Demand: Testing for Substitution Effects Using State Panel Data." *Review of Industrial Organization* 22, no. 1: 1–25.

Nelson, Phillip. 1974. "Advertising as Information." *Journal of Political Economy* 82, no. 4: 729–754.

New Brewer. 1996. "Here's Looking at You." January-February: 13–23.

New Brewer. 1996. "Do the Small Brewers of the 30s Compare to Today's Craft Brewers?" March-April: 67–70.

Newsweek. 1953. "Pabst Goes West." November 30: 85.

Newsweek. 1957. "Hamm—and Beer." July 22.

Newsweek. 1958. "Why It's Pabst's Blatz." August 11: 62.

Newsweek. 1978. "The Battle of the Beers." September 4: 60–70.

Newsweek. 1981. "Heileman's Super Suds." August 10: 53.

Newsweek. 1982. "Big Beer's Titanic Brawl." August 16: 48–50.

Newsweek. 1986. "Beer Wars Round Two." June 9: 51.

Newsweek. 1987. "A New Thirst for Brew Pubs." February 9: 49.

Newsweek. 2002. "Few Carbs, Less Taste." December 9: 93.

New York Times. 1978. "U.S. Indicts Schlitz for Tax Fraud and Illegal Practices in Business." March 16.

New York Times. 1979. "The Titans of Beer Head to Head: A Battle Full of Foam and Fury." April 29.

New York Times. 1982. "American Beer: How Changing Tastes Have Changed It." May 12.

New York Times. 1983. "Brewer Tries a New Image." August 27.

New York Times. 1988. "The Mellow Art of the Micro-Brewer." April 10.

New York Times. 1988. "And Now from Japan, the Hot New Dry Beers." July 10: 8.

New York Times. 1991. "Heileman in Chapter 11, but Upbeat." January 25.

New York Times. 1992. "Coors Files Suit Over Ads by Anheuser-Busch." August 14.

New York Times. 1992. "Court Rejects Coors Bid to Block Ads by Busch." August 20.

New York Times. 1993. "Miller Closing New York State Plant." December 2.

Niskanen, W. A. 1962. The Demand for Alcoholic Beverages. Ph.D. dissertation, University of Chicago.

Ohsfeldt, Robert L., and Michael A. Morrisey. 1997. "Beer Taxes, Workers' Compensation, and Industrial Injury." *Review of Economics and Statistics* 79, no. 1: 155–160.

Oregonian. 1997. "Widmer Joins King of Beers Realm." April 18.

Oregonian. 1995. "Free Speech Includes Beer Labels, High Court Rules." April 20.

Ornstein, Stanley I. 1981. "Antitrust Policy and Market Forces as Determinants of Industry Structure: Case Histories in Beer and Distilled Spirits." *Antitrust Bulletin* 26, no. 2: 281–313.

Ornstein, Stanley I., and Dominique M. Hanssens. 1985. "Alcohol Control Laws and the Consumption of Distilled Spirits and Beer." *Journal of Consumer Research* 12, no. 2: 200–213.

Oster, Sharon M. 1999. *Modern Competitive Analysis.* Oxford University Press.

Pautler, Paul A. 2001. Evidence on Mergers and Acquisitions. Working Paper 243, Bureau of Economics Research, Federal Trade Commission.

Pearson, E. S. 1990. *'Student:' A Statistical Biography of William Sealy Gosset.* Clarendon.

Peles, Yoram. 1971a. "Economies of Scale in Advertising Beer and Cigarettes." *Journal of Business* 44, no. 1: 32–37.

Peles, Yoram. 1971b. "Rates of Amortization of Advertising Expenditures." *Journal of Political Economy* 79, no. 5: 1032–1058.

Pepall, Lynn, Daniel J. Richards, and George Norman. 2002. *Industrial Organization and Contemporary Theory and Practice.* South-Western.

Perkins, Wesley. 2003. *The Social Norms Approach to Preventing School and College Age Substance Abuse: A Handbook for Educators, Counselors, and Clinicians.* Jossey-Bass.

Pesendorfer, Martin. 2003. "Horizontal Mergers in the Paper Industry." *Rand Journal of Economics* 34, no. 3: 495–515.

Phelps, Charles. 1988. "Death and Taxes: An Opportunity for Substitution." *Journal of Health Economics* 7, no. 1: 1–24.

Phelps, Charles. 1997. *Health Economics.* Addison-Wesley.

Phelps, Charles, and G. Fai Leung. 1993. "My Kingdom for a Drink?" In Economics and the Prevention of Alcohol-Related Problems. Research Monograph 25, National Institute on Alcohol Abuse and Alcoholism.

Pindyck, Robert S., and Daniel L. Rubinfeld. 1991. *Econometric Models & Economic Forecasts.* McGraw-Hill.

Pogue, Thomas F., and Larry G. Sgontz. 1989. "Taxing to Control Social Costs: The Case of Alcohol." *American Economic Review* 79, no. 1: 235–243.

Porter, Michael E. 1976. "Interbrand Choice, Media Mix, and Market Performance." *American Economic Review* 66, no. 2: 398–406.

Porter, Michael E. 1979. "The Structure Within Industries and Companies' Performance." *Review of Economics and Statistics* 61, no. 2: 214–227.

Porter, Michael E. 1980. *Competitive Strategy: Techniques for Analyzing Industries and Competitors.* Free Press.

Porter, Michael E. 1985. *Competitive Advantage: Creating and Sustaining Superior Performance.* Free Press.

Pratten, C. F. 1971. *Economies of Scale in Manufacturing Industry.* Cambridge University Press.

Pride, William M., and O. C. Ferrell. 2003. *Marketing Concepts and Strategies,* twelfth edition. Houghton Mifflin.

Printers' Ink. 1958. "Schlitzmen Are Toning Down Schlitztalk as Bud Takes Lead in Beer Sales." February 7: 1.

Printers' Ink. 1959. "Bud, Schlitz Brew 59 Sales Battle." February 6: 57.

Printers' Ink. 1962. "Does the Label 'Change' the Taste?" January 12: 55–57.

Printers' Ink. 1962. "Beer Makers Brew '61 Sales Record." January 19: 26.

Printers' Ink. 1963. "What's Missing in Beer Marketing?" November 29: 25–41.

Printers' Ink. 1964. "Beer: On the Move at Last?" January 31: 21.

Printers' Ink. 1965. "It's Better to Switch than Slide." March 12: 7.

Printers' Ink. 1966. "Beer Going Flat Again?" February 11: 22.

Printers' Ink. 1966. "What Is Gablinger? Scientist and Beer." December 23: 41.

Printers' Ink. 1967. "Big Get Bigger: Bud, Schlitz, and Pabst Pull Ahead." February 10: 11.

Prugh, Thomas. 1986. "Point-of-Purchase Health Warning Notices." *Alcohol Health and Research World* 10, no. 4: 36.

Rasmusen, Eric. 1994. *Games and Information: An Introduction to Game Theory.* Blackwell.

Reichert, Tom, Jacqueline Lambiase, Susan Morgan, Meta Carsarphen, and Susan Zovina. 1999., "Cheesecake and Beefcake: No Matter How You Slice It, Sexual Explicitness in Advertising Continues to Increase." *Journalism and Mass Communication Quarterly* 76, no. 1: 7–20.

Restaurant Business. 2000. "Brew pubs." March 1: 51.

Rewoldt, Stewart H., James D. Scott, and Martin R. Warshaw. 1973. *Introduction to Marketing Management: Text and Cases*. Irwin.

Rhodes, Christine P. 1995. *Encyclopedia of Beer*. Henry Holt.

Robertson, James D. 1978. *The Great American Beer Book*. Warner Books.

Robertson, James D. 1984. *The Connoisseur's Guide to Beer*. Jameson Books.

Rogers, John D., and Thomas K. Greefield. 1999. "Beer Drinking Accounts for Most Hazardous Alcohol Consumption Reported in the U.S. *Journal of Studies on Alcohol* 60, no. 6: 732–739.

Rogers, Stuart. 1992. "How a Publicity Blitz Created the Myth of Subliminal Advertising." *Public Relations Quarterly* 37, no. 4: 12–17.

Ronnenberg, Herman W. 1998. "The American Brewing Industry since 1920." In R. Wilson and T. Gourvish, eds., *The Dynamics of the International Brewing Industry Since 1800*. Routledge.

Rubin, Secretary of the Treasury v. Coors Brewing Co. 1995. No. 93–1631, April 19.

Saffer, Henry. 1991. "Alcohol Advertising and Alcohol Abuse: An International Comparison." *Journal of Health Economics* 10, no. 1: 65–69.

Saffer, Henry. 1993. "Alcohol Advertising and Alcohol Abuse: A Reply." *Journal of Health Economics* 12, no. 2: 229–234.

Saffer, Henry. 2002. "Alcohol Advertising and Youth." *Journal of Studies on Alcohol* 14 (supplement), March: 173–181.

Saffer, Henry and Frank Chaloupka. 2000. "The Effect of Tobacco Advertising Bans on Tobacco Consumption, *Journal of Health Economics* 19, no. 6: 1117–1137.

Salent, Stephen W., S. Switzer, and Robert J. Reynolds. 1983. "Losses from Horizontal Merger: The Effects of an Exogenous Change in Industry Structure on Cournot-Nash Equilibrium." *Quarterly Journal of Economics* 98, no. 2: 185–213.

Samuel, Delwen. 1996. "Ancient Egyptian Cereal Processing: Beyond the Artistic Record." *Cambridge Archeological Journal* 3, no. 2: 276–283.

Sass, Tim. 2004. The Competitive Effects of Exclusive Dealing: Evidence from the U.S. Beer Industry. Working paper, Department of Economics, Florida State University.

Sass, Tim, and David Saurman. 1993. "Mandated Exclusive Territories and Economic Efficiency: An Empirical Analysis of the Malt-Beverage Industry." *Journal of Law and Economics* 36, no. 1: 153–177.

Sass, Tim, and David Saurman. 1995. "Advertising Restrictions and Concentration: The Case of Malt Beverages." *Review of Economics and Statistics* 77, no. 1: 66–81.

Scarborough Research Company. 2002. "Sports Fans Make Surprising Choices in Beers and Wines According to Scarborough Research." www.scarborough.com.

Scherer, F. M. 1970. *Industrial Market Structure and Economic Performance*. Rand McNally.

Scherer, F. M. 1973. "The Determinants of Industrial Plant Size in Six Nations." *Review of Economics and Statistics* 55, no. 2: 135–145.

Scherer, F. M. 1980. *Industrial Market Structure and Economic Performance*. Rand McNally.

Scherer, F. M. 1996. *Industry Structure, Strategy, and Public Policy*. HarperCollins.

Scherer, F. M., Alan Beckenstein, Erich Kaufer, and R. Dennis Murphy. 1975. *The Economics of Multi-Plant Operation: An International Comparisons Study*. Harvard University Press.

Scherer, F. M., and David Ross. 1990. *Industrial Market Structure and Economic Performance*. Houghton Mifflin.

Schmalensee, Richard. 1972. *The Economics of Advertising*. North-Holland.

Schmalensee, Richard. 1977. "Using the H-Index of Concentration with Published Data." *Review of Economics and Statistics* 59, no. 2: 168–193.

Schmalensee, Richard. 1978. "Entry Deterrence in the Ready-to-Eat Breakfast Cereal Industry." *Bell Journal of Economics* 9, no. 2: 305–327.

Schmalensee, Richard. 1982. "Product Differentiation Advantages of Pioneering Brands." *American Economic Review* 72, no. 3: 346–365.

Schmalensee, Richard. 1986. "Advertising and Market Structure." In J. Stiglitz and F. Matthewson, eds., *New Developments in the Analysis of Market Structure*. MIT Press.

Schmidt, Peter. 1985–86. "Frontier Production Functions." *Econometric Reviews* 4, no. 2: 289–328.

Seattle Post Intelligencer. 1980. "Getting Buy on the BEER Necessities." April 28.

Seldon, Barry J., R. Todd Jewell, and Daniel M. O'Brien. 2000. "Media Substitution and Economies of Scale in Advertising." *International Journal of Industrial Organization* 18, no. 8: 1153–1180.

Selvanathan, E. A. 1995. "The Effects of Advertising on Alcohol Consumption: An Empirical Analysis." In E. Selvanathan and K. Clements, eds., *Recent Developments in Applied Demand Analysis*. Springer.

Seplaki, Les. 1982., *Antitrust and the Economics of the Market: Text, Readings, Cases*. Harcourt Brace Jovanovich

Shapiro, Carl. 1980. "Advertising and Welfare: Comment." *Bell Journal of Economics* 11, no. 2: 749–752.

Shepherd, William G. 1967. "What Does the Survivor Technique Show about Economies of Scale?" *Southern Economic Journal* 34, no. 1: 113–122.

Shepherd, William G. 1990. *The Economics of Industrial Organization*. Prentice-Hall.

Shepherd, William G. 1997. *The Economics of Industrial Organization*. Prentice-Hall.

Sheth, Jagdish N., Bruce I. Newman, and Barbara L. Gross. 1999. *Consumption Values and Market Choices: Theory and Applications*. South-Western.

Shih, Ko Ching, and C. Ying Shih. 1958. *American Brewing Industry and the Beer Market: A Statistical Analysis and Graphic Presentation*. W. A. Krueger.

Shy, Oz. 1995. *Industrial Organization: Theory and Applications*. MIT Press.

Siegfried, John, J., and Laurie Beth Evans. 1994. "Empirical Studies of Entry and Exit: A Survey of the Evidence." *Review of Industrial Organization* 9, no. 2: 121–155.

Silberberg, Eugene. 1985. "Nutrition and the Demand for Tastes." *Journal of Political Economy* 93, no. 5: 881–900.

Simon, Carl P., and Lawrence Blume. 1994. *Mathematics for Economists*. Norton.

Slade, Margaret E. 1998. "Beer and the Tie: Did Divestiture of Brewer-Owned Public Houses Lead to Higher Beer Prices?" *Economic Journal* 104, no. 448: 565–602.

Slade, Margaret E. 2004. "Market Power and Joint Dominance in U.K. Brewing." *Journal of Industrial Economics* 52, no. 1: 133–161.

Slemrod, Joel. 1990., "Optimal Taxation and Optimal Tax Systems." *Journal of Economic Perspectives* 4, no. 1: 157–178.

Sleuwaegen, Leo, and Wim Dehandschutter. 1986. "The Critical Choice between the Concentration Ratio and the H–Index in Assessing Industry Performance." *Journal of Industrial Economics* 35, no. 2: 193–208.

Sloan, Frank A., Bridget A. Reilly, and Cristoph M. Schenzler. 1994. "Tort Liability versus Other Deterring Careless Driving Policies." *International Review of Law and Economics* 14, March: 53–71.

Smith, J. B., and. W. A. Sims. 1985. "The Impact of Pollution Charges on Productivity Growth in Canadian Brewing." *Rand Journal of Economics* 16, no. 3: 410–423.

Solow, R. M. 1967. "The New Industrial State or Son of Affluence." *The Public Interest* 9, fall: 100–108.

Spence, A. Michael. 1980. "Notes on Advertising, Economies of Scale, and Entry Barriers." *Quarterly Journal of Economics* 95, no. 3: 493–507.

Sports Illustrated. 1988. "Sports and Suds: The Beer Business and the Sports World Have Brewed Up a Potential Partnership." August 8: 69–82.

St. Louis Post-Dispatch. 2002. "Bud Makes Sure Super Bowl Isn't Miller Time." February 3.

Stack, Martin. 2000. "Local and Regional Breweries in America's Brewing Industry, 1865 to 1920." *Business History Review* 74, no. 3: 435–463.

Standard and Poor's DRI. 2001. "The Tax Burden on the Brewing Industry." January 17. www.rollbackthetax.org.

Stigler, George J. 1955. "Mergers and Preventive Antitrust Policy." *University of Pennsylvania Law Review* 104, no. 1: 176–184.

Stigler, George J. 1958. "The Economies of Scale." *Journal of Law and Economics* 1, no. 1: 54–71.

Stigler, George J., and Becker, Gary S. 1977. "De Gustibus Non Est Disputandum." *American Economic Review* 67, no. 2: 76–90.

Stout, Emily M., Frank A. Sloan, Lang Liang, and Hester H. Davies. 2000. "Reducing Harmful Alcohol-Related Behaviors:Effective Regulatory Methods." *Journal of Studies on Alcohol* 61, no. 3: 402–412.

Sutton, John. 1991. *Sunk Costs and Market Structure: Price Competition, Advertising, and the Evolution of Concentration.* MIT Press.

Sutton, John. 1999. *Technology and Market Structure: Theory and History.* MIT Press.

Swaminathan, Anand. 1998. "Entry into New Market Segments in Mature Industries: Endogenous and Exogenous Segmentation in the U.S. Brewing Industry." *Strategic Management Journal* 19, no. 4: 389–404.

Symeonidis, George. 2002. "Cartel Stability with Multiproduct Firms." *International Journal of Industrial Organization* 20, no. 3: 339–352.

Tegene, Abebayehu. 1990. "The Kalman Filter Approach for Testing Structural Change in the Demand for Alcoholic Beverages in the U.S." *Applied Economics* 22, no. 10: 1407–1417.

Tenn, Steven. 2003. Estimating Promotional Effects with Retailer-Level Scanner Data. Bureau of Economics, Federal Trade Commission.

The U.S. Beer Market: Impact Databank Review and Forecast. 2002. M. Shanken Communications.

Thompson, Henry. 2001. *International Economics: Global Markets and International Competition.* World Scientific.

Time. 1982. "A Beer Hall Brawl for Third Place." April 26: 50.

Tin International. 1981. "Schmidt and Sons Buys Henry Ortlieb Brewing." July: 277.

Tirole, Jean. 1988. *The Theory of Industrial Organization.* MIT Press.

Tollison, Robert D. 1983. "Antitrust in the Reagan Administration: A Report from the Belly of the Beast." *International Journal of Industrial Organization* 60, no. 2: 211–221.

Tremblay, Carol Horton, and Davina Ling. 2003. AIDS Education, Condom Demand, and the Sexual Activity of American Youth. Working paper, Oregon State University.

Tremblay, Carol Horton, and Victor J. Tremblay. 1988. "The Determinants of Horizontal Acquisitions: Evidence from the U.S. Brewing Industry." *Journal of Industrial Economics* 37, no. 1: 21–45.

Tremblay, Carol Horton, and Victor J. Tremblay. 1995a. "The Impact of Cigarette Advertising on Consumer Surplus, Profit, and Social Welfare." *Contemporary Economic Policy* 13, no. 1: 113–124.

Tremblay, Carol Horton, and Victor J. Tremblay. 1995b. "Advertising, Price, and Welfare: Evidence from the U.S. Brewing Industry." *Southern Economic Journal* 62, no. 2: 367–381.

Tremblay, Carol Horton, and Victor J. Tremblay. 1996. "Firm Success, National Status, and Product Line Diversification: An Empirical Examination." *Review of Industrial Organization* 11, no. 6: 771–789.

Tremblay, Carol Horton, and Victor J. Tremblay. 1999. "Reinterpreting the Effect of an Advertising Ban on Cigarette Smoking." *International Journal of Advertising* 18, no. 1: 41–50.

Tremblay, Victor J. 1983. The Effects of Firm Behavior and Technology on Firm Size: A Case Study of the U.S. Brewing Industry. Ph.D. dissertation, Washington State University.

Tremblay, Victor J. 1985a. "A Reappraisal of Interpreting Rising Concentration: The Case of Beer." *Journal of Business* 58, no. 4: 419–431.

Tremblay, Victor J. 1985b. "Strategic Groups and the Demand for Beer." *Journal of Industrial Economics* 34, no. 2: 183–198.

Tremblay, Victor J. 1987. "Scale Economies, Technological Change, and Firm Cost Asymmetries in the U.S. Brewing Industry." *Quarterly Review of Economics and Business* 27, no. 2: 71–86.

Tremblay, Victor J. 1993a. "The Organizational Ecology of Strategic Groups in the American Brewing Industry: A Comment." *Industrial and Corporate Change* 2, no. 1: 91–98.

Tremblay, Victor J. 1993b. "Consistency between the Law and Its Enforcement: The Case of Mergers." *Antitrust Bulletin* 38, no. 2: 327–348.

Tremblay, Victor J. 1995. "Alcohol Advertising and Alcohol Abuse: Comments on Econometric Evidence." In S. Martin, ed., *The Effects of the Mass Media on the Use and Abuse of Alcohol*. Department of Health and Human Services, Public Health Services, National Institute on Alcohol Abuse and Alcoholism.

Tremblay, Victor J. 2001. Informative and Persuasive Advertising in Markets with Search Costs and Product Differentiation. Working paper, Department of Economics, Oregon State University.

Tremblay, Victor J. 2003. Advertising, Welfare, and Supermodularity. Working paper, Department of Economics, Oregon State University.

Tremblay, Victor J., and Carlos Martins-Filho. 2001. "A Model of Vertical Differentiation, Brand Loyalty, and Persuasive Advertising." In M. Baye and J. Nelson, eds., *Advances in Applied Microeconomics: Advertising and Differentiated Products*, volume 10. JAI.

Tremblay, Victor J., and Kumiko Okuyama. 2001. "Advertising Restrictions, Competition, and Alcohol Consumption." *Contemporary Economic Policy* 19, no. 3: 313–321.

Tremblay, Victor J., and Steven Polasky. 2002. "Advertising and Brand Loyalty in Models with Subjective Product Differentiation." *Review of Industrial Organization* 20, May: 253–265.

USA Today. 1993. "A Macro Demand for Microbrews." October 8.

USA Today. 1994. "Tapping Micros' Success." October 21–23.

USA Today. 2002. "'Social Norming' May Be Strategy for Good Behavior." May 27.

U.S. Department of Agriculture and U.S. Department of Health and Human Services. 1995. *Nutrition and Your Health: Dietary Guidelines for Americans*, fourth edition. www.health.gov.

U.S. Department of Justice. 1968. *Merger Guidelines*. May 30.

U.S. Department of Justice. 1982. *Merger Guidelines*. June 30.

U.S. Department of Justice. 1984. *Merger Guidelines*. June 29.

U.S. Department of Justice and Federal Trade Commission. 1992. *Horizontal Merger Guidelines*.

U.S. Department of Justice and Federal Trade Commission. 1997. *Horizontal Merger Guidelines*. April 8.

Van Munching, Philip. 1997. *Beer Blast: The Inside Story of the Brewing Industry's Bizarre Battles for Your Money.* Times Books.

Vardanyan, Michael, and Victor J. Tremblay, 2004. The Measurement of Marketing Efficiency in the Presence of Spillovers: Theory and Evidence. Working paper, Department of Economics, Oregon State University.

Varian, Hal. 1980. "A Model of Sales." *American Economic Review* 70, no. 4: 651–659.

Varian, Hal. 1992. *Microeconomic Analysis.* Norton.

Veblen, Thorstein. 1899. *The Theory of the Leisure Class.* Macmillan.

Vives, Xavier. 1999. *Oligopoly Pricing: Old Ideas and New Tools.* MIT Press.

Waldman, Don E. 1986. *The Economics of Antitrust: Cases and Analysis.* Little, Brown.

Wallace, Lawrence, and William DeJong. 1995. "Mass Media and Public Health: Moving the Focus from the Individual to the Environment." In S. Martin, ed., *The Effects of the Mass Media on the Use and Abuse of Alcohol.* Department of Health and Human Services, Public Health Services, National Institute on Alcohol Abuse and Alcoholism.

Wall Street Journal. 1968. "Justice Department Drops Suit Challenging Rheingold Merger." June 5.

Wall Street Journal. 1973. "G. Heileman Brewing and Justice Agency Settle Antitrust Suit." June 14.

Wall Street Journal. 1973. "Colorado's Coors Family Has Built an Empire on 1 Brand of Beer." October 26.

Wall Street Journal. 1974. "Pepsi Co.'s Rheingold to Close Brooklyn Unit if a Buyer Isn't Found." January 7.

Wall Street Journal. 1974. "Coors Loses Bid to Reverse FTC In P-Fix Case." June 6.

Wall Street Journal. 1973. "G. Heileman Brewing and Justice Agency Settle Antitrust Suit." June 14.

Wall Street Journal. 1974. "Schaefer Says Its Unit Negotiating to Make Market 2 Piel Beers." December 18.

Wall Street Journal. 1975. "Bob Uihlein Restored the Gusto to Schlitz after a Sale Spell." January 3.

Wall Street Journal. 1975. "Minneapolis Firm Says It Settled Price Suit with Schlitz Brewing." June 27.

Wall Street Journal. 1975. "Falstaff, Its Chairman Charged in Suit by Two Former Aids." August 12.

Wall Street Journal. 1975. "Philip Morris's Miller Is Suing Jos. Schlitz Over Beer Brand Name." November 3.

Wall Street Journal. 1976. "A-B Strike Ends after 95 Days as Bottlers Ratify Pact." June 7.

Wall Street Journal. 1976. "A-B Says Questionable Payments May Total $2.7 Million." September 3.

Wall Street Journal. 1977. "SEC Accuses Schlitz Brewing of Making at Least $3 Million in Illegal Payments." April 8.

Wall Street Journal. 1977. "Jos. Schlitz, Others Charged with Fixing Beer Prices in Hawaii." June 9.

Wall Street Journal. 1977. "Hurt by 3–Month Strike, Anheuser-Busch Tries to Regain Budweiser's Market Share." June 28.

Wall Street Journal. 1977. "Collapsed Brewer Files Suit against A-B Inc." November 14.

Wall Street Journal. 1977. "Jos. Schlitz Is Sued by Three Breweries for Alleged Discounts." December 12.

Wall Street Journal. 1978. "A-B Inc. Has Another Entry to Soothe Qualms on Low-Calorie Products." February 13.

Wall Street Journal. 1978. "Schlitz Brewing as Expected, Is Indicted for Illegal Practices in Marketing Beer." March 16.

Wall Street Journal. 1978. "Schlitz Bows to Order Sought by SEC in Suit on Dubious Payments." July 10.

Wall Street Journal. 1978. "Schlitz Agrees to Pay $750,000 In Civil Penalties." November 2.

Wall Street Journal. 1979. "Brewers' Battle." March 14.

Wall Street Journal. 1979. "A. Coors Co. to Begin Distribution in Arkansas." October 2.

Wall Street Journal. 1981. "Stroh Brewery Closes Merger with Schaefer." May 14.

Wall Street Journal. 1983. "Heileman Plans Big Expansion Into South, Setting Stage for Bruising Beer-Sales Fight." February 3.

Wall Street Journal. 1983. "New Little Breweries Cause Some Ferment in the Beer Business." March 15.

Wall Street Journal. 1983. "G. Heileman Completes Purchase of Some Assets of Pabst and Olympia." March 21.

Wall Street Journal. 1986. "Iroquois Agrees to Sell Trademarks, Inventory of Champale, Inc. Unit." November 4.

Wall Street Journal. 1987. "Heileman Accepts Bid of $1.26 Billion From Bond, Will Operate Autonomously." September 24.

Wall Street Journal. 1988. "Coors Light's Success Imperils Flagship Brand." February 9.

Wall Street Journal. 1988. "In a World of Millers and Buds, Coors Beer Has to Play Catch-Up." November 3.

Wall Street Journal. 1988. "Second String: Coors Beer Forced to Keep Playing Catch-Up Game." November 3.

Wall Street Journal. 1989. "Heileman Unveils a Dry Malt Brew, Called Colt 45 Dry." March 29.

Wall Street Journal. 1989. "Coors Discusses Buying Stroh Assets, as Brewers Try to Survive Beer Wars." August 1.

Wall Street Journal. 1989. "Coors to Buy Beer-Related Assets of Stroh." September 26.

Wall Street Journal. 1989. "Alcohol Firms Retain Campus Presence." October 6.

Wall Street Journal. 1989. "Anheuser-Busch, Slugging It Out, Plans Beer Price Cuts." October 26.

Wall Street Journal. 1989. "Coors Hits a Snag in Plans to Acquire Stroh, but Many Still Expect Accord." December 19.

Wall Street Journal. 1991. "Stroh Brewing Co.: Company Is Still Interested in Heileman Despite Rebuff." August 19.

Wall Street Journal. 1993. "Small Regional Brewers Inject New Foam into a Beer Market That Had Gone Flat." March 5.

Wall Street Journal. 1993. "Existing Distributors Are Being Squeezed By Brewers, Retailers." November 22.

Wall Street Journal. 1996. "Who Really Makes That Cute Little Beer? You'd Be Surprised." April 15.

Wall Street Journal. 1996. "Liquor Industry Is Divided Over Use of TV Ads." June 12.

Wall Street Journal. 1996. "TV Beer Ads May Be Caught in a Backlash." June 14.

Wall Street Journal. 1996. "Stroh Brewing Co.: G. Heileman Is Purchased in $290 Million Transaction." July 2.

Wall Street Journal. 1997. "Anheuser's Sales Practices under Probe—Justice Agency Charges Brewer Abuses Its Top Market Position." October 2.

Wall Street Journal. 1998. "Amid Probe, Anheuser Conquers Turf." March 9.

Wall Street Journal. 1998. "Big Brewers Find Price War Seems to Have No End." July 2.

Wall Street Journal. 2001. "Diageo Unit Buys Pabst Facility." November 27.

Wall Street Journal. 2002. "Healthy Brew: Beer, It Seems, Is Good For You." August 13.

Wall Street Journal. 2002. "Coors's Pitch to Young Is Paying Off—Sexy New Ads Help Sales of Light, but Market Share Has a Long Way to Go." November 6.

Wechsler, Henry, and Bernice Wuethrich. 2002. *Dying to Drink: Confronting Binge Drinking on College Campuses.* Rodale.

Weinberg, Robert S. 1978a. "Beer Wars." *Beverage World*, May: 32–34: 56.

Weinberg, Robert S. 1978b. "The Economics of the Malt Beverage Production/ Distribution System 1976." St. Louis: R.S. Weinberg and Associates, August 8.

Weinberg, Robert S. 1980. "Beer Prices and Costs." St. Louis: R.S. Weinberg and Associates, May 30.

Weinberg, Robert S. 1998. *The Brewing Industry at a Crossroads*, St. Louis: The Office of R.S. Weinberg, November 2.

Weinberg, Robert S. 1999. *Factors That Will Determine the Future of Third Tier Players in the United States Malt Beverage Market: 1999–2001.* Office of R.S. Weinberg.

Weinberg, Robert S. 2002. *Examine the Present in Light of the Past for the Purposes of the Future*, St. Louis: The Office of R.S. Weinberg, April 22.

Weiss, Leonard W. 1966. "An Evaluation of Mergers in Six Industries." *Review of Economics and Statistics* 47, no. 2: 172–181.

Weiss, Leonard W. 1976. "Optimal Plant Size and the Extent of Suboptimal Capacity." In R. Mason and P. Qualls, eds., *Essays on IO in Honor of Joe S. Bain*. Ballinger.

Wharff, Jeffrey Craig. 1995. Firm Conduct: The Case of the U.S. Malt Beverage Industry. Ph.D. dissertation, American University.

Wilcox, G. B., D. Shea, and R. Hovland. 1986. "Alcoholic Beverage Advertising and the Electronic Media." *Communications and the Law*, February: 31–41.

Wilson, R. G., and T. R. Gourvish, eds.. 1998. *The Dynamics of the International Brewing Industry Since 1800*. Routledge.

Wolaver, Amy M. 2002. "Effects of Heavy Drinking in College on Study Effort, Grade Point Average, and Major Choice." *Contemporary Economic Policy* 20, no. 4: 415–428.

Wolinsky, Asher. 1987. "Brand Names and Price Discrimination." *Journal of Industrial Economics* 35, no. 3: 255–268.

World Drink Trends 2003. 2002. Commission for Distilled Spirits, World Advertising Research.

Xia, Yin, and Steven Buccola. 2003. "Factor Use and Productivity Change in the Alcohol Beverage Industries." *Southern Economic Journal* 70, no. 1: 93–109.

Young, Douglas J. 1993. "Alcohol Advertising Bans and Alcohol Abuse: Comment." *Journal of Health Economics* 12, no. 2: 213–228.

Young, Douglas J., and Thomas W. Likens. 2000. "Alcohol Regulation and Auto Fatalities." *International Law and Economics* 20, no. 1: 107–126.

Materials on the Web

ABC News. "Is Bigger Better? Beer Makers May Have More Deals Brewing." June 4, 2002. http://abcnews.go.com

Alaskan Brewing Company: www.alaskanbeer.com

American Brewing History: www.beerhistory.com

Anchor Brewing Company: www.anchorbrewing.com

Anheuser-Busch Brewing Company: www.anheuser-busch.com

Association of Brewers: www.beertown.org

Beer trivia and history: www.allaboutbeer.com, www.beerhistory.com, www.beerinfo.com, www.beernotes.com, and www.realbeer.com

Beer Institute: www.beerinstitute.org

Beer Marketer's Insights: www.beerinsights.com

Beer rankings: www.allaboutbeer.com, www.gabf.org, www.ratebeer.com, www.realbeer.com

Beverage Marketing: www.beveragemarketing.com

Boston Beer Company: www.bostonbeer.com

Brewers' Association of America: http://65.23.136.214/

Bureau of Alcohol, Tobacco, and Firearms: www.atf.treas.gov

Capital Brewery Company: www.capital-brewery.com

Carolina Beer and Beverage: www.carolinablond.com

Cascade Brewers Guild: www.cascadebrewersguild.org

City Brewing Company: www.citybrewery.com

Coors Brewing Company: www.coors.com

Deschutes Brewing Company: www.deschutesbrewery.com

D. G. Yuengling & Son, Inc.: www.yuengling.com

Distilled Spirits Council of the United States: www.discus.org

Full Sail Brewing Company: www.deschutesbrewery.com

F. X. Matt Brewing Company: www.saranac.com

Hale's Ales Ltd: www.halesales.com

Harpoon Brewery: www.harpoonbrewery.com

High Falls Brewing Company: www.highfalls.com

Hudepohl-Schoenling Brewing Company: www.littlekings.com

Jackson, Michael: www.beerhunter.com

Jacob Leinenkugel Brewing Company: www.leinie.com

James Page Brewing Company: www.pagebrewing.com

Latrobe Brewing Company: www.labatt.com

Left Hand Brewing Company: www.lefthandbrewing.com

Master Brewers Association of America: www.mbaa.com

Mendocino Brewing Company: www.mendobrew.com

Miller Brewing Company: www.millerbrewing.com

Modern Brewery Age: www.breweryage.com

Mothers Against Drunk Driving: www.madd.org

New Belgium Brewing Compapny: www.newbelgium.com

North Coast Brewing Company: www.ncoast-brewing.com

Pabst Brewing Company: www.pabst.com

Pete's Brewing Company: www.peteswicked.com

Pittsburgh Brewing Company: www.pittsburghbrewery.com

Portland Brewing Company: www.macsbeer.com

Pyramid Brewing Company: www.pyramidbrew.com

Redhook Ale Brewery: www.redhook.com

Siebel Institute of Technology and World Brewing Academy: www.siebelinstitute.com

Sierra Nevada Brewing Company: www.sierra-nevada.com

Spoetzl Brewery: www.shiner.com

Stone Brewing Company: www.stonebrew.com

Stoudt's Brewing Company: www.stoudtsbeer.com

Tabernash/Left Hand Brewing Company: www.lefthandbrewing.com

Uinta Brewing Company: www.uintabrewing.com

U.S. Department of Justice, Bureau of Alcohol, Tobacco, Firearms, and Explosives: www.atf.treas.gov

Victory Brewing Company: www.victorybeer.com

Widmer Brewing Company: www.widmer.com

Wine Institute: www.wineinstitute.org

Index